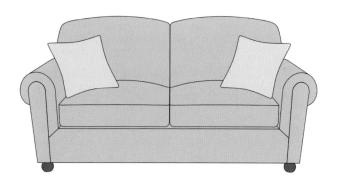

STEP-BY-STEP
home
DESIGN&DECORATING

STEP-BY-STEP
home
DESIGN&DECORATING

CLARE STEEL

London, New York, Munich,
Melbourne, Delhi

Illustrator Tim Loughhead
Step-by-step photography Kate Davis
Location photography Carolyn Barber
Editor Susannah Steel
Designer Anne Fisher

DK UK AND US
Project Editor Robert Sharman
Senior Art Editor Glenda Fisher
Editorial Assistant David Fentiman
US Editors Margaret Parrish, Rebecca Warren
US Consultant Michael Fasulo
Design Assistants Danaya Bunnag, Jade Wheaton
Managing Editor Dawn Henderson
Managing Art Editor Christine Keilty
Senior Presentations Creative Caroline de Souza
Senior Jacket Creative Nicola Powling
Senior Production Editor Jennifer Murray
Senior Production Controller Claire Pearson
Creative Technical Support Sonia Charbonnier
Publisher Mary-Clare Jerram

DK INDIA
Senior Editors Alicia Ingty, Dorothy Kikon
Senior Art Editor Neha Ahuja
Project Designer Era Chawla
Designer Anjan Dey
Managing Editor Glenda Fernandes
Managing Art Editor Navidita Thapa
DTP Designer Sourabh Challariya
Senior DTP Designer Tarun Sharma
DTP Manager Sunil Sharma

First published in the United States in 2012
by DK Publishing, 375 Hudson Street, New York, New York 10014
12 13 14 15 16 10 9 8 7 6 5 4 3 2 1

001—179007—Mar/2012

Published in Great Britain by Dorling Kindersley Limited.

A catalog record for this book
is available from the Library of Congress.

ISBN 978-0-7566-8976-6

Printed and bound in China by Hung Hing

Discover more at www.dk.com

CONTENTS

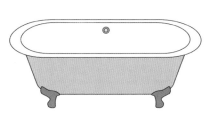

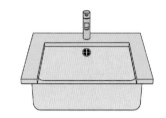

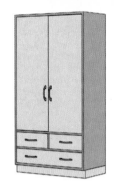

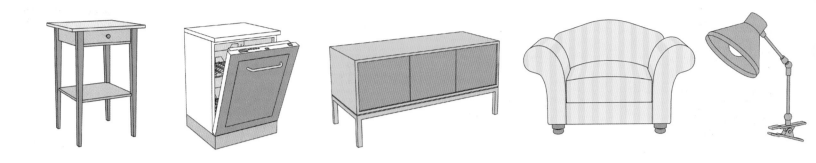

LAUNDRY ROOM 328

OUTSIDE SPACE 346

APPENDICES

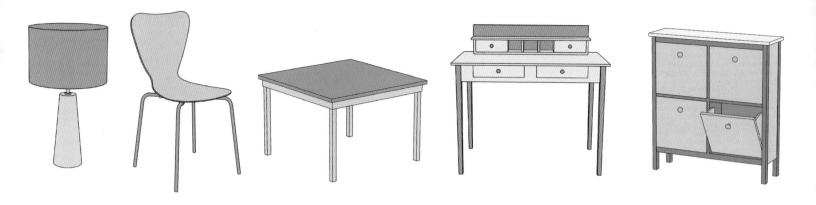

FOREWORD

Over the past 15 years, I have worked for a broad selection of interiors magazines as a stylist and writer, creating room sets to inspire readers, and nuts-and-bolts features on just about everything related to homes and property.

During this period, I moved three times. Each house I bought was in a different state of repair, and each time I became more ambitious. The first house required a minor makeover; the second needed some character added to it, and the latest, a 1920s duplex, had to be completely gutted—new electrical, plumbing, windows, the whole ball of wax!

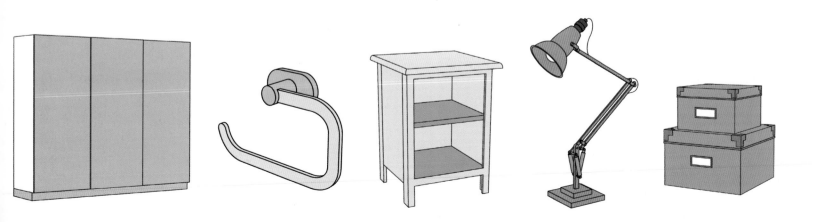

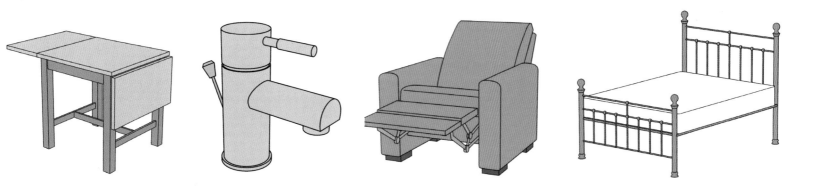

I approached each project relying on the knowledge I'd begun to build up and the experience I'd gained through work, but life would have been much easier if I had had a book like this one from the very beginning.

We all know that designing and decorating a home can be expensive, time-consuming, and, at times, stressful, which is why I have worked with DK Publishing to create this step-by-step approach that will, hopefully, save you time, money, and a lot of stress.

The goal is to take you all the way through the practical side of the process, so that you can do the work on your home in the right order and make informed choices about materials and finishes before you buy.

Every material you might need is covered—from faucets to carpets—to suit every home's style and every homemaker's approach and tastes. In these guides, you'll find lots of information to help you stick to your budget, too. There are also practical projects—presented step by step, naturally—to help you tackle home improvement tasks and create unique features for your home.

Aside from including practical details, the decorative side of transforming a home is tackled with gusto in this book. The processes you need to go through to create a defined style for your home are broken down into a step-by-step process in a way that's achievable, affordable, and appealing to you and your family. There are mood board

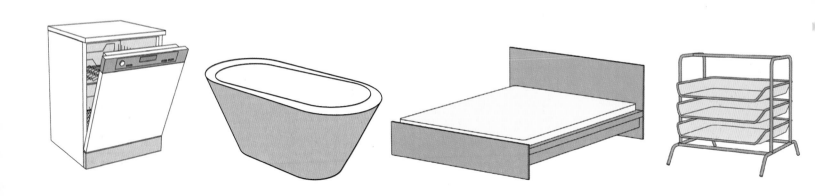

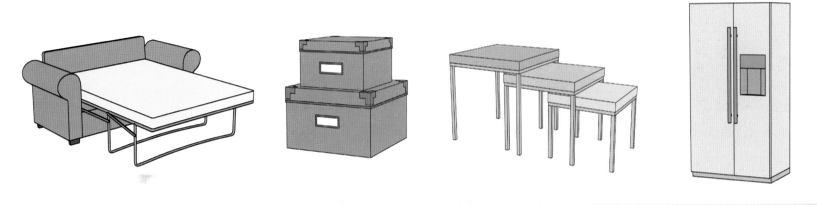

tutorials whereby you learn how to pull your room's color scheme and layout together so that it works practically and decoratively. There are also "5 ways with…" features to inspire ideas and help you find design suggestions that will work for your home.

In short, whether you're a beginner to transforming a home or a seasoned renovator like me, I think you'll find this book an indispensible guide and an inspiration to be more ambitious with your home's makeover than you might otherwise have been.

Clare

Clare Steel

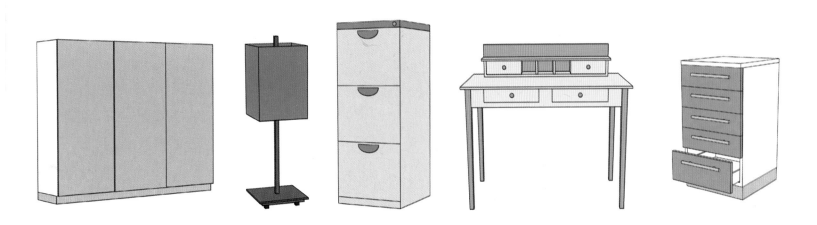

HOW TO USE
THIS BOOK

This book is designed to plot a logical course through the designing and decorating of your home. Everything in the book is presented step by step, making it the perfect reference for any would-be designer who doesn't know where to start, or for any budding renovator eager to make sure that their comprehensive overhaul is planned and executed to perfection.

If you are opening this book for the first time, begin with "Where do I start?" on pages 14–17. The principles discussed here are relevant to any, and every, room and reading this will provide a useful introduction to the most fundamental things you should consider when approaching any redecorating job.

Thereafter, there is a chapter for every room in the house, including outside space. The sequence in which each chapter is structured represents a suggestion for how to approach the work. You may find that, in places, it suits you to approach tasks in a different order and often this will be entirely possible. It is, however, recommended that you at least read the features that open each chapter—"What to do when...," "Create a mood board," and "Layout considerations"—before you undertake any work. Doing so will help you to identify any likely problems or complications from the outset.

There follows a brief introduction to the various types of feature that appear in this book.

WHAT TO DO WHEN...

There is a logical order in which any redecorating job should be approached. Failing to observe this can cause problems and could result in you having to redo work. These features guide you through the correct process for each room. The text assumes a fairly comprehensive renovation, involving sheetrock, replacing windows, and so on; if you are undertaking a more minor refurbishment, you will only need to focus on the parts that concern you.

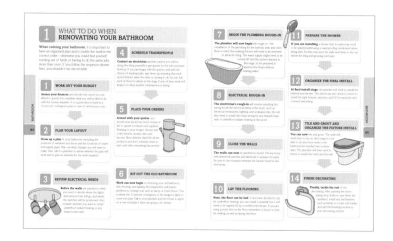

CREATE A MOOD BOARD

Next, you'll find the process by which you will decide on the room's new appearance, focusing on color, texture, pattern, and style. You may already have strong ideas about how you want the room to look. Or, on the other hand, you may not know where to start. If you are in the former camp, these features will allow you to check that your ideas work as a coherent scheme and find out sooner rather than later if anything doesn't work; if the latter is the case, they will guide you through the whole process to help you come up with the perfect scheme for your room.

LAYOUT CONSIDERATIONS

Your ideal room should not only look amazing; but it should also offer perfect functionality. These features will get you thinking about how you will use the room and ensure that you arrange the component parts in such a way that everything works smoothly and nothing is awkward. Not everyone notices a well-thought-out room, but they certainly notice one that hasn't been well planned; these features will help ensure yours is the former.

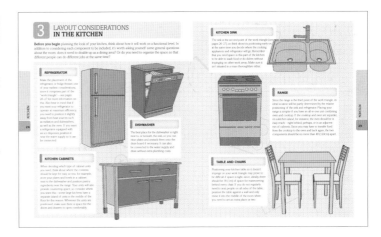

CHOOSE A...

There is a lot of choosing involved in redecorating a room: walls, flooring, lighting, furniture, appliances, fixtures, fittings. Much of this book is devoted to helping you make these decisions and choosing the options that are best for you and your home. This book is not a catalog and cannot hope to be comprehensive in showing every variation of faucet, light fixture, armchair, or refrigerator. Instead, the goal has been to present every generic option, without going into the sort of subtle variations that can only be explored by comparing specific brands and models.

When comparing materials, certain qualities are invariably important, and this is why icons are included throughout that show at a glance how each material rates in those categories. "Durability" is represented by a hammer icon, "maintenance" by a brush. A low, medium, or high rating is denoted by the icon appearing singly, as a pair, or in triplicate. The goal is always to state, within the accompanying text, whether a material is low-, medium-, or high-priced. This approach provides a useful

at-a-glance guide, although please keep in mind that most materials vary in quality and that a material identified as typically "highly durable" or "low maintenance" may not always live up to this billing, depending on the type you opt for or the supplier you use.

🔨🔨🔨 Highly durable	🖌🖌🖌 High maintenance
🔨🔨 Medium durability	🖌🖌 Medium maintenance
🔨 Low durability	🖌 Low maintenance

OTHER FEATURES

The other features that appear in this book are less fundamental to the process of designing and decorating a room, but should provide plenty of inspiration.

"Plan the perfect..." features look at a handful of small spaces in the home and show you how to approach them. Many of the subjects—outdoor kitchens; walk-in closets— will not be applicable to every home; others, however, such as the kitchen work triangle, are much more universal.

"Ways with..." features—i.e., "5 ways with…," "6 ways with…" and so on—demonstrate several approaches to a particular design idea, such as displaying art, creating a feature wall, or using the space under the stairs.

Projects also appear throughout the book, with step-by-step instructions and photography showing you how to undertake many home improvement and craft-based projects.

WHERE
DO I START?

Whether you've moved into a new home or are redesigning and decorating a room in your existing home, planning your scheme step by step gives you the best chance of making it a success. Whichever room you're thinking about, there are some key points you need to consider before you get going.

1 THINK ABOUT DIRECTION

The direction a room faces has an important effect on the amount and type of light it gets and the mood this creates. Bear this in mind when considering your color scheme.

NORTH-FACING ROOM

A north-facing room is light-starved and the light it gets is cool. You can enliven a dark, north-facing room by using light, warm shades of color.

SOUTH-FACING ROOM

Rooms facing south may be flooded with light and the quality of light is warm. You can temper a very bright, sunny room by using cool colors.

EAST-FACING ROOM

This is flooded with sunlight in the morning, but tonally cooler in the afternoon. Your colors need to work in both environments, so compare the effect of the changing light.

WEST-FACING ROOM

This is tonally cooler in the morning than in the afternoon. Again, your chosen colors need to suit both kinds of light.

2 CONSIDER TIME OF DAY

What time of day do you usually use the room and, therefore, how do you want it to "feel"? Consider this when planning your colors—walls, floors, furniture, and accessories.

MORNING

If it's a room you principally use in the morning, you may wish to decorate it so that it feels bright and invigorating.

EVENING

If it's a room you use to relax in the evening, you might want it to feel soothing and calming. It may not see much natural light, so consider the effect of electric lights on your colors.

DAY AND NIGHT

If the room is used in the day and evening, choose colors that will ensure that the room feels comfortable at all times.

Flooded with light A south-facing room is bathed in warm light throughout the day. Using cool colors as your basis offsets this to create a clean, sleek, fresh feel. You could go supercool with white walls and floors and cream furniture and accessories.

Morning colors Experiment with swatches of color that feel invigorating—colors that encourage you to wake up and welcome the day.

Evening colors You may wish to consider calming, restful colors that will help to create an environment in which you can unwind.

Day and night colors Compare versatile colors that will enable you to achieve the feel you want at all times of the day, and compare how the colors react to the changing light.

This will help you to decide not only how to decorate your room, but also what you can do to influence how large or small the room feels. Good proportions aren't just about high ceilings or generous width and length—large, sparsely dressed windows in a smaller room can also contribute to how spacious the room feels.

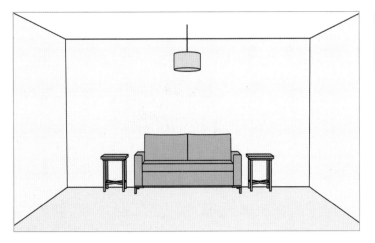

Deepen and widen Make a narrow, low-ceilinged room feel wide and bright by keeping both your flooring and walls a light color.

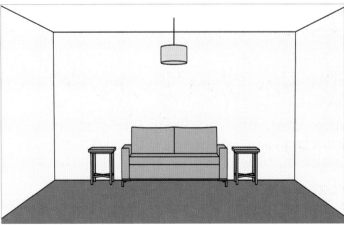

Widen Make a small, low-ceilinged room seem wider by matching a dark floor with a light-colored ceiling and surrounding walls.

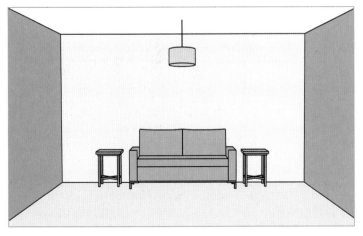

Narrow and make taller A low-ceilinged, wide space that lacks unity can be made to feel narrower, taller, and more cohesive with dark opposing walls and a light floor and ceiling.

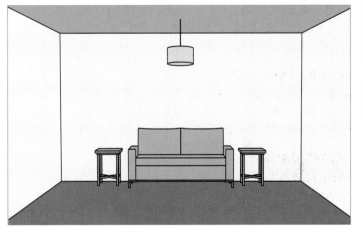

Widen and lower A large, lofty room can be made to feel cozy and more intimate with a dark floor and ceiling and light-colored walls.

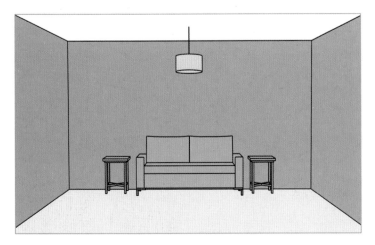

Narrow and deepen You can make a bright, large impersonal space feel warmer and more contained with a light floor and ceiling and dark-colored walls.

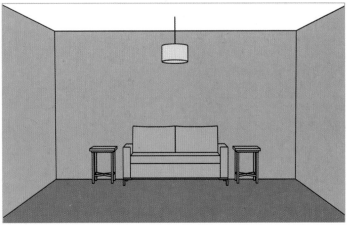

Narrow, deepen, and lower Make a large, low-ceilinged room feel cozy and intimate by matching a dark floor and walls with a light-colored ceiling.

4 COMBINE COLORS

Your color choice will be based on the direction, use, and proportions of your room, but it's your combination of colors that will enable you to achieve the balance you desire.

LIGHT TO BOLD
Light, cool colors make a room feel more spacious, but can also make it seem less inviting. So for a small, north-facing room with cream walls and light-colored neutral furnishings, add an injection of extra interest with a bold-colored rug.

BOLD TO LIGHT
Warm, deep colors make a room feel welcoming, but can also make it feel smaller. So take a large, south-facing room and treat it to bold, dark walls, but temper this with white or neutral flooring and cool, stylish furniture, perhaps with some textural interest.

Light-colored walls can make a space feel larger.

Neutral floors complement the light-colored walls.

Bold accessories add interest and warmth.

Bold walls make a room feel cozy and welcoming.

Understated floors offset the darker walls.

Cool accessories keep the room feeling fresh.

5 CREATE A FOCAL POINT

Nominating a feature within a room to be the focal point will help you to bring your scheme together. The focus may be an obvious feature that's part of the existing architecture of the room, or something that you create yourself to draw the eye and anchor the room. You can create or enhance a focal point in a number of ways, some of which are shown below.

Create contrast The recessed wall behind this shelving is painted in a vibrant contrasting color, which draws the eye. The objects on the shelves are also carefully chosen and artfully placed to enhance the effect.

Embellish The existing fireplace surround is further highlighted by dramatic art and impressive artifacts.

Construct The dark-colored panel and large ornate mirror bring the focal point of the room to the stylish bathtub, creating a unified and relaxing mood.

Dress The French windows in this simple room are dressed with showy monochrome curtains, which draw the eye to the light.

6 SELECT FURNITURE

Use what you've learned about style and color to choose your furniture and consider your room's proportions to get the size and shape of your items right. Don't forget comfort!

THINK ABOUT HEIGHT

A room with a low ceiling suits low items of furniture best, so if your ceiling's low, choose a low-backed sofa or a bed that's low to the floor, such as a futon. Rooms with high ceilings can house a tall, ornately framed bed, or even a four-poster bed, and still feel balanced.

ADD INTEREST

If your room's general scheme is fairly plain in terms of color and pattern, or if its architecture is uninteresting, you can use furniture to introduce curvaceous shapes and finishes and to add texture in its upholstery and materials. Choose sofas, chairs, tables, and beds with this in mind.

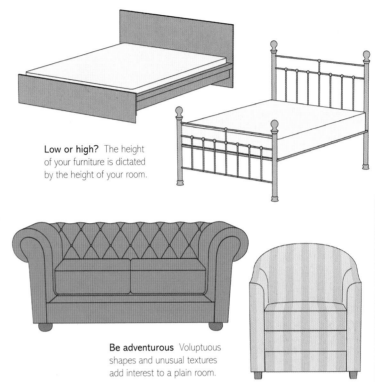

Low or high? The height of your furniture is dictated by the height of your room.

Be adventurous Voluptuous shapes and unusual textures add interest to a plain room.

7 LAYER IT UP

The style of your room should not be conjured up artificially so that your whole house becomes a slave to a single overworked theme or so that each room has a contrived individual look. Ideally, your rooms should evolve slowly, so you might come up with a basic scheme and build from there over a period of weeks or months—layer by layer.

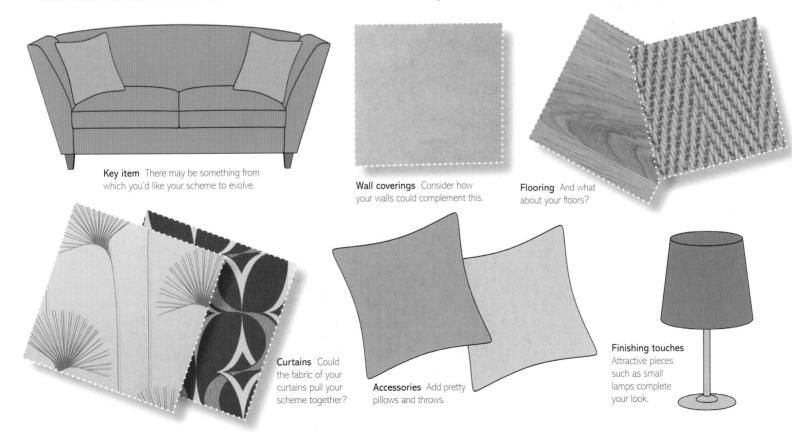

Key item There may be something from which you'd like your scheme to evolve.

Wall coverings Consider how your walls could complement this.

Flooring And what about your floors?

Curtains Could the fabric of your curtains pull your scheme together?

Accessories Add pretty pillows and throws.

Finishing touches Attractive pieces such as small lamps complete your look.

KITCHEN

1 WHAT TO DO WHEN RENOVATING YOUR KITCHEN

The sheer number of components involved in redesigning a kitchen means that it requires careful scheduling. The majority of your time will probably be spent preparing for the kitchen to be installed, but if you do this job properly, the rest of the renovation should run smoothly. Get your redesign right the first time with this step-by-step approach.

1 PLAN YOUR LAYOUT

Use graph paper to draw a plan to scale of your kitchen. Include windows and doors and all measurements. Then plan the position of cabinets, appliances, and electrical points. Moving the plumbing, gas supply, or electrical points for appliances will increase costs, as will having the washing machine, dishwasher, and sink in different locations.

2 CONSIDER THE LIGHTING

The right lighting is vital, especially bright task lighting in food preparation areas. Put dimmable lighting in the dining area and also include inviting ambient lighting, if possible.

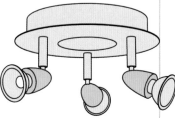

3 VISIT A KITCHEN DESIGNER

When you know your layout and budget, get input on kitchen design from an in-store service or from an interior designer or architect. If you can, visit a total of three designers to compare prices and pick out clever design ideas.

4 ORDER YOUR KITCHEN

You'll be given the choice of booking your own contractor or having the kitchen company's workmen install your kitchen when you order it. The latter is a wise choice—although sometimes not the cheapest option—since someone familiar with the design will install it more quickly, and can easily resolve any problems with a delivery, such as the odd missing piece. If you choose your own electrician, carpenter, and plumber instead, book them now. Order appliances now, too.

5 REMOVE YOUR OLD KITCHEN

Once the delivery date is confirmed (and not before), get your old kitchen removed. The installer you've booked could do this for you at an extra cost, but make sure that this price also includes the disposal of the old kitchen. Coordinate any gas, electrical, and/or plumbing removals with qualified tradespeople.

6 BEGIN THE ROUGH-IN

The new electrical wiring and pipes need to be installed now. Double-check the position of all the electrical receptacles, both behind appliances and at work surface level. The electrician—if not the kitchen company's installer—will need a set of the finalized plans to get this right.

7 LAY THE KITCHEN FLOOR

If your floor is uneven, the appliances and cabinets won't sit neatly, so have it leveled once any underfloor work has been completed. If you're having underfloor heating, it can be installed at this point. Then lay the new floor and keep it well protected while the rest of the work is completed.

8 PLASTER AND PAINT

Wiring and plumbing make a mess of walls, so they may have to be patched. Once the plaster is dry, give the ceiling, walls, and woodwork a coat of primer and a couple of coats of paint. This will save you from having to worry about splattering your new kitchen with paint later.

9 TAKE DELIVERY OF THE KITCHEN

Even if the kitchen company's workmen are installing your kitchen, it's worth checking off all the boxes yourself when your units arrive. Open up every box to make sure that all the hinges and screws are included. Check the units for damage, too, and have them replaced as soon as possible if there are any problems.

10 INSTALL THE CABINETS AND COUNTERTOPS

If your kitchen arrives flat-packed, assemble it carefully to prevent warping later on. Begin with base units in one corner, making sure that each fits well and is level before moving on. Either the workmen or you can then install the countertop.

11 INSTALL THE SINK AND APPLIANCES

The kitchen contractor will install the sink once the countertop is in place, unless you have chosen a composite or Corian® countertop, perhaps with an integral sink, which must be measured before being factory-cut. Allow a gap of a couple of days for this process to take place. With the sink in place, the faucets can then be connected. Wood or stone countertops may need to be treated with oil or sealed once in place. Then have a professional connect and check all your appliances.

12 INSTALL THE BACKSPLASH

Install the backsplash, ensuring that it is templated (measured) before being set in place to allow for the electrical receptacles. The walls may need to be touched up after this.

13 FINAL INSTALL—ELECTRICAL AND PLUMBING

Any wiring or plumbing that hasn't been taken care of can be completed now, including any light fixtures.

14 TAKE CARE OF FINAL DETAILS

Finishing touches like baseboards (or toe kicks) can be installed now, as can crown trim, doors, drawers, door handles, and so on. Check that everything works properly, from appliances to soft-closing drawers.

2 CREATE A MOOD BOARD FOR YOUR KITCHEN

Working on a mood board for your kitchen is, in many ways, simpler than for other rooms, because much of the room will be dominated by cabinet doors, drawer fronts, and countertops. Spend time now carefully considering whether you want a homey, chic and contemporary, or traditional-style kitchen, using the mood board to help you build up your theme and achieve the look you want.

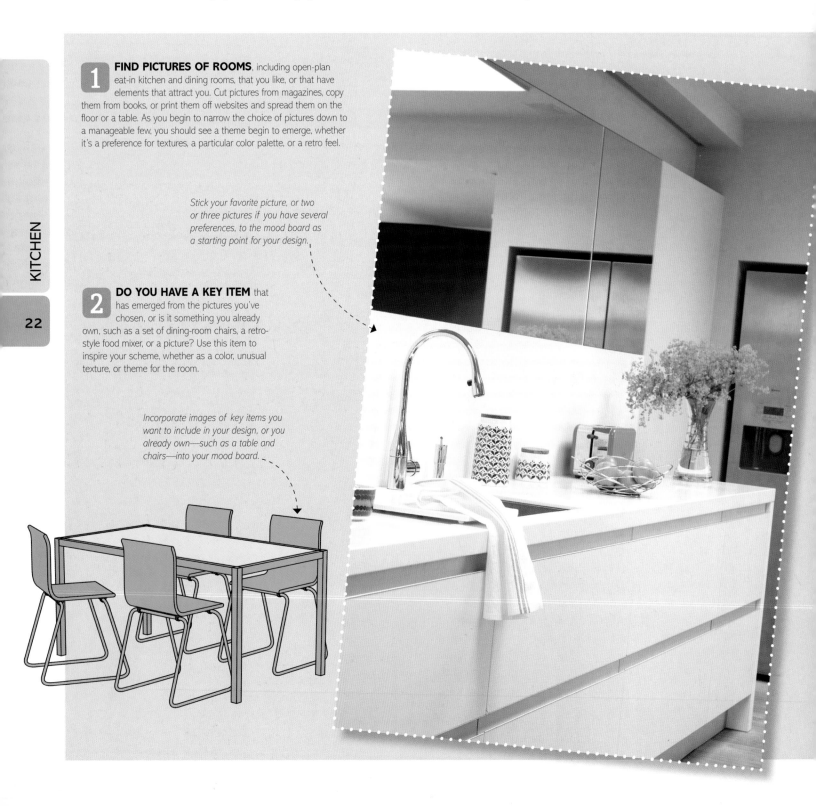

1 **FIND PICTURES OF ROOMS**, including open-plan eat-in kitchen and dining rooms, that you like, or that have elements that attract you. Cut pictures from magazines, copy them from books, or print them off websites and spread them on the floor or a table. As you begin to narrow the choice of pictures down to a manageable few, you should see a theme begin to emerge, whether it's a preference for textures, a particular color palette, or a retro feel.

Stick your favorite picture, or two or three pictures if you have several preferences, to the mood board as a starting point for your design.

2 **DO YOU HAVE A KEY ITEM** that has emerged from the pictures you've chosen, or is it something you already own, such as a set of dining-room chairs, a retro-style food mixer, or a picture? Use this item to inspire your scheme, whether as a color, unusual texture, or theme for the room.

Incorporate images of key items you want to include in your design, or you already own—such as a table and chairs—into your mood board.

3 **PICK A BACKGROUND WALL COLOR** that will enhance the look of the cabinets you like, or that zones the room into dining and cooking areas. Some walls will be partly covered with a backsplash, so consider the color of these, too. They don't have to match, but there should be a cohesion between them and the cabinets. Attach a tile, paint colors, and any other samples to the mood board for reference.

If your units will be bright or glossy, pick an understated or neutral color as a background shade for the walls.

Think about including at least two accent colors in your scheme.

An accent color can be a subtle variation of, or a dramatic contrast to, your background wall color.

4 **INTRODUCE TWO ACCENT COLORS** that link visually to your background color, and consider adding a third accent color in small splashes. Play around with the proportions of the color combinations using fabric and paint swatches and floor samples to see if they work successfully.

Pick a strong contrasting accent color if you want touches of bright, bold detail.

5 **ADD PATTERN & TEXTURE** with a grainy wood countertop or cabinet doors, for example, or with patterned tiles, wallpaper, a fabric blind, a natural stone for tiles and walls, or a composite countertop. Include roughly woven storage baskets, grained wood cutting boards, or ribbed china bowls for added texture. Stick wallpaper and fabric swatches and pictures of tiles and flooring and countertop surfaces to the mood board to find the look you're aiming for.

If your kitchen is large, add pattern with wallpaper, for example, but don't add more than two patterns to the room.

Select a range of materials and different textures as options for the floor, walls, countertops, and storage.

6 **CHOOSE NEW FURNITURE** such as a table, chairs, a sideboard, or extra storage. Shape and size are just as important as looks, so check carefully before you buy to see if the pieces will sit comfortably in the room. Also use the color and textural elements of your mood board to check which material your furniture should be made from.

7 **ADD THE FINISHING TOUCHES** such as light fixtures, pictures, and china; stick pictures of your choices to your mood board. If you like to revamp rooms regularly, pick plain and textured accessories and add splashes of an accent color with the odd item here and there to unite the whole scheme.

Accessories in an accent color or contemporary material add to a fun, creative look.

Consider buying colored dishes and flatware to make your color scheme more cohesive.

3 LAYOUT CONSIDERATIONS IN THE KITCHEN

Before you begin planning the look of your kitchen, think about how it will work on a functional level. In addition to considering each component to be included, it's worth asking yourself some general questions about the room: does it need to double up as a dining area? Or do you need to organize the space so that different people can do different jobs at the same time?

REFRIGERATOR

Make the placement of the refrigerator, or fridge-freezer, one of your earliest considerations, since it comprises part of the "work triangle"—see pages 26–27 for more information on this. Also bear in mind that if you want your refrigerator to operate at maximum efficiency, you need to position it slightly away from heat sources such as radiators and dishwashers, as well as the oven. If you want a refrigerator equipped with an ice dispenser, position it near the water supply so it can be connected.

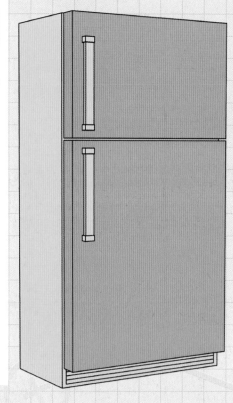

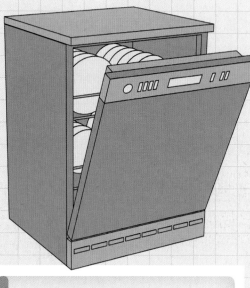

DISHWASHER

The best place for the dishwasher is right next to, or beneath, the sink, so you can rinse plates and unstack them onto the drain board if necessary. It can also be connected to the water supply and drain without extra plumbing costs.

KITCHEN CABINETS

When deciding which type of cabinet units you need, think about where the contents should be kept for easy access: for example, store your plates and bowls in a cabinet next to the dishwasher and position pantry ingredients near the range. Your units will also provide countertop space, so consider where you want this—some large kitchens have a separate island of units in the middle of the floor for this reason. Wherever the units are positioned, make sure there is space for the doors and drawers to open comfortably.

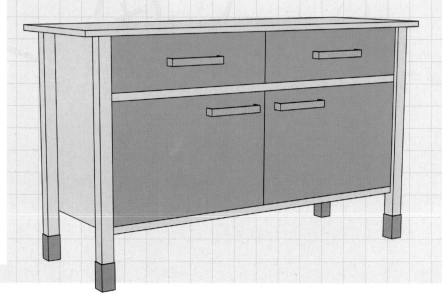

KITCHEN SINK

The sink is the second point of the work triangle (see pages 26–27), so think about its positioning early on, at the same time you decide where the cooking appliances and refrigerator will go. Remember that you need space in this part of the kitchen to be able to wash food or do dishes without impinging on other work areas. Make sure it isn't situated in a main thoroughfare either.

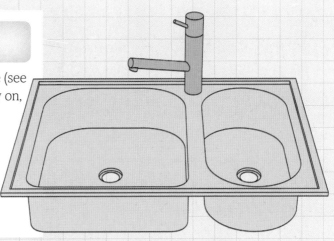

RANGE

Since the range is the third point of the work triangle, its ideal location will be partly determined by the relative positioning of the sink and refrigerator. Placing your range is simpler if you have an all-in-one unit combining oven and cooktop. If the cooktop and oven are separate, on a kitchen island, for instance, the oven should be in easy reach—right behind, perhaps, or in an adjacent run of cabinets. Since you may have to transfer food from the cooktop to the oven and back again, the two components should be no more than 4ft (120cm) apart.

TABLE AND CHAIRS

Positioning your kitchen table so it doesn't impinge on your work triangle may prove to be difficult if space is tight, since, ideally, there should be 3ft (1m) of space for maneuvering behind every chair. If you do not regularly need to seat people on all sides of the table, position the table against a wall and only move it into the middle of the room when you need to set an extra place or two.

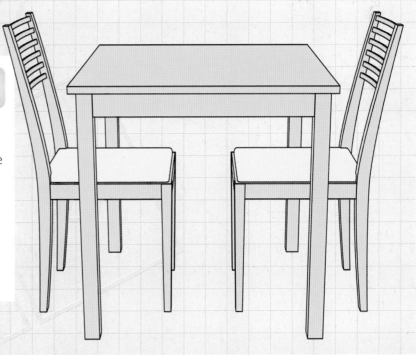

PLAN THE PERFECT
KITCHEN WORK TRIANGLE

To create a smoothly functioning kitchen, it is helpful to understand the concept of the work triangle. This states that there are three key points in any kitchen: a cooking area (the range), a food storage area (the refrigerator), and a cleaning area (the sink). Here's how to plan your space around these three points.

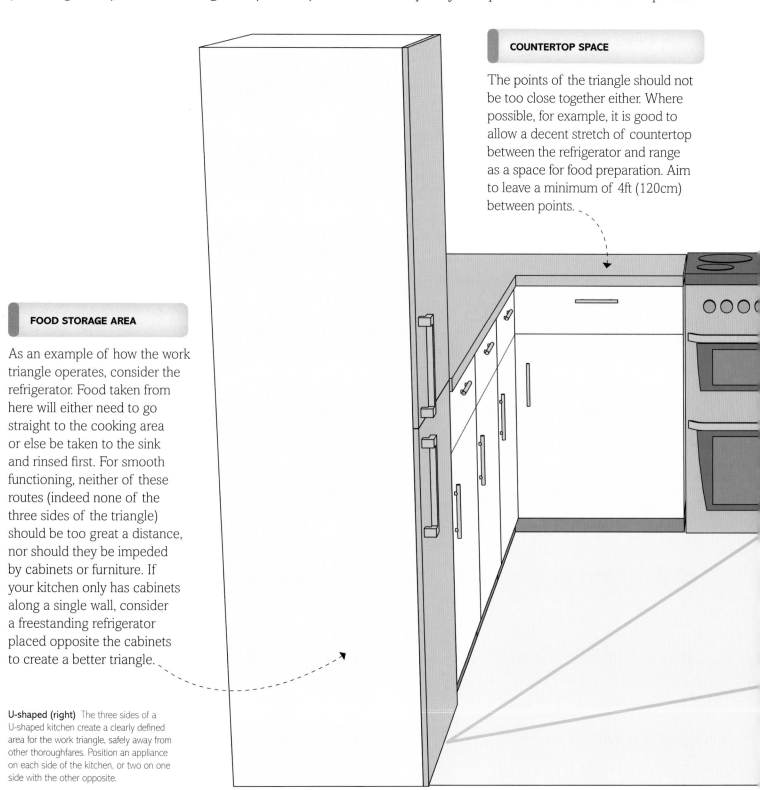

COUNTERTOP SPACE

The points of the triangle should not be too close together either. Where possible, for example, it is good to allow a decent stretch of countertop between the refrigerator and range as a space for food preparation. Aim to leave a minimum of 4ft (120cm) between points.

FOOD STORAGE AREA

As an example of how the work triangle operates, consider the refrigerator. Food taken from here will either need to go straight to the cooking area or else be taken to the sink and rinsed first. For smooth functioning, neither of these routes (indeed none of the three sides of the triangle) should be too great a distance, nor should they be impeded by cabinets or furniture. If your kitchen only has cabinets along a single wall, consider a freestanding refrigerator placed opposite the cabinets to create a better triangle.

U-shaped (right) The three sides of a U-shaped kitchen create a clearly defined area for the work triangle, safely away from other thoroughfares. Position an appliance on each side of the kitchen, or two on one side with the other opposite.

COOKING AREA

When cooking, you need to be able to get ingredients from the refrigerator quickly and easily and also to transfer dirty pots and pans to the sink or surrounding countertop. With this in mind, the maximum recommended distance between points of the work triangle is 10ft (3m), in a straight line.

CLEANING AREA

Moving from the refrigerator to the sink to rinse your food, on to the cooking area, then back to the sink with your dirty pots—all of this is made much simpler if you can avoid any thoroughfares intruding on the work triangle. Another thing that will aid economy of movement is locating your dishwasher as close as possible to the sink, so that any pans left to soak have to travel the shortest distance possible afterward.

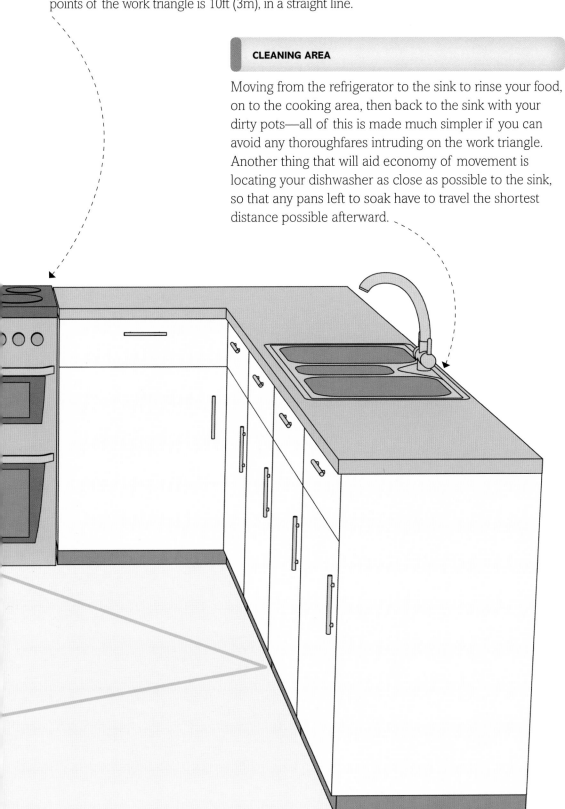

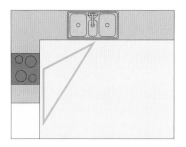

L-shaped In an L-shaped kitchen where the cabinets run along two adjacent walls, two points of the triangle should be located along one wall and the other along the second wall. Think carefully about which appliances should go together.

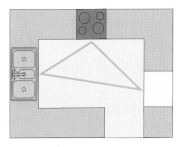

G-shaped A G-shaped kitchen can be laid out much like a U-shaped kitchen, with an appliance on each of the three sides, or alternatively you can position one of the points of the triangle within the peninsula.

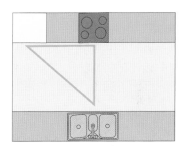

Galley Galley kitchens tend to be a thoroughfare, making the work triangle imperfect, but in all other respects you can create a smoothly functioning workspace by positioning two appliances along one wall and the other opposite.

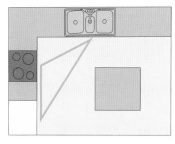

Island feature If you add an island feature to an L- or U-shaped kitchen, you can either use the island as the site for the sink or range, or else put the appliances against the walls and simply position the island so it does not encroach on the work triangle.

4 CHOOSE KITCHEN CABINETS

Choosing your kitchen cabinets requires careful planning so that you get the right configuration to suit your needs perfectly. Start by asking yourself whether you prefer built-in or freestanding cabinets, and then consider individual elements—what storage do you need, and what finish do you want for the doors?

1 BUILT-IN OR FREESTANDING

Two factors will influence your choice: the look, and your budget. Built-in kitchens are streamlined and use space effectively, but freestanding kitchens can be a cheaper option, with lower installation costs, so you may be able to afford a better-quality kitchen.

BUILT-IN

Built-in kitchens—where runs of cabinets are installed along the wall—maximize storage and use space efficiently, so they are practical for all room sizes. Buy the cabinets separately and hire a trusted contractor to install them, or opt for a specialized company that will take care of everything from design through to installation.

FREESTANDING

Freestanding kitchens can comprise separate stand-alone cabinets, drawers, islands, and other cabinets. They are flexible, since you can add to them or rearrange the layout—and even take them with you if you move. Freestanding cabinets work best in larger kitchens, since they don't use space as efficiently as built-in versions.

2 CHOOSE YOUR BASIC CABINETS

Built-in kitchens can include base and wall cabinets, and possibly tall cabinets, which should meet all storage requirements. Consider exactly what you want to store and how often you'll want to access it before you buy.

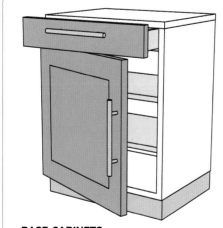

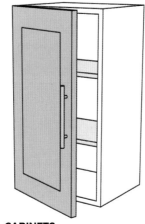

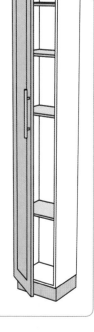

BASE CABINETS

Cabinets between the floor and countertop range in size from 12in (30cm) to 39in (100cm) wide. High-line cabinets have single or double doors, usually with shelves inside; drawer-line cabinets feature one or more drawers.

WALL CABINETS

Wall-mounted cabinets are also 12in (30cm) to 39in (100cm) wide and vary in height (pick according to the height of your ceiling). Leave a gap of at least 18in (45cm) between the countertop and the underside of the cabinet.

HIGH CABINETS

These floor-to-ceiling cabinets include narrow pull-out cabinets, which provide easy access to stored items, and pantry cabinets with shelves that can store practically anything from food to china. Both types of cabinet finish level with the tops of wall cabinets, and provide valuable extra storage space while taking up minimal floor space.

3 CHOOSE STORAGE OPTIONS

A wide selection of internal fixtures and storage accessories for cabinets and drawers will help to keep your contents secure and surfaces clutter-free. Note down what needs to be stored and how often it is used to determine the type of storage you need.

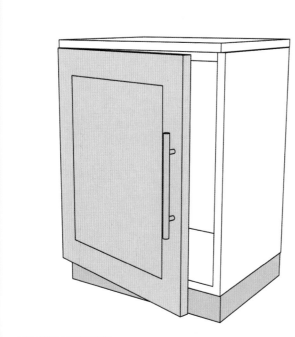

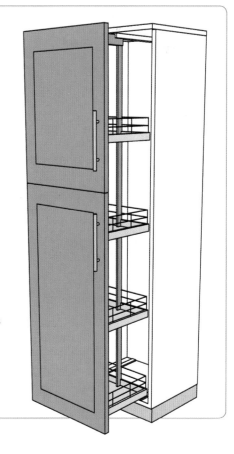

CABINET OPTIONS

Standard cabinets may suit all your storage needs, but if not, you could add at least one wide cabinet of 24in (60cm) or more. If you want, you can also include half-depth cabinets for small items like canned goods and spices.

PULL-OUT PANTRY

Tall pull-out pantry storage cabinets incorporate wire baskets on runners, making spices, cans, and groceries easy to spot and reach for. They are available in various widths and look best positioned by a refrigerator. Ideally, they should also be near a counter or a table so the contents are easier to load and unload.

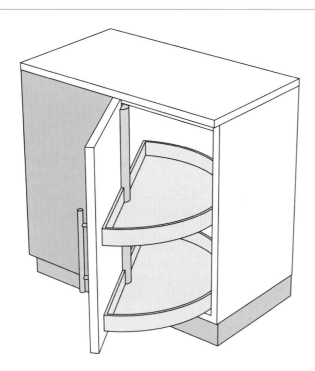

CAROUSEL

A carousel helps you utilize corner space that would otherwise be difficult to access. They are available as rectangular units with semicircular shelves (shown above) or L-shaped units with three-quarter-circular shelves that spin all the way around.

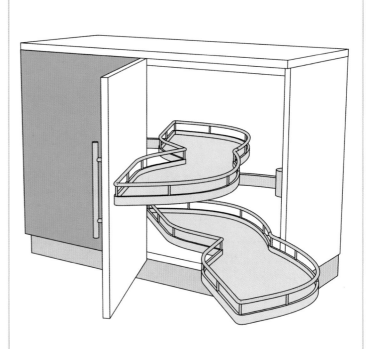

PULL-OUT CORNER UNIT

Another great way of making use of otherwise restricted corner space, these units have shelves mounted on a hinged arm. With the door open, the shelves will swing out, giving you easy access to the entire contents.

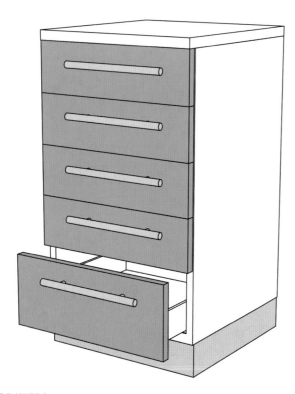

DRAWERS

The traditional method of kitchen storage, drawers can be used for anything from cutlery and dish towels to fine china. Drawer units are best located low enough so that you can see into the drawers when they are opened.

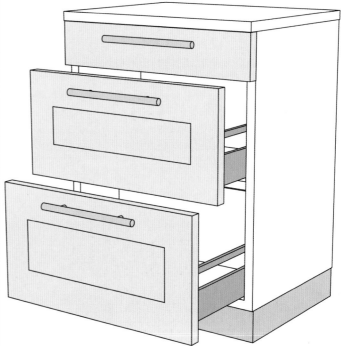

EXTRA-DEEP DRAWERS

Fashionable in contemporary kitchens, these oversized drawers are deep enough to hold stacked-up dinnerware, saucepans, and electrical appliances. Opt for a soft-close mechanism, which ensures that the drawers close gently and quietly to minimize any accidents or noise.

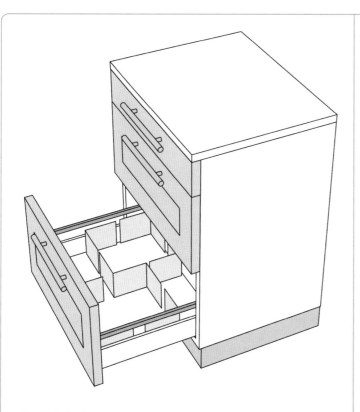

DRAWER DIVIDERS

Wood or plastic inserts, which separate and secure various items in drawers, include cutlery and utensil trays, knife blocks, and plate holders—vertical pegs that prevent stacks of plates from being disturbed when the drawer is moved.

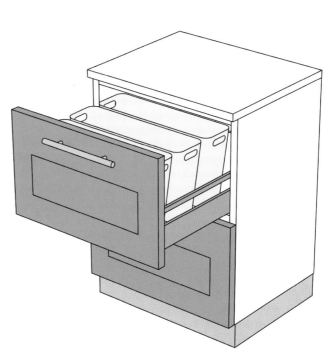

PULL-OUT BASKETS

Keep your recycling organized and out of sight with baskets that slide out on runners, concealed behind doors or drawer fronts. Make sure the number of compartments is appropriate for the recycling program in your area.

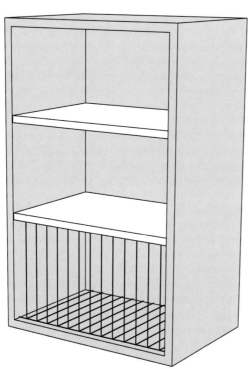

PLATE RACK

The benefit of a plate rack is that it keeps plates separated and upright so they are less likely to gather dust. It is a practical buy if you have expensive dinnerware that you want on show and that you would rather not stack. Often built into a wall unit, a plate rack can be an insert for deep drawers.

WINE RACK

A wine rack allows bottles of wine to rest lying down. Available in varying sizes, this feature can be installed inside wall or base cabinets, as a pull-out from a cupboard door, or installed as a separate unit, often as an infill between two wider cabinets.

4 CHOOSE DOORS

The appearance and style of a kitchen depends very much on the style of the cabinet doors. Manufacturers offer a choice of solid doors, which can be paneled or flush, or glass-paneled doors with various types of surround.

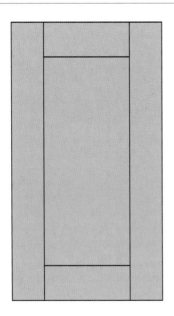

SOLID

Flat, flush doors are sleek, contemporary, and easy to keep clean. Paneled doors consist of a sunken panel surrounded by a frame. Shaker-style doors suit all types of kitchen, and tongue-and-groove and arched panels are ideal for traditional design schemes.

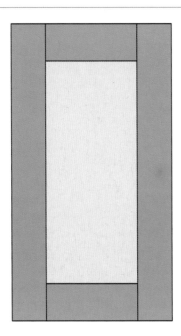

GLASS PANEL

Glass-paneled doors are often used alongside solid doors in wall units to provide contrast. Frosted glass is popular, but go for clear glass if you want to display the items inside. The cabinets may also be lit from within, providing a gentle glow that illuminates the contents.

5 CHOOSE THE FINISH

The material and color you choose for the cabinet doors are the crucial factors in creating your look. In a large room, you could try two coordinating shades or finishes, such as painted or clear finished wood—but avoid using more than two.

WOOD LAMINATE

Cost-effective laminated wood doors are made by heat-bonding patterned paper onto MDF; veneered doors consist of MDF covered with a thin layer of real wood.

SOLID WOOD

Warm wood is environmentally friendly, and the doors are available in finishes from pale ash through to deep mahogany. The high quality is reflected in the price.

PAINTED

Made from solid wood or coated MDF, painted doors are often found in country-style kitchens. The doors can be finished in any paint color you like.

HI-GLOSS

Made from MDF onto which a high-gloss thermofoil layer has been glued at high pressure, these shiny flush doors are available in many colors.

STAINLESS STEEL

This tough material creates an industrial, contemporary look. The doors are made from MDF wrapped in brushed steel. The overall effect is very striking, if expensive.

GLASS

Choose from frosted or clear glass with a wood or MDF frame. These doors are available as single-framed panels or paned windows, which suit traditional rooms.

6 | CHOOSE HARDWARE

Stylish hardware can make all the difference, transforming an ordinary kitchen into something special, or helping to create a particular effect. Use identical hardware throughout for a streamlined effect and to keep the scheme from looking messy.

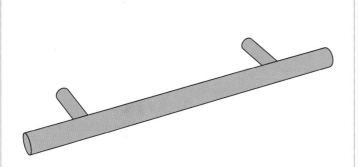

BAR PULL

Bar pulls are angular in shape and are available in various lengths and finishes. Opt for a sleek, minimalist finish if you have a contemporary kitchen, or pick more intricate designs if you have chosen a classic scheme.

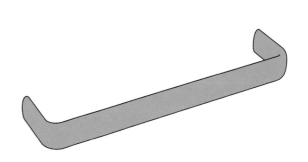

D AND BOW

D pulls are simple and stylish, with a softer look than bar pulls due to their curved corners. Bow pulls are similar, but consist of a single, sweeping curve. Both of these styles are available in various lengths, thicknesses, and profiles.

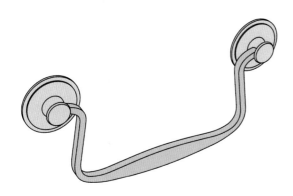

DROP PULLS

Drop-pendant, drop-bar, and drop-ring pulls are used almost exclusively in traditional kitchens and are hinged, unlike other types of pull. Simply lift them up and pull to open drawers and cabinets.

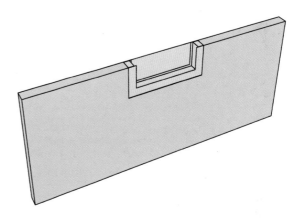

RECESSED PULLS

Also known as integrated pulls, recessed pulls create a flush, streamlined effect and are a trademark of an ultramodern kitchen. They are usually positioned at the tops of drawers and cabinets and include molded grooves and metal-inset pulls.

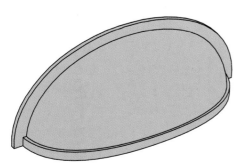

CUP PULLS

These traditional metal pulls are typically found on drawers rather than cabinets. Available in brushed nickel, chrome, or antique brass, they often feature in Shaker-style kitchens, where they add a stylish finishing touch.

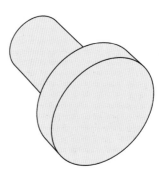

KNOBS

If you want to choose from the widest selection of sizes, materials, and shapes, opt for a traditional knob design. Pick wood or porcelain finishes for a classic kitchen, or brushed or polished metal to give your cabinets a contemporary twist.

5 CHOOSE COUNTERTOPS

A good-quality countertop can really lift the look of a kitchen—even if you have chosen plain cabinets on a budget—so it's worth spending as much as you can afford on it. Keep in mind that you get what you pay for in terms of quality, and always follow the manufacturer's care instructions carefully so it wears well.

CHOOSE THE MATERIAL

The range of countertop materials to choose from is vast, and there can be a huge variation in the quality of each type. Check the durability of the material you prefer and whether it is suitable for use around the cooktop and sink before you buy.

GRANITE
Expensive and extremely hard-wearing, granite is available in a polished high-gloss finish or a honed matte finish. It won't need to be resealed for 10 years or so.

COMPOSITE STONE
Made of resin, minerals, and acrylic, medium-priced, hard-wearing composite stone comes in a range of colors. Choose a smooth or slightly grainy textured surface.

LAVA STONE
Lava stone is a natural volcanic stone that can be glazed in any color or finish. It is very expensive, but it is claimed that nothing can damage its surface.

WOOD
Medium to high in price, hardwood gives a warm look. Choices vary from pale beech to dark wenge. Reseal the wood annually, or sooner if it starts to lose its sheen.

GLASS
Mid- to high-priced toughened glass is scratch-, heat-, and acid-resistant, and may crack only if heavy objects are dropped onto it. Choose tinted or colored glass.

STAINLESS STEEL
Popular in professional kitchens, medium-priced stainless steel is durable, hygienic, and can be made in almost any shape and size. Any scratches will add to its appeal.

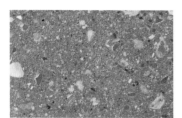

CONCRETE
High-priced concrete countertops are set on site or cast using a template made to your specification. Different finishes are available. Treat with sealant before use.

CORIAN®
This high-priced surface has a semi-matte, nonporous finish that is extremely hard-wearing. It is easy to care for and any scratches can be removed professionally.

LAMINATE
Laminate countertops come in many guises including wood, stone, and granite effect. They are not as hard-wearing as the real thing, but are a much cheaper option.

CARING FOR A COUNTERTOP

Follow these tips to keep your countertops in good condition.

Clean wood countertops with a soft cloth and warm soapy water. Wipe up spills immediately.

For granite countertops, use a nonabrasive neutral detergent and dry it with a chamois cloth to maintain the shine. Use steel wool to clean drain board grooves, a water-based stain remover to remove wine and tea stains, and an alkaline degreaser to remove grease and oil.

Clean Corian® using a kitchen spray and a cloth. Remove hard water marks with a limescale remover and grease and red wine with detergent. You may need to use bleach to remove tea and coffee stains.

Use a soft cloth and warm soapy water to clean laminate surfaces. Remove stubborn marks with a cream cleaner or a mild bleach solution. Use a bleach solution on stronger stains like red wine.

To treat glass, concrete, or stainless steel, wipe with a soft cloth and soapy water to remove marks. Polish with a microfiber cloth to give shine. Use baby oil on stainless steel to keep it looking new.

For composite and stone, use a soft, damp cloth and a mild detergent.

6 CHOOSE A BACKSPLASH

You should choose your backsplash at the same time as your work surface. You don't have to use the same material, but you should pick something that complements it. Whether you choose to have a small backsplash tile or a whole wall of your chosen material is a matter of personal taste.

CHOOSE THE MATERIAL

Your backsplash material, above all else, needs to be practical and easy to clean. However, it's also a good opportunity to add interest to your walls, so consider adding color with glass, pattern with tiles, or warmth with wood.

TILED

Probably the most popular choice, tiles are easy to clean and stain-resistant, although you should steer clear of unglazed finishes, since they are porous and will stain if splashed. If you have a large kitchen, consider using bigger tiles for your backsplash.

GLASS

A good choice for modern kitchens, tempered-glass backsplashes are usually custom-made, although you can buy precut panels that normally come in 28in (70cm) widths. They come in a huge range of colors; look for those that are UV stable so they won't fade.

WOOD

A solid wood backsplash will need to be treated regularly—either every three months, or when you notice that it has lost its sheen—so that it continues to repel water and oil splashes. It is not suitable for use behind a cooktop, since it may become scorched.

STAINLESS STEEL

Stainless steel is extremely hard-wearing, hygienic, and easy to clean. Its surface may scratch over time, but that is part of its appeal and complements its tough, industrial look. Stainless-steel backsplashes are available in various sizes.

5 WAYS WITH
BACKSPLASHES

A new backsplash can transform an existing kitchen for a fraction of the budget you would need if you were to replace all your kitchen cabinets. You don't have to choose a plain backsplash; there are unusual effects or materials you can opt for if you want to make the backsplash the focal point of your kitchen.

SUBWAY TILES

Subway tiles are traditional-shaped tiles that look just as good in contemporary kitchens as in rustic ones. Adhere the tiles to the wall in a horizontal pattern, and consider extending this backsplash effect behind all the countertops if you like the look.

CONSIDER USING a colored tile grout for a bold contemporary look.

PATTERNED TILES

For an eclectic look, try a patchwork arrangement of vintage-style tiles in a range of patterns.

MIRROR

In small, dark kitchens, a mirrored backsplash will bounce light around the room, although it is not suitable for use behind a cooktop.

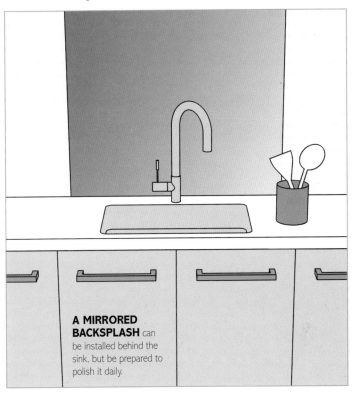

A MIRRORED BACKSPLASH can be installed behind the sink, but be prepared to polish it daily.

FEATURE WALLPAPER

Create a striking feature wall by wallpapering your wall, then covering it with a protective glass panel.

KITCHENS ARE PRONE to excessive moisture, so choose a mold-resistant paper.

MIRRORED MOSAIC

Mirrored mosaic tiles will give your kitchen a glamorous feel and, like a mirrored backsplash, will reflect light around a small space.

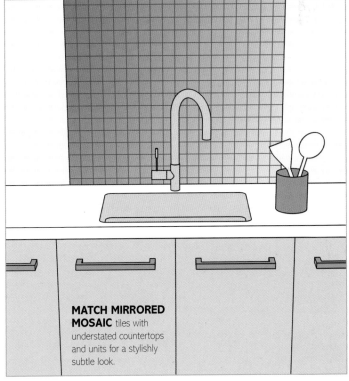

MATCH MIRRORED MOSAIC tiles with understated countertops and units for a stylishly subtle look.

7 CHOOSE A KITCHEN SINK

In addition to thinking about which fixtures and material you would prefer when choosing your kitchen sink, it's also worth considering what you intend to use the sink for—are you an avid cook, or someone who doesn't spend much time in the kitchen?—and how much counter space you can afford to sacrifice for it.

1 DECIDE ON THE TYPE OF SINK

To choose a sink, figure out the size of the cabinet or unit it will sit in (it must be big enough to house the bowl), the depth and width of the counter, and what you will use the sink for; if you cook most nights, you'll need at least a sink and a half.

SINGLE SINK

If you have a compact kitchen, or rarely use your sink, a single bowl will be more than adequate. Single sinks are available in various designs and come in a range of sizes and shapes.

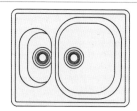

ONE-AND-A-HALF SINKS

A one-and-a-half sink allows you to perform more than one task at any time. The full-sized bowl can be used for washing dishes and the smaller half sink for rinsing them and for food preparation.

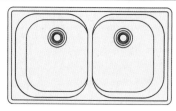

DOUBLE SINK

Double sinks have two bowls with the same dimensions, although sometimes the second bowl is slightly smaller. This allows you to deal with bigger jobs at the same time, such as washing dishes and soaking pans.

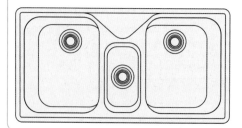

TWO-AND-A-HALF SINKS

This type of sink, with two large bowls and a small third bowl, which can be used for food preparation or for a garbage disposal unit, gives you the most washing options. Its size means it is only really suitable for larger kitchens.

DRAIN BOARDS

Some people have a strong preference for having the drain board on one side of the sink rather than the other. However, it is usually more important to think about which configuration will best suit your space. Go for the arrangement that seems the least disruptive in the way it affects the run of countertop.

2 DECIDE ON THE MOUNTING

Some sinks are designed to be mounted beneath the counter,top and look much more streamlined than those that are surface-mounted. However, surface-mounted sinks are easier to install and are therefore usually the cheaper option.

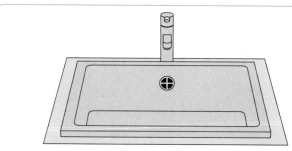

INSET

Inset sinks are fixed into place so that the rim of the sink stands slightly above the countertop. They are available in a wide range of sizes and designs, with various drain board options, and are suitable for use with all countertop materials.

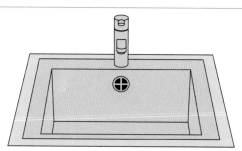

FLUSH-MOUNTED

A flush-mounted sink has a fine lip around its edge that sits on a recessed inset cut into the countertop to give a near seamless edge. A silicon seal holds the sink in place and makes the area around it watertight. It is not suitable for wood or laminate counters.

UNDERMOUNTED

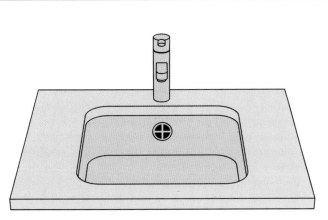

This sink, as its name suggests, is installed beneath the counter surface to leave the edge of the counter on show. It can only be used with solid counters such as stone or Corian®, and if you want a drain board you will need to have some grooves cut or routed into the surface of your counter.

INTEGRAL

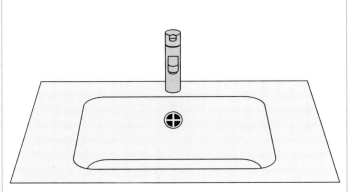

Made from the same piece of composite or stainless steel as your countertop, integral sinks give a sleek look that is hygienic, since there aren't any seams. This can be expensive and you will need to have grooves cut or stamped into the surface to create a draining area.

FARM SINK

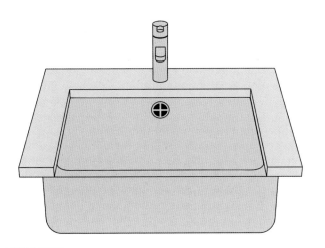

Typically rectangular in shape, these sinks are good work sinks that provide a classic country look as well. These sinks sit below the countertop, with the front of the sink on show.

CHOOSE THE FINISH

The choice of sink finishes available is vast. Choose a hard-wearing option that will be easy to clean; some materials show stains and scratches more readily, while others look as good after years of use as they did on day one. Check, too, if it complements the counter, which is the real showpiece.

STAINLESS STEEL

The most popular choice, stainless steel is durable, hard-wearing, and easy to look after. Prices can vary hugely, from low to high, depending on the design and quality.

PORCELAIN

Heat-, stain-, and scratch-resistant, a porcelain sink is a robust mid-price choice, although there is a minor risk that a heavy item dropped on it could cause it to crack.

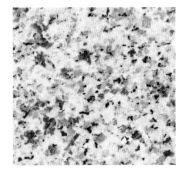

GRANITE

Granite sinks are made of 80–85% ground natural granite mixed with resin. Although expensive, they are hard-wearing and available in a wide range of colors.

CORIAN®

This solid surface sink has a hard-wearing semi-matte, nonporous finish and is medium to high in price. Any scratches have to be removed professionally.

COMPOSITE

Made from resin, minerals, and acrylic, this mid-priced sink has a smooth or grainy texture. It comes in a range of colors (in hard-water areas, pale colors may stain).

COPPER

Although an expensive choice for sinks, copper offers good antibacterial properties. Keep it clean with soap and water. In hard-water areas, dry it with a soft cloth after use.

8 CHOOSE
KITCHEN FAUCETS

Picking the right kitchen faucet is mainly a matter of choosing the style you prefer; whether the sink has predrilled faucet holes will also influence choice. Kitchens often have a high-pressure water supply, so most types of faucet will work (if water pressure is low, however, designs with pull-out sprays won't work effectively).

1 CHOOSE THE TYPE

Unless your choice of faucet is predetermined by the sink you've chosen (with predrilled holes), you need to prioritize which style you prefer and the extent of your budget.

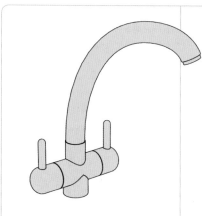  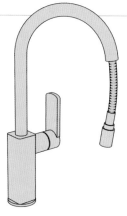 

MIXER

This single faucet with controls on each side mixes hot and cold water within its body. It is available as a single-hole, three-piece, bridge mixer, or wall-mounted option.

SINGLE LEVER

A single-lever faucet operates in a similar way to a mixer faucet, but has one lever to alter the temperature and control the water flow. Its neat design makes it easy to clean.

PULL-OUT

Larger than standard faucets, pull-out faucets require high water pressure and feature a pull-out spray head on a flexible hose for rinsing dishes and fresh produce.

PILLAR

Suitable for two-hole sinks, this pair of matching faucets supply hot and cold water independently. Pillar faucets are a traditional design with crosshead or lever handles.

2 CHOOSE THE FINISH

There is a wide choice of faucet finishes available, so what you choose will depend on the color of your sink, appliances, and other elements of the kitchen, and whether you prefer a sleek and shiny finish or a contemporary matte finish.

   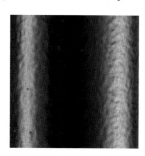 

CHROME

A popular choice in a range of prices, shiny chrome faucets suit contemporary and traditional kitchens. Chrome is easy to keep clean, but water spots will show.

BRASS

Mid- to high-priced polished or antiqued brass faucets add warmth to traditional and country-style kitchens. Brass retains its appearance for many years.

BRUSHED METAL

Brushed chrome or nickel is a mid- to high-priced choice. It won't show water marks as much as shiny surfaces, and works well with appliances in a similar finish.

POWDER-COATED BRASS

Black or white faucets made of powder-coated brass can look striking paired with certain sinks and countertops. They are available in a range of prices.

OIL-RUBBED BRONZE

Available in a range of prices, this attractive dark finish, which changes over time as the yellow metal starts to show through the coating, suits traditional kitchens.

CHOOSE
A REFRIGERATOR

Your kitchen layout and the amount of vertical or floor space you have will dictate whether you choose a combined fridge-freezer or separate units. Decide their proportionate sizes—how much fresh food do you need to store, and how much frozen?—and consider energy-efficient models before you buy.

1 CHOOSE THE APPLIANCE

If your refrigerator and freezer will both sit under a countertop, you may want to choose matching (but not combined) appliances. If, however, you need your under-counter cabinet space for extra storage, a combined fridge-freezer is best.

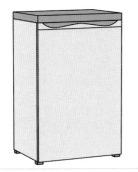

UNDER-COUNTER MODELS

A separate refrigerator and freezer are a practical choice for a kitchen that doesn't have full-height units. These appliances can even be positioned within a kitchen island. They don't have to sit side by side, although it's easier if they do.

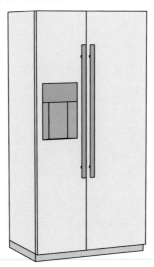

SIDE-BY-SIDE FRIDGE-FREEZER

Large side-by-side fridge freezers are around 6ft (2m) tall and are usually configured with the two appliances combined side by side. The fridge tends to be about twice the width of the freezer. They are available in a wide range of colors, and often feature water coolers and ice makers, which means they may require minor plumbing.

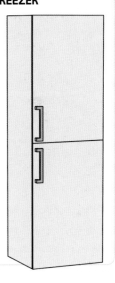

STACKED FRIDGE-FREEZER

Stacked fridge-freezers are a popular choice for both built-in and freestanding kitchens and are available in a variety of fridge and freezer sizes and configurations. The refrigerator will usually be at least as big as the freezer compartment— often bigger. Having the fridge above the freezer is the most ergonomic arrangement, since it minimizes the need to bend down.

2 CHOOSE THE LOOK

It is likely to be one of the largest items in your kitchen, so the appearance of your fridge-freezer requires careful consideration. An integrated model will give a more streamlined look, while a stylish freestanding model can make a good focal point.

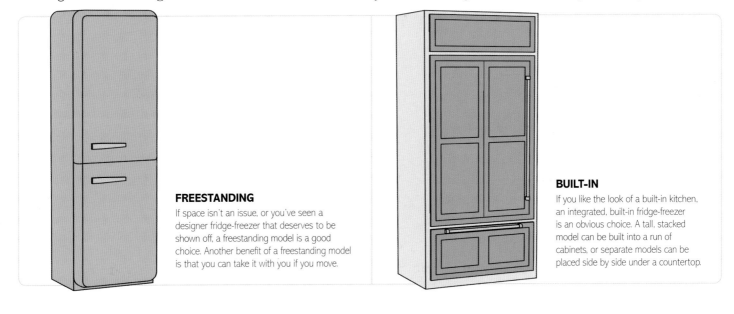

FREESTANDING

If space isn't an issue, or you've seen a designer fridge-freezer that deserves to be shown off, a freestanding model is a good choice. Another benefit of a freestanding model is that you can take it with you if you move.

BUILT-IN

If you like the look of a built-in kitchen, an integrated, built-in fridge-freezer is an obvious choice. A tall, stacked model can be built into a run of cabinets, or separate models can be placed side by side under a countertop.

10 CHOOSE A STOVE

Picking the right stove is more complicated than choosing other appliances in your kitchen, because it needs to do so much: you need to consider various cooking functions, from broiling to baking, the fuel type, cooktop and oven configurations, and whether you want a self-cleaning function or not.

1 DECIDE WHAT OVEN COMPARTMENTS YOU NEED

When considering the oven compartments you need, take into account how many people you cook for, and how often. Is a single oven enough? Or do you need two ovens running at different temperatures, or a broiler and oven running simultaneously?

SINGLE

Ideal for small kitchens, single ovens tend to have a broiler built within them, which means you can't use the oven and broiler functions at the same time. Some gas models have lift-up lids that double as a backsplash.

DUAL

Dual ovens are configured with either a smaller oven above a larger-capacity oven or two medium ovens stacked vertically. The large oven may be multifunctional (offering a range of heating modes), while the smaller top oven will typically be an economy model featuring a broiler function.

PROFESSIONAL STYLE RANGE

A range is typically freestanding and is larger than a standard stove—sometimes up to 5ft (150cm) wide. Originally quite traditional in design, ranges are now available in more contemporary designs. Most models feature twin ovens side by side, although there are some that have a separate broiler compartment.

FREESTANDING OR BUILT-IN

A stove can either be freestanding or built into your kitchen cabinets. What you choose will largely depend on the look of your kitchen—built-in stoves are a better match for a sleek, contemporary design, while freestanding ranges give a more relaxed look.

FREESTANDING

Invariably used in freestanding kitchens, freestanding stoves can also be used with built-in cabinets if you leave space. Choose from standard stoves, which are 24in (60cm) wide, to professional style ranges. They are available with gas or electric fuel and in a range of styles, from contemporary to retro.

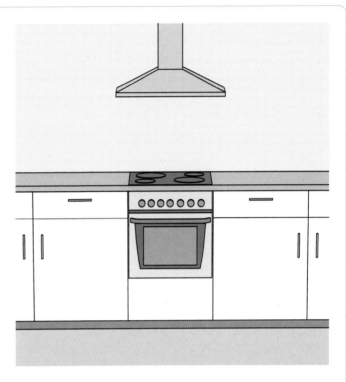

BUILT-IN (STACKED)

In a built-in kitchen, a built-in oven is good for maintaining the overall look, and if yours is a small space where layout choices are limited, it will often make sense to choose a combined model where the cooktop is positioned directly over the oven. Single- and double-oven options are available.

BUILT-IN (SEPARATE)

If you have space, you may find it more convenient to locate your oven and cooktop separately. Having the oven built into a run of high cabinets at eye level is a particularly good option, since you can open the oven or check on its contents without having to bend down.

3 CHOOSE THE FUEL TYPE

Ranges are available in single- or dual-fuel combinations. Electric- and fan-assisted ovens can be combined with a gas cooktop, or you could choose induction burners with a convection oven, or a gas cooktop with a gas oven.

STOVE

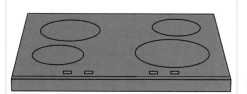

CERAMIC

Easy-to-clean ceramic cooktops have a glass surface with heating elements beneath. The heat is quickly conducted, but isn't as easy to control as gas. Use cast-iron or ferrous pans with this cooktop.

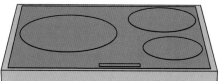

INDUCTION

A magnetic field created between a coil beneath the surface of an electric induction cooktop and a pan heats the pan very quickly and cools almost immediately when turned off. Use cast-iron or ferrous saucepans.

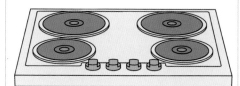

ELECTRIC PLATE

Electric plates provide excellent heat distribution by conducting all heat evenly into the base of a pan, making this a cost-effective option. Any flat-based pans—especially cast-iron—are suitable.

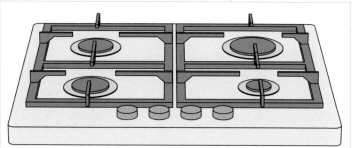

GAS

Gas cooktops typically have four burners of varying sizes, although there are also larger versions (if you choose a range with a gas cooktop, it could easily have six or even eight burners). Gas is still a popular choice, since it is easy to control and provides a visible heat source.

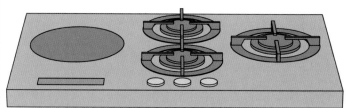

COMBINATION

You can also buy combination cooktops—two gas burners and two electric is a basic example. Or you can go for something more adventurous by mixing an electric cooktop with a gas wok burner. The advantage of this type of cooktop is that it gives you a choice of cooking styles and fuel sources.

OVEN AND BROILER

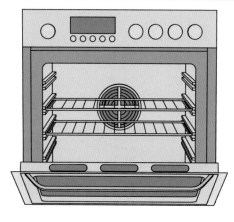

ELECTRIC

Conventional electric ovens are controlled by a thermostat in the middle of the oven, making it slightly hotter at the top and cooler at the bottom. They can take a while to reach the required cooking temperature, so should be preheated. Fan-assisted convection ovens circulate heat quickly, creating a more even temperature.

GAS

Gas ovens are heated by a flame at the bottom of the cavity. The hot air circulates as it rises to create different heat zones, with the highest temperature at the top and the lowest at the bottom. Gas ovens are especially good for baking cakes, since they give off moisture during cooking.

4 CHOOSE A HOOD

Oven hoods are vital for getting rid of steam and cooking smells. Available in a range of designs, they come as extraction hoods, which extract the air from the room, or recirculation hoods, which merely filter it. Many models can be installed as either.

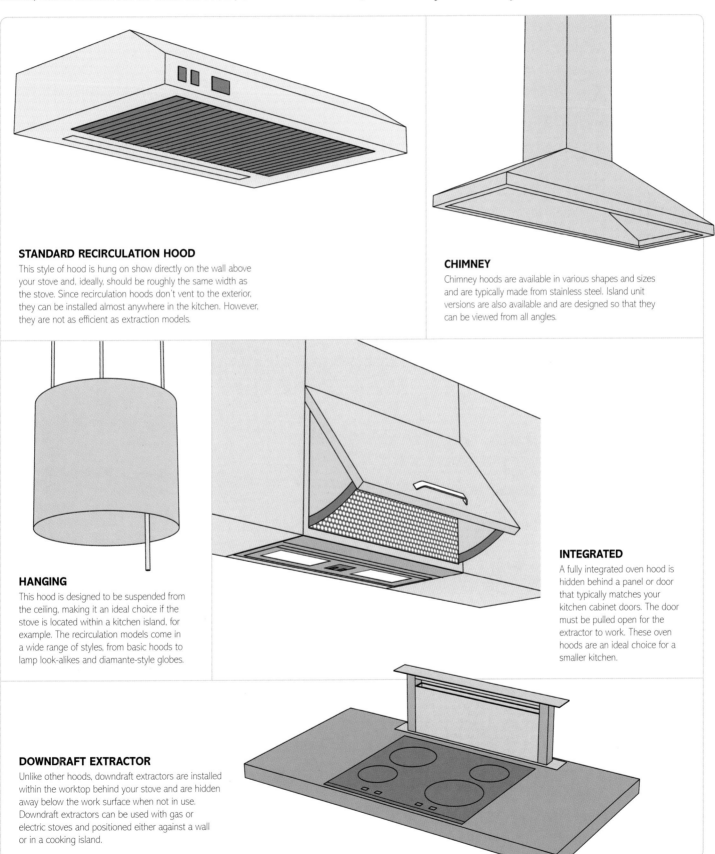

STANDARD RECIRCULATION HOOD

This style of hood is hung on show directly on the wall above your stove and, ideally, should be roughly the same width as the stove. Since recirculation hoods don't vent to the exterior, they can be installed almost anywhere in the kitchen. However, they are not as efficient as extraction models.

CHIMNEY

Chimney hoods are available in various shapes and sizes and are typically made from stainless steel. Island unit versions are also available and are designed so that they can be viewed from all angles.

HANGING

This hood is designed to be suspended from the ceiling, making it an ideal choice if the stove is located within a kitchen island, for example. The recirculation models come in a wide range of styles, from basic hoods to lamp look-alikes and diamante-style globes.

INTEGRATED

A fully integrated oven hood is hidden behind a panel or door that typically matches your kitchen cabinet doors. The door must be pulled open for the extractor to work. These oven hoods are an ideal choice for a smaller kitchen.

DOWNDRAFT EXTRACTOR

Unlike other hoods, downdraft extractors are installed within the worktop behind your stove and are hidden away below the work surface when not in use. Downdraft extractors can be used with gas or electric stoves and positioned either against a wall or in a cooking island.

11 CHOOSE
A DISHWASHER

When it comes to choosing a dishwasher, you need to consider not only its look and capacity, but also whether it can be integrated into a run of cabinets, whether it is energy- and space-efficient, how much noise it makes, and if it has a range of cycles to suit your family's needs.

1 CHOOSE THE MODEL

When planning your kitchen you may automatically include a regular-sized dishwasher in your layout, but this isn't the only option available, and may not be the most suitable model for your kitchen or lifestyle.

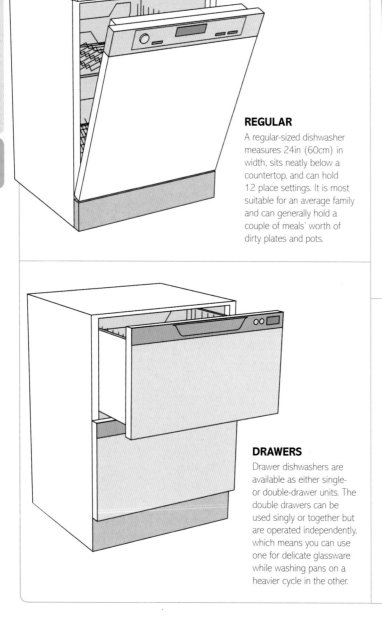

REGULAR

A regular-sized dishwasher measures 24in (60cm) in width, sits neatly below a countertop, and can hold 12 place settings. It is most suitable for an average family and can generally hold a couple of meals' worth of dirty plates and pots.

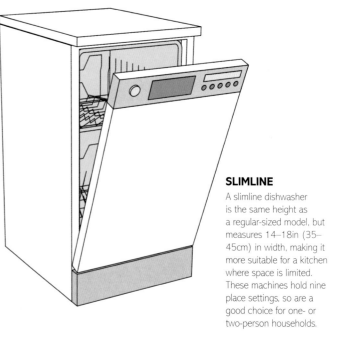

SLIMLINE

A slimline dishwasher is the same height as a regular-sized model, but measures 14–18in (35–45cm) in width, making it more suitable for a kitchen where space is limited. These machines hold nine place settings, so are a good choice for one- or two-person households.

DRAWERS

Drawer dishwashers are available as either single- or double-drawer units. The double drawers can be used singly or together but are operated independently, which means you can use one for delicate glassware while washing pans on a heavier cycle in the other.

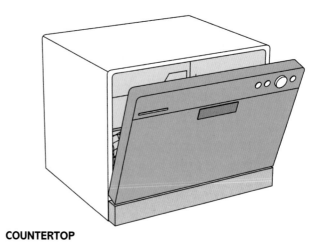

COUNTERTOP

A countertop dishwasher is around 20in (50cm) wide and 18in (45cm) high, so it is an ideal choice for smaller kitchens or single-person households. It is designed to sit on top of a countertop.

2

CHOOSE THE LOOK

If you choose a floor-standing dishwasher that will sit beneath the countertop, you'll need to consider whether you want to have it free-standing, built-in, or concealed.

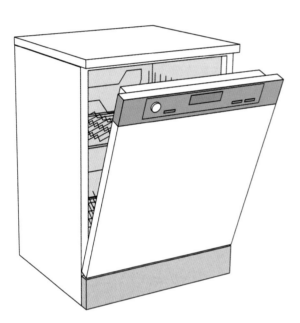

FREESTANDING
One of the main advantages of a freestanding dishwasher is that you can take it with you when you move. Most models are available in white, but if you want yours to be more contemporary looking, you can buy models with a more stylish door shape and finish, such as stainless steel.

SEMI-INTEGRATED
Semi-integrated dishwashers are partially covered by a kitchen cabinet door up to drawer line height, with the control panel above it on show. The advantage of these models over fully integrated ones is that you can observe the control panel while the machine is running to keep track of the cycle process.

FULLY INTEGRATED
Fully integrated dishwashers—including the controls—are concealed behind a cabinet door. Look for a machine with a light that shines on the floor when it's on so you can check that the cycle is running.

DISHWASHERS AND ENERGY EFFICIENCY

Check the ENERGY STAR label when shopping for your dishwasher to find an energy-efficient model. Would investing in a more eco-friendly machine be the right choice for you?

● An eco-friendly model uses on average 10 percent less energy than a dishwasher with a poorer energy efficiency rating. Whether your concern is for the planet or your electricity bill, it's worth considering.

● An energy-efficient dishwasher typically has low water consumption levels: some models use less water than you would washing by hand. It's especially worth monitoring water consumption levels if you are on a water meter.

● Look for machines that have an "eco" or "energy save" program. This will be the cycle that uses the least water and energy, typically washing dishes at a lower temperature.

12 CHOOSE FLOORING

The floor in your kitchen is likely to suffer from more wear and tear than flooring in any other room in your home, so choose something that can deal with all your requirements. In addition to choosing something that looks good, you also need to consider how much maintenance it will require.

1 CHOOSE THE LOOK

Flooring that's suitable for a kitchen broadly falls into three types: tiled, wood, and seamless. Tiled and poured floors create a contemporary look and can withstand the most wear; wood and tiles are good choices if you want an informal, rustic look.

TILED

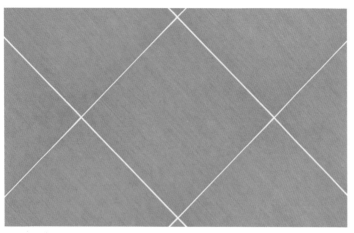

A tiled floor is the classic choice for a kitchen. When choosing tiles, consider the size and finish: large tiles make a space look contemporary, while smaller tiles give a room a more traditional feel. The more grouting there is, the more cleaning the floor will require.

WOOD

Wood floors should be well sealed, and must be able to withstand both the foot traffic of a busy space and the raised moisture levels of a cooking area. Planks can appear visually longer and wider, so are a good choice for small and narrow kitchens.

SEAMLESS

Seamless designs, which include sheet vinyl, rubber, and linoleum, and poured floors like concrete and resin are essentially one piece of flooring without any seams. The latest sheet flooring designs are very upmarket and a good choice for small areas.

CHECKLIST

● **When calculating the amount** of tiles, hardwood, or laminate flooring you need for your project, add at least 10 percent extra to the total amount as a contingency.

● **If you are laying tiles,** particularly large tiles, your subfloor must be perfectly level. If you have floorboards, you will need to cover them first with marine plywood.

● **If you have a sound, flat concrete floor** or an existing flat tiled floor, you can lay new tiles right on top, but check first that the raised level of the new floor will not obstruct any doors or other moveable items in the room.

2 CHOOSE THE MATERIAL

The material you choose will largely depend on your budget and whether you prefer the look and solidity of tiles or a warmer, softer feel like vinyl or rubber. If you are installing underfloor heating, check which materials are suitable to use with it first.

TILES

PORCELAIN

Hard-wearing porcelain is a versatile choice available in a variety of prices, designs, and glazed and unglazed finishes. Seal unglazed tiles before and after grouting.

CERAMIC

Ceramic tiles are good for large areas. Available in a variety of colors, shapes, and textures, they are cheap, hard-wearing, stain-resistant, and don't need sealing.

QUARTZ COMPOSITE

If you want a coordinated look for your countertops and floor, this may be a good choice. It doesn't stain, hides dirt, and rarely chips or cracks, but it is expensive.

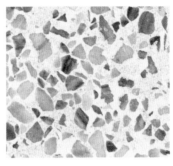

TERRAZZO

This expensive flooring is made of marble chips set into cement with a color pigment added. Endless combinations of colors and finishes can be achieved.

CONCRETE

Extremely hard-wearing but costly, concrete tiles are available in various sizes with a polished or matte finish. The polished effect is easier to clean, so suits a kitchen.

TERRA-COTTA

Medium-priced terra-cotta is very porous so the tiles must be sealed to prevent staining. Choose from a range of shapes such as classic square or brick-shaped tiles.

TRAVERTINE

Though expensive, this natural stone floor is available in either a sleek, polished finish or a rustic, tumbled look with soft edges and a spongelike appearance.

LIMESTONE

These expensive tiles range from chalky white to honey in color, and often reveal details of fossils within. Choose polished gloss tiles or rougher, matte finishes.

SLATE

The uneven "chipped" surface of black or gray slate sometimes has flecks of gold or orange, and always creates a dramatic look. It is medium to high in price.

LAMINATE

These laminated decorative fiberboard tiles are available in a range of colors and designs, including slate and travertine, and are a low- or medium-cost option.

VINYL

Vinyl gives an authentic look of the material it mimics. Prices depend on the brand. Cheaper versions have self-adhesive backing, so are easy to stick to the floor.

RUBBER

Medium-priced rubber comes in a range of colors and textures. Smoother surfaces are easy to clean; low-profile textures, like studs, provide extra grip underfoot.

WOOD

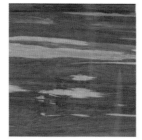

HARDWOOD
Good medium- to high-cost choices that will not react to heat and moisture include mahogany, walnut, and teak. Buy presealed or seal with lacquer or linseed oil.

ENGINEERED WOOD
The construction of this medium-priced wood (layers of hard- and softwood boards topped with hardwood lumber) makes it less likely to warp than hardwood.

BAMBOO
Bamboo is medium- to high-cost and eco-friendly. While moisture-tolerant, it still needs to be sealed. It can either be left in its natural color or stained.

LAMINATE
Low- to medium-cost laminate planks have realistic textured finishes and detailing to give the appearance of real boards like oak, maple, and teak.

VINYL
Wood-effect vinyl looks authentic and is easier to care for than the real thing. It is available in a range of prices. Expensive vinyls should be professionally installed.

SEAMLESS

CONCRETE
A poured concrete floor is installed whole, then polished into a perfectly smooth surface. It is an expensive option, but comes in a range of colors and is durable.

RESIN
An expensive poured resin flooring offers a seamless finish. Highly contemporary, it's available in both matte and gloss finishes and a range of colors.

RUBBER
Practical, hardwearing, and warm underfoot, medium-cost rubber comes in a huge range of colors and textures—the smoother surfaces are easier to keep clean.

VINYL
Modern sheet vinyl is cheap or mid-priced and is available in a huge range of designs that reproduce the look and texture of many different floor surfaces.

LINOLEUM
Medium-priced linoleum is made of natural, sustainable ingredients. It is easy to clean and scratches or dents only if heavy objects are dropped on or dragged across it.

ZONING YOUR KITCHEN FLOOR

If you have a large open-plan kitchen with dining space, dividing the dining and cooking floor areas into separate zones will make your scheme look more successful.

- **Choose a rug in colors** that match the palette of your kitchen and place it beneath the table and chairs. Make sure that you buy a rug large enough so all the chair legs can stand on it comfortably, even when they are pulled out.

- **Stay away from light-colored flooring** or a rug with a deep pile or weave that will retain dropped food, and choose a material that's easy to clean.

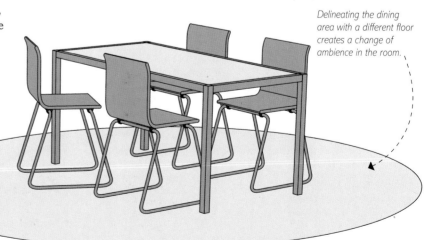

Delineating the dining area with a different floor creates a change of ambience in the room.

NATURAL MATERIALS
like wood can bring visual
warmth to an otherwise sleek
and shiny modern kitchen.

13 CHOOSE WALL COVERINGS

If you want to make your kitchen look visually stimulating, think about using more than one material on the walls: a mixture of decorated walls could look more interesting and may help your budget. Just remember, though, that your walls should complement rather than eclipse your kitchen cabinets.

1 CHOOSE THE MATERIAL

When considering different materials for your kitchen, you should always bear in mind how much cleaning and maintenance each surface will require and whether it might be splashed by water or food.

TILES

Tiles are a practical choice for a kitchen, especially behind the sink and cooktop, where they can be easily cleaned if splashed. There are a wide range of designs, colors, and finishes available to suit both traditional and contemporary kitchens.

PAINT

Paint can be used on all walls in a kitchen, but if you're planning to use it near the sink or cooktop, choose one—such as kitchen & bathroom paint—that resists moisture and wipes clean easily, and avoid textured paints, which won't be so easy to wipe down.

WALLPAPER

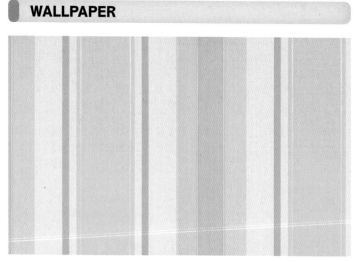

As with paint, it's worth choosing wallpaper that can withstand moisture if you're using it in the kitchen. It's best not to use these papers near a cooking or wet area; if you do, a clear glass backsplash over the top gives you the best chance of keeping it protected.

PANELING

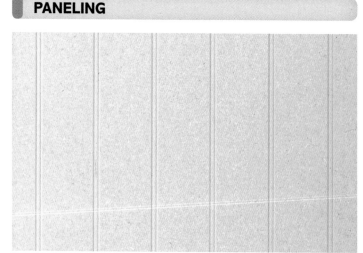

If you want a rustic look, paneling is a good choice and a less expensive alternative to tiles. It needs to be well protected with a varnish, oil, or paint to resist moisture. Although it will withstand use around a wet area, it should not be used behind a cooktop.

2 CHOOSE THE TYPE

The type of material you pick will very much be dictated by the style of your house and the kitchen units themselves. If you are going to choose a combination of materials, make sure that they complement each other.

TILES

CLASSIC

Plain, square, or rectangular tiles are a low- to medium-cost choice. For a contemporary look, use gray grout—it looks good and doesn't show dirt.

SUBWAY

Give your kitchen a retro look with medium-priced subway tiles. Typically made of ceramic with a gloss or matte surface, they have a straight or beveled edge.

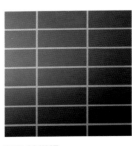

MOSAIC

Good for contemporary spaces, medium- to high-cost mosaic tiles come in a range of materials and finishes such as stone, ceramic, or glass.

MELAMINE

Low-cost melamine panels are available in a selection of plain colors and patterned designs. They can be used on all walls except those behind a gas cooktop.

LARGE FORMAT

You may only need one row of large tiles (31 x 31in/80 x 80cm) to create a backsplash, but your walls do need to be perfectly flat. They come in a range of prices.

PAINT

KITCHEN & BATHROOM

These medium- to high-priced paints withstand moisture and often offer mold protection, too. They are only available in a limited range of color choices.

MATTE

Unless your kitchen is badly ventilated, use matte emulsion on all walls except those behind a sink and cooktop. This paint is available in a range of prices.

SEMI-GLOSS

With a surface that can easily be wiped, medium-priced semi-gloss paints are a good choice. Their subtle sheen helps to reflect light around the room.

EGGSHELL

Tough and washable, mid-priced eggshell paint can be used on all surfaces in a kitchen, including baseboards and any wood paneling, as well as walls.

BLACKBOARD PAINT

If you have a contemporary kitchen and enough light and space to paint a wall black, create a chalkboard using low- to medium-cost blackboard paint.

WALLPAPER

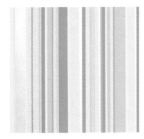

VINYL

Medium-priced vinyl wallpapers are designed for rooms with a higher moisture content, although don't use them behind a sink.

PLAIN OR PATTERNED

Standard wallpapers come in a range of prices. If you want to use it behind the sink or oven, protect it with a clear glass panel.

PANELING

WAINSCOT

Medium-priced wainscot panels can be painted, so pick a paint with a soft sheen to match that of your baseboards.

TONGUE & GROVE

Cover this low- to medium-priced paneling in a paint suitable for a kitchen, such as eggshell. Don't install it behind a cooktop, however.

14 CHOOSE KITCHEN LIGHTING

Kitchen lighting needs to be chosen with precision because it's the one area of the home—other than a workshop or home office, perhaps—where you need spaces to be lit well enough for you to work. Include ambient lighting, too, and accent lighting to show off any design elements.

1 CHOOSE YOUR LIGHTING

How you light your kitchen depends to some degree on how big it is. If it's a tiny room, you will probably want to focus on ambient and task lighting. If the room is large, or part of an open-plan living space, you can be more creative.

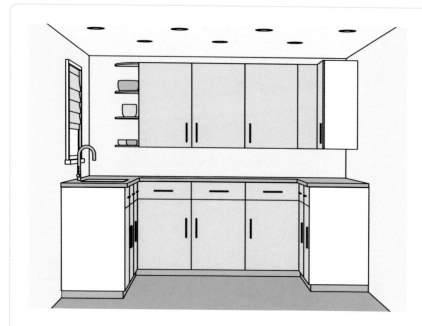

AMBIENT
Most kitchens have overhead lighting in addition to task lighting. If you have a large open-plan, eat-in kitchen and living space, adding a dimmer switch will allow you to lower the brightness of the overhead lighting once the cooking is over and the eating begins.

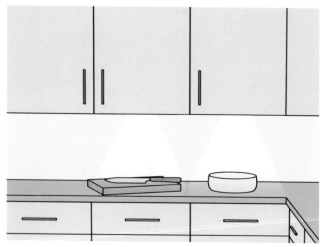

TASK
Task lighting is a must for a kitchen, whatever its size. Position it directly over the countertop so that no shadows are cast as you bend forward to chop vegetables, for example. If your kitchen is small and lighting options are limited by your budget, designate a task area—ideally near the cooktop—and ensure that it is lit well.

ACCENT
Accent lighting can make a room seem larger. Place lights on the underside, on top of and inside glass-paneled wall cabinets, and at baseboard level to stretch your space and highlight your kitchen's design. Or use accent lighting as you would in a living room, focusing spotlights on pictures or an impressive range, for example.

2 CHOOSE YOUR LIGHT FIXTURES

It is important to create a space where you and your family will enjoy spending time, as well as one that is practical for cooking. The goal should be to choose a combination of fixtures that will cover all your lighting needs.

CEILING LIGHTS

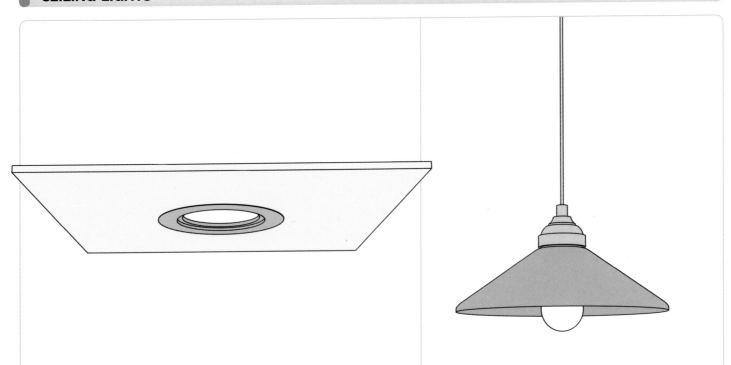

RECESSED DOWNLIGHTS
Recessed downlights provide a feeling of natural daylight, which is good in a room where you may spend a lot of time, and their virtually flush design makes them good for low-ceilinged rooms. Install them with a dimmer switch so that you can lower the light levels when you want.

PENDANT
Pendant lights work particularly well in kitchens if they are hung low over an island unit (but not a cooktop), countertop, or dining table. Consider hanging a line of three for a more interesting and illuminating option. Look for extractor fan options that look like pendant lighting.

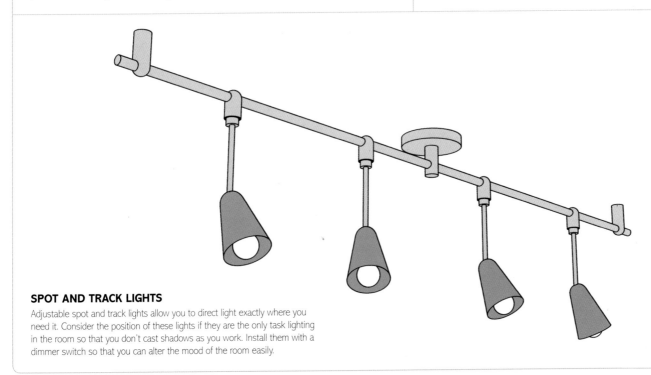

SPOT AND TRACK LIGHTS
Adjustable spot and track lights allow you to direct light exactly where you need it. Consider the position of these lights if they are the only task lighting in the room so that you don't cast shadows as you work. Install them with a dimmer switch so that you can alter the mood of the room easily.

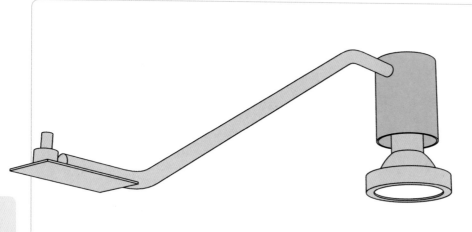

OVER CABINET

Swan-neck fixtures are installed at the front of the top of wall cabinets to cast light down onto the doors and illuminate preparation areas. Or, you can have lights concealed on top of the cabinet—they simply light the space above the unit. Both types create decorative accent lighting in the evening.

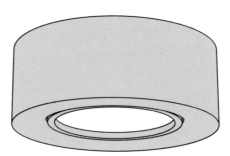

UNDER CABINET

Under-cabinet lighting provides task lighting when you are preparing food and also creates decorative additional lighting if you are dining in the kitchen. The lights should be mounted toward the middle of the underside of a wall cabinet so that the light is evenly distributed and doesn't cast shadows.

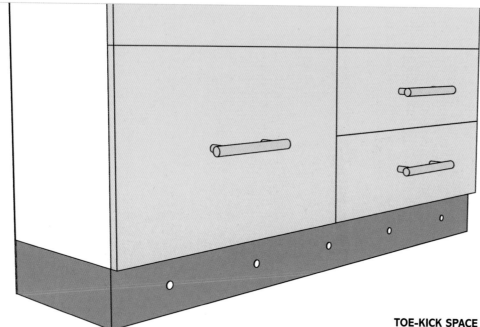

TOE-KICK SPACE LIGHTING

Highlight your kitchen floor using toe-kick space lights. These lights are available as LEDs or halogen lamps, and come in a range of designs installed in the plinth panel around the bottom of your kitchen cabinets.

15 CHOOSE WINDOW TREATMENTS

Before you choose your kitchen window treatment, decide if you want the window treatment to hide or show off the view outside? Second, does the window sit near a sink and require something that can withstand splashing? And, finally, how much impact should the window treatment make decoratively?

1 CHOOSE THE TYPE

Kitchen window treatments must be practical because they are subjected to more humidity than window treatments in most other rooms. Consider, too, how easy your choice will be to keep clean, since over time it will become greasy and dust-covered.

BLINDS

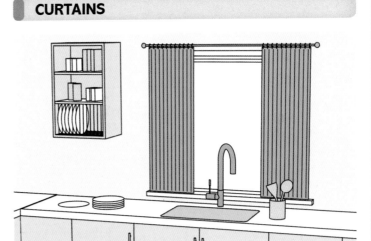

Blinds are a popular choice in a kitchen, since they can sit neatly within the recess of a window and are less likely to get splashed. Choose a fabric that's mold-resistant and easy to wipe, and add decorative detail with pattern or a sculpted lower edge.

CURTAINS

If you want curtains in your kitchen, choose ones that are machine-washable, since curtains are likely to pick up kitchen odors, grime, and dust. If you have two windows in your kitchen, choose a blind for the cooking area and curtains for the dining area.

SHUTTERS

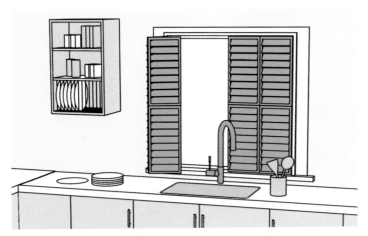

A practical choice in a kitchen, shutters can easily be wiped clean. Choose from full-height, tier-on-tier, or café-style shutters, which only cover the bottom half of your window. Opt for a white or pale wood finish if you want to reflect light.

FILM

Window film offers complete privacy without blocking out all natural light. It can be bought by the yard or made to measure, and is easily attached to your interior windowpanes. It is a good choice for a small space when you don't want a fancy window treatment.

2 CHOOSE THE STYLE

Kitchens are busy, often small rooms and typically need window dressings in a simple style. However, that doesn't mean they have to be plain—you can add pattern or texture with both fabric and wood finishes.

BLINDS

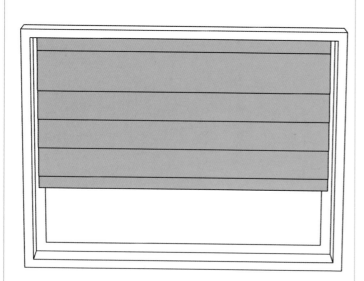

ROMAN

If you want your kitchen to feel cozy rather than functional, consider a Roman blind. These blinds are available in a wide choice of fabrics, although you may want to consider using a patterned rather than plain design, so it doesn't show marks so easily.

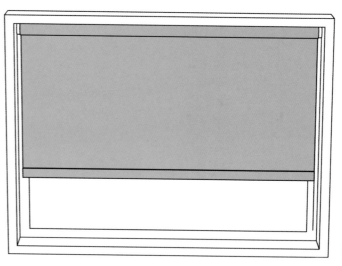

ROLLER

Roller blinds are a fairly inexpensive option, so are a good choice in kitchens with wider windows. You can have roller blinds made to measure, although most ready-made blinds can be cut to size and, providing you're fairly handy, they are easy to install. Choose blinds made from moisture-resistant fabrics.

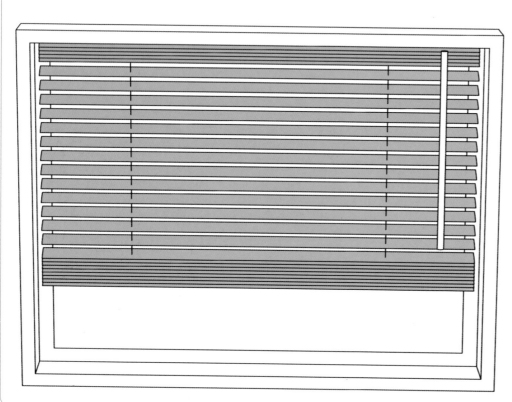

VENETIAN

Made from metal or wood, Venetian blinds are an easy-to-clean, functional choice for your kitchen. They will give your windows a streamlined look, which is ideal if you have a contemporary kitchen. They're available in a choice of materials, colors, and slat widths.

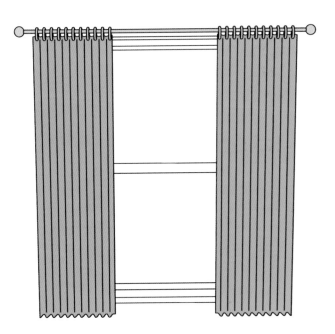

SILL LENGTH

Sill-length, or just below sill-length, curtains in a washable cotton are a good choice for small, recessed windows in a kitchen. Choose light fabrics that can be washed or find patterns that will hide grime or splashes—but be aware that this curtain length can look old-fashioned, so pick your fabric design carefully.

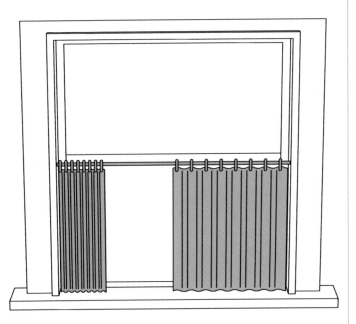

CAFÉ CURTAINS

Café curtains are hung from a rod or curtain wire that is installed inside the window recess either halfway down a window, or aligned with the central horizontal frame between two panes of glass. They are designed to screen the lower half of the window to offer privacy, but still allow light in and enable you to see out.

SHUTTERS

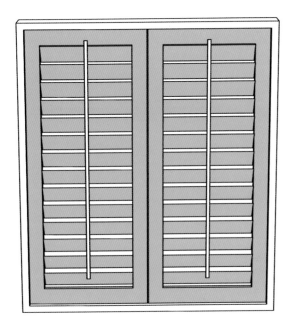

LOUVER

Depending on the wood or paint finish you choose, louvered shutters suit most kitchen styles, whether traditional or contemporary. If your window is behind your sink, make sure that you will be able to open the shutters without hitting the faucet.

FILM

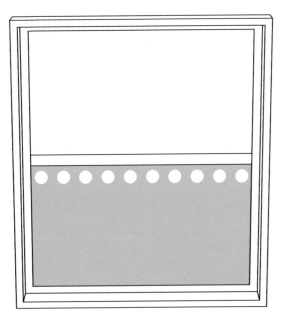

PLAIN OR PATTERNED

If you are opting for window film, give some thought to whether you want to add interest with a pattern or motif, or whether you are happy to keep it plain. If you are teaming the film with another window dressing, such as curtains, for which you are using a patterned fabric, make sure to avoid a clash of patterns.

MAKE
A ROMAN BLIND

Like roller blinds, Roman blinds allow more natural light into a room than thick curtains or drapes, but they dress a window more extravagantly than a simple roller blind. The cords and rods attached to the reverse of the blind enable it to be pulled into neat folded pleats when not covering the window.

WHAT YOU NEED

- Fabric with a straight weave
- Lining material
- Tape measure and ruler
- Scissors
- Pins
- Iron
- Velcro
- Sewing machine
- Roman blind kit
- Pencil or pen
- Glue
- Level and screwdriver

1 CUT THE FABRIC AND LINING

1 MEASURE YOUR WINDOW to determine what size the finished blind needs to be. You will need to decide whether the blind will hang inside or outside the window recess.

2 CUT OUT THE FABRIC, adding 6in (15cm) to the length and 3in (8cm) to the width. Then cut out the lining material: this needs to be the same length as the main fabric (6in/15cm longer than the final length of the blind) but the width should only be that of the final blind—no extra allowance is needed.

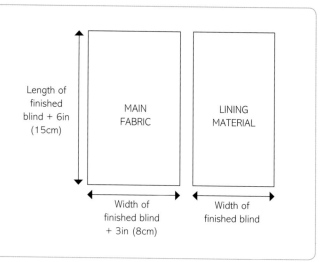

Length of finished blind + 6in (15cm)

MAIN FABRIC

LINING MATERIAL

Width of finished blind + 3in (8cm)

Width of finished blind

2 STITCH ON THE LINING

1 PLACE THE FABRIC face down on a flat surface and lay the lining over the top. Align the edges of the two fabrics on both sides and pin them together (there will be slightly more fabric than lining).

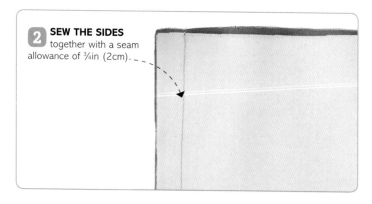

2 SEW THE SIDES together with a seam allowance of ¾in (2cm).

3 TURN THE JOINED FABRICS inside out so the fabric is the right way around. Lay the blind on a flat surface and make sure that the extra strip of fabric at either side of the lining is ¾in (2cm) on each side. Use a hot iron to press the fabric edges flat.

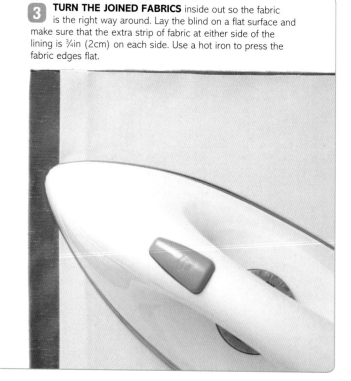

3 ATTACH THE VELCRO

1 FOLD THE TOP of the blind over: the fold should be 1¼–1½in (3–4cm), depending on how wide your Velcro is.

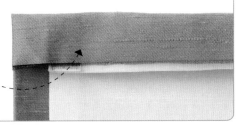

2 TRIM THE EDGE of the fabric, if necessary, to neaten it, then press the fold flat with the iron.

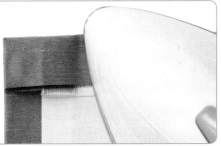

3 FOLD THE TOP CORNERS into triangles, tuck them under the pressed fold, and pin one half of the Velcro onto the fabric fold.

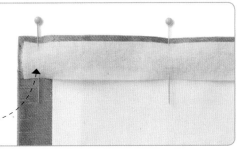

4 SEW THE VELCRO in place.

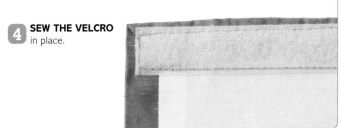

4 SEW ON THE TAPES

1 TO DETERMINE WHERE to attach the tapes (which comprise the pockets for the rods), you need to divide the blind into sections. A blind with three rods needs to be divided into three equal sections plus another section that is half the size. You should also make allowance for the headrail at the top of the blind.

To calculate the positions of the tapes, begin with the intended final length of your blind, as determined at step 1. Subtract 2in (5cm) for the headrail. Then divide the resulting figure by 3.5 (relating to the three equal sections plus one half-size section; if your blind is to have four rods, divide the figure by 4.5 instead).

The example (right) shows how this would work for a blind 44in (110cm) long. Subtracting 2in (5cm) for the headrail gives you a figure of 42in (105cm). Dividing this by 3.5 gives you a figure of 12in (30cm). This will be the size of your three full-sized panels.

Again, you need to make allowance for the headrail, so measure 2in (5cm) from the top of the blind, then measure and mark (using a pencil or pen) a line 12in (30cm) below. Mark two more lines at 12in (30cm) intervals. The bottom of the blind once hemmed will be 6in (15cm) below the lowest tape; you can mark this line now if you want, but you should still check that it is correct by holding the blind up to the window (see step 5) before hemming.

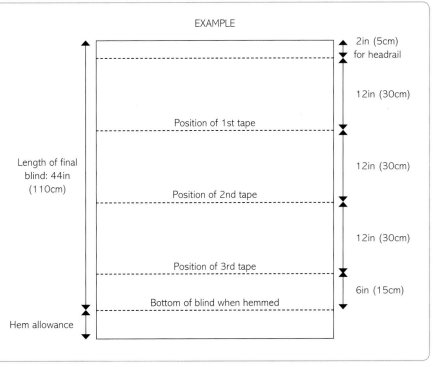

EXAMPLE

Length of final blind: 44in (110cm)

Hem allowance

2in (5cm) for headrail

12in (30cm)

Position of 1st tape

12in (30cm)

Position of 2nd tape

12in (30cm)

Position of 3rd tape

6in (15cm)

Bottom of blind when hemmed

2 PIN THE THREE LENGTHS of tape onto the lining at the marked points.

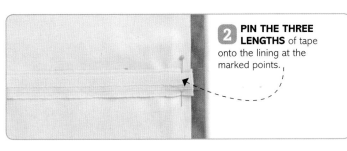

3 SEW THE TAPES onto the blind.

5 FOLD OVER THE BASE

1 **HOLD THE BLIND** up to the window to check where the bottom edge needs to be and mark a line with pins. (If you marked the bottom edge at step 4 and you are satisfied that your line is in the correct place, you will not need to mark it again.)

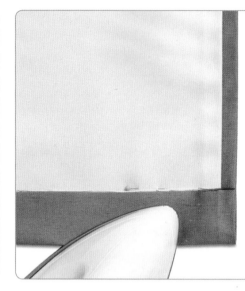

2 **FOLD OVER THE BOTTOM** of the fabric so it sits just below the line of pins and press it flat with the iron.

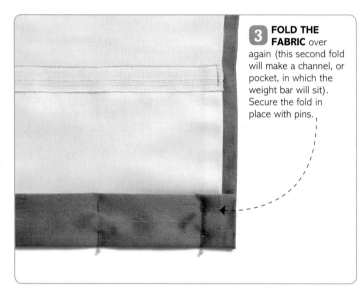

3 **FOLD THE FABRIC** over again (this second fold will make a channel, or pocket, in which the weight bar will sit). Secure the fold in place with pins.

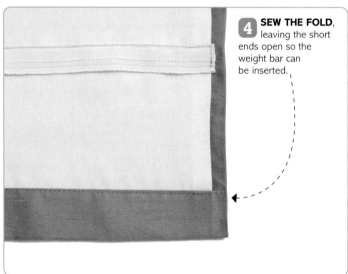

4 **SEW THE FOLD,** leaving the short ends open so the weight bar can be inserted.

6 INSERT THE WEIGHT BAR AND RODS

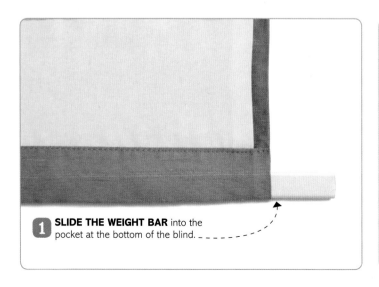

1 **SLIDE THE WEIGHT BAR** into the pocket at the bottom of the blind.

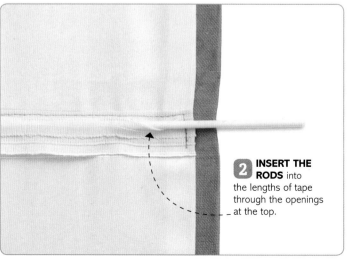

2 **INSERT THE RODS** into the lengths of tape through the openings at the top.

7

PREPARE THE BLIND FOR MOUNTING

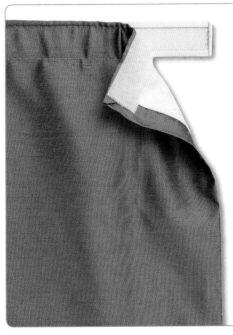

1 GLUE THE OTHER LENGTH of Velcro to the blind mechanism, then attach the mechanism to the blind by firmly pressing the two lengths of Velcro together.

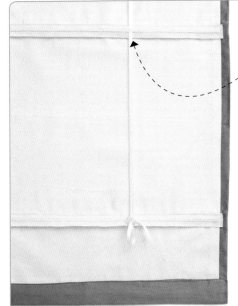

2 THREAD THE BLIND, making sure the cords pass through each length of tape at the same point.

8

ATTACH THE BRACKETS

1 TO GAUGE THE RIGHT HEIGHT of the brackets on the window, measure the position of the brackets on the blind and transfer these measurements to the window frame or recess. Draw a straight line between the two points using a level.

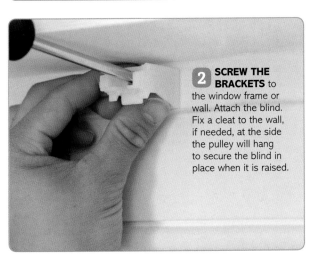

2 SCREW THE BRACKETS to the window frame or wall. Attach the blind. Fix a cleat to the wall, if needed, at the side the pulley will hang to secure the blind in place when it is raised.

17 CHOOSE
A KITCHEN TABLE AND CHAIRS

A table and chairs are key pieces of furniture—whether they will be going in your kitchen, a dining room, or an open-plan living area. Think about whether you would rather prioritize a convivial atmosphere or spacious dining, and whether you prefer a sophisticated, integrated look or a more relaxed setting.

1 DECIDE ON TABLE SIZE

At a minimum, your table needs to be large enough to accommodate your usual number of diners, and if you regularly have guests you should also think about the logistics of fitting extra people in. The space available is the other major consideration and, particularly in a kitchen, you need to ensure there will be plenty of room to maneuver around it once it is in place.

2 CHOOSE SHAPE OF TABLE

Most tables are either round (circular or oval), square, or rectangular. You will usually find that one shape suits the dimensions of your room better than the others, but think too about the number of diners and which shape will best accommodate them.

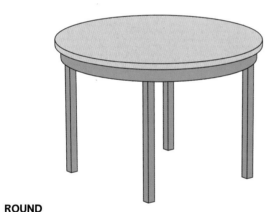

ROUND

Good for sociable dining, a round table allows everyone sitting around it to see and talk to each other easily. You can fit different numbers of chairs around a round table without leaving anyone stuck on a corner or at one end of the table.

SQUARE

Square tables are suited to square rooms, since they make the most of the available space. If the table is only ever used to seat four or fewer people, the equal length of its sides means that each person has plenty of elbow room while eating.

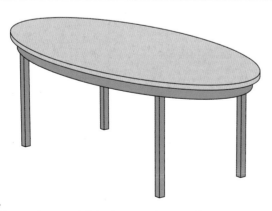

OVAL

Oval tables are often a good choice for rectangular rooms. If you entertain large groups, or if the number of people at your table often varies, the curved ends of an oval table make it easy to accommodate everyone without anyone have to sit on a corner.

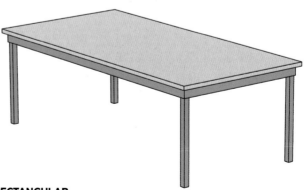

RECTANGULAR

Since most rooms are rectangular, this shaped table may well make the best use of space. These designs are available in a wide selection of lengths and widths to suit your room's dimensions, and even the smallest design can seat more than four people comfortably.

3 CHOOSE TYPE OF CHAIR

If you like a streamlined, coordinated look, choose chairs that match your table. If you prefer your dining area to have a less formal atmosphere, go for chairs that aren't a perfect match, or choose a selection of different styles for a fun, individual look.

WITH ARMS

If you have space around your table, chairs with arms provide the most comfortable option. Where space is at a premium, purchase just one or two chairs with arms. Position them at the head, or at either end, of a table and use armless chairs elsewhere.

WITHOUT ARMS

The most popular and practical choice, chairs without arms sit comfortably side by side around a table. They also come in practically every material and style, although sizes will vary, so check the dimensions before choosing what to buy.

FOLDING

A good choice for rooms where space is tight, folding chairs fold down to be stored away when you don't need them. They're also handy if you have extra dinner guests. Do keep in mind that you'll need room to store them, though.

STACKABLE

Stackable chairs are designed to stack on top of each other so that they only take up the floor space of one chair rather than four when you're not using them—although you may choose to buy them for their design rather than practicality. They are available in a wide range of styles.

While the material of your table and chairs should match, or at least complement, the look of your kitchen furniture, also think about how durable it will be, how much it costs, if the material is comfortable to sit on, and whether it will age well.

TABLES

WOOD
Medium-priced solid wood lasts for years. If the top is damaged, it can be sanded and refinished. As a natural material there will be variations in the grain and color.

WOOD LAMINATE
Wood-laminate tables have a textured grain effect that looks and feels like real wood. A low-cost option, it costs less than the real thing, but is not as hard-wearing.

METAL
Medium-priced metal tables usually have a metal frame and legs and a wood or glass tabletop for a contemporary look; the brushed metal creates an industrial feel.

GLASS
A medium-cost glass table visually expands a space. Like a metal table, it is usually a combination of two materials: a tempered glass tabletop with wood or metal legs.

PLASTIC
Available in a range of prices, a plastic table can easily be wiped clean, so is ideal if you have children. Clear acrylic, a type of plastic, is more suited to grown-up dining.

CHAIRS

WOOD
Wood is a practical, medium-cost choice. Wood chairs can become uncomfortable after sitting on them for long periods of time, so you may want to add seat cushions.

UPHOLSTERED
Medium-priced upholstered chairs tend to have a foam-filled seat and back, so feel comfortable. Choose leather or removable washable covers if you have children.

PLASTIC
Low-cost plastic can easily be wiped clean, which makes it a good low-maintenance choice. However, it is not comfortable to sit on for long periods of time.

RATTAN
Rustic-looking, medium-cost, woven rattan is not completely rigid, so is comfortable to sit on. Cheaper versions may unravel over time; if you pay extra, it will last for years.

CHECKLIST

● **Where will the table go**, and how you will use it? An eat-in kitchen looks best if the table and chairs coordinate with the kitchen cabinets. If the table will be used for more than just eating (doing homework, for instance), make sure the tabletop is hard-wearing.

● **Will the table fit?** Lay a newspaper template of the table on the floor to find out. Allow at least 24in (60cm)—and ideally 36in (90cm)—between the table and any walls.

● **Table heights vary**, so if you're buying your dining chairs separately, take careful measurements of the different items to get the correct height.

EXTENDING TABLES

If space in your kitchen or dining room is tight, or you don't need a large table for everyday use, an extendable dining table that can be made bigger or smaller may give you the flexibility you need. There are many different types available, made to extend and retract in all kinds of different ways; a few of the most commonplace are shown below. Extending tables are available in all the standard shapes you would expect, and in a range of sizes and materials, so you won't be limited in your choice.

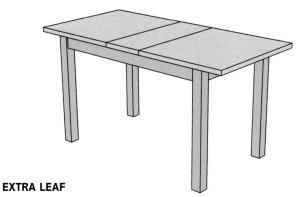

EXTRA LEAF

An extra section (the leaf) in the same material can be added to increase the size of a table. Extra leaves are most commonly kept concealed under the tabletop when they are not in use. Some tables have more than one leaf; four leaves can turn a four-seater table into an impressive 16-seater.

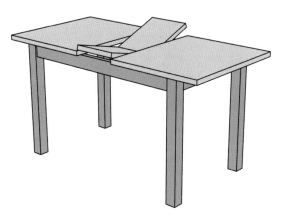

BUTTERFLY EXTENSION

Dining tables with a butterfly extension are similar to those with an extra leaf. The two top panels of the table slide apart to reveal a central "butterfly" extension panel that is pulled up and out—typically enough space to seat two more people.

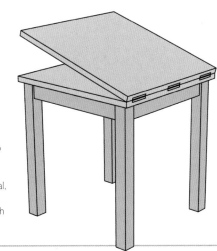

FLIP TOP

The surface area of a flip-top dining table can be doubled by unfolding the hinged top. For the legs to remain central, you either have to slide the top along, or rotate it through 90 degrees.

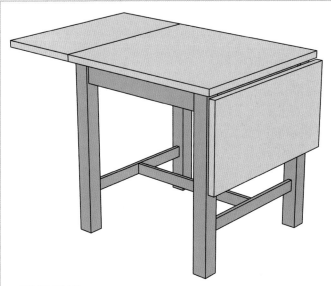

DROP LEAF

A drop-leaf table has a fixed tabletop section in the center and two folded leaves that can be lifted up at one or both sides, depending on how much extra seating you need. The leaves are supported by brackets underneath the tabletop. A drop-leaf table often also features a concealed drawer in which you can store flatware.

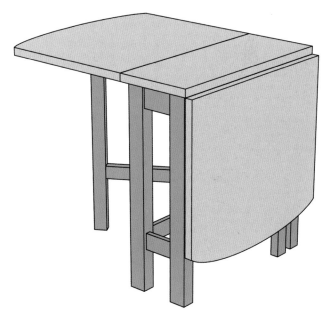

GATE LEG

A variation on the drop-leaf style, a gate-leg table has hinged legs that swing out (like a gate) to support extensions that, when not in use, can be folded down at the side. The sturdy support provided by these gate legs means that the extensions can be fairly large, and often these tables convert from something extremely slimline to a table that can comfortably seat several people.

MAKE CUSHIONS
FOR KITCHEN CHAIRS

You can transform plain kitchen chairs, and make them much more comfortable, with colorful cushions. The best way to ensure that these work with your overall color scheme, and that they fit your chairs snugly, is to make them yourself. These tie-on cushion pads are both simple to create and stylish.

WHAT YOU NEED

- Brown paper
- Scissors
- Pins
- Colored fabric—use curtain-weight cotton material
- Rickrack
- Needle and thread
- Sewing machine (optional)
- Polyester batting
- Cover buttons (4 per cushion)
- Button maker (optional)

1 MAKE A TEMPLATE

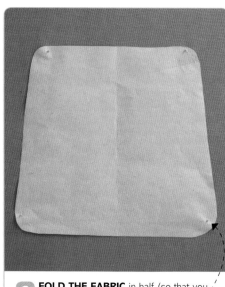

1 MEASURE THE SEAT of one of your kitchen chairs and make a template from brown paper. Place the cutout on the chair seat to check that the dimensions are accurate. Trim the template with scissors, if necessary.

2 FOLD THE FABRIC in half (so that you will cut out two fabric shapes) and pin the template onto one end of the fabric.

2 CUT THE FABRIC

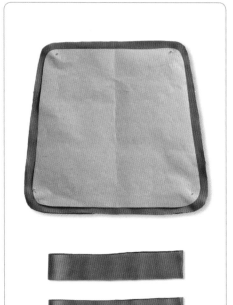

CUT AROUND the template, leaving at least ½in (1cm) of seam allowance at the edges. With the fabric still folded over (keep the fold of the fabric vertical), cut out the cushion ties: measure and cut two strips 3in high and 8in long (7 x 20cm). Once unfolded, each strip should measure 3 x 16in (7 x 40cm).

3 ATTACH THE BORDER

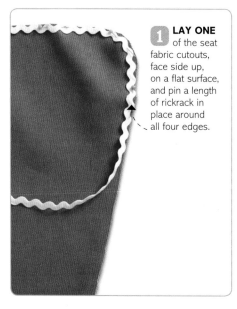

1 LAY ONE of the seat fabric cutouts, face side up, on a flat surface, and pin a length of rickrack in place around all four edges.

2 SEW THE RICKRACK to the edge of the fabric.

4 MAKE THE FABRIC TIES

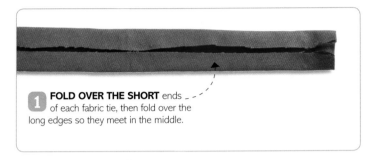

1 **FOLD OVER THE SHORT** ends of each fabric tie, then fold over the long edges so they meet in the middle.

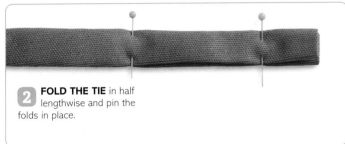

2 **FOLD THE TIE** in half lengthwise and pin the folds in place.

3 **SEW ALONG** the outer edges of each tie to make a neat seam.

5 SEW THE SEAT COVER

1 **FOLD THE SEAMED TIES** in half and position them on top of the fabric cutout (with the rickrack face up). The folded ends of the ties should overhang the back of the seat cutout near each corner. Hold each tie in place with a pin at the corners.

2 **PLACE THE SECOND FABRIC** cutout, reverse side face up, over rickrack fabric cutout and ties, and pin the two cutouts together around the edges.

3 **SEW THE FABRIC CUTOUTS** together. Leave a hole at one side of the seat cover that is large enough to pull the cover through it to turn it inside out.

6 FILL THE SEAT CUSHION

1 TURN THE CUSHION the right way around by pulling it through the hole in the side.

2 FILL THE SEAT CUSHION with enough polyester batting to make it comfortable to sit on, without overstuffing it.

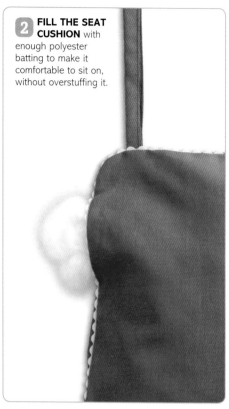

3 SEW UP THE HOLE at the side of the cushion with a needle and thread.

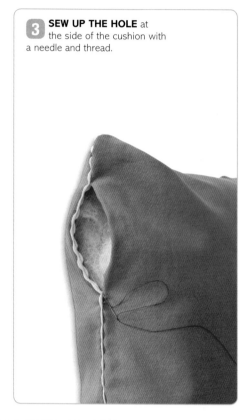

7 DECORATE THE SEAT CUSHION

1 CUT OUT FOUR CIRCLES of fabric that are twice the size of each cover button. Cover the head of each button with a fabric circle, fold over the edges of the fabric beneath the button head, and snap the back of the button on to hold the fabric in place (use a button maker, if necessary).

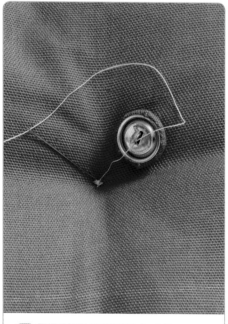

2 THE FOUR BUTTONS should be positioned equidistant from each other on the cushion. Mark the position of each button with a couple of simple stitches. Then attach each button to the cushion: using double thread, sew through the fabric, batting, and button shank from the back.

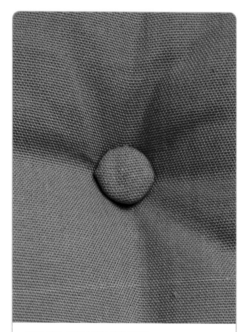

3 TIE OFF THE BUTTON at the back of the cushion. Each sewn-on button should make an attractive indent in the front of the cushion.

7 WAYS TO
REFRESH A TIRED KITCHEN

If your kitchen is looking a little tired, give it a fresh new look by making some small changes, such as replacing cabinet hardware or changing the color of a wall. If you are feeling more ambitious, you can make bigger changes that, although they will require a little more time and effort, can create more impact.

CREATE A FEATURE WALL

Add interest to your kitchen by painting or wallpapering one wall in an eye-catching color or pattern.

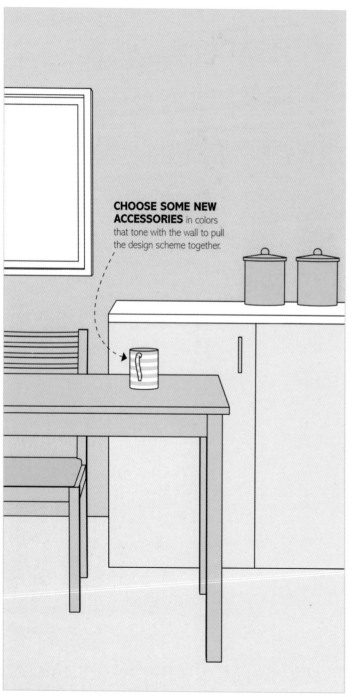

CHOOSE SOME NEW ACCESSORIES in colors that tone with the wall to pull the design scheme together.

CHANGE CABINET HARDWARE

Update the look of your cabinets by adding new hardware. The simplest option is to look for designs that will cover existing holes.

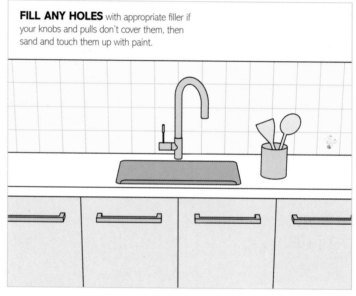

FILL ANY HOLES with appropriate filler if your knobs and pulls don't cover them, then sand and touch them up with paint.

REPLACE DOORS

For a real transformation, replace cabinet doors and drawer fronts. Make sure the size of the new ones is correct for your units.

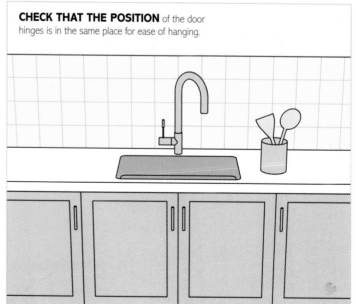

CHECK THAT THE POSITION of the door hinges is in the same place for ease of hanging.

REPLACE THE BACKSPLASH

A new backsplash can make a big difference to the look of a kitchen, especially if you choose a material different from your old one.

REPLACE COUNTERTOPS

Replacing your countertops can completely change the look of your kitchen. Swap them for any material your budget can accommodate.

IF YOUR COUNTERTOP is a good fit, lift it out and use it as a template for your new countertop.

REVAMP TILES

Give your existing tiles a makeover using tile paint, which is available in a range of colors, or by adding decorative tile transfers.

CONSIDER REGROUTING your tiles if the grout is looking dirty.

CHANGE THE WINDOW TREATMENT

Update your window by adding a new blind. If your window overlooks a neighbor's house or the street, add window film.

REPAINT AND COVER
A KITCHEN TABLE

If you have a table that needs reconditioning, or an unexciting table that requires a little character, renovate and paint it—and cover the top with oilcloth if it is in poor condition—to give it a fresh look. If you use water-based wood paint, finish with a layer of acrylic lacquer or varnish for added durability.

WHAT YOU NEED

- Sandpaper (medium grade)
- Tack cloth
- Paint for interior wood
- Paintbrush
- Oilcloth cut to size (the edges of the cloth should hang approximately 1in/3cm over the sides of the table)
- Iron (plus fabric to cover the oilcloth)
- Staple gun

1 SAND THE TABLE

1 LIGHTLY SAND THE LEGS and the sides of the table frame to give the wood enough "tooth" for the paint to adhere to. If the table is old, choose a coarser sandpaper; if it is new, use fine sandpaper.

2 WIPE DOWN all the sanded areas with a tack cloth to remove any wood dust.

2 PAINT THE TABLE

1 PAINT THE TABLE LEGS with a first coat of paint, following the direction of the wood grain as you paint.

2 PAINT THE FRAME and the edges under the tabletop. When the paint has dried (see the manufacturer's instructions), apply a second coat to all the painted areas. For a shabby chic look, lightly sand the wood for a distressed appearance instead of painting it a second time.

LAY THE OILCLOTH

1 **PLACE THE OILCLOTH**, reverse side down, on an ironing board between two pieces of fabric and use a cool iron to smooth out any deep creases.

2 **LAY THE OILCLOTH** over the tabletop, fold over one end, and secure it at one point underneath the tabletop using the staple gun.

3 **MOVE AROUND TO THE OPPOSITE** side of the table, fold the other end of the oilcloth down, gently pulling it taut, and secure it in place with a staple.

```
        7    1    5

12                  9


4                   3


10                  11

     6    2    8
```

4 **FOLLOW THIS SUGGESTED** tightening sequence (above) to staple the rest of the fabric to the underside of the tabletop, leaving the corners unstapled.

4 FOLD IN THE CORNERS

1 **FOLD ONE CORNER** of the oilcloth in half to make a triangular shape.

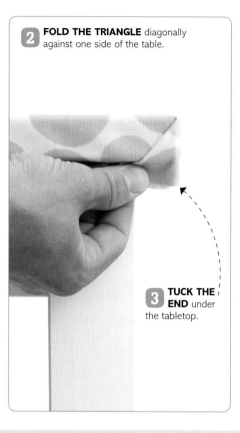

2 **FOLD THE TRIANGLE** diagonally against one side of the table.

3 **TUCK THE END** under the tabletop.

4 **SECURE IT** in place with the staple gun.

ANOTHER WAY TO FOLD

1 **ALTERNATIVELY**, draw the two sides of the oilcloth together at the corner to make a triangular shape with a central fold.

2 **FOLD THE TRIANGLE** straight under the tabletop.

3 **SECURE IT** in place with the staple gun.

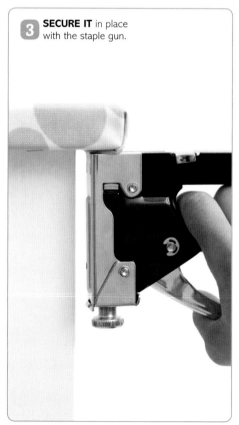

REPAINT
KITCHEN CABINETS

To update your kitchen quickly and easily, repaint your cabinet doors (if they are wood) and replace the handles. If it's permitted in your area, oil-based paint is best for this job, since kitchen furniture gets lots of wear and tear; if you use a water-based wood paint, add a coat of water-based lacquer over the dried paint.

WHAT YOU NEED

- Screwdriver
- Wood filler
- Fine finishing sandpaper
- Tack cloth
- Kitchen cabinet handles
- Pencil
- Ruler
- T-square (optional)
- Drill
- Paint for interior wood
- Paintbrush

1 REMOVE THE DOOR

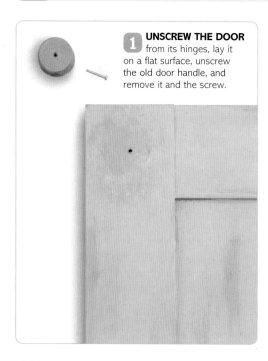

1 UNSCREW THE DOOR from its hinges, lay it on a flat surface, unscrew the old door handle, and remove it and the screw.

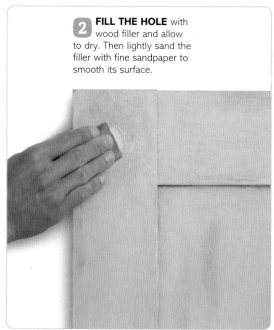

2 FILL THE HOLE with wood filler and allow to dry. Then lightly sand the filler with fine sandpaper to smooth its surface.

2 SAND DOWN THE DOOR

1 SAND DOWN the whole door with more sandpaper to get rid of any imperfections in the wood to give a smooth, fine finish, and to provide a "tooth" for the paint to adhere to.

2 RUB DOWN the wood with a tack cloth to wipe off any loose dust.

1 **HOLD** the new handle against the side of the door to see where you would like to position it.

2 **MARK WITH A PENCIL** where the top and bottom of the handle will be fastened. Draw a horizontal centerline with a ruler on the wood from each point to the side edge of the door.

3 **DRAW A VERTICAL CENTERLINE** between the two horizontal centerlines. Use the ruler or T-square to ensure that the line is straight by measuring the distance from the edge of the door to the top and bottom of the vertical line.

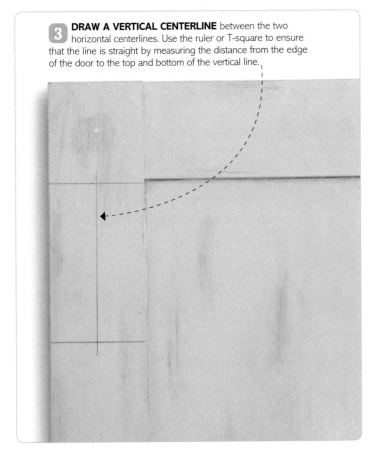

4 **DRILL A HOLE** at each point where the horizontal and vertical lines cross.

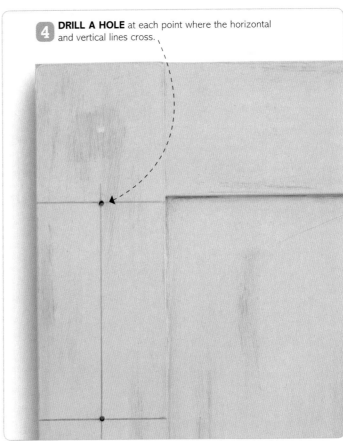

KITCHEN

79

4 APPLY TWO COATS OF PAINT

1 PAINT THE EDGES of the door first, following the grain of the wood.

2 IF YOU HAVE SHAKER-STYLE DOORS, paint the central panel next, ensuring that you get enough paint into the corners.

3 PAINT the horizontal top and bottom edge panels next.

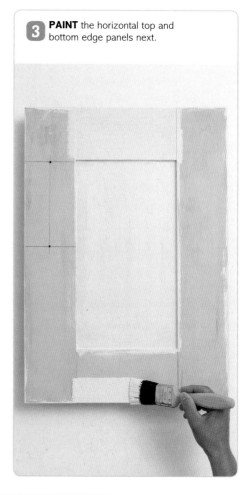

4 FINALLY, PAINT THE VERTICAL EDGE panels. This sequence gives a neater finish and highlights the wood grain. Allow the first coat to dry before painting the second coat.

5 ATTACH THE HANDLES

FASTEN THE HANDLE to the front of the door with screws and a screwdriver, and then screw the door back onto its cabinet hinges. Repeat the same process with the remaining kitchen cabinet doors and drawers.

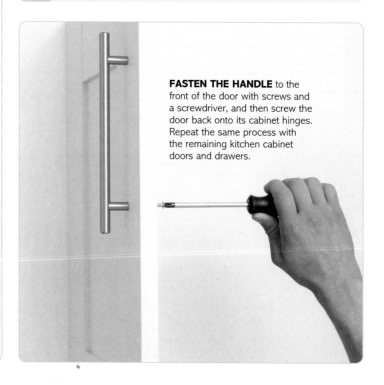

BEFORE

BATHROOM

WHAT TO DO WHEN
RENOVATING YOUR BATHROOM

When redoing your bathroom, it is important to have an organized plan and to tackle the work in the correct order—otherwise you could find yourself running out of funds or having to do the same jobs more than once. If you follow the sequence shown here, you shouldn't run into trouble.

1 WORK OUT YOUR BUDGET

Assess your finances and decide how much you can afford to spend, then establish what you will be able to do with the money available. It is a good idea to build in a 10 percent contingency plan in case of unforeseen costs.

2 PLAN YOUR LAYOUT

Draw up a plan of your bathroom, including the positions of windows and doors and the locations of waste and supply pipes. Plan out what changes you will want to make, then call in a plumber to advise whether the plan will work and to give an estimate for the work required.

3 REVIEW ELECTRICAL NEEDS

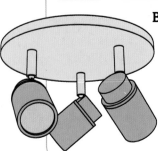

Before the walls are patched or tiled, you need to decide where the lights and extractor fan will go, and where the switches will be positioned. Also consider whether you want to install underfloor radiant heating or any heated towel racks.

4 SCHEDULE TRADESPEOPLE

Contact an electrician and tiler (unless you will be doing the tiling yourself) to get quotes for the jobs you have lined up. If you are happy with the quotes, and with the choice of tradespeople, sign them up, ensuring that each person knows when the other is coming to do his job. Ask each of them to advise at this stage if any of their work will impact on what another tradesperson is doing.

5 PLACE YOUR ORDERS

Armed with your quotes, you should now know how much money is left to spend on fixtures and supplies. Working to your budget, choose and order fixtures, shower, tiles, and faucets. Note delivery dates for all the products and don't schedule work to start until after everything has arrived.

6 RIP OUT THE OLD BATHROOM

Work can now begin on removing your old bathroom, tiles, flooring, and lighting. Be prepared for unforeseen problems to emerge now, such as damp or rotten floors. This is where the 10 percent contingency in the budget is likely to come into play. Talk to your plumber and electrician to agree on a new schedule if there are going to be delays.

7 BEGIN THE PLUMBING ROUGH-IN

The plumber will now begin the rough-in—the installation of the plumbing for the bathtub, sink, and toilet. Bear in mind that existing fixtures will need to be removed to allow for tiling. The water supply might need to be turned off and the system drained at this stage, so be prepared to spend a few hours without running water.

8 ELECTRICAL ROUGH-IN

The electrician's rough-in will involve installing the wiring for all the electrical items in the room, such as electrical receptacles, lighting, and ventilation fan. He will also need to install the initial wiring for any heated towel racks or underfloor radiant heating at this point.

9 CLOSE THE WALLS

The walls can now be patched or closed. Fill any holes with sheetrock patches and skimcoat to prepare for paint. Be sure to use moisture-resistant tile backer board in wet tiled areas.

10 LAY THE FLOORING

Next, the floor can be laid. If you have decided to opt for underfloor heating, you can install it yourself, but it will need to be signed off by a certified electrician. If you are using porous tiles on the floor, remember to factor in time for sealing, as well as laying, the floor.

11 PREPARE THE SHOWER

If you are installing a shower stall, its walls may need to be waterproofed using a waterproofing membrane before being tiled. Do this now, since the walls need time to dry out before the tiling and grouting can begin.

12 ORGANIZE THE FINAL INSTALL

At final install stage, the plumber will need to install the bathtub and shower. The electrician also needs to return to install the light fixtures, switches, and GFI receptacles and connect everything.

13 TILE AND GROUT AND ORGANIZE THE FIXTURE INSTALL

You can now tile and grout. The work will need time to dry, so don't expect to be able to do any more work in the bathroom for another two to three days. The plumber will then need to return to install the toilet and the sink.

14 FINISH DECORATING

Finally, tackle the rest of the decorating. After painting the room (using drop cloths in case there are splashes), install any last features, such as blinds or a toilet roll holder, and add the finishing touches to your decorating scheme.

2 CREATE A MOOD BOARD
FOR YOUR BATHROOM

Making up a mood board before you begin to refurbish a bathroom will not only help you to finalize the design of your layout, but it will also encourage you to inject the room with style, personality, and color, which might otherwise be overlooked in your search for fixtures and practical buys like tiles. Here's a guide to follow for creating a useful bathroom mood board.

1 **FIND PICTURES OF BATHROOMS YOU LIKE** in magazines and books, and even on hotel websites. Tear out, take a color copy, or print out any you like and stick a few favorites to the board; you may want to take different elements from a few images as inspiration for your design. Note down what you don't like about your current bathroom so you don't repeat the same mistakes.

As a starting point, think about whether you would like your bathroom to look contemporary and minimalist or you would prefer a period style, for example.

2 **DO YOU HAVE A KEY ITEM** at the top of your wish list—a free-standing bathtub, a designer shower, or gorgeous wall tiles, or an ornate sink that you already own, for example—that you really must include? Use this piece as inspiration for the rest of your design.

Your favorite item may influence whether your bathroom will look traditional or modern.

3 **CHOOSE YOUR FIXTURES**, starting with the bathtub, which will dictate the shape and finish of both your toilet and sink, and the faucets and shower fixtures, too. Before you go any further with your design, you need to finalize your choice of these items.

Stick pictures of fixtures that you like to the mood board so you can refer back to them as you build your ideas.

4 **CHOOSE A BACKGROUND COLOR** for the bathroom: if a large percentage of your bathroom walls will be tiled, pick the tiles first, since they will greatly influence other colors in the room. Your main consideration should be to make the room light and bright enough so that you can see clearly to put on makeup or shave. If your bathroom receives lots of natural daylight or you install effective lighting, you can choose darker wall tiles or paint colors.

Stick a sample tile, or a picture of the tiles, to the mood board as a color reference.

Select possible colors for any untiled walls, picking either neutral, toning, or contrasting shades.

Buy towels in an accent color that is a variation of, or a dramatic contrast to, your base color.

Choose two or three colors to give yourself several options.

5 **INTRODUCING ACCENT COLORS** into a bathroom doesn't have to be complicated. Ideally, there should be two accent colors and no more than three—with the third as a washcloth, perhaps, or an arrangement of pretty bath bottles. Experiment with the proportions of the color combinations to see if they work together using tile or paint swatches and floor samples.

6 **CHOOSE STORAGE**, whether you have room for freestanding or built-in furniture or just storage boxes. Bear in mind that any mirrored or reflective surfaces will make your space feel bigger. Shapes and size are important, too: figure out whether the pieces you like will be a comfortable fit.

Wicker baskets can be used to store clean towels and bathroom supplies and hide laundry to be washed.

Refer back to your color palette to decide the colors of your accessories.

7 **ADD FINISHING TOUCHES** such as towels, pictures, and bath mats. These items don't have to coordinate exactly with your main theme, but they do need to lift the look of the room and highlight particular areas, such as a stylish sink or shower. These final touches will seal the room's success; the mood board will help you get this last element right.

3 LAYOUT CONSIDERATIONS IN THE BATHROOM

A bathroom requires careful planning, so before thinking about how you'd like it to look, consider the practical issues—how the room will be used, and which individual components will work best. Will more than one person regularly use the room at the same time? Do you need to make space for double sinks? Should you install a separate shower? How can the room be organized to make it work well for everyone?

BATHTUB

Plan the room's layout and functionality around the tub, since it is the biggest item and you may have little choice about where it will sit. If space is an issue, choose a tub that sits against a wall, and ideally in a corner. If you have a larger room, consider installing a freestanding bathtub, but check first with your plumber that it won't cause drainage issues. Consider, too, where the tub spout and knobs will be positioned: freestanding tubs, for example, don't usually have these fittings attached, so they will have to be attached to the wall or be "floor standing." If your bathtub is to have a shower above it, the tub should be positioned against the wall and screened to prevent water spillage.

SINK

Ideally, the sink should sit within easy reach of the toilet, and with a solid wall (rather than, say, a window) behind so that you can hang a mirror above it. Before choosing a sink and locating the best position for it, give some thought to the storage you'll need. If storage space is tight, consider getting a vanity unit with a sink set into, or sitting on, a shelving unit or cabinet, rather than opting for a simple pedestal sink. This choice may affect your layout, so check the dimensions of the unit carefully first to make sure it will fit into the bathroom plan.

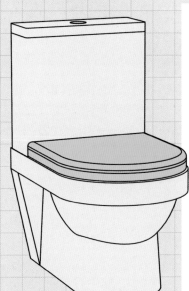

TOILET

It's important to consider waste and vent piping when locating a toilet. Positioning a toilet on an outside wall isn't a good idea in cold climates, as waterlines can freeze, causing pipes to burst. It's best to install a toilet near a window or extractor fan, either across from or next to the sink for convenience. If the toilet will sit on an interior wall, bear in mind that the wall may need to be built out to hide soil and vent pipes. This thicker area can be at partial height to provide a shallow shelf behind the toilet. As with all plumbing fixtures, the configurations and sizes for toilets vary, so if space is an issue, shop around before buying.

STORAGE UNITS

Bathrooms benefit from as much storage space as possible. Include shelving for toiletries, towel rails, and hooks for clothes or bathrobes—all within reach of the bath or shower. A wall-hung cabinet for bottles, medicines, and cleaning products is also useful, as are shelves to stack unused towels. Or have storage space built behind a bathtub panel and accessed via a small door. For a streamlined look, pick vanity units or cabinets below the sink with plenty of storage space.

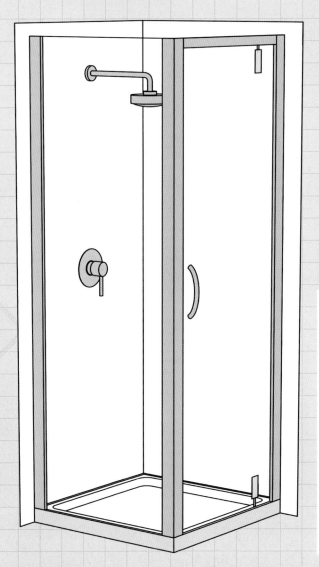

SHOWER

If space allows, install a separate shower, particularly if this is your only bathroom. Sit it along the same wall as the tub and choose a shower base the same depth for a streamlined look, and to make plumbing and drainage easier. If you have space, a walk-in shower looks luxurious. If your ceiling slopes, put the shower in the tallest part of the room (and take the extra height of the shower tray into account).

4 CHOOSE A BATHTUB

When it comes to choosing a bathtub, you need to consider how much space you have, and how you will use it—do you like to spend hours soaking, or prefer to shower? You also need to think of practicalities: a deep bathtub may look luxurious, but it will take longer to fill and weigh more than a conventional bathtub.

1 CHOOSE THE SHAPE

The shape of the bathtub you choose depends on the size and proportions of your bathroom. For example, your awkwardly shaped bathroom may be most suited to a corner bathtub, or you may only have room for a standard rectangular tub.

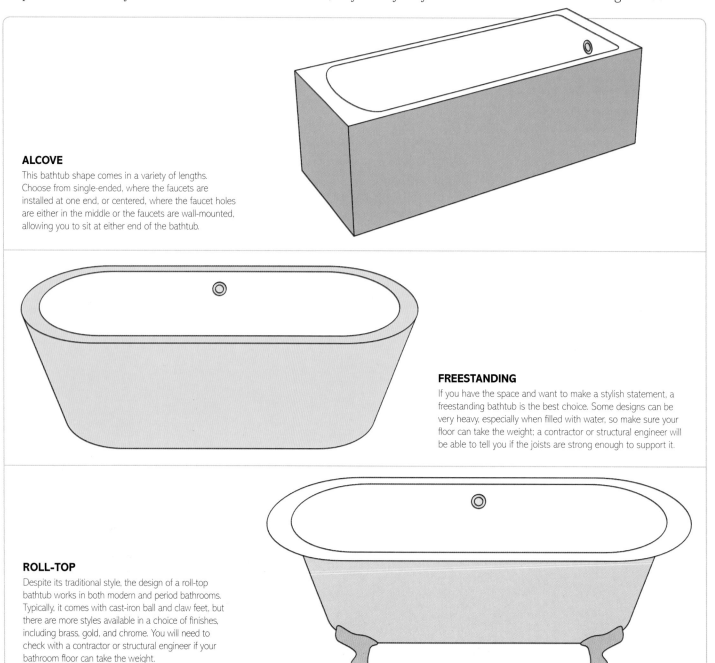

ALCOVE
This bathtub shape comes in a variety of lengths. Choose from single-ended, where the faucets are installed at one end, or centered, where the faucet holes are either in the middle or the faucets are wall-mounted, allowing you to sit at either end of the bathtub.

FREESTANDING
If you have the space and want to make a stylish statement, a freestanding bathtub is the best choice. Some designs can be very heavy, especially when filled with water, so make sure your floor can take the weight; a contractor or structural engineer will be able to tell you if the joists are strong enough to support it.

ROLL-TOP
Despite its traditional style, the design of a roll-top bathtub works in both modern and period bathrooms. Typically, it comes with cast-iron ball and claw feet, but there are more styles available in a choice of finishes, including brass, gold, and chrome. You will need to check with a contractor or structural engineer if your bathroom floor can take the weight.

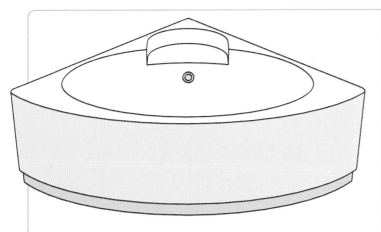

SHOWER BATHTUB

If you are going to have a shower attachment over the bathtub, consider a shape that provides extra showering space. These bathtubs are either L-shaped or bowed to make one end of the bathtub roomier.

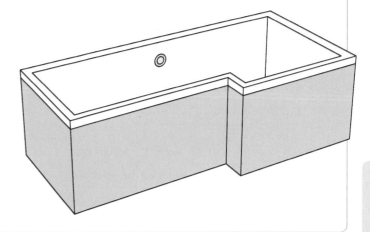

CORNER BATHTUB

Corner tubs range in size from small and space-efficient to large and dramatic. They don't require the long wall that other tubs do, however, they do require more floor space and use more water than standard tubs, and you may not be able to lie down in them comfortably.

2 CHOOSE THE MATERIAL

If you want to make a style statement, look for a bathtub in a "stand-out" unusual material and be prepared to pay for it. If practicality and a low budget are higher up on your list, shop for an eye-catching bathtub shape in a cheaper material.

ACRYLIC

A popular choice, acrylic is warm to the touch, lightweight, and durable, so can be made into a variety of shapes and sizes. It's a relatively inexpensive option.

STEEL

Heavy, hard-wearing, medium-cost steel is usually only available in a rectangular shape. Its vitreous enamel surface is impact-, scratch-, and acid-resistant.

CAST-IRON

Medium-priced and heavy, a cast-iron bathtub is extremely strong, but it cools hot water quickly. It has a durable surface that is impact- and scratch-resistant.

COPPER

Although an expensive option, a copper bathtub is a style statement. It also heats up instantly when in contact with warm water and retains the warmth for longer.

WOOD

Available in good-looking woods like ash, walnut, teak, and iroko, this expensive option has a finishing coat that strengthens the structure and provides a durable finish.

SOLID-SURFACE MIX

Usually a mix of stone and resin, this high-cost bathtub is very tough and hard-wearing, and can be molded into any shape. Choose from a variety of colors.

WHIRLPOOL AND SPA BATHTUBS

If you are replacing your bathtub, look for models with whirlpool or spa systems (or both, known as hydro systems) built in.

Spa bathtubs

● Spa bathtubs have low-profile nozzles set into the base of the bathtub; these pump air bubbles into the water, creating a gentle, fizzing massage effect.

Whirlpool bathtubs

● Whirlpool bathtubs have jets set around the sides of the tub. A powerful pump, usually situated beneath the tub, pushes a mix of air and water through the jets, creating an invigorating massage effect that can be controlled with a turbo or electronic controls.

● Whirlpool bathtubs are easier to keep clean, since a cleaning solution can be passed through the pipework (many spa systems can only be cleaned after being soaked in cleaning solution).

● Putting in one of these tubs is as easy as installing a regular tub: the piping is already in place. However, the junction box for the power supply must be installed by a certified electrician.

5 CHOOSE
A SHOWER

Installing the right shower can make all the difference in helping you get your day off to a good start or wind down completely at the end of it. Assess your space, consider all the options, and don't forget to check that your preferred choice will work with your water supply before you finalize your decision.

1 CHOOSE YOUR SHOWER ARRANGEMENT

There are plenty of ways to create a stylish, practical showering area. Depending on the space available, you have the choice of installing a shower over your bathtub, installing a stall shower or walk-in enclosure, or creating a dedicated wet room.

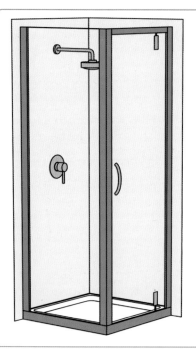

STALL SHOWER

If you are having a shower enclosure separate from your bathtub, a stall shower with a prefabricated base is usually the simplest and most cost-effective way of doing it. A separate shower, without a bathtub, is fine in an en suite or second bathroom but it is not advisable to remove the household's only bathtub to accommodate a stand-alone shower unit.

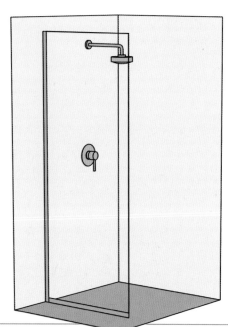

WET ROOM

Ideal for bigger areas, walk-in showers and wet rooms have become very popular in recent years and are contemporary, stylish, and spacious. A wet room needs to be waterproofed, with a shower drain set into a sloping floor.

TUB SHOWER

If your bathroom is very small with no space for a separate shower, you may need to install a tub shower above the bathtub and add a shower curtain or screen.

2 DECIDE ON SIZE AND SHAPE

While a wet room will be custom-fitted to suit your space, there is a finite range of stall shower shapes and sizes to choose from. Here are the main options. (If you are combining your shower area with your bathtub, see pages 90–91 for bathtub shapes.)

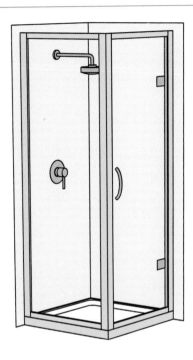

SQUARE

Square shower bases are very versatile, since they can be positioned in a corner, along a wall, or in the center of a large room. They are available in a range of sizes, although it is worth picking the largest size your bathroom can accommodate, to make your showering experience less cramped.

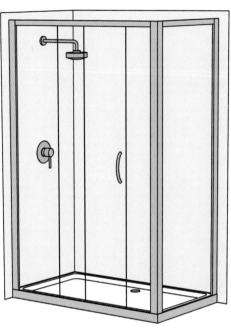

RECTANGULAR

A rectangular-shaped shower is the perfect choice if you have a bit more space to play with in your bathroom. The benefit of these shower bases is that they give you more room to move around while you're showering. Like square shower bases, they are available in many different sizes.

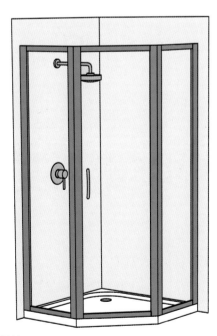

PENTAGONAL

Essentially square in shape, but with a triangular section on one side of the base sliced away, this type of shower is a space-saving solution to suit a smaller bathroom. The shower is designed to be tucked neatly into one corner of the bathroom to take up minimal floor space.

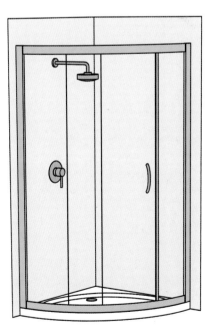

QUADRANT

Also suitable for compact areas, this type of shower base is curved rather than angular at the front. It requires a matching curved shower screen, and together the base and screen give a smoother look to a bathroom. Offset quadrant bases provide a little more space in which to shower than a regular quadrant base.

3 CHOOSE A SCREEN

A shower screen can add a touch of class to your bathroom, as well as protecting the surrounding area from water damage. What you go for will largely be dictated by your choice of shower arrangement, but there are still things you need to consider.

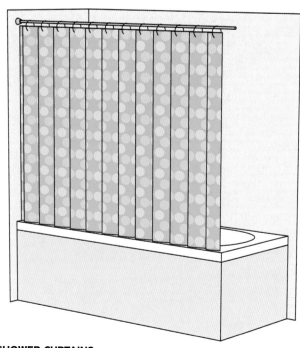

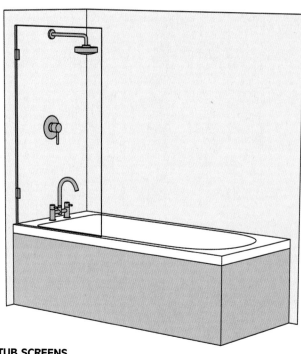

SHOWER CURTAINS

Shower curtains, designed to hang over a bathtub, can be hung on rings from either a straight, L-shaped, or circular shower rail. Made from polyester or PVC, they are inexpensive and are available in a huge range of colors and prints. Some versions have a second layer, in a more attractive fabric, that hangs outside the bathtub.

TUB SCREENS

These transparent screens are attached to the wall at the end of a bathtub where the shower is positioned and sit flush against the long outside edge of the bathtub. Made from tempered safety glass, they may be straight or curved in shape and hinged for easy cleaning. Folding screens are also available.

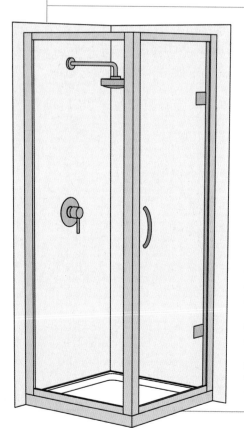

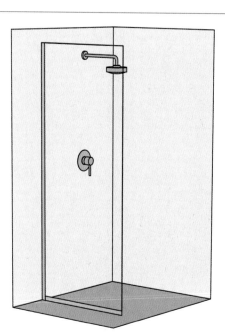

SHOWER DOORS

There are several types of door you can choose for a shower cubicle. Pivot and hinged doors require some space in front to swing open, whereas sliding doors and bifold doors can be folded inward, and so are perfect for small bathrooms. For a more contemporary finish, consider a frameless style.

SHOWER SCREENS

A fixed, full-height straight or curved glass screen—or a combination of both—will make a stylish statement in a wet room or for a walk-in shower. Opt for a frameless design, complemented by sleek chrome fixtures, if you want to create a chic, minimalist look in your bathroom.

4 CHOOSE YOUR SHOWERHEAD

The showerhead you choose is very much down to personal preference but, in making the decision, consider who will be using the shower and their needs, as well as the look you want to go for and how spacious or cramped the shower enclosure is.

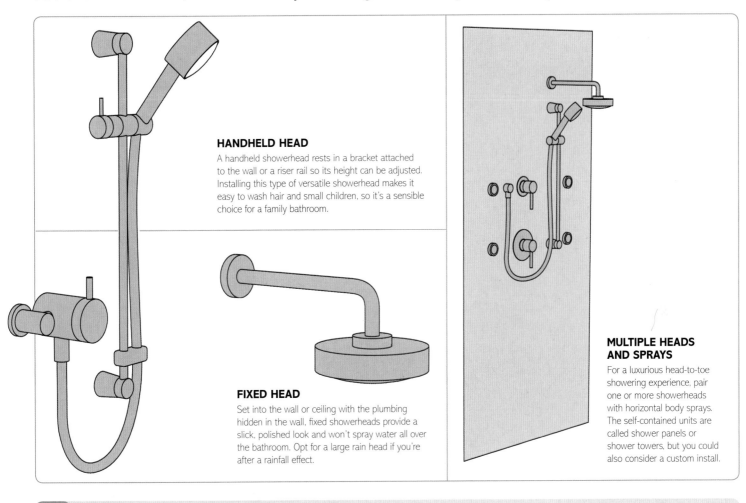

HANDHELD HEAD

A handheld showerhead rests in a bracket attached to the wall or a riser rail so its height can be adjusted. Installing this type of versatile showerhead makes it easy to wash hair and small children, so it's a sensible choice for a family bathroom.

FIXED HEAD

Set into the wall or ceiling with the plumbing hidden in the wall, fixed showerheads provide a slick, polished look and won't spray water all over the bathroom. Opt for a large rain head if you're after a rainfall effect.

MULTIPLE HEADS AND SPRAYS

For a luxurious head-to-toe showering experience, pair one or more showerheads with horizontal body sprays. The self-contained units are called shower panels or shower towers, but you could also consider a custom install.

5 CHOOSE YOUR CONTROLS

Besides finding the functionality you like best in terms of knobs and/or levers, the most fundamental question when choosing valves to regulate the flow and temperature of your shower is "concealed or exposed."

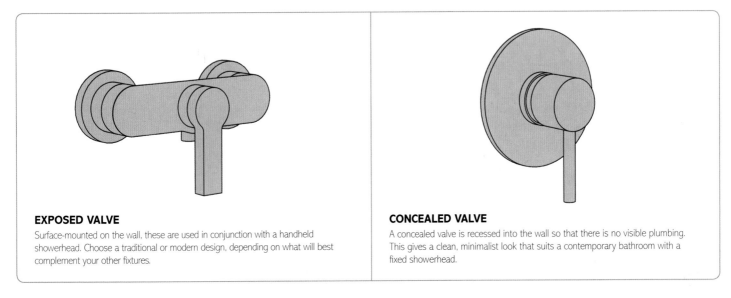

EXPOSED VALVE

Surface-mounted on the wall, these are used in conjunction with a handheld showerhead. Choose a traditional or modern design, depending on what will best complement your other fixtures.

CONCEALED VALVE

A concealed valve is recessed into the wall so that there is no visible plumbing. This gives a clean, minimalist look that suits a contemporary bathroom with a fixed showerhead.

6 CHOOSE A BATHROOM SINK

The size of your bathroom and the suite you choose may predetermine your choice of sink, but with so many different shapes and styles available, where to start? Consider practical issues, such as storage needs and how many people use the bathroom at one time, as well as the look you want to achieve.

CHOOSE THE TYPE

Each of these basic sink types comes in a range of styles, from square, contemporary shapes to curvaceous lines suited to traditional rooms. Sizes vary, too, with big sinks for family use and small sinks best for bathrooms where space is an issue.

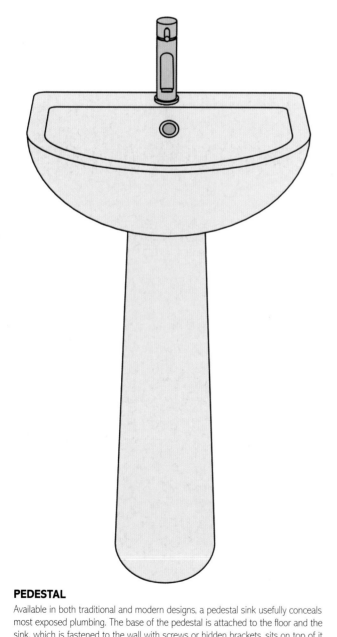

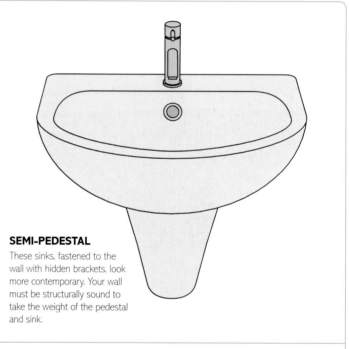

SEMI-PEDESTAL
These sinks, fastened to the wall with hidden brackets, look more contemporary. Your wall must be structurally sound to take the weight of the pedestal and sink.

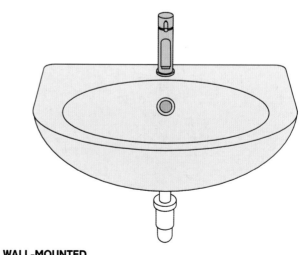

PEDESTAL
Available in both traditional and modern designs, a pedestal sink usefully conceals most exposed plumbing. The base of the pedestal is attached to the floor and the sink, which is fastened to the wall with screws or hidden brackets, sits on top of it.

WALL-MOUNTED
Wall-mounted sinks are usually attached directly to the wall using concealed brackets. However, if the wall is not structurally sound enough to take the sink's weight, you may need a mounting frame hidden within the wall itself.

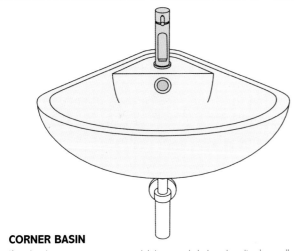

CORNER BASIN

If you're short on space, a corner sink is a good choice, since its shape allows it to sit neatly in the corner of the room and take up less floor space. More often than not, these sinks are wall-hung, although you can find some with pedestals.

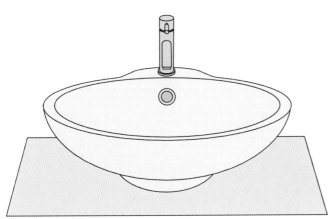

COUNTERTOP

This style of sink sits on top of a piece of furniture—either a cabinet, table, or specially made unit. It comes in a wide range of shapes, including round, oval, and square, and a selection of materials such as ceramic, glass, and natural stone.

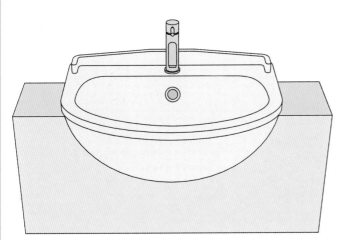

SEMI-RECESSED

Semi-recessed sinks require minimal space on your countertop, making them ideal for smaller bathrooms. They are designed to be fastened into a cavity within a slim worktop or storage cabinet, with the front of the sink overhanging the worktop.

VANITY UNIT

Vanity units sit underneath a sink (which is inset) and act as a pedestal, as well as offering storage of one or two door cabinets or drawers. They are available in a wide range of materials and designs, with floor- or wall-mounted options.

CUSTOM BASIN UNIT

A custom-fitted sink cabinet is made to measure to make the most of your bathroom's space. Much like a vanity unit in its design, this type of sink can sit on top of the unit or be sunk into the worktop.

When choosing faucets for your bathroom, style is just one consideration. You should also check that your preferred options will work with your water supply (standard pressure is fine for most modern faucets but some require a higher pressure), as well as being compatible with your sink or bathtub.

1 CHOOSE THE TYPE

Before you choose which type of faucet you need, first decide whether it must be—or you want it to be—mounted on the bathtub or sink, the counter surface, or the wall. (If your sink or bathtub has predrilled holes, your decision is already made.)

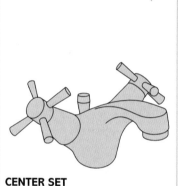
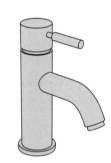

CENTER SET
Hot and cold water are mixed inside this faucet, and its temperature can be regulated by separate controls, which makes it a good choice for a family bathroom.

SINGLE LEVER
With a single faucet and lever handle that controls the temperature and water flow, single lever faucets are easy to control with one hand and very neat in appearance.

PILLAR
An old-fashioned pair of pillar faucets supply hot and cold water separately. These faucets can be useful in restorations.

WALL-MOUNTED
Wall-mounted faucets are ideal for center-drained tubs (but do require concealed plumbing). Check the faucet's length and position are suitable for your tub or basin.

2 CHOOSE THE FINISH

Bathroom faucets are available in many different finishes, so what you choose will depend on the color of your sink or bathtub and other elements of the bathroom, and whether you prefer a sleek and shiny or matte finish.

CHROME
Shiny chrome suits contemporary and traditional bathrooms, and is relatively easy to keep clean, although water spots do show. It is available in a range of prices.

POLISHED BRASS
Medium to high in cost, and often only available in traditional styles, these faucets add a touch of luxury. They work well if teamed with warm natural stone tiles.

BRUSHED METAL
Best in contemporary bathrooms, mid- to high-priced brushed metal faucets don't show water marks so easily—a bonus if you live in a hard-water area.

POWDER-COATED BRASS
Black faucets to match a black sink create a dramatic feature. Made of powder-coated brass, and low to high in cost, they feature chrome levers or other details.

OIL-RUBBED BRONZE
Prices vary for this dark-coated brass finish. Over time, the yellow brass beneath the coating will start to become visible, giving the fixture a timeworn quality.

CHOOSE A TOILET

While the toilet might not be the focal point of your bathroom, you should still pay attention to its design. By doing so, you will ensure that it fits in with the rest of the room's scheme, might save you valuable space if you need it, could be easier to clean, and may help you economize on water usage.

CHOOSE THE TYPE

The type of toilet you choose will largely depend on whether you prefer a contemporary or traditional look to the room. You will also need to consider where it will be placed, and whether you prefer the look of a one- or a two-piece toilet.

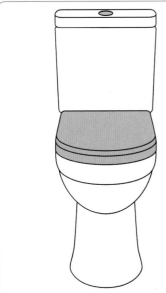

TANK TOILET
An inexpensive option, this style is easiest to install and hides more plumbing than other designs. In the one-piece version, the tank is fused to the pedestal; in a two-piece, the tank rests on it. The flush is operated by a push button or lever on the tank.

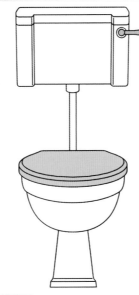

HIGH WALL
The pedestal for this style of old-fashioned toilet rests on the floor and is connected with a pipe to the tank, which is mounted high on the wall. The high wall style of toilet typically has a lever flush in keeping with its classic design.

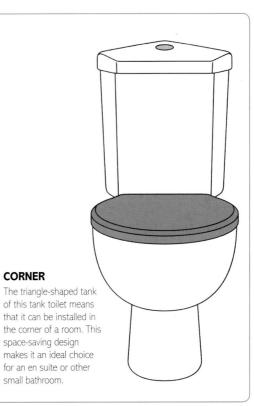

CORNER
The triangle-shaped tank of this tank toilet means that it can be installed in the corner of a room. This space-saving design makes it an ideal choice for an en suite or other small bathroom.

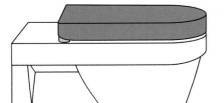

CONCEALED TANK
The tank for this modern, easy-to-clean toilet is concealed in a special carriage built into the wall behind the toilet. It's a good choice if space is tight.

BIDETS

Bidets are available in a choice of both modern and traditional styles, and are come in floor-standing or wall-mounted designs. More commonplace in Europe than in the US, they are nonetheless worth considering if you have children or elderly people in your family who find a bathtub or shower too difficult to negotiate on a daily basis. Bidets are best positioned next to the toilet.

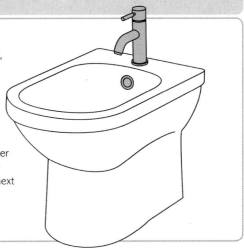

9 CHOOSE FLOORING

One of the most important considerations when decorating your bathroom is the flooring you use. Not only does it need to look good, but it also should be nonslip, durable, easy to clean, comfortable to walk on in bare feet, and, most importantly, moisture- and humidity-resistant.

1 CHOOSE THE LOOK

Wood, tiles, and seamless flooring can all look contemporary, while the former two are better choices for a period-style room. Tiles and seamless flooring stand up better to moisture; wood is less water-resistant, but is a viable option if you love the look.

TILED

Floor tiles come in a range of materials—including porcelain, ceramic, and vinyl—and colors and sizes. Although tiles may seem like an obvious choice, they are hard and cold underfoot, so might be best if teamed with underfloor heating.

SEAMLESS

Vinyl and rubber sheets are a popular seamless flooring for a bathroom, although poured resin is also a good option. Ideal for small spaces, its lack of joins gives it a neat finish. However, if the floor becomes damaged, the whole floor has to be replaced.

WOOD

The color and texture of wood creates a nice contrast to sleek plumbing fixtures and gives continuity if wood floors are used elsewhere in the house. If your bathroom gets wet and humid, avoid solid wood and opt for laminate, engineered wood or vinyl look-alikes.

CHECKLIST

- **If you are laying tiles,** you can tile directly onto concrete or existing tiles (provided they are sound and level), but be aware that doing this will raise the level of your floor significantly, as will underfloor heating. You may have to remove and shave the bottom of the door before rehanging it.

- **A wood framed floor** must have a subfloor installed over it before you can tile. The simplest way to achieve this is to screw down marine plywood boards.

- **Make sure that any gaps** between planks or tiles are well sealed to stop water from seeping through to rooms below.

2 CHOOSE THE MATERIAL

What you choose depends on whether you prefer the classic look and feel of tiles or something softer, like vinyl or rubber. If you are having underfloor heating installed, check which materials are suitable to use with it first.

TILES

PORCELAIN

Porcelain is a versatile, very hard-wearing choice in a range of prices and designs, including mosaic. Seal unglazed tiles before and after grouting.

CERAMIC

Cheap compared to natural stone and porcelain, ceramic tiles are a good choice for larger areas, They are also hard-wearing and won't need sealing.

QUARTZ COMPOSITE

Expensive quartz composite has a luxurious look and is available in a wide range of colors, including black, white, gray, red, and blue. It rarely chips or cracks.

SEAMLESS

RESIN

Poured resin, available in a range of colors, is highly contemporary. It is laid directly onto concrete subfloors or special marine plywood, but not floorboards.

RUBBER

A practical choice, medium-priced rubber is hard-wearing and warm underfoot, and comes in a range of colors and textures. Low-profile textures provide extra grip.

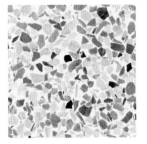

TERRAZZO

High-cost terrazzo (marble chips set into cement with a color pigment added) comes in many colors and finishes. When wet, this surface may become slippery.

VINYL

Available in a range of patterns and prices, vinyl tiles are water-resistant so are ideal for a bathroom. More expensive vinyls are best left for a professional to install.

RUBBER

Medium-priced rubber tiles are available in a huge range of colors and different textures. These tiles are a good choice for family bathrooms.

VINYL

Low- to medium-priced modern sheet vinyl comes in a range of designs that reproduce the look and texture of material such as wood, stone, metal, and glass.

LINOLEUM

Made of natural and sustainable ingredients, this medium-priced floor is easy to clean and naturally resistant to bacteria and fungus, so is an ideal choice.

WOOD

HARDWOOD

A hardwood floor must be installed perfectly, with no gaps for moisture. It is not a good option if the floor will get very wet. It is medium to high in cost.

ENGINEERED WOOD

The construction of this medium-priced wood (layers of hard and softwood boards topped with a layer of hardwood) means it is less likely to warp.

BAMBOO

Medium to high in price, bamboo has moisture-resistant qualities and does not shrink, expand, or warp. It's eco friendly, too. It should be sealed before use.

LAMINATE

Some laminate wood planks are designed for bathrooms and have a moisture-resistant core, although they are still not moisture-proof. Laminate is low to medium in cost.

VINYL

Wood-effect vinyl will give an authentic look and is easier to care for than real wood. Prices depend on the brand; cheaper versions are self-adhesive.

10 CHOOSE WALL COVERINGS

Decorated bathroom walls, particularly around wet areas, need to be water-resistant and easy to clean. However, you don't have to stick to one material—for example, wallpaper can be combined with tiles to good effect. In small bathrooms, think, too, about ways to stretch the space visually.

1 CHOOSE THE MATERIAL

If your bathroom is very small with no window you can open, your choice must be practical and water-resistant; if you have more space and ventilation, why not choose less obvious materials with which to decorate your bathroom.

TILES

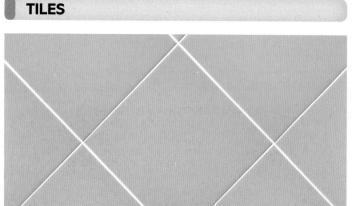

Tiles are the most practical choice for a bathroom, especially on the walls of shower stalls and around bathtubs and sink backsplashs. Choose from porcelain or ceramic, glass, natural stone, and mosaics.

PAINT

Although you shouldn't paint areas that are going to get wet—where you shower, for instance—paint is a good way to add color to your bathroom, and can be changed fairly quickly and easily when you want to update the look of the room.

WALLPAPER

Use wallpaper only on walls that don't come in direct contact with water. Look for a paper specifically designed for use in bathrooms. Alternatively, consider using wallpaper behind a sheet of clear glass, which will go some way toward protecting it.

PANELING

Wood or MDF paneling itself is not water-resistant, but if you coat it with a tough paint suitable for woodwork in bathrooms, it can withstand a high degree of dampness and some minor splashing. It is ideal for creating a period feel.

2 CHOOSE THE TYPE

If you want to choose a mixture of different materials for your bathroom walls, consider each one in combination with another material. Will the tiles you choose complement the paneling you like, or will painted walls work with the tiles you prefer?

TILES

CLASSIC

Square ceramic or porcelain tiles can be used in any bathroom. Those on a budget can opt for plain white, but a huge range of colors and patterns are available.

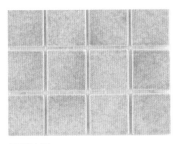

SUBWAY

Typically made of ceramic with a gloss or matte surface, medium- to high-priced subway tiles have a straight or beveled edge and come in a variety of colors.

MOSAIC

Medium- to high-cost mosaic tiles come in a range of materials, including natural stone, ceramic, travertine, and glass, and a variety of finishes such as silver and mirror glass.

LARGE FORMAT

To use large-format (31 x 31in/80 x 80cm) tiles you need flat walls. This tile is better in a medium- or large-sized room, since its size dwarfs the proportions of a smaller room.

PAINT

KITCHEN & BATHROOM

These medium- to high-priced paints are made to withstand moisture and often mold, too. They are available in a limited number of colors.

MATTE

If your bathroom is well ventilated and the painted walls won't get splashed with water, using a water-based matte emulsion shouldn't be a problem. Prices vary greatly.

SATIN

You can use medium-priced satin paints if your room is well ventilated. The subtle sheen of these paints can help to reflect light in small or dark bathrooms.

EGGSHELL

Medium-priced eggshell paint can be used for walls and for woodwork and metalwork such as baseboards and radiators. It is washable and has a near-matte finish.

WALLPAPER

VINYL

Low to medium in cost, vinyl wallpapers in various designs are specially made for use in bathrooms, but are not recommended for wet areas—for example, next to the tub.

PLAIN OR PATTERNED

If you like a standard wallpaper design that isn't specifically for a bathroom, check that your ventilation is good, and be prepared for the wallpaper to lift in places. Prices vary.

PANELING

 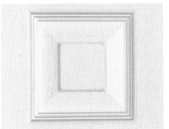

WAINSCOT

Medium-cost wainscot paneling can be used just as effectively in a bathroom as other rooms. if painted, pick a paint with a soft sheen.

TONGUE & GROVE

If this paneling is painted with a water-resistant paint, it can be used next to a bathtub and behind a sink, but don't use it in a shower. It is low to medium in price.

TILE AND GROUT
BATHROOM WALLS

The sequence below shows how to tile around two sides of a bathtub, but the principles can be applied to creating a backsplash around a sink, and other simple tiling jobs. After the old tile is removed, check the concrete board for any cracks or chips; either fill in the cracks or replace the concrete board, if necessary.

WHAT YOU NEED

- Tiles
- Tile spacers
- Tile adhesive
- Serrated hand trowel
- Tile cutter or wet saw
- Grout spreader, or spatula
- Grout
- Rounded sponge
- Cloth
- Silicone sealant

1 PLAN THE PLACEMENT

PLAN HOW TO ARRANGE the tiles by propping the first row up against the wall around the edge of the bathtub. Use whole tiles, placing tile spacers in between, and ascertain whether these will fill the space. If you will need to add cut tiles, leave a gap in the corner.

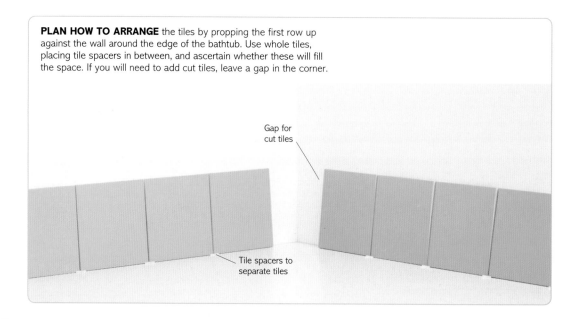

Gap for cut tiles

Tile spacers to separate tiles

2 SET THE FIRST TILES

1 APPLY THE ADHESIVE with a serrated hand trowel. (If the applied adhesive is flat and smooth, the tiles won't adhere to it properly.) Work in sections of approximately 3ft square (1m square) or, if the area you are tiling is small, apply adhesive to each tile.

2 STICK THE FIRST ROW of whole tiles to the wall. Place a tile spacer between each tile so that the gaps are all equal.

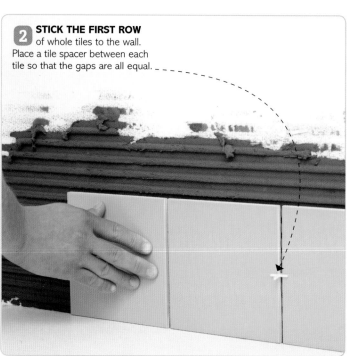

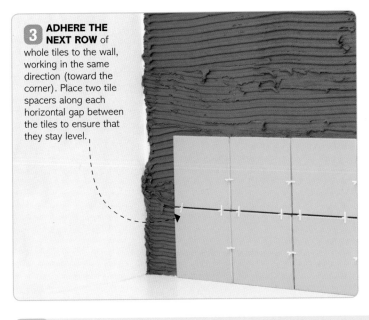

3 ADHERE THE NEXT ROW of whole tiles to the wall, working in the same direction (toward the corner). Place two tile spacers along each horizontal gap between the tiles to ensure that they stay level.

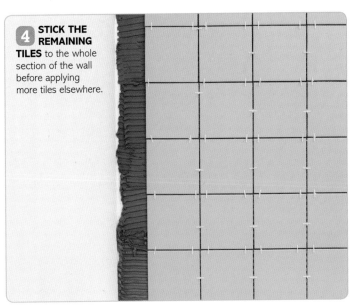

4 STICK THE REMAINING TILES to the whole section of the wall before applying more tiles elsewhere.

3 MEASURE AND CUT THE CORNER TILES

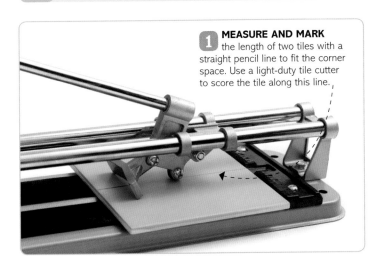

1 MEASURE AND MARK the length of two tiles with a straight pencil line to fit the corner space. Use a light-duty tile cutter to score the tile along this line.

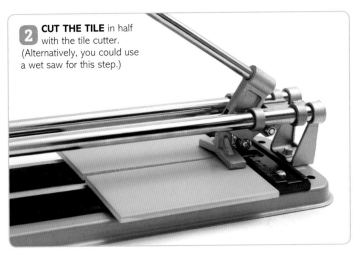

2 CUT THE TILE in half with the tile cutter. (Alternatively, you could use a wet saw for this step.)

4 TILE THE CORNERS

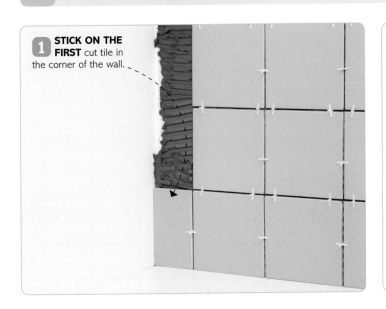

1 STICK ON THE FIRST cut tile in the corner of the wall.

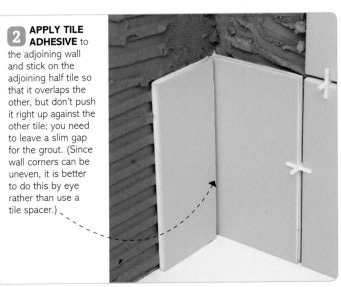

2 APPLY TILE ADHESIVE to the adjoining wall and stick on the adjoining half tile so that it overlaps the other, but don't push it right up against the other tile; you need to leave a slim gap for the grout. (Since wall corners can be uneven, it is better to do this by eye rather than use a tile spacer.)

5 TILE THE ADJOINING WALL

1 SET A ROW of whole tiles in place along the bottom of the adjoining wall, inserting tile spacers between the tiles.

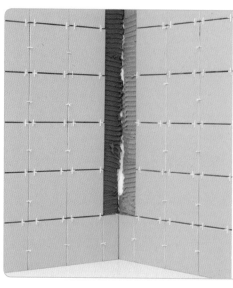

2 APPLY SOME MORE TILE ADHESIVE and stick the remaining whole tiles to the wall in ascending rows.

3 MEASURE, CUT, AND STICK the remaining tiles to the corner area. Then allow the tile adhesive to dry (see manufacturer's instructions).

6 FILL THE GAPS WITH GROUT

1 ONCE THE ADHESIVE IS DRY, remove the tile spacers. Then load the grout spreader or spatula with grout and spread it in a diagonal direction across the surface of the tiles. Work in small sections (3ft square/1m square), pushing the grout into the gaps and smoothing it down with the spatula.

2 GROUT DRIES QUICKLY, so sponge away any residual grout on the tiles before working on another section. Again, move in a diagonal direction as you wipe down the tiles.

3 **SPREAD GROUT** evenly over all the corner tiles using the grout spreader or spatula.

4 **USE A FINGER**, if necessary, to smooth the grout between the cut tiles in the corner for an even finish.

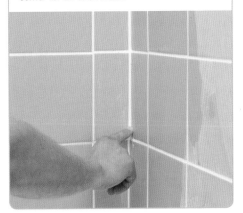

5 **WHEN THE GROUT IS DRY**, polish the tiles with a clean cloth to remove the last of the excess grout.

7 SEAL THE BASE OF THE TILES

1 **APPLY THE SILICONE SEALANT** evenly around the base of the tiles where they make contact with the edge of the bathtub.

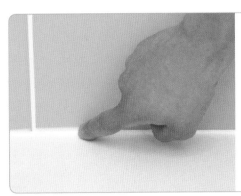

2 **USE A WET FINGER** to smooth the silicone out to make it look as neat as possible.

5 WAYS WITH
TILE PATTERNS

If you want to add pattern and interest to a bathroom, the easiest and most practical way to do this is with tiles. Decide if you want a modern, colorful, retro, or unusual look, and then pick tiles—whether rustic handmade, machine-made, metalic, glass, resin, or mosaic—that will best suit your scheme.

FEATURE WALL

Create a feature behind your bathtub with a panel of tiles that contrast with the base color of the room. As in any other room, create just one focal wall, while leaving the others plain.

IF YOU WANT TO MAKE color a dynamic element of the tiled area, limit yourself to no more than three colors.

GRADUATION

Start at the bottom of a wall with a row of dark-colored tiles and gradually work up the wall using paler shades of the same color.

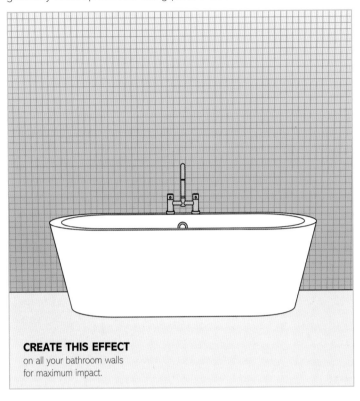

CREATE THIS EFFECT
on all your bathroom walls for maximum impact.

PATCHWORK

Create a patchwork wall using a mixture of tiles with different patterns. Try to stick to a limited color palette for the best effect.

STRIPES

Add interest to a painted wall with wide bands of tiles to create a striped effect. The tiled stripes can run vertically or horizontally.

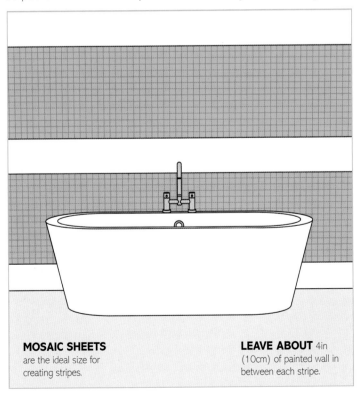

MOSAIC SHEETS
are the ideal size for creating stripes.

LEAVE ABOUT 4in (10cm) of painted wall in between each stripe.

BORDER

Add a border around the top of your tiled wall. Either use a specific border tile with a pattern, or a tile in a different color.

IF YOU WANT TO CREATE the illusion of height, add a vertical border to draw the eye upward.

5 WAYS WITH
CLEVER BATHROOM STORAGE

Space is often wasted in bathrooms, particularly small ones. However, there are clever storage options available that are functional yet good-looking, and will help to keep a bathroom free from clutter. None of these options will compromise the overall design and look of your bathroom.

BENEATH THE SINK

If you've chosen a bowl sink with a finished exterior face, practically any table will do as a washstand. Find a stand with drawers and shelves that will provide storage space for towels and toiletries.

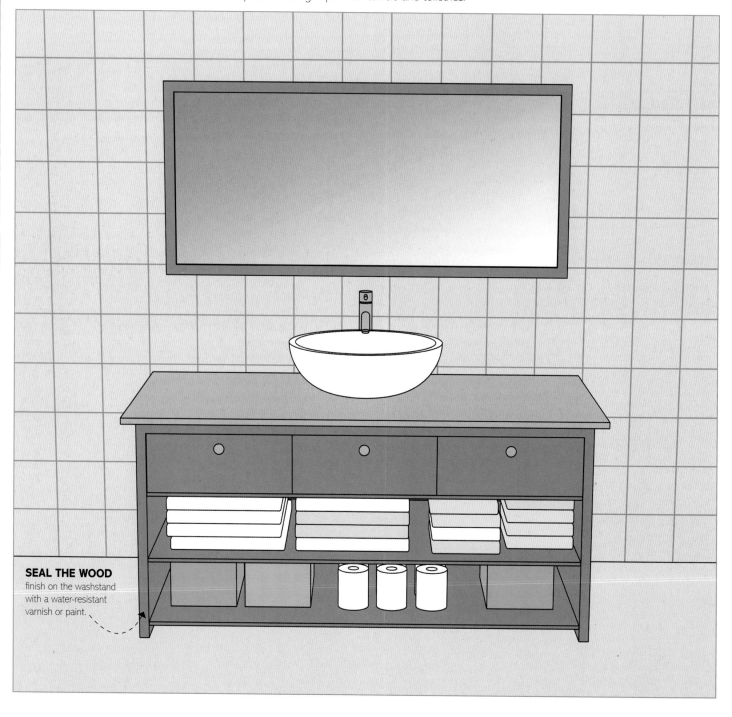

SEAL THE WOOD finish on the washstand with a water-resistant varnish or paint.

END OF BATHTUB

Create storage for smaller items such as bottles and toilet-paper rolls by building shelves in the unused space at the end of a bathtub.

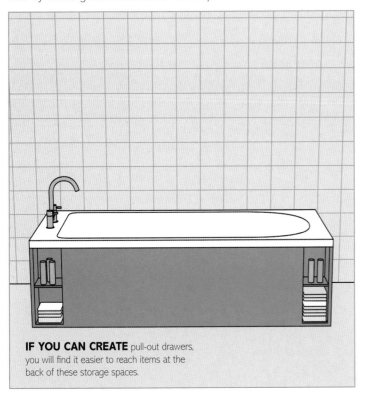

IF YOU CAN CREATE pull-out drawers, you will find it easier to reach items at the back of these storage spaces.

BEHIND A BATHTUB PANEL

Side bathtub panels that can be pulled open at the top can provide practical storage for cleaning products and other tall bottles.

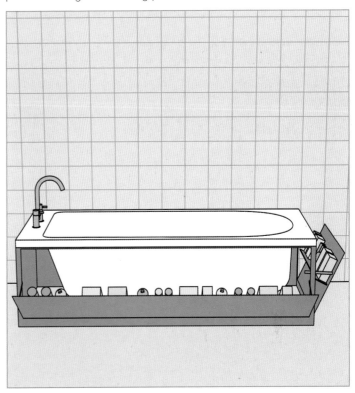

BEHIND THE DOOR

Towel racks aren't just for walls. Here, they have been attached to the back of a bathroom door for maximum space efficiency.

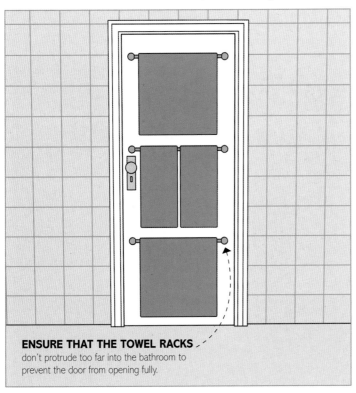

ENSURE THAT THE TOWEL RACKS don't protrude too far into the bathroom to prevent the door from opening fully.

RECESSED CUBBIES

When building a shower or wet room, create recessed, tiled cubby holes in the wall to hold shampoo and body wash bottles, and soap.

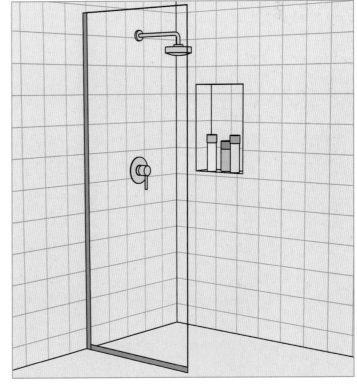

11 CHOOSE BATHROOM LIGHTING

Bathrooms need to be well lit so that they feel bright and welcoming and you can see what you're doing if you're shaving or applying makeup. However, bathroom lights also need to cope with the amount of moisture generated, particularly if you have a shower in the room, so make sure you choose suitable fixtures.

1 DECIDE ON A STYLE OF LIGHTING

Most bathrooms are fairly compact so you may be limited in your choice of lighting. In this room, your primary focus should be on getting the ambient and task lighting right.

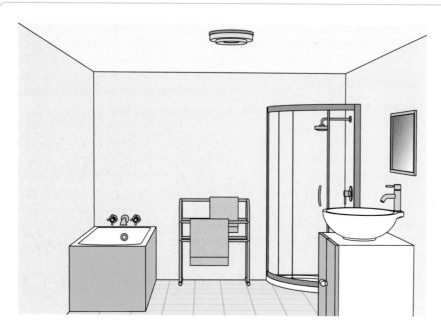

AMBIENT
Your overhead lighting should account for the ambient lighting within the room, and it needs to be bright enough for you to see what you're doing, morning and night. Consider wall lights or candles if you want to lay back and relax in the bathtub.

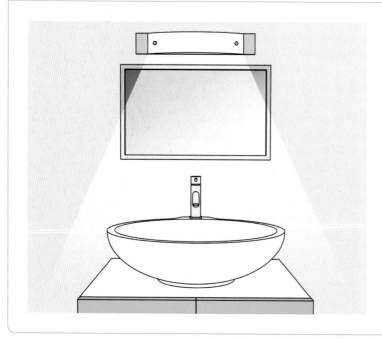

TASK
Task lighting in a bathroom can include strong overhead downlights installed in the ceiling. Ideally, you should place one task light above the sink, another above the bathtub, and a third above the shower. Also place a bright light above the mirror over your sink.

2 CHOOSE YOUR LIGHT FIXTURES

There's nothing worse than a poorly lit bathroom—it makes the room feel cold, unwelcoming, and smaller than it really is. So, make sure you get a good combination of lighting types within the room, space and budget permitting.

CEILING LIGHTS

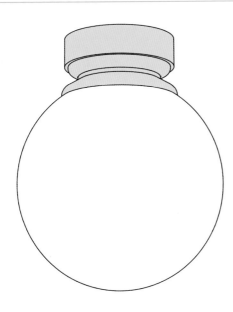

CEILING LIGHT

A central ceiling light, provided it is used in combination with other types of lighting, will provide good levels of ambient lighting in a bathroom. For safety reasons, the light itself must be enclosed or flush. A prominent fixture is not the best choice if your bathroom has a low ceiling.

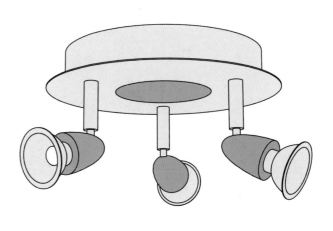

SPOTLIGHTS

Spotlights are good for providing both task and accent lighting in a bathroom; their adjustable heads mean you can direct the light exactly where you need it. Choose from individual heads, or bars or plates with two to four heads that can be adjusted independently of each other.

RECESSED DOWNLIGHTS

Recessed downlights offer high levels of practical lighting in a bathroom, and their unobtrusive design makes them perfect for a small or low-ceilinged bathroom. If you are using these lights over a shower or bathtub, you will need to purchase sealed downlights.

FLOOR LIGHTS

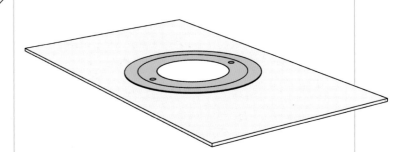

RECESSED UPLIGHTS

Highlight your bathroom walls using recessed floor uplighters. Install them near to the wall around the edges of the room to create subtle shafts of light that will illuminate your chosen wallcovering. A dimmer switch will also allow you to vary the height the light travels and create different moods in the room.

WALL-MOUNTED LIGHTS

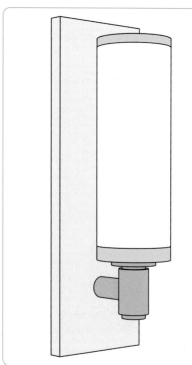

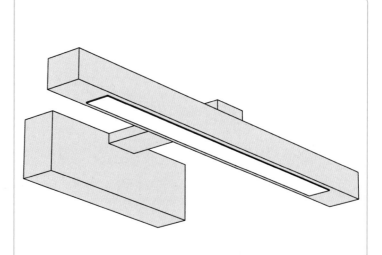

WALL SCONCES

Used in addition to a central ceiling light or downlights, wall sconces can provide a soft atmospheric light and also add interest to your room's decorating scheme. Install them in alcoves, on each side of a mirror, or even above a bathtub.

OVER MIRROR LIGHT

These lights provide bright task lighting. The design is often long and slim with an electrical receptacle in one end. They typically work independently from other lighting in the bathroom. Some bathroom mirrors have lighting built into them that works in the same way.

SAFETY OPTIONS

When it comes to bathroom lighting, it's safety first. You need to make sure that your light fixtures are appropriate, safe to use, and correctly positioned. Electrical equipment used in bathrooms must be protected against the inevitable condensation, humidity, and sprays of water that come with the territory.

While it is always best to have a certified electrician do the electrical installation, it is still important to understand some of the safety options available for lighting fixtures used in bathrooms.

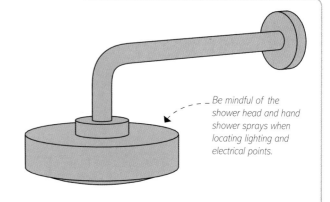

Be mindful of the shower head and hand shower sprays when locating lighting and electrical points.

- **A good rule of thumb** to use when selecting lighting for wet areas such as the bathroom is to check the UL (Underwriter's Laboratory) listing. The UL establishes testing criteria for lighting fixtures and rates fixtures based on how well suited they are for areas where there is a risk they will be exposed to moisture. Ratings are: Wet, Damp, and Dry.

- **Wet-rated fixtures** should be used in locations where there is the risk of contact with direct flowing water or moisture, for instance, in near showers and bathtubs.

- **Damp-rated fixtures** are suitable for areas where there is a risk of exposure to condensation. This can include downlights, surface-mounted ceiling lights, and wall sconces that will be positioned near steamy showers, bathtubs, or saunas.

- **Dry-rated fixtures** should only be used in areas where there will be a low chance of exposure to moisture vapor. An example of such an area would be a large, well ventilated bathroom.

In addition to the UL rating, other considerations may apply when you are deciding where to locate electrical items in the bathroom.

- **If you choose vanity lights** with electrical receptacles integrated on them, be sure that the receptacle is a GFCI (Ground Fault Circuit Interrupter). This is a special outlet that disconnects power to the outlet if it comes into contact with water.

- **If you are including a steam shower** or sauna in your renovated bathroom you should be aware that special "vapor-proof" fixtures are available. The fixtures are sealed with gaskets to prevent steam from migrating into the ceiling and causing damage.

12 CHOOSE WINDOW TREATMENTS

Above all, the window treatment you choose for your bathroom needs to offer privacy and insulation. Pick a design that allows you to open and close the window easily to let steam escape, is resistant to moisture itself, and looks good, too.

1 CHOOSE THE TYPE

The size of your bathroom and window will largely determine the type of window treatment you choose, and whether you want a purely practical or more decorative option. Choose a material that is washable or, at the very least, can be wiped easily.

BLINDS

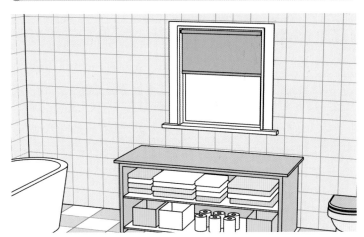

Blinds will give your windows a neat, streamlined look, and are a good choice for smaller bathrooms. Make sure that the material—whether wood, faux wood, or fabric—is resistant to moisture and easy to clean. Also ensure that its fixtures block as little light as possible.

CURTAINS

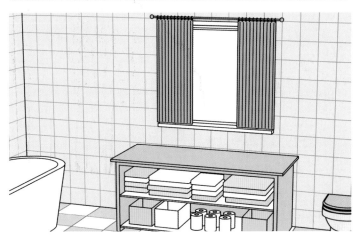

Only really suitable for large or well-ventilated bathrooms, curtains should be made from a machine-washable fabric and washed often to prevent mold caused by hot, humid surroundings. Use a curtain rod that's wider than the window to pull the curtains back fully.

SHUTTERS

Solid shutters are available in limited designs, but louvered shutters come with two or three panels in a choice of styles including full-height and tier-on-tier. Louvered shutters are ideal for bathrooms, since they can be tilted open and shut for light, privacy, and insulation.

FILM

Window film offers complete privacy without blocking out all natural light. It can be bought by the yard or made to measure, and is attached to interior windowpanes with a water and detergent solution. Choose from plain frosted or colored film.

2 CHOOSE THE STYLE

What you choose for your bathroom window is dictated to some degree by the size of your room: the smaller the room, the simpler the window treatment—and any pattern on it—should be. It should complement the look of the bathroom fixtures, too.

BLINDS

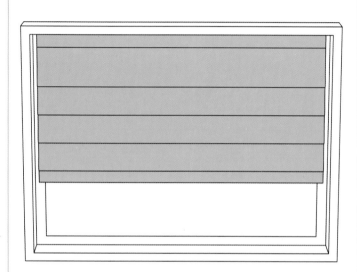

ROMAN

Unless your bathroom is very well ventilated, a Roman blind should be made from a fabric that is not susceptible to mildew in hot and humid rooms. The benefit of choosing a fabric blind is that it allows you to add pattern to a room that might otherwise be fairly plain—although keep the fabric plain if your bathroom tiles are patterned.

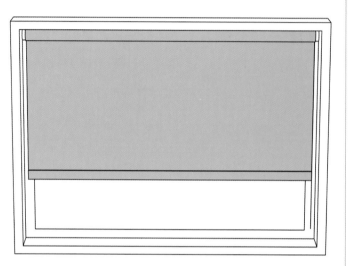

ROLLER

Roller blinds are a fairly inexpensive option, and, providing you're good at home improvement, are easy to install. You can have roller blinds made to measure, although most ready-made blinds can be cut to size. Choose blinds that are made from moisture-resistant fabrics.

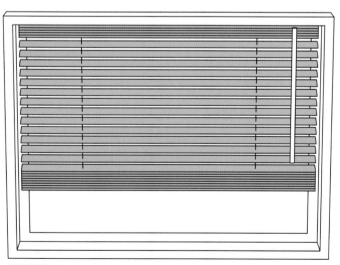

VENETIAN

Made from metal or wood, the adjustable slats of a Venetian blind allow you to control the amount of light coming through the window, in addition to providing privacy. They are available in a choice of materials, colors, and slat widths.

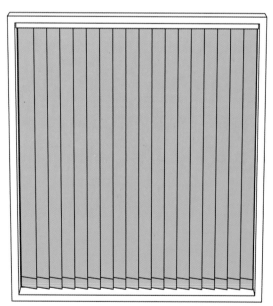

VERTICAL

Best suited to modern bathrooms with large windows, vertical blinds consist of long strips of fabric that can be tilted or drawn. They produce the optical effect of distorting the human form, which is good for maintaining privacy. The blinds come in a range of colors and fabrics; look for those that are moisture- and mold-resistant.

SHUTTERS

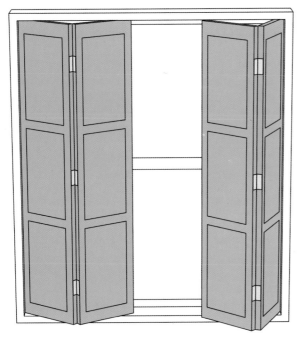

SOLID

Solid shutters are designed to be closed shut at night and folded back against the wall during the day. In addition to full-height shutters, you can choose half- or three-quarter height, which can be kept closed at all times for privacy, while still letting in light.

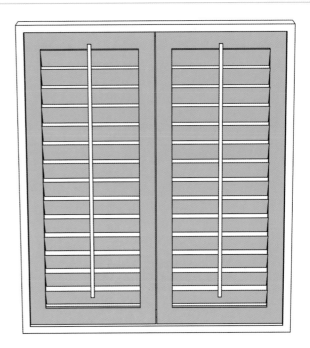

LOUVER

The adjustable slats of louvered shutters make them a good choice for bathrooms. The best options are tier-on-tier shutters or full-height shutters with a midrail so you can control the top and bottom sections independently. They are available in a wide choice of wood or paint finishes.

CURTAINS

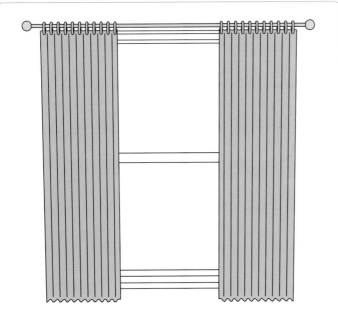

SILL LENGTH

Slimline sill-length—or just below sill-length—curtains in a washable cotton can be used to introduce a decorative theme to your bathroom. For example, a flower design will give your bathroom a country feel, while blue and white stripes can lend a nautical flavor. You may need to team them with a blind or window film to offer some privacy.

FILM

PLAIN OR PATTERNED

If your bathroom window looks directly into a neighbor's house, use a plain or patterned film that completely obscures the window. For upstairs bathrooms that aren't overlooked, you can choose film with a cutout design such as circles, stars, or another motif to add a decorative touch.

MAKE
A ROLLER BLIND

To dress a window simply yet stylishly, put up a handmade roller blind. Before starting, decide if you want it to roll from the back of the roller close to the window (for better light blockage when closed) or from the front, with the shade facing into the room. Decide, too, on which side you want the pulley mechanism to hang.

WHAT YOU NEED

- Roller blind kit
- Screwdriver
- Ruler or tape measure
- Hand saw
- Fabric
- Scissors
- Fabric stiffener
- Iron
- Triangle
- Sewing machine, or needle and thread
- Pencil
- Double-sided adhesive tape

1 ATTACH THE BRACKETS

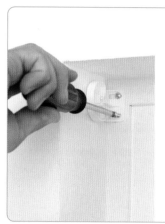

1 SCREW THE BRACKETS to either side of the inside of the window frame at the top. Use a ruler or tape measure, if necessary, to check that the brackets are the same height.

2 CUT THE ROLLER to size with a saw, and check it fits in the brackets.

2 PREPARE THE FABRIC

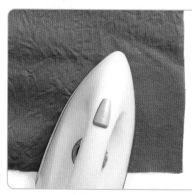

1 CUT THE FABRIC to fit the dimensions of the window recess, adding 12in (30cm) to the length for hem allowance and to ensure coverage of the roller, plus an extra 2in (5cm) to both the length and width, in case the fabric shrinks when stiffened. Stiffen the fabric according to the manufacturer's instructions, and allow to dry. Iron flat with a hot iron, or according to the manufacturer's instructions.

2 CUT THE FABRIC exactly to size, using a triangle to ensure that the corners are absolutely square. The width of the stiffened fabric should be identical to that of the roller (excluding the brackets).

3 STITCH THE HEM

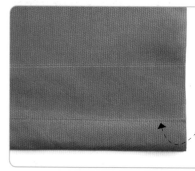

1 LAY THE FABRIC on a flat surface, right side face down. To make the hem that will hold the bottom weight bar, measure the width of the bar, then fold the bottom edge of the fabric over so the depth of the fold is slightly more than the width of the bar. Sew along this raw edge to make an open seam.

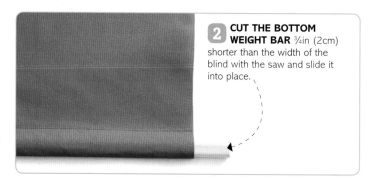

2 CUT THE BOTTOM WEIGHT BAR ¾in (2cm) shorter than the width of the blind with the saw and slide it into place.

4 ATTACH THE FABRIC

1 **LAY OUT THE FABRIC** on a flat surface, wrong side down if the blind is to unroll from the back of the roller, right side down if the blind will roll down at the front of the roller. Mark a horizontal line ½in (12mm) from the top edge of the fabric.

2 **POSITION A LENGTH** of double-sided adhesive tape at the top edge of the blind along the marked line.

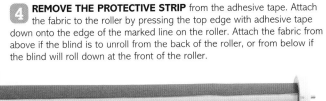

3 **LAY THE ROLLER** on a flat surface with the pulley positioned on the correct side. Mark a pencil line along the length of the roller—this line must be true or the fabric will not hang straight.

4 **REMOVE THE PROTECTIVE STRIP** from the adhesive tape. Attach the fabric to the roller by pressing the top edge with adhesive tape down onto the edge of the marked line on the roller. Attach the fabric from above if the blind is to unroll from the back of the roller, or from below if the blind will roll down at the front of the roller.

5 MOUNT THE ROLLER

ROLL UP THE ROLLER by hand and slot it into the brackets. If necessary, pull the blind up and down using the pulley until you achieve the right tension.

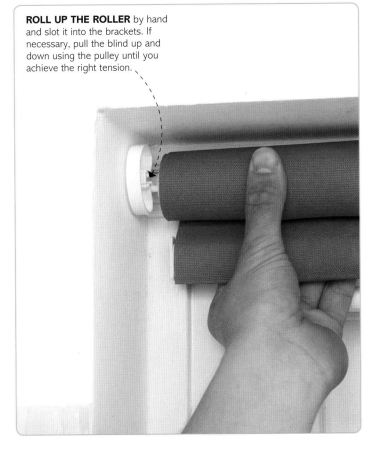

6 WAYS TO
REFRESH A TIRED BATHROOM

If you want to give your bathroom a fresh new look without having to change the plumbing fixtures, remove tiles, or revise the layout, there are some simple changes that you can make—they can all be easily completed in a weekend.

MIRRORS

Hang mirrors in different sizes and shapes on a wall. Stagger them in height and group them in odd numbers to create a stylish collection.

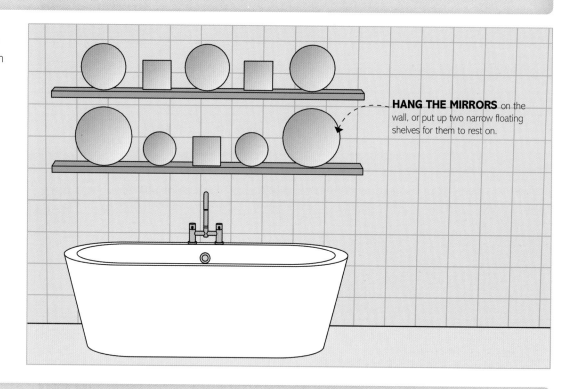

HANG THE MIRRORS on the wall, or put up two narrow floating shelves for them to rest on.

WALLPAPER

Create a feature wall using moisture-resistant vinyl patterned wallpaper, or add a panel of glass to protect a standard wallpaper.

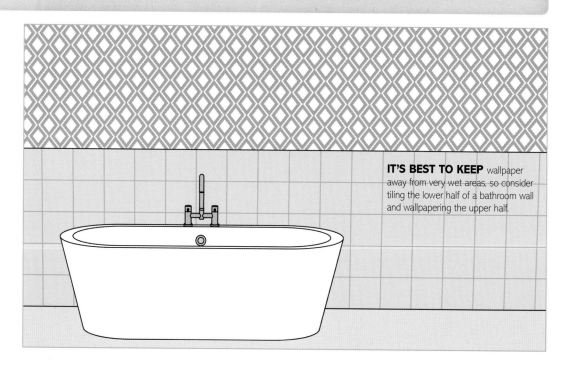

IT'S BEST TO KEEP wallpaper away from very wet areas, so consider tiling the lower half of a bathroom wall and wallpapering the upper half.

SHOWER CURTAIN

Replacing your shower curtain is quick and easy, and can make a big difference in the look of your bathroom.

CHOOSE A SHOWER CURTAIN that is machine-washable so it stays fresh.

WALL PANELING

Cover old walls or dated, but firmly attached, tiles with wood paneling. Give the paneling a coat of oil-based paint to make it water-resistant.

FINISH OFF THE TOP of the paneling with a narrow wood shelf for displaying bottles and pictures.

PAINTED WALL

Paint just one wall in a new color to brighten up your bathroom and create visual interest. Choose a light shade if your bathroom is small.

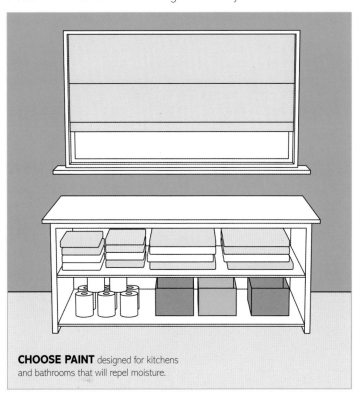

CHOOSE PAINT designed for kitchens and bathrooms that will repel moisture.

WINDOW TREATMENT

Update your window by giving it a new treatment. Choose a colorful roller blind or a window film with a decorative design.

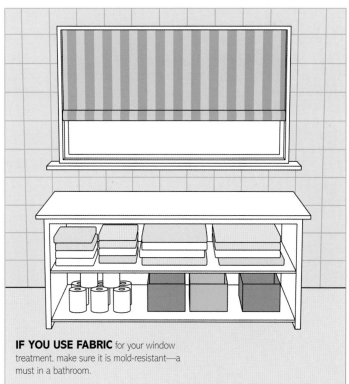

IF YOU USE FABRIC for your window treatment, make sure it is mold-resistant—a must in a bathroom.

PLAN THE PERFECT
EN SUITE BATHROOM

If you're adding an en suite bathroom to your bedroom, it's wise to try to link the two spaces visually so they look coordinated and streamlined. There are many ways to do this, some more subtle than others, while also choosing the right practical fixtures for the bathroom suite. Follow these tips to find out how.

ACCESSORIZE

Your bedroom is likely to be a very personal space and there's no reason this shouldn't continue into the bathroom. A bathroom feels more welcoming if there are pictures on the walls, pretty bathroom bottles, or towels in a complementary color scheme.

CHOOSING WINDOW TREATMENTS

Although the window treatments will need to reflect what's in your bedroom, it's not practical to have bulky curtains or fussy blinds in a small bathroom, since you need as much light as possible in the room. Choose a blind that is the same material as your bedroom curtains, or pick out a color in the fabric. If your bedroom look is contemporary, you don't have to find something that matches exactly; opt for window film or shutters if they will suit the bathroom window.

GET THE RIGHT SHOWER SCREEN

What you use to screen your shower area will have a major impact on how big your bathroom suite feels. Steer clear of a shower curtain, since it looks cheap, is too bulky in a small space, and tends not to be effective. Equally, decorated or frosted tempered shower panels will visually divide the space, making it seem smaller. The best choice is plain glass panels that you can look right through.

CHOOSING FLOORING

Choose a floor for the bathroom that tones with that of your bedroom. It doesn't have to be the same material (carpet will not be water-resistant enough), but if you can find tiles, rubber, or even vinyl in a shade similar to that used for the bedroom floor, the two spaces will merge smoothly.

HANG A MIRROR

Hang a mirror above the sink that matches the width of the sink to give the bathroom suite a balanced look. Consider covering a whole wall with mirrored panels or antiqued glass to make the space seem bigger. If you have a bathtub, glaze the wall above it or hang a supersized mirror there. As a general tip, hanging a mirror adjacent to or opposite from a window heightens the light reflected around the room.

GET GOOD LIGHTING

You may have soft mood lighting in your bedroom, but in a bathroom suite the lighting needs to mimick daylight so you can see what you're doing. Good lighting also helps a space to feel bigger. Use downlights positioned above the sink and shower or bathtub. Additional lighting around the mirror will also prove useful.

DECIDE ON A COLOR SCHEME

If you want your bathroom suite to feel spacious, choose a lighter shade of the color used for the bedroom walls to stretch the space visually. If your bedroom is fairly plain, you can break all the rules by choosing a much bolder color scheme for the en suite bathroom, using brightly colored or patterned tiles, for example. Anything with a sheen will subtly reflect light and help the space to feel larger.

GET GOOD STORAGE

If your bathroom suite is doubling up as a dressing area, good storage is a must. Open shelving may keep things handy for you, but will look messy and make the space feel cluttered and smaller. If you have wall space, opt for shallow, wall-hung cabinets with doors to hide anything you don't want to display. With space at such a premium, a vanity unit can also provide valuable low-level storage.

FINDING FURNITURE

Getting the right furniture for your bathroom is key. For example, a traditionally furnished bedroom with an en suite bathroom decorated in a contemporary style will jar. So make it your goal that any furniture, such as a vanity unit, matches the style of the bedroom. You may have to adapt the furniture, if necessary, perhaps painting or varnishing it to make it water-resistant.

LIVING ROOM

1 WHAT TO DO WHEN
RENOVATING YOUR LIVING ROOM

If you are redesigning your living room from scratch, it's vital to approach the work in a particular order. If you follow this sytematic approach, you'll avoid problems and won't have to redo jobs that have already been done, and so save yourself money. Follow the plan here to get it right the first time.

1 DETERMINE YOUR BUDGET

How much can you afford to spend to get the look you want? If your budget is tight, concentrate on basics—fireplace, doors, flooring, moldings, and woodwork—and upgrade any cheap accessories later. Allow for a contingency of at least 10 percent in addition to your proposed budget.

2 PLAN THE LAYOUT

Draw a scale plan with doors or walls to be moved or removed, windows added, or fireplaces installed, and where electrical receptacles, lights, light switches, TV antenna, built-in audio, phone jacks, and the flue for a wood burning stove will go.

3 CONSIDER THE HEATING

If you are replacing radiators, are they currently in the best position and big enough for the room? Will removing walls or doors mean you need to increase the heating in the room? Or think about removing radiators altogether in favor of underfloor radiant heating.

4 SCHEDULE TRADESPEOPLE

Contact an electrician, HVAC contractor, carpenter or millworker, and painter to get quotes. You may also need a general contractor if you are knocking down walls. Ask how the work other tradespeople will be doing might impact on their jobs so you can get everyone in at the right time.

5 GET APPROVAL

If you are making structural changes, get approval from your local building department. The same applies if you plan to replace original windows, for example, and live in a historical preservation area.

6 PLACE YOUR ORDERS

Once your quotes are in, order flooring, doors, woodwork, radiators, and windows. Paint, wallpaper, carpet, and light fixtures can all be ordered later.

7 GUT THE ROOM

Strip any wallpaper to see if the walls or ceiling need to be patched. Rip out old flooring, woodwork, moldings damaged beyond repair, unwanted fireplaces (or unblock a fireplace, if needed), old electrical wiring, radiator pipes, and walls you have approval to demolish (be sure to provide appropriate supports to keep the room safe).

8 INSTALL NEW HEATING—ROUGH-IN

Have plumbing installed for water-fed underfloor heating or new radiators first, since this is a disruptive job.

9 INSTALL THE ELECTRICAL WIRING—ROUGH-IN

The electrician will install wiring beneath the floors and into the walls and ceiling for all the electrical fixtures. If you are having a security system installed, have this system wired now.

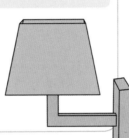

10 INSTALL THE FIREPLACE—ROUGH-IN

Wiring, gas piping, or a chimney lining for a fireplace happen now, so a mantle and/or gas fireplace can be installed after the walls are patched—or get an existing chimney swept.

11 INSTALL NEW WINDOWS

Install new windows, or prepare existing windows now so they're ready to be painted.

12 PATCH THE WALLS AND CEILING

Patch and repair openings in sheetrock or plaster walls. Apply plaster skim coating and sand in preparation for the wall finish.

13 LAY THE FLOORING

Lay tiles or a wood floor—or a subfloor if you are having carpet laid.

14 TACKLE THE MILLWORK

When the plaster is dry, install baseboards, crown trim, doors, door trims, and chair and picture rails. Make sure the carpenter knows the position of all plumbing and wires.

15 DECORATE

Fill fine cracks, paint ceilings, walls, and woodwork, and wallpaper—in that order.

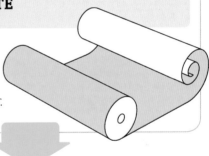

16 ORGANIZE THE FINAL INSTALL

The electrician and HVAC contractor can return to install radiators, light fixtures, and electrical receptacles, and finalize underfloor heating. The fireplace can be finished off.

17 ADD FINISHING TOUCHES

Put up curtain rods or blinds, attach door hardware, and lay the carpet to finish the room.

2 CREATE A MOOD BOARD
FOR YOUR LIVING ROOM

A living room is generally regarded as the most public space in a house, since it is the room that most visitors will be invited into. So it pays to get your color scheme absolutely right. The best way to get the look right the first time is to create a mood board filled with colors, textures, and items that really suit the proportions, orientation, and atmosphere of your living room.

1 FIND PICTURES OF ROOMS YOU LIKE and stick one or two of your favorites to your mood board. Be realistic about recreating the same look— the layout, light, and proportions of your room may be very different from those in the picture you prefer.

Pick pictures of living rooms that reflect something of your personality, and not just current trends.

2 DO YOU HAVE A KEY ITEM that you absolutely love and want to include in the room as your starting point for the scheme? It might be a picture, a rug, or even a keepsake. Or perhaps you have an existing piece of furniture such as a sofa that has to be included in the design? Use this as your starting point instead, either as inspiration for colors, patterns, or shapes, or as something to build a theme around.

Using a favorite item as a starting point for your inspiration will give your living room character and individuality.

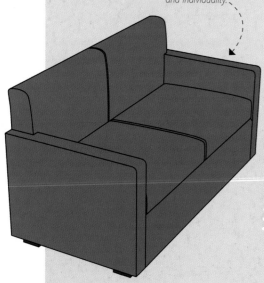

3 **PICK A BASE COLOR** for your walls or floors, since these areas will form the largest block of color in your room. Paint the best sample color or pin your favorite wallpaper sample onto the mood board, ensuring it's in proportion to how it will be used in the room (so, if you're painting all four walls, paint the whole board in your test color). If you like the effect, use that as the starting point for your color palette.

When you choose your background color, consider whether a lighter tone might be easier to live with over the long term.

Choose two, or a maximum of three, accent colors and stick or paint the samples on top of your base color to see if they all work together.

4 **INTRODUCE ACCENT COLORS** that are subtle variations of your base color or a dramatic contrast to it (or both). One color will be your main accent shade, used, perhaps, in a wallpaper design on a chimney breast, or as a sofa cover. A second accent color should be used less, in throw pillows, lampshades, or vases. A third color might just be a shade variation visible in the pattern of a throw pillow.

A contrasting color, if needed, should be used minimally in a scheme.

5 **ADD PATTERN & TEXTURE,** which can be as subtle or as overt as you like. No room absolutely has to include pattern, but those that do tend to be more interesting. If pattern is not your thing, introduce texture with items like a wooden table and a faux fur throw arranged over the back of a chair or across a sofa.

Add images of patterned items like pillows to the board to see if they lift and complement your scheme.

If you want to add texture with a carpet, rugs, or throws, stick samples to the board to check that they look right visually.

6 **CHOOSE FURNITURE** that you'd like to include (assuming you are replacing existing pieces). Here, color comes into play—use the tricks you've learned above to pick the right shade of fabric or type of wood. When it comes to shape, revisit the colors and patterns on your mood board. Will a traditional piece of furniture with curvaceous lines sit more comfortably in your scheme than a contemporary piece?

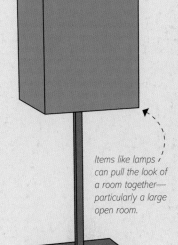

Items like lamps can pull the look of a room together— particularly a large open room.

7 **ADD FINISHING TOUCHES** such as throw pillows, lampshades, vases, and ornaments. These items will help to personalize your room and make it individual to you. These subtle touches can make or break a room's success, and the mood board will help you plan this effectively: collect ideas for what you'd like to add and stick pictures to the board to see if they match your theme, design, and color palette.

Your accessories needn't match perfectly, but they do need to suit the style of the room.

3 LAYOUT CONSIDERATIONS IN THE LIVING ROOM

Planning the layout of your living room is all about creating zones for different activities – from relaxing around the fireplace or watching television to reading or listening to music. This can be predominantly achieved with the positioning of furniture. However, in getting the functionality of the room right, you also need to ensure that the room looks both attractive and welcoming. Follow these layout tips to find out how.

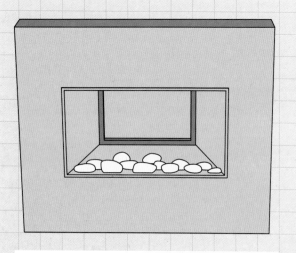

FIRE

If your room is a blank canvas and you can choose where to put a fireplace, establish which will be your focal wall. If your room is square, place the fireplace centrally on the wall. If you have a long thin room divided into a seating area and a dining area, place the fire centrally in one half of the room.

SOFA

If your living room has a fireplace, it's natural to group the seating around it. In many modern homes, the fire as a focal point of the room has now been replaced by a TV, and sofas and chairs are usually gathered around it in the same way. Whichever is the case in your home, a single sofa is best placed opposite the focal wall in a central position. A pair of sofas look best adjacent to the focal wall at either side of the fireplace or TV, or at right angles to each other (in a square room, one sofa could sit opposite the focal wall and the other opposite the window). Ensure that the sofas are the correct proportions for the room and that there is enough space between them to manoeuvre around easily.

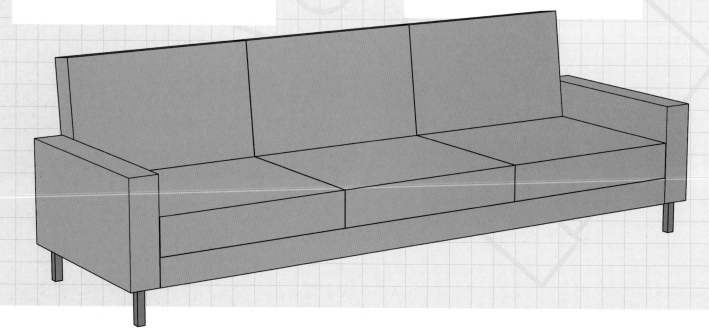

COFFEE TABLE

Adding a coffee table to a living room does more than just create a surface to put things on: it makes a second focal point or zone for sociable relaxation. The best place for a coffee table is centrally in front of the most used seat in the room, whether a sofa or a pair of armchairs, and within reach of any other seats. Don't be tempted to squeeze in a large table that won't let you move around comfortably.

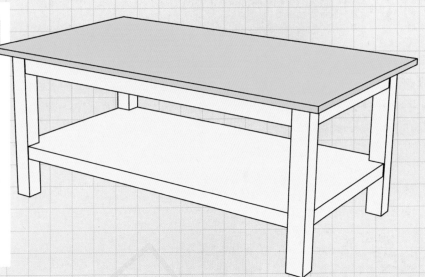

TV/MEDIA UNIT

If there's no fireplace in your living space, it's likely that your TV will form the focal point of the room. If the room is small and there's little space for a large TV, a wall-hung model is a good, if not particularly attractive, option. Before you choose which wall to put it on, decide how to group your seating. Then choose a spot where everyone can see the screen when seated. Don't hang it too high, since you'll be sitting or lying down to watch the TV. If you have enough space, or you have a fireplace in the room, the TV will fit better in a corner.

ARMCHAIR

Two sofas are preferable to a sofa and an armchair, since they are more comfortable, but if you only have space for a sofa and an extra armchair or two, the trick is to position them correctly. Create a comfortable arrangement around your focal point so that when people are seated everyone else is visible. In a long, thin room, an armchair can also be positioned separately from this central grouping to create a reading zone in a corner or at the end of the room.

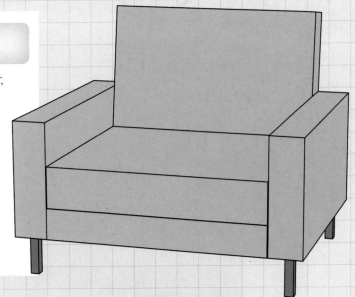

4 CHOOSE FLOORING

When choosing a floor that will fit in with the design scheme of your living room, you also need to consider how practical it will be for your lifestyle. For instance, do you have children who like to play in the living room, and do you allow pets in there, or is it purely a space for grown-up relaxation?

1 CHOOSE THE LOOK

The type of flooring you choose will have a big impact on the atmosphere of your living room. Think about whether you want the cozy, relaxed feel of carpet, sleek and contemporary or rustic tiles, or wood floors, which strike a balance between the two.

TILED

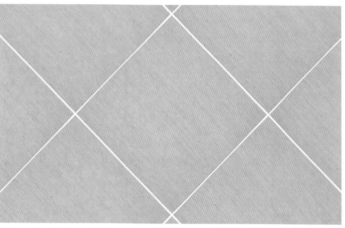

Tiled floors are easy to care for and clean. They feel cool underfoot in the summer and, if teamed with underfloor heating, warm in winter. Shiny tiles reflect light, but show marks; matte finishes disguise smudges, but aren't good for dark rooms. Budget for area rugs when using tile.

WOOD

Wood floors are particularly good at adding warmth and character to a room, and are available in a wide range of tones. Paler tones create a light, relaxed, contemporary space, while darker toned woods create a scheme that's more formal.

CARPET

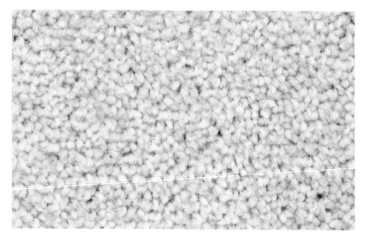

Don't just think of carpets in terms of color—consider the material and finish, too. A luxurious deep velvet pile will give a living room a traditional look, whereas something such as a loop pile or a natural floor covering like jute or coir will give it a modern feel.

SEAMLESS

An ideal choice for large, open-plan living rooms, poured concrete and poured resin flooring provide a seamless look without joins to give a slick, unfussy, and contemporary look. Lighter gloss finishes stretch space visually, but also show up marks and smudges.

2 CHOOSE THE MATERIAL

The material you pick will depend on your lifestyle and how much you use the room. Your decision may also be affected by whether the room leads on to an outdoor space; if not, you can choose something less practical and in a lighter color.

TILED

PORCELAIN
Porcelain flooring is low to medium in price, easy to keep clean, and has a smooth, nonporous surface—though it can feel cold and hard underfoot.

CERAMIC
Ceramic tiles are cheap, so are a good choice if you have a large area to tile. They won't stain and don't need sealing, so they are easy to look after.

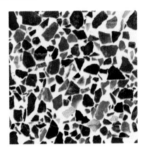

TERRAZZO
High-cost terrazzo tiles are extremely durable, with a highly polished finish, which can make them slippery. They must be installed by a professional.

CONCRETE
A popular but expensive choice for modern, open-plan living rooms, concrete is available in a variety of natural concrete colors and in a polished or matte finish.

TERRA-COTTA
Medium-priced natural terra-cotta is very porous, so needs sealing, but gives a warm rustic look and doesn't feel as hard or cold underfoot as other natural tiles.

TRAVERTINE
An expensive natural stone, this has a sleek, polished, modern finish or a natural, tumbled look with soft edges and a sponge-like, more traditional appearance.

LIMESTONE
These expensive tiles are a good choice for living room color schemes. If your room leads out to the yard, use limestone in both areas for a cohesive look.

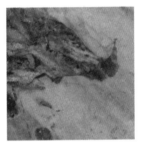

SLATE
Medium to high in cost, slate tiles tend to be black or gray, which means that they work well in both modern and traditional decorating schemes.

LAMINATE
Laminate floor tiles come in a range of colors and designs, including slate and travertine, and offer a cheaper or medium-priced alternative to the real thing.

WOOD

HARDWOOD
Hardwoods can be sanded to remove any scratches and scuffs. This medium to expensive option feels firmer underfoot than a floating engineered wood floor.

SOFTWOOD
If you want to paint your wood floor, softwood is a cheap or medium-priced option. Although it may dent and mark, it can be repaired easily.

ENGINEERED WOOD
Medium-priced engineered wood can be installed as a floating floor with an underlay—a good choice for uneven floors and floors that require acoustic protection.

BAMBOO
Bamboo flooring is made from grass, but looks like wood. It can be installed as a floating floor or glued or nailed down. It is medium to high in price.

LAMINATE
Many laminate wood planks, which are cheap or average in price, have realistic textured finishes and detailing that give the appearance of real boards.

CARPET

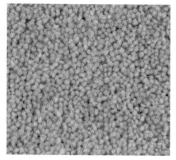

TWIST PILES

Medium-priced twist piles have a coarse, rugged appearance, are hard-wearing, come in plain colors, heathers, or patterns, and are made of wool or man-made fibers.

VELVET PILE

Despite its luxurious appearance, this medium- to high-cost carpet is surprisingly hard-wearing, and its dense, low-cut pile gives a soft smooth appearance.

BERBER

This low- to medium-priced option is a popular alternative to coir and sisal floors with its similar looks, but has the warmth, comfort, and durability of natural wool.

SAXONY

A deep, dense pile that feels soft and smooth underfoot and gives a classic look. It is best used in rooms with low foot traffic, and is medium to high in price.

COIR

The surface of hard-wearing, low-cost coir is nonslip, so is a good choice if you have children who like to run around indoors. However, it can feel rough underfoot.

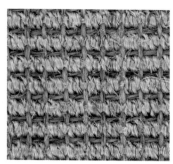

SISAL

Sisal is hard-wearing, has a fine texture and a subtle sheen, is of average price, and is available in a range of weaves and colors, so adds both color and texture to a room.

JUTE

With its flat woven designs, jute is a neat-looking, medium-priced option for living rooms. It is softer than other natural floor coverings, though not as hard-wearing.

SEAGRASS

Medium-priced woven seagrass has a chunky appearance. Its natural waxy texture makes it stain-resistant, so it's a good choice for a busy room.

SEAMLESS

CONCRETE

Although expensive, poured polished concrete gives a stylish, contemporary look and is extremely durable. Choose from a range of shades, including red and green.

RESIN

High-cost poured resin flooring is very contemporary. Its seamless matte or gloss finish suits both large open-plan living rooms and awkward spaces.

LIGHT-COLORED FLOORING combined with a darker color on the walls can make a room feel narrower and taller.

STAIN
A WOOD FLOOR

If you want to give inexpensive pine floorboards the look of rich mahogany or walnut wood, or you want to disguise a well-worn floor, use a wood stain. To prepare the room, tape up doors so the dust won't penetrate the rest of the house, and open all the windows to allow for as much ventilation as possible.

WHAT YOU NEED

- Hammer
- Wood filler (optional)
- Face mask
- Professional sanding machine
- Vacuum cleaner or broom and dustpan
- Protective gloves
- Old cloth
- Mineral spirits or tack cloth
- Masking tape

- Wood stain or wood dye
- Large paintbrush
- Clear polyurethane wood varnish

1 PREPARE THE FLOOR

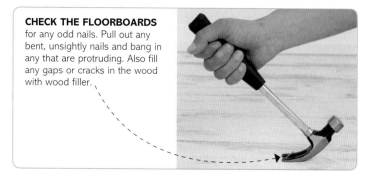

CHECK THE FLOORBOARDS for any odd nails. Pull out any bent, unsightly nails and bang in any that are protruding. Also fill any gaps or cracks in the wood with wood filler.

2 SMOOTH THE FLOORBOARDS

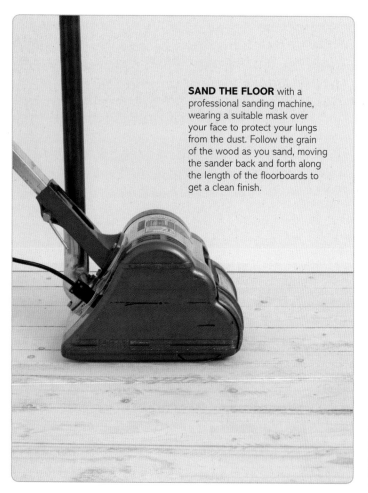

SAND THE FLOOR with a professional sanding machine, wearing a suitable mask over your face to protect your lungs from the dust. Follow the grain of the wood as you sand, moving the sander back and forth along the length of the floorboards to get a clean finish.

3 DUST THOROUGHLY

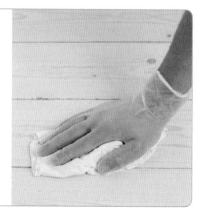

VACUUM UP THE DUST with a vacuum cleaner, or sweep it clean with a broom. Then put on protective gloves and wipe down the floorboards with a piece of cloth soaked in mineral spirits or use a tack cloth.

4 PROTECT WITH TAPE

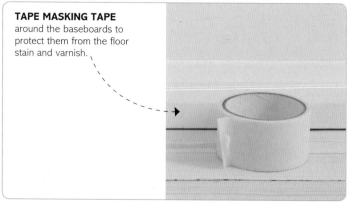

TAPE MASKING TAPE around the baseboards to protect them from the floor stain and varnish.

5 STAIN THE WOOD

APPLY THE STAIN with a cloth, working in short sections across the floor. If your boards are very light, or relatively new, stain the very edges of the floorboards with a paintbrush first and wipe off the excess stain quickly with a cloth. Then apply the stain across the rest of the floor in the usual way.

6 APPLY THE VARNISH

DEPENDING ON THE DEPTH OF COLOR you want, or if the floor looks a little patchy, repeat the staining process. Then apply 2–3 coats of clear polyurethane varnish (see the manufacturer's instructions) to the boards. Use a paintbrush for corners and small areas, or a mop with an applicator pad for large areas.

5 CHOOSE WALL COVERINGS

You don't have to limit yourself to one type of wall decoration for a living room—a combination of two or three types will give a plain, boxy room a much more interesting look. Choose something that both suits the period of your home in terms of material and design, and one that you can live with for the long term.

1 CHOOSE THE MATERIAL

Your living room will be subject to a certain amount of wear and tear, especially if you have children, so look for the toughest finishes you can find: pick a paint or wallpaper that can be wiped down easily, or paneling that is simple to fill and repair.

PAINT

The wide choice of paint colors available allows you to create almost any look fairly quickly and inexpensively. Your walls will need to be in good condition for paint to look its best, since it won't hide cracks or any uneven surfaces. Apply two to three coats of paint.

WALLPAPER

Wallpaper is sold in a range of colors, plains, patterns, and finishes. Plain wallpaper provides a tougher surface than painted sheetrock. Patterned wallpapers add interest to plain walls, and textured wallpapers (left white or painted) are good for imperfect walls.

PANELING

Paneling can give your walls a range of looks, from traditional-style paneling made from solid wood or MDF to simple tongue-and-groove boards or flat wood veneer panels for a retro look. All but the veneers can be stained, varnished, or painted to suit a scheme.

CHECKLIST

● **Prepare your walls correctly.** Whether they are being painted or papered, cracks and holes need to be filled and sanded back and any unevenness should be smoothed.

● **Do you have enough wallpaper?** Buy an extra 10% as a contingency, and make sure that it's from the same batch so the colors match perfectly. If you use a patterned wallpaper, make sure you have enough extra paper to match the pattern repeat.

● **If you are attaching** paneling to your walls, use a pipe and cable detector to check whether there are live wires or pipes behind the plasterwork.

2 CHOOSE THE TYPE

Paint is sold in various formats, each giving a different effect, and wallpaper is available in a variety of finishes and textures. If you've chosen to panel your walls, pick something that's going to be practical and produce the right look.

PAINT

MATTE
Water-based nonreflective matte emulsion suits modern- and traditional-style living rooms, and is available in an endless choice of colors. Prices vary greatly.

SATIN
Satin paints are a good medium-priced choice for family rooms, since marks can be wiped off easily. The subtle sheen can help to reflect light in the room.

METALLIC
Medium-priced metallic emulsion paints bring a touch of luxury and come in a range of colors. Try using metallic paint on a feature wall like a chimney breast.

SUEDE EFFECT
Suede-effect medium-priced emulsion has miniscule grains that give a brushed-suede effect. Apply it in short random brush strokes to achieve the textured finish.

WALLPAPER

PLAIN OR PATTERNED
Use plain wallpapers as an alternative to paint on walls with fine surface cracks. Patterned paper comes in a huge range of designs and colors; prices vary greatly.

FLOCK
With its raised velvet texture, this medium- to high-cost paper is typically available in rich and opulent colors to add drama. It is more expensive than other wallpapers.

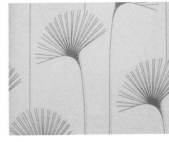

METALLIC
Patterned wallpapers with a metallic sheen help to reflect light around a room, so are ideal for smaller and darker living rooms. They range in price from medium to high.

TEXTURED
Medium-priced textured wallpapers are available in a choice of raised designs. Some embossed wallpapers also have a colored pattern.

PANELING

TONGUE & GROOVE
Cheap or averagely priced, this paneling is usually made of pine, but you can buy MDF designs. Usually attached to the lower half of a wall, you can also install it full height.

FLAT WOOD VENEER
If you like the mid-century look, medium to expensive wood veneer panels are the ideal choice. Iron-on wood veneer on a thin sheet of MDF is the best option.

WAINSCOT PANELING
Medium-priced wainscot paneling works equally well in contemporary or country-style rooms. Paint it in a soft sheen that matches your baseboards.

PAINT WALLS

The technology behind modern paints makes them vastly superior to old-fashioned paints (which had to be applied in one direction and then another), so it is now easier to achieve the best finish. You may need to apply several coats depending on the quality and color of the paint and the original color of your wall.

LIVING ROOM

140

WHAT YOU NEED

- Drop cloths
- Masking tape
- Wall filler and sandpaper (optional)
- Dish detergent and soap or tack cloth
- Sponge
- Wall paint
- Small- or medium-sized paintbrush
- Roller and tray

1 PREPARE THE AREA

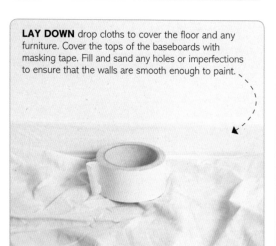

LAY DOWN drop cloths to cover the floor and any furniture. Cover the tops of the baseboards with masking tape. Fill and sand any holes or imperfections to ensure that the walls are smooth enough to paint.

2 CLEAN THE WALLS

IF YOU ARE PAINTING a kitchen or bathroom, wipe down the walls using a sponge dipped in soapy hot water. For other walls, clean dust from the wall with a tack cloth.

3 PAINT THE EDGES OF THE WALL

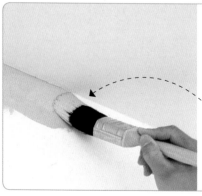

1 CAREFULLY PAINT along the upper edge of the wall where it meets the ceiling with a paintbrush. Paint at a fairly steady speed (not too slowly), so the paint goes on smoothly and your hand doesn't wobble.

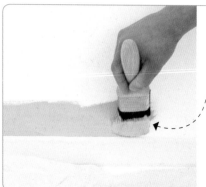

2 PAINT ALONG THE BOTTOM of the wall where it meets the baseboard. The masking tape will protect the baseboard from any excess paint brushed over it.

3 PAINT THE CORNERS and sides of the walls next, using the same brush to work the paint right into the crevices and down the edge of each wall.

4 PAINT THE REST OF THE WALL

1 **USE A THICK PILE ROLLER** to cover the remaining area of the wall. This type of roller will ensure that the paint goes on thickly and smoothly, and gives a slight textural effect.

2 **TURN THE ROLLER SIDEWAYS** to paint the uppermost and lowest areas of the wall. Check the manufacturer's instructions for how much time to allow the paint to dry, then apply a second coat.

6 WAYS WITH
FEATURE WALLS

Every room, and a living room in particular, needs a focal point. One way to do this is to create a feature wall that will help to make your room's design scheme more cohesive. If you have a particular theme, period, style, or color scheme for the room, use this as a starting point for your wall feature.

WALLPAPER

Use a patterned wallpaper to create a stunning panel or wall in a color that tones with the predominant color of your other walls.

MIRRORS

Add interest to slim wall spaces by hanging mirrors vertically. Use odd numbers for a more pleasing look.

A SIMILAR EFFECT can be created with pictures, too.

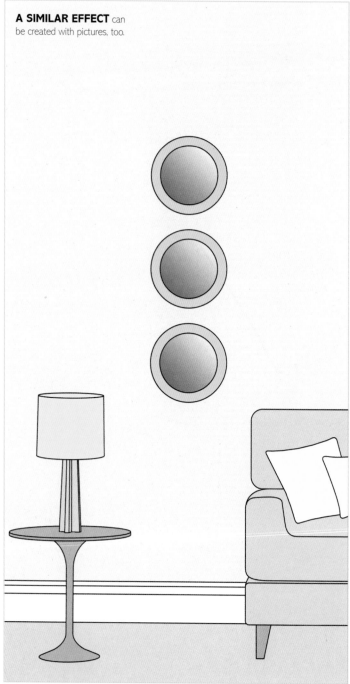

STICKERS

Stylish wall stickers can be used to change the look of your room fairly quickly and do not require you to be creative.

FOR LARGER DESIGNS, you will need an extra pair of hands to help you press the stickers onto your wall.

PLATES

Hang plates with different styles, shapes, and designs. Make the display cohesive by sticking to a color palette of three or four shades.

DRAW AROUND each plate to create a template and play around with different configurations. Then attach the plates with disk plate hangers.

PHOTO WALL

Create a picture gallery with different-sized frames that match in style or color. Choose black-and-white photos for a really unified effect.

WOOD PANELS

Cover MDF panels with iron-on wood veneer or paint and attach them to the wall to create a modern patchwork design.

FOR A MORE INTERESTING design, use panels of different sizes.

10 WAYS WITH
ART

You've probably invested plenty of money in your pictures and photos, so why not put some serious thought into how you should hang them? Achieving the right look can create a much more effective display than a slapdash approach. Decide which of these 10 options best suits your own artwork and home.

MIXTURE OF FRAME SHAPES

Group together a mixture of pictures in differently sized and shaped frames for an eye-catching effect. Keep the display as symmetrical as possible so that each picture stands out in its own right.

CREATE A UNIFIED LOOK by keeping your display tightly spaced.

GROUPING

Hanging a group of four pictures of exactly the same size in a tight group gives the illusion of one larger picture.

ONE LARGE PIECE

Make the most of a large expanse of wall by hanging one large picture centrally for dramatic effect.

THE SIZE OF YOUR ARTWORK shouldn't be wider than the piece of furniture it hangs above.

OFFSET

You don't always have to hang pictures in a straight line; hanging them slightly offset from one another gives a less formal look.

THIS EFFECT WORKS BEST if the frames match in terms of proportion, if not shape.

TRIPTYCH

Hang a triptych—where one picture is divided into three sections, which are framed and fixed to the wall next to each other.

Fill a whole wall with a collection of pictures and paintings. The frames and picture styles don't have to match, but a cohesive theme—whether color or subject matter—will make the design more successful.

ON A SHELF

For a more relaxed display, sit pictures on a floating shelf or picture shelf, allowing them to lean against the wall.

USE A MIXTURE of sizes and shapes, but find a cohesive color theme for best results.

TALL PIECE

One tall picture, or a line of smaller pictures hung vertically, will draw the eye upward and add a feeling of height to a room.

LIGHT IT UP

Illuminate your artwork with a picture light. Attach the picture light directly to the frame or to the wall immediately above the picture.

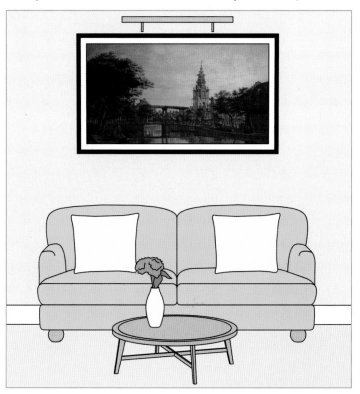

TONAL TO ROOM COLORS

If you position a picture at a focal point within a room, make sure it contains at least one color that matches your decorating scheme.

HANG
A PICTURE FRAME

A framed picture usually looks best if it is hung centrally on a wall, although if you hang it above a fireplace, it works best visually if the picture is centered vertically as well as horizontally. You may need someone to help you position the picture correctly on the wall before you mark where it should hang.

WHAT YOU NEED

- Tape measure
- Pencil
- 2 picture rings and plates, or screw eyes
- Bradawl
- Screwdriver

- Picture wire
- Pliers (optional)
- Level (optional)
- Picture hook and nail or screw (size depends on weight of the frame)
- Hammer (or drill if using a screw)

1 ATTACH THE PICTURE RINGS AND PLATES

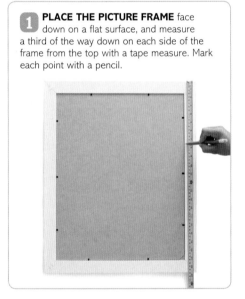

1 PLACE THE PICTURE FRAME face down on a flat surface, and measure a third of the way down on each side of the frame from the top with a tape measure. Mark each point with a pencil.

2 IF YOU ARE USING a picture ring and plate, place the plate against the pencil mark and make holes in the frame through the two circles in the plate with a bradawl. If you are using a screw eye, make a hole with the bradawl at the point of each pencil mark.

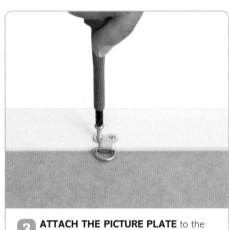

3 ATTACH THE PICTURE PLATE to the wooden frame with screws, using a screwdriver, or insert the screw eyes.

2 ATTACH THE WIRE

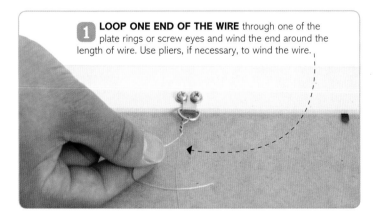

1 LOOP ONE END OF THE WIRE through one of the plate rings or screw eyes and wind the end around the length of wire. Use pliers, if necessary, to wind the wire.

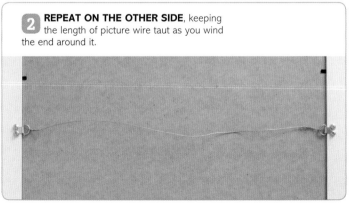

2 REPEAT ON THE OTHER SIDE, keeping the length of picture wire taut as you wind the end around it.

INSTALL THE HOOK AND PUT THE PICTURE IN PLACE

1 HOLD THE PICTURE up to the wall where you want to hang it. Make sure it is centered and then mark the central point of the top of the frame on the wall with a pencil.

2 PLACE THE FRAME face down on a flat surface again, pull the picture wire taut in the center, and measure the distance from the top of the taut wire to the top of the picture frame with a tape measure.

3 MEASURE THE SAME DISTANCE below the mark on the wall, making another pencil mark at the lower point. Use a level, if necessary, to ensure that the second mark is directly below the first mark.

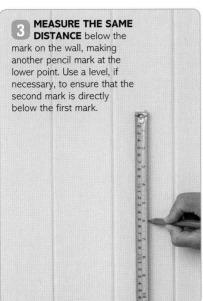

4 PLACE THE BOTTOM of the picture hook where the pencil mark is (since the hook is where the wire hangs from), hammer the nail into the wall, then hang the picture. If the frame is heavy, use a screw and a drill instead.

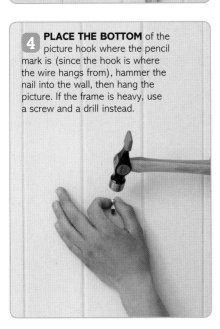

6 CHOOSE A SOFA

You may be tempted to choose a sofa on looks and size alone, but paying attention to how it's made will give you a clue to its longevity. Good-quality sofas comprise hardwood, coil springs, and expensive wool batting; cheaper ones are made from softwood frames, webbing (not coils), and foam.

1 DECIDE ON SIZE

Sofas come in many sizes, from compact two-seaters to sprawling sectional sofas that can easily seat whole families. Measure your space and estimate what sofa size will work best for you; next, lay down a newspaper template, based on those dimensions. Living around this template for a couple of days will show you whether this is in fact the right size.

2 CHOOSE THE STYLE

A sofa is often a living room's dominant feature, so the design you choose will dictate the room's style. Stick to a traditional model if you are furnishing a period room, but consider combining old with new if your tastes are more contemporary.

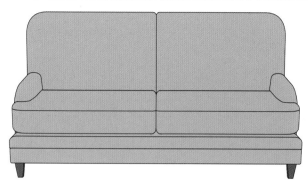

CLASSIC
A classic sofa is ideal for a traditional room, and is a sofa for sitting on rather than slouching across. Look for details such as plump cushions, angular arms, and curved wooden legs. Darker colors and striped or checked upholstery will give a more formal look.

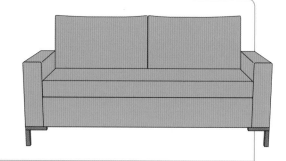

CONTEMPORARY
Streamlined contemporary sofas suit minimally decorated rooms. Look for square, boxy shapes, firm cushions, and plain feet in metal or wood. For an informal look, go for a low back. Add throw pillows if you want to lounge on it.

TRADITIONAL
This sofa style is a popular, family-friendly choice, with its high back and neat slim arms that are either straight or have a slight curve. The seat and back cushions are commonly foam-filled, with comfort being the priority.

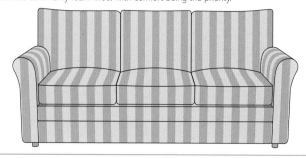

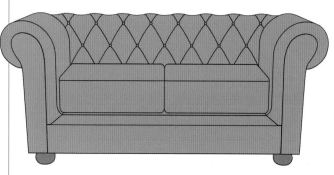

CHESTERFIELD
A very traditional design, this sofa will also suit contemporary rooms, particularly if it is upholstered in distressed leather or fabric. The height and angle of the back and arms make it comfortable for adults to sit up on, but it is not ideal for lounging.

BUTTON BACK
Button-back detailing on the sofa back or cushions hints at a traditional style, making this type of sofa ideal for a period home. Or choose a model in an angular, streamlined shape to add interest to a contemporary scheme.

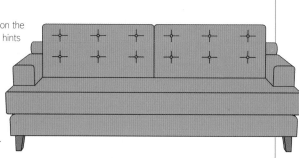

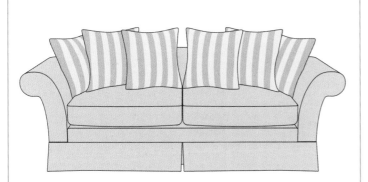

INFORMAL

An informal sofa has its legs hidden beneath a skirt and a selection of throw pillows rather than larger overstuffed back cushions. A sofa like this should be bought for comfort over looks, and the cushions will need plumping frequently to keep them neat.

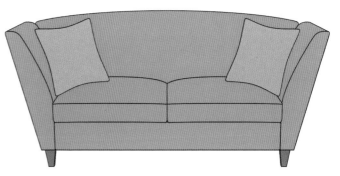

CURVED BACK

Midway between a contemporary and traditional style sofa, this neat, formal model has a high curved back dropping down to steep, slightly angled arms at either end, which are ideal for reclining against.

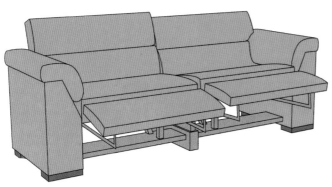

RECLINER

Recliner sofas feature single seat sections within their backs that recline and include a footrest that rises up so that you can lounge in ultimate comfort, if not style. They are available as two- or three-seaters, with one or two seats able to recline.

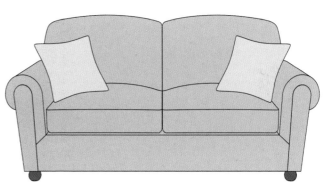

COUNTRY

The emphasis of this sofa is on comfort. It is curvy, with plump cushions and scrolled arms, and is normally upholstered in patterned—usually floral—fabric, often with removable covers.

CORNER SOFA

L-shaped corner sofas are most approriate for large and open-plan rooms, where they can be placed against two adjoining walls to fill a perhaps otherwise insignificant corner, or positioned in the center of the room to separate the living area from the rest of the room.

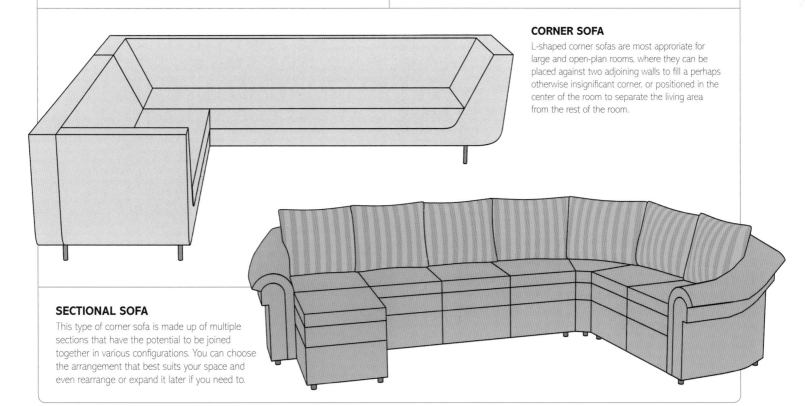

SECTIONAL SOFA

This type of corner sofa is made up of multiple sections that have the potential to be joined together in various configurations. You can choose the arrangement that best suits your space and even rearrange or expand it later if you need to.

3 CHOOSE THE MATERIAL

The material you choose for your sofa doesn't just dictate its look—it also affects its price, longevity, and maintenance. So, before you fall in love with a particular fabric, find out whether it is an affordable and practical choice.

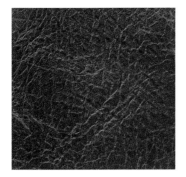

LEATHER

High-priced leather comes in a whole range of finishes, from soft and polished to distressed for an antique feel. Do not place a leather sofa next to a radiator or window.

100% COTTON

Cotton is durable and strong, but fades and can stain easily, wrinkle, or stretch. Premium-grade cotton keeps its looks for longer. It is a medium-priced choice.

FORMAL VELVET

Although expensive, velvet is luxurious and soft. It is made from natural fibers such as silk or cotton, which drape better and will last longer, or synthetics such as rayon.

CHENILLE

This very soft, medium-priced textured fabric is either 100% polyester or a blend of cotton, rayon, and polyester. Deep pile chenille is susceptible to crushing.

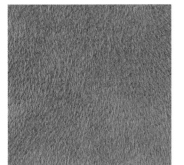

MICROFIBER

A very fine but hard-wearing polyester fiber, low-cost microfiber has the look and feel of velvet or suede. Its advantage is that it can be wiped easily with a damp cloth.

FAUX SUEDE

A cheap option, faux suede is 100% polyester, but feels and looks similar to the real thing. It is easy to clean and is more resistant to spillages than leathers.

WOVEN DESIGNS

Woven designs come in a huge range of weaves and weights, so they vary greatly in price and durability. Designs include stripes, checks, florals, and damasks.

FAUX LEATHER

This medium-priced man-made material is treated to look like leather, but doesn't age as well. However, it is easier to clean and is pretty durable.

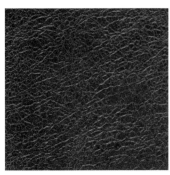

NUBUCK

This expensive type of leather is similar to suede, but is durable—a good alternative to classic leather upholstery. It can be dyed and pretreated to protect it from stains.

WOOL/FELT

This material, available in a range of solid colors, may be 100% wool or a mix of wool and polyester; prices vary accordingly. It has a stylish, flat appearance.

LINEN

Ideal for informal sofas and loose covers, linen has similar properties to cotton, but doesn't fade and is less resilient. It ages well, but is expensive and tends to wrinkle.

SLEEPER SOFAS

A sleeper sofa may be your best option and a useful investment if you want to host guests in relative comfort, but don't have rooms to spare. Points to consider include how big the bed can be without having to buy a conspicuously large sofa, whether it's more important to have a good sofa or a good bed, and whether you will need to move the sofa in order to convert it to a bed, making weight an issue. There are many types available, with a range of ingenious mechanisms; below are four of the most common options.

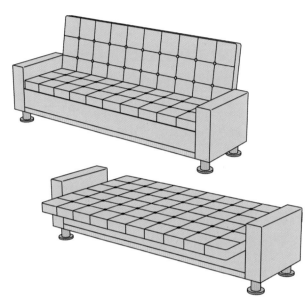

BENCH STYLE

The simplest of sleeper sofas, bench-style models have a mattresslike base and back, the latter of which folds down to create an instant bed. Of all the models, this type is the one model that can be as comfortable as any normal bed and, if you're likely to fold the bed back into a sofa only occasionally, it's the best choice.

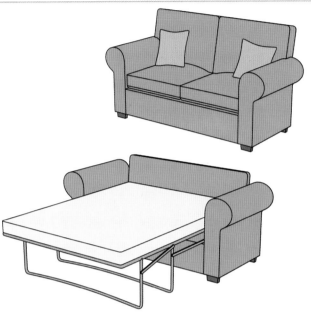

PULL-OUT

The most common type of sleeper sofa, this model looks like a standard sofa and is available in a range of styles. The bed frame and mattress, which are folded and concealed inside the sofa base, are pulled up and outward to form the bed. It may include storage space to store a quilt and pillows, and is usually very heavy.

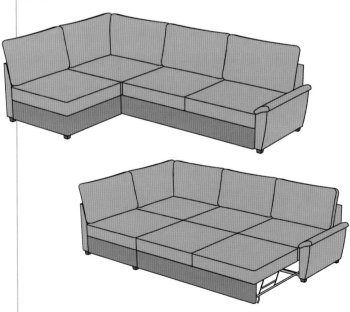

CORNER

Corner sleeper sofas typically comprise a two-seater sofa and a chaise that forms the corner unit. The bed section comes out from the base of the sofa section, either with a pull-out action (see above right) or as a pop-up trundle. These sleeper sofas also sometimes feature storage space, which is useful for storing bed linens.

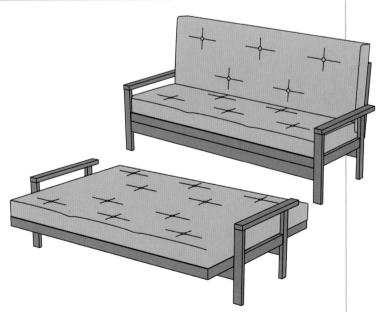

FUTON

A futon-style sleeper sofa usually has a frame that is made of wood or metal and a choice of mattress thicknesses and materials. The two basic types are bi-fold (shown above), which fold back like bench-style sleeper sofas, and tri-fold, whereby the mattress is folded into three sections to make a more compact sofa.

7 CHOOSE ARMCHAIRS

Living room chairs should complement your sofa, but they don't have to be the same shape, fabric, or color, so look around for a range of designs and different looks before you make your final choice. Consider, too, whether they will be decorative or provide extra seating if there isn't space for a second sofa.

1 CHOOSE THE STYLE

The type of chair you choose should complement its surroundings and the style of the room. Size is also important: if you have a small room, opt for a compact design, since a wide Chesterfield chair will dominate it.

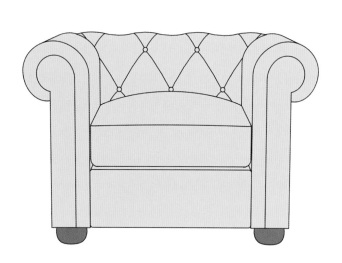

CHESTERFIELD

A classic design, the Chesterfield chair suits both traditional and contemporary rooms. The height and angle of its back and arms mean that it's comfortable to sit upright in and read, and its robust design makes it a good choice for family homes.

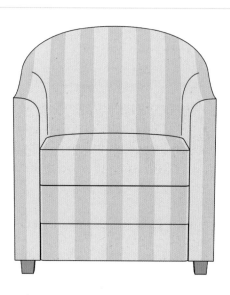

CLUB

With solid arms and a continuous semicircular back, the club chair's compact shape means that you can often fit two into a room. Its simple design makes it suitable for contemporary and traditional homes, and its light weight makes it easy to move.

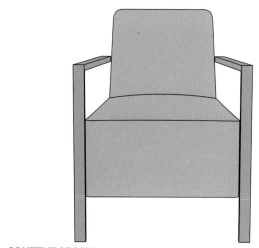

CONTEMPORARY

Sleek contemporary armchairs are ideal for minimally decorated rooms. Look for compact shapes, square angles, and straight arms and feet in metal or wood. Stick to plain fabrics in neutral tones and accessorize with patterned cushions for interest.

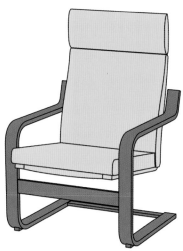

CANTILEVER

This chair has a bent frame (normally made from wood) rather than back legs, which provides support and resilience. Despite its skeletal frame, the design is surprisingly robust. The high back also provides great support, making it an ideal reading chair.

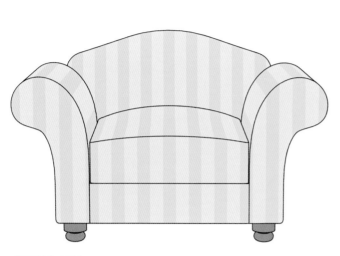

SCROLL ARM

As its name would suggest, this type of chair has elegantly curved arms and a high curved back. It is comfortable to sit on, but is definitely not for slouching in, so it is more suited to traditional, formal living rooms.

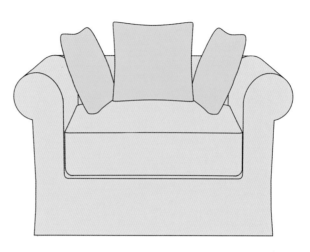

INFORMAL

An informal armchair has a fairly traditional shape and its legs are hidden beneath a fabric skirt. Instead of a back cushion, it's more likely to have a selection of throw pillows and a slip cover. This design is prefect for sinking into to relax.

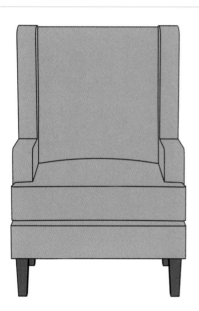

WING CHAIR

A classic style, this armchair has a high winged back, scrolled arms, and turned legs, which are often on casters. Despite its upright features, this is a comfortable chair design that suits contemporary as well as traditional rooms.

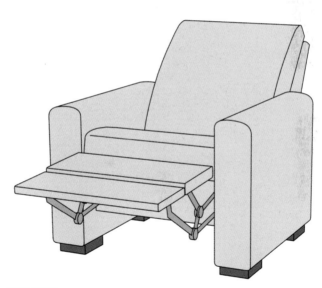

RECLINER

This chair design has a reclining back with a footrest that rises up so that you can lounge in ultimate comfort. Manual and electric versions are available, with some modern recliners also featuring a massage action. Styles are becoming more varied.

2 CHOOSE THE MATERIAL

The choice of fabric materials for living rooms chairs is essentially the same as that for sofas (p.152), but that doesn't necessarily mean that the fabric you choose for your chairs has to match that of your sofa. In fact, if you don't want the furniture to resemble a three-piece suite, this is a good opportunity to pick a contrasting fabric or pattern.

COVER
A SOFA WITH THROWS

With layered throws, custom-made to fit your sofa, this method gives a neater overall appearance than a single loose throw and stays in place much more effectively. You can use the same fabric or complementary fabrics for the different layers.

WHAT YOU NEED

- Fabric for underlayer—use curtain-weight cotton material
- Fabric for 2 overlayers—use curtain-weight cotton material (can be the same fabric or a complementary one)
- Scissors
- Sewing machine, or needle and thread
- Iron
- Pins
- Narrow rods (optional)

1 MEASURE AND CUT

MEASURE each layer separately. The underlayer is the biggest piece of fabric, since it needs to cover the whole sofa, reaching almost to the floor on all four sides. The second layer is long but narrow, since it needs to pass over both arms and along the entire width of the sofa in between. The final, top layer should be the exact width of the seats and long enough to cover the sofa from front to back, reaching almost to the floor on both sides. Allow for hems and for a few inches of fabric to be tucked in at the seat edges.

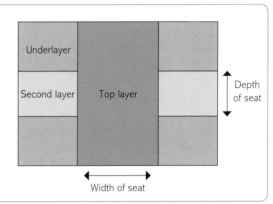

Underlayer

Second layer

Top layer

Depth of seat

Width of seat

2 JOIN THE FABRIC

1 TO MAKE THE NECESSARY WIDTH of fabric for the underlayer, you will almost certainly need to join together multiple lengths. To join, place the pieces together, right sides facing each other, and then sew a ¾in (2cm) seam.

2 OPEN UP and lay flat. Press the seam to one side.

3 SEW AGAIN to secure, creating a flat seam.

3 HEM THE SIDES

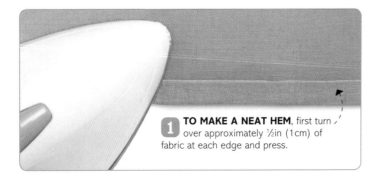

1 TO MAKE A NEAT HEM, first turn over approximately ½in (1cm) of fabric at each edge and press.

2 TURN THE FIRST HEM over again so that the raw edge is concealed. Do likewise with the hem directly opposite. At each corner, fold a triangle of fabric in at a 45° angle. (if you want, you can trim some of the fabric away from the corner first to reduce the bulk).

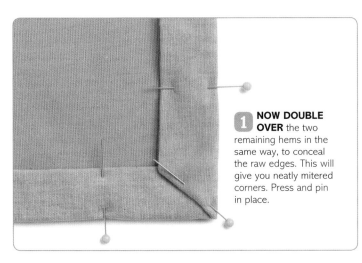

1 NOW DOUBLE OVER the two remaining hems in the same way, to conceal the raw edges. This will give you neatly mitered corners. Press and pin in place.

2 SEW THE HEMS on all four sides.

4 MAKE THE OVERLAYERS

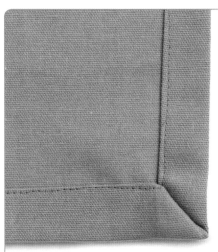

REPEAT THE ABOVE steps to make the second layer, and again to make the top layer. Depending on the size of your sofa, you may not need to join together multiple lengths of fabric this time.

5 ARRANGE THE THROWS

DRAPE THE UNDERLAYER over the entire sofa, tucking a few inches of fabric in at the edges of the seat to hold it in place. Lay the long second layer over both arms and along the seats, again tucking it in at the sides. Add the top layer over the seats and back, tucking in at the back (narrow rods, pushed down into the gaps at the edges of the seat cushions, can help keep the throws in place).

8 CHOOSE LIVING ROOM FURNITURE

The choice and price ranges of living room furniture available may at first seem overwhelming. Start by considering what material you want the furniture to be made of, and if you want it already assembled or are happy for it to arrive flat-packed. Then consider what pieces of furniture you actually need.

1 CHOOSE THE MATERIAL

The material of your living room furniture will really set the style for the room. Chunky solid wood, for instance, will give your room a rustic, country style, while sleek glass or acrylic will create a more modern, contemporary feel.

SOLID WOOD

Medium-priced wood furniture comes in a range of modern and traditional designs. Since it is a natural material, there will be variations in the grain and color.

VENEER

This low- to medium-cost furniture is made of thin layers of wood glued to a base—typically particleboard or MDF. It is more lightweight than solid wood.

METAL

This medium-priced furniture often has a metal frame and legs with a glass or wood tabletop, giving a contemporary look; brushed metal has a more industrial feel.

GLASS

This medium-priced or expensive furniture gives the illusion of light and space, although it is often molded from one piece of glass so can be heavy to lift or move.

ACRYLIC

Like glass, medium-priced acrylic furniture is usually transparent and typically molded from a single sheet. Acrylic designs suit modern living rooms well.

2 CHOOSE THE PIECES

Other than a sofa, there are no hard and fast rules about what furniture you should have in your living room, so what you choose is really down to the size of your room and whether you need table surfaces, storage, or areas for displays.

COFFEE TABLE

Available in various sizes and shapes, including square, rectangle, oval, and round, coffee tables are also available with a choice of storage options. Choose from a single-shelf table for storing magazines, for example, a table with drawers for filing documents, or one with a lift-up top in which to store more bulky items.

CONSOLE TABLE

Console tables are more decorative than practical, although those with drawers can be used to store small items. Their height makes them a useful surface on which to stand a table lamp. Place the table against a wall or behind a sofa.

SIDE TABLE

A side table is designed to sit to the side of a sofa or armchair, and be used as a surface on which to rest a lamp for task work and any reading material or drinks, for example. They are sold in various widths, so check the size you need before you buy.

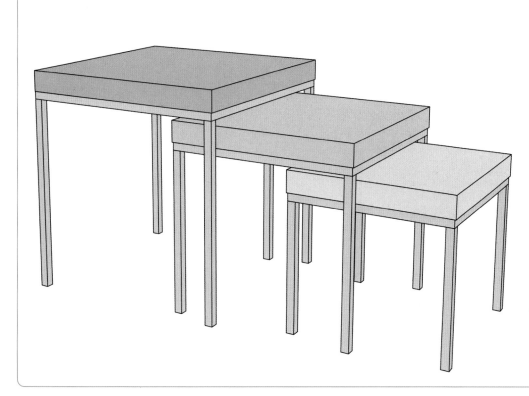

NEST OF TABLES

This useful piece of furniture comprises a nest of two or three different-sized tables neatly tucked inside each other. They can be pulled out when needed to provide extra table surfaces.

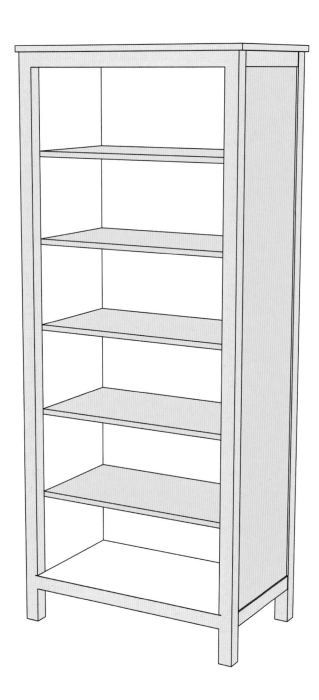

BOOKCASE

A bookcase can also be used to display ornaments, collections, and photos, in addition to books. Make sure the space between the shelves is deep and tall enough to house your possessions before you purchase the item.

SHELVING UNIT

Similar to a bookshelf, open shelving is available in a huge range of designs, sizes, and finishes. In addition to providing you with practical storage, this type of shelving can also be used as a divider between living zones.

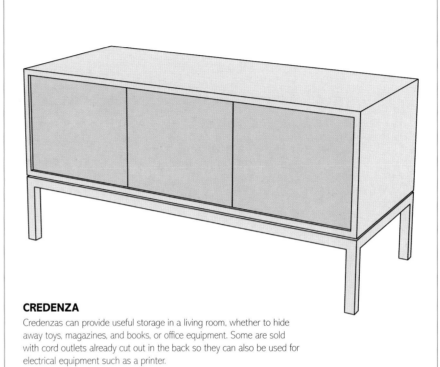

CREDENZA

Credenzas can provide useful storage in a living room, whether to hide away toys, magazines, and books, or office equipment. Some are sold with cord outlets already cut out in the back so they can also be used for electrical equipment such as a printer.

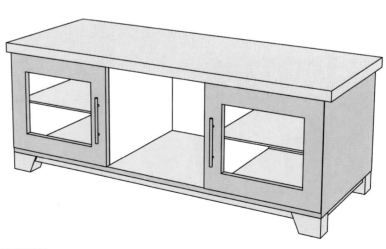

TV STAND

These low units are designed so that you can sit a TV on top and and house your home entertainment systems and games equipment on the shelf, or in the cupboard, below. You can also buy corner TV stands, which will fit neatly into a corner of your room, if space is an issue.

CABINET

Cabinets come in a wide range of heights and widths, and typically have an open, solid, or glazed front, or a mixture of the two. Those with shelves or glazed doors can be used to display ornaments or family photos.

6 WAYS WITH
SHELVING

Living room shelves don't have to be used only for practical storage; they can also be used for displaying a variety of attractive accessories and personal mementoes. If you do fill the shelves predominantly with books, try arranging the books by color and size to make them look organized and attractive.

FLOATING SHELVES

Supported by concealed supports, floating shelves offer an unfussy, modern look. Use them on their own, or group them together.

CONSIDER ATTACHING several floating shelves to the wall in either a vertical or staggered arrangement.

PICTURE RAIL HEIGHT

If you don't want your shelves to be the center of attention or the focal point of your living room, hang them at picture rail height.

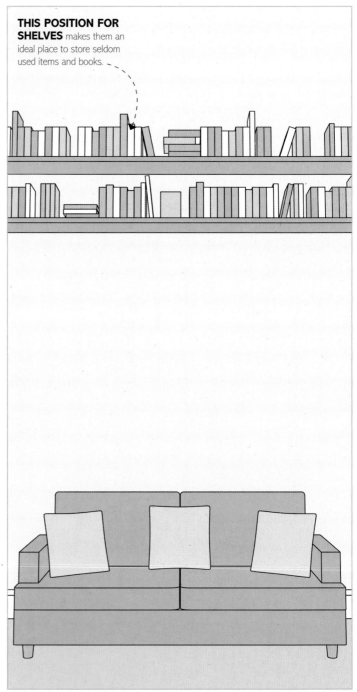

THIS POSITION FOR SHELVES makes them an ideal place to store seldom used items and books.

BOX SHELVES

Hang box-style shelves in groups of even numbers to give your wall a neat, symmetrically balanced look.

WHOLE WALL

Hang shelving across an entire wall. This type of shelving needs to be kept organized or your whole room will end up feeling cluttered.

ALCOVES

An alcove is an ideal place for shelves. If you hang shelving in two alcoves on the same wall, make sure they match, for a streamlined look.

CHECK THAT your books, photos, and accessories give a balanced display if you put up shelves in alcoves on the same wall.

ROOM OPENING

The space around your door frame or room opening is rarely put to good use, so install some shelves and add valuable storage space.

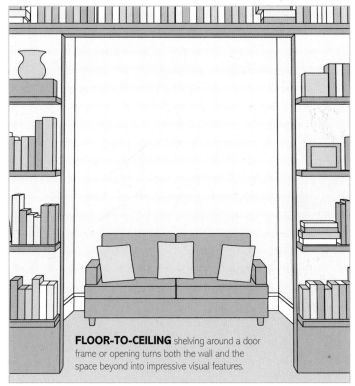

FLOOR-TO-CEILING shelving around a door frame or opening turns both the wall and the space beyond into impressive visual features.

INSTALL
WALL SHELVES

Before you install your wall shelves, it's worth attaching the brackets to the shelf before checking where you want to position the shelf against the wall (rather than holding up just the brackets). In this way, you can space the whole piece visually first to ensure the best result.

WHAT YOU NEED

- Wooden shelves (your choice of wood and thickness)
- Brackets
- Tape measure
- Pencil
- Bradawl
- Screwdriver
- Level
- Drill
- Wall anchors (choose wall anchors appropriate for your wall type; size should correspond to the screw size)
- Screws

1 ATTACH THE BRACKETS

1 PLACE THE BACK OF THE SHELF on a flat surface and butt the shelf brackets up against the underside of the shelf. Judge by eye where the brackets should be positioned.

2 MEASURE THE DISTANCE of each bracket from the edge of the shelf with a tape measure to check each is equidistant from the end. The top and base of the brackets must also be parallel.

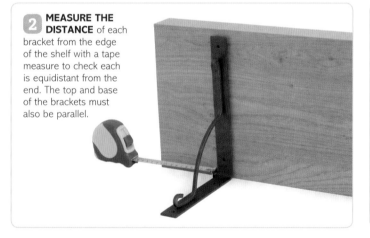

3 MAKE LIGHT PENCIL MARKS for the bracket holes on the underside of the shelf. Attaching the brackets in this "side on" position ensures that they sit flush with the back of the shelf.

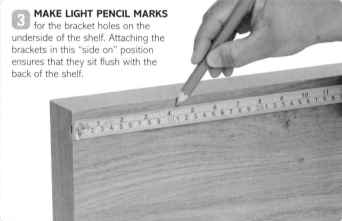

4 USE A BRADAWL to make holes in the underside of the shelf over the pencil marks. If necessary, turn the shelf, face side down, onto a flat surface to do this.

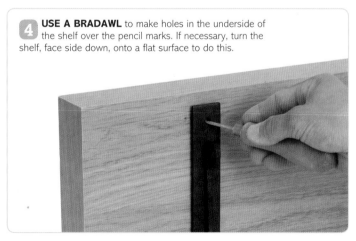

5 INSERT THE SCREWS through the brackets into the holes, and screw the brackets to the underside of the shelf.

2 MARK THE POSITION

1 **HOLD THE SHELF** (with the brackets attached) up to the wall to see where you want to position it. Place a level along the length of the shelf to make sure it is level.

2 **MARK THE BRACKET** holes on the wall with a pencil.

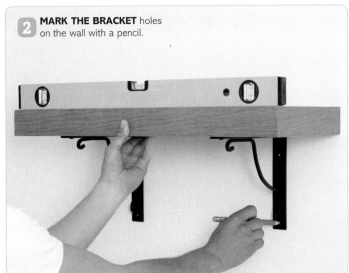

3 MOUNT THE SHELVES

1 **DRILL HOLES INTO THE WALL** over the pencil marks. Select the drill bit that corresponds to the size of the wall anchors.

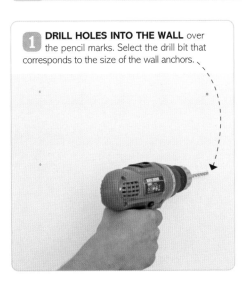

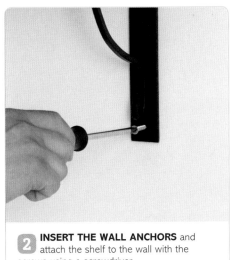

2 **INSERT THE WALL ANCHORS** and attach the shelf to the wall with the screws using a screwdriver.

BUILD
ALCOVE SHELVES

These "floating" shelves (wherein no bracket is visible) comprise wood strips sandwiched between two pieces of plywood. Alcove walls are not always "true," or straight, so measure the width of the alcove at both back and front, at the height where the shelf will be positioned, before cutting your shelf to size.

WHAT YOU NEED

- MDF boards (about ⅜in/9mm thick for standard alcove shelf size)
- ¾ x ¾in/2 x 2cm wood strips
- Hand saw or jigsaw
- Wood glue
- Brads
- Hammer
- Nail punch
- Wood filler
- Sandpaper
- Level

- Drill and drill bits
- Wall anchors
- Screws
- Caulk
- Primer and paint for interior wood
- Paintbrush

1 CUT TWO BOARDS

MEASURE THE DIMENSIONS of the alcove wall, then transfer the measurements onto a plank of MDF and cut out two identically sized pieces of MDF with a saw. Sand the edges with sandpaper to give a smooth finish.

2 MARK EACH BOARD

1 TO ALLOW SPACE for the attached wood strips on the wall to sit inside the shelf, mark at least one and half times the width of a strip from either end of the board. Do the same thing along the back of the board.

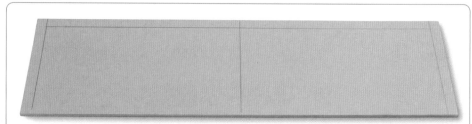

2 DRAW OUT A GRID on the first board where all the internal wood strips will be attached. Allow for two short strips to be attached at either end of the shelf and at least one in the middle. (These wood strips must be shorter than the depth of the shelf.) Repeat this grid on the other side of the board so you will know where to hammer brads into the wood strips.

3 ATTACH THE WOOD STRIPS

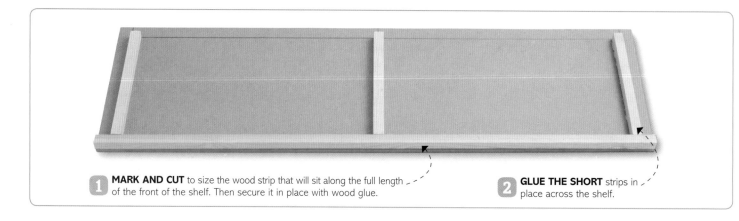

1 MARK AND CUT to size the wood strip that will sit along the full length of the front of the shelf. Then secure it in place with wood glue.

2 GLUE THE SHORT strips in place across the shelf.

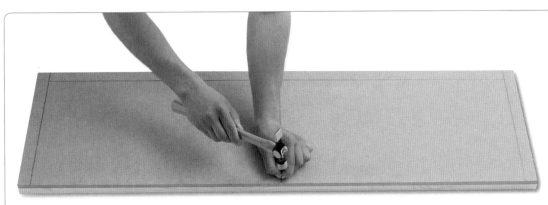

3 TURN OVER THE SHELF and hammer brads approximately 4in (10cm) apart through the boards into the wood strips. Press the brads below the level of the shelf with a nail punch and hammer.

4 ATTACH THE SECOND BOARD

1 TURN THE SHELF back over and place wood glue on all the strips.

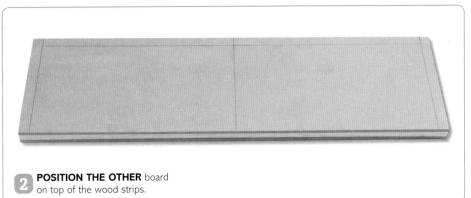

2 POSITION THE OTHER board on top of the wood strips.

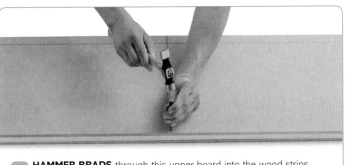

3 HAMMER BRADS through this upper board into the wood strips, again approximately 4in (10cm) apart, and press the brads below the level of the MDF boards with the nail punch and hammer.

4 COVER THE BRAD HOLES—and any other gaps or holes in the boards—with wood filler. Do this on both sides of the shelf.

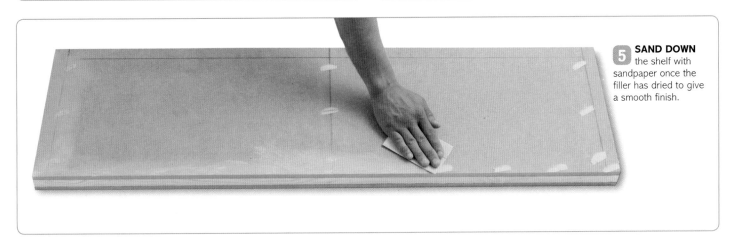

5 SAND DOWN the shelf with sandpaper once the filler has dried to give a smooth finish.

5 ATTACH SUPPORTS TO THE WALL

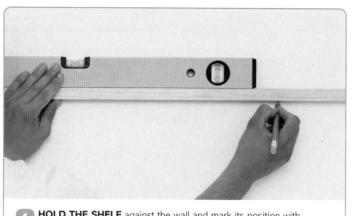

1 **HOLD THE SHELF** against the wall and mark its position with a few pencil marks. Cut a length of wood strip to fit the back wall and hold it up to the wall. Check that it is level using a level, and draw a pencil line underneath the length of wood strip.

2 **DRILL HOLES** in the wood strip to be mounted on the wall—these should be evenly spaced and no more than 18in (45cm) apart. Countersink each hole if you have the appropriate drill bit. Reposition the strip and use a small drill bit to drill through the strip and into the wall.

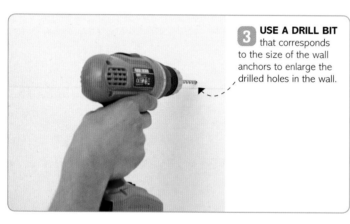

3 **USE A DRILL BIT** that corresponds to the size of the wall anchors to enlarge the drilled holes in the wall.

4 **SCREW THE WOOD STRIP** to the wall with wall anchors and screws using a screwdriver.

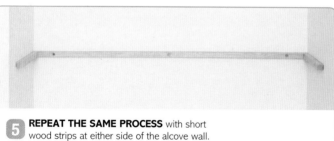

5 **REPEAT THE SAME PROCESS** with short wood strips at either side of the alcove wall.

6 **SLIDE THE SHELF** onto the supports, and fill any gaps between the edge of the shelf and the wall with caulk.

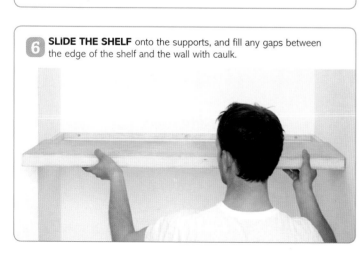

6 PAINT THE SHELF

APPLY A COAT of suitable primer first and then paint the shelf.

9 CHOOSE **LIGHTING**

The trick to planning a lighting scheme for your living room is to create a number of moods with different lighting levels. If the room's proportions aren't as good as they could be, good lighting can help with this, too. Also, choose lighting that looks as good switched off as it does switched on.

1 DECIDE ON A STYLE OF LIGHTING

There's no one approach to lighting a living room; your goal should be to combine task, ambient, and accent lighting to conjure up different levels of light, depending on what you will be using the room for and how you want the space to feel.

AMBIENT

Ambient lighting is all about creating atmosphere. It might be that your main overhead light, when dimmed, can create a relaxing mood, or you might want to turn off the overhead light and substitute it with soft pools of light from an even spread of table lamps that you have positioned around the room.

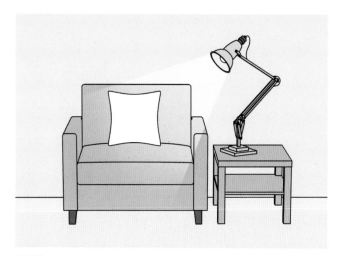

TASK

Task lighting in a living room can either be bright overhead lighting—usually a pendant or surface-mounted ceiling light—or a swing arm or table lamp. Having a dimmer switch installed with your overhead light will allow you to increase the light levels for task work and decrease them when you want to relax.

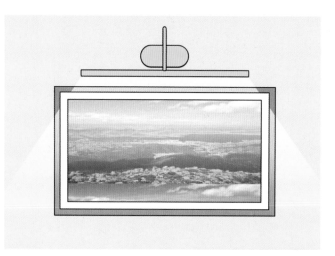

ACCENT

Accent lighting is used to create a particular lighting effect; use it to draw attention to attractive architectural details or to highlight a favorite picture, piece of sculpture, or piece of furniture. You can also use accent lighting to play with, and improve, the proportions of your room.

CHOOSE YOUR LIGHT FIXTURES

It is wise to go for a combination of light fixtures in a living room, but the mix you go for should depend on the lighting effects you want to create, the period of your house, your decorating style, and how coordinated you want your room to look.

CEILING LIGHTS

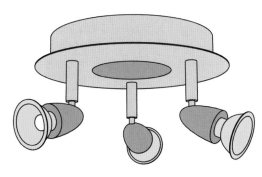

PENDANT LIGHT

A pendant with a shade can be just as much of a show-stopping fixture as a chandelier would be—big shades in bold colors can have a large impact on a contemporary scheme. If you've opted for a more traditional look with a smaller, perhaps fussier shade, don't rely on the pendant as your only source of light—it's likely that it won't be bright or atmospheric enough.

SPOTLIGHTS

In a contemporary room, spotlights can be used as both ceiling lights and on walls and at floor level to provide accent lighting. However you choose to use them, it is vital that they are installed with a dimmer switch so you can easily alter the mood of the room; you'll find it hard to relax in a brightly lit room.

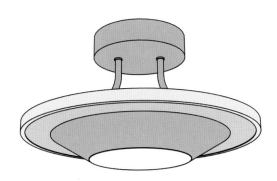

SURFACE-MOUNTED CEILING LIGHT

A surface-mounted ceiling light in a living room should be an attractive feature, so if you have a large room with a high ceiling, pick a piece that matches the room's proportions. Smaller, low-ceilinged rooms can still carry off a surface-mounted ceiling light, but it should be one that sits fairly snugly against the ceiling.

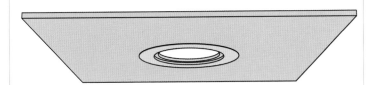

RECESSED DOWNLIGHTS

In a north-facing or low-ceilinged contemporary space, recessed downlights will create an effect resembling real daylight. However, these downlights should be teamed with other sources of light, such as table lamps, and installed with a dimmer switch so that you can lower the light levels when you want to.

STATEMENT LIGHTING

If you have a big room, choose a statement piece for its decorative impact rather than how well it lights the room. Consider chandeliers—modern or traditional—or a line or cluster of bold pendants. Whatever you choose, you'll still need other lights within the room to get the right balance, but keep these other elements subtle so that they don't battle for attention with your statement piece.

WALL-MOUNTED SCONCES

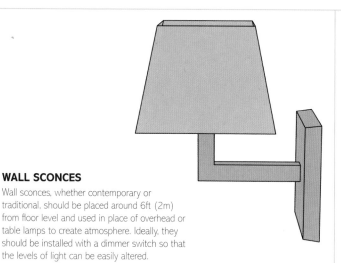

WALL SCONCES

Wall sconces, whether contemporary or traditional, should be placed around 6ft (2m) from floor level and used in place of overhead or table lamps to create atmosphere. Ideally, they should be installed with a dimmer switch so that the levels of light can be easily altered.

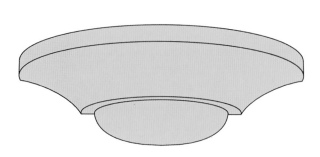

WALL UPLIGHTS

Wall uplights, like wall sconces, are used to create softer pools of light than overhead lighting would and can be combined with table lamps to create a relaxing space. They also play a part in improving the proportions of the room—the light from them is thrown upward, making a ceiling seem higher that it really is.

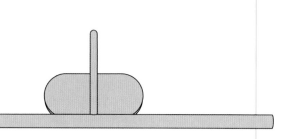

PICTURE LIGHTS

The living room is the one place where you're likely to have a favorite piece of art on display, and the best way to show it off is with a picture light, which should sit just above or below it. Look for a fixture that matches the others in your room in terms of material and finish for the best effect.

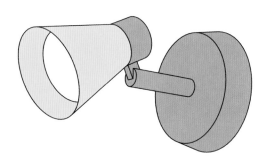

SINGLE SPOTLIGHTS

Single spotlights are typically used to highlight areas of a room or things in it—from architectural details to pieces of art. Limit yourself to no more than one spotlight per room (or per zone in a very large room), otherwise the drama you may be hoping to create will be dampened.

LAMPS

FLOOR LAMPS

Floor lamps usually sit comfortably behind an armchair to provide task lighting for reading or craft projects. However, contemporary lamps can also be bought for decorative effect and look just as good lighting up a dark corner. Experiment with different shades before you buy to make sure the light thrown off is right for your space, both in terms of color and strength.

TORCHIERE LAMPS

Just as wall uplights project light upward to the ceiling, torchiere lamps perform the same trick in enhancing the space in a low-ceilinged room, or showing off the proportions of a room with a high ceiling. Choose one with adjustable light levels for the best effect.

TABLE LAMPS

Table lamps are a must-have in a living room, however contemporary, because they allow you to take the light down to the lowest level and create soft pools of relaxing light. Dot the lights evenly around so the whole room can be adequately lit by them, and switch off all the overhead lights.

10 CHOOSE WINDOW TREATMENTS

Of all the rooms in your house, the living room is the one room where you may want to introduce luxurious fabrics to make a stylish, individual statement and heighten the sense of comfort and relaxation. However, if you want a more contemporary, understated look, choose something more subtle.

1 CHOOSE A TYPE

It may be that you want to put more than one type of treatment on your living room windows. Doing so will introduce a layered look to the room. But which should you match up, and which should you hang on its own?

BLINDS

If you prefer a streamlined look, or you have a small living room, blinds are a neat choice. Roller and Roman blinds are available in a wide choice of colors and designs, and Venetian blinds come in a choice of materials and colors. Team with curtains for a layered look.

CURTAINS

A classic choice for living rooms, curtains are available in a wide range of fabrics, patterns, styles, and headings so they can be used in both traditional and modern homes. Curtains can be matched with blinds and also shutters, if chosen carefully.

SHUTTERS

A streamlined choice for modern rooms, solid shutters are available in limited designs. Louvered shutters can be designed with two or three panels, and styles include full-height, café-style, and tier-on-tier. They are also ideal for bay and arched windows.

CHECKLIST

● **Can your living room** be viewed from the outside? If so, consider using a translucent fabric such as muslin, voile, or lace net that offers privacy while still letting in light.

● **Think about the amount** of space around your window and make sure that you will be able to pull back curtains fully or open shutters—by doing so you can make the room seem larger and let in more light.

● **If you live on** a busy street, consider curtains made from a heavy-weight fabric such as velvet, which can help eliminate street noise.

2 CHOOSE A STYLE

If your living room is traditional and the space light and large, extravagant, layered dressings can give a luxurious feel. Minimal contemporary rooms often suit more modest window dressings, although you can still layer them for a more relaxed look.

BLINDS

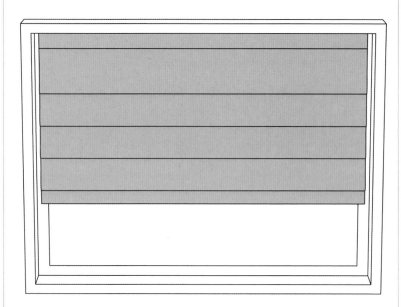

ROMAN

Available in a wide choice of fabrics that are suitable for modern and traditional-style living rooms, Roman blinds are particularly attractive when matched with curtains. The blinds hang flat against the window when lowered and fold neatly together when raised, making them feel more sumptuous than other blinds.

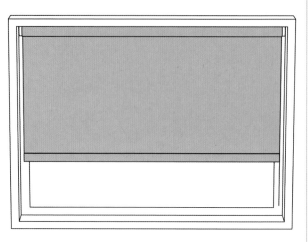

ROLLER

Roller blinds tend to give a more modern look and, since they are a fairly inexpensive option, are a good choice for bay windows. Available in a wide range of colors and designs, they can be pulled up or down smoothly to block out or let sunlight in. Many ready-made roller blinds can be cut smaller to fit your window.

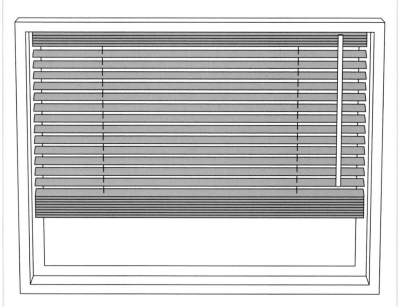

VENETIAN

Venetian blinds have adjustable slats that you can open and close, allowing you to control the amount of light coming through the window, in addition to offering privacy. They are available in a choice of materials, colors, and slat widths. White wood will give your room a fresh feel, while darker shades of wood will make it feel warm and cozy.

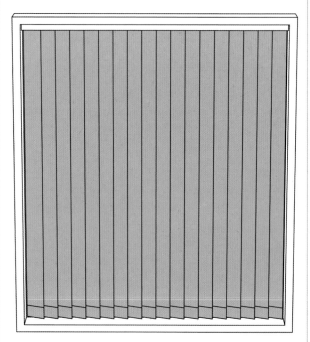

VERTICAL

More suited to contemporary-style rooms, vertical blinds are a good choice if you have full-length windows or sliding doors. They're available in a wide range of colors and fabrics, and are made up of vertical strips of fabric that can be tilted or drawn.

CURTAINS

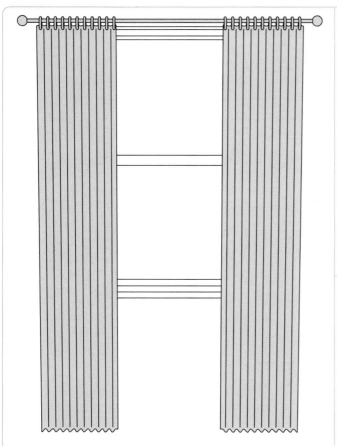

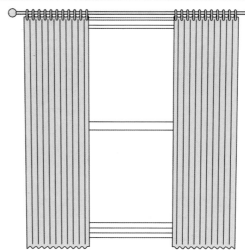

SILL LENGTH
Sill-length, or just below sill-length, curtains are a neater option if you have small windows. These are also worth considering if a radiator sits directly below your window. This curtain length can look old-fashioned, so pick the fabric carefully.

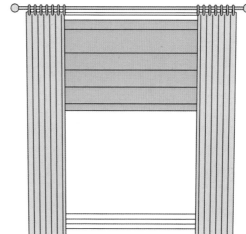

DRESS CURTAINS
Dress curtains are narrower than normal curtains and not designed to be drawn. Use them to add a decorative touch at a window where you've had to use blinds for practical or privacy purposes. They are particularly good for dressing bay windows if you are on a budget.

FULL LENGTH
Fully lined, full-length curtains can be an expensive option, but not only will they make an impact to your room's scheme, but they can also help keep heat in the room, too. Match them with Roman blinds to create a luxurious feel—an ideal look for large bay windows.

SHUTTERS

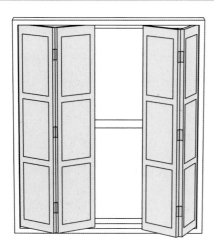

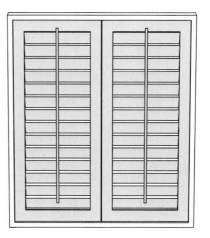

SOLID
Solid shutters are a popular choice for period homes, although that's not to say that they don't suit contemporary rooms, too. They are designed to be folded back against the wall during the day and closed shut at night, so may not be the best option if you require privacy during the day.

LOUVER
Louvered shutters allow you to control the amount of light coming into the room and provide privacy. Full-height shutters look stylish, although you may only need to use café-style shutters, which screen only the lower part of the window, offering privacy at street level, while still allowing light into the room.

7 WAYS WITH
CURTAIN HEADERS

Whether you decide to have plain or patterned curtains, you can make them more appealing by choosing interesting curtain headers. Whether you buy the curtains ready-made, make them yourself, or have a professional make them for you, choose a style that suits the look of the room where they will hang.

DOUBLE PLEAT

If you have long curtains, use double-pleat headers so they hang in orderly folds, yet with a more relaxed look than triple-pleats.

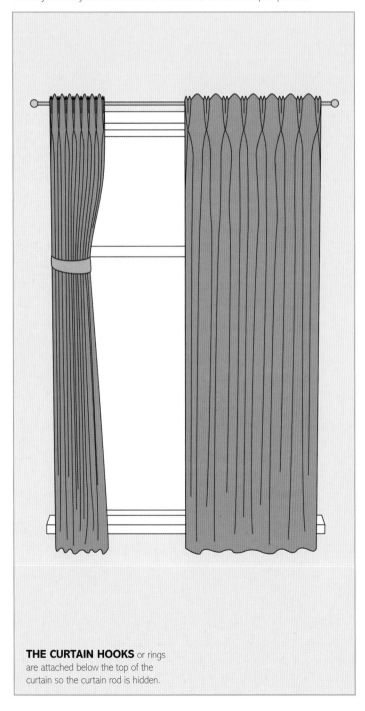

THE CURTAIN HOOKS or rings are attached below the top of the curtain so the curtain rod is hidden.

EYELET

This modern look has metal eyelets punched through the top of the curtain at regular intervals, which are threaded onto a curtain rod.

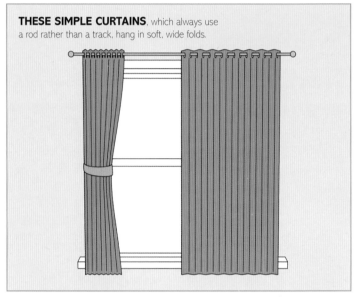

THESE SIMPLE CURTAINS, which always use a rod rather than a track, hang in soft, wide folds.

INVERTED PLEAT

Curtains with inverted, or box, pleats look neat, and their minimalist appearance makes them a good choice for contemporary rooms.

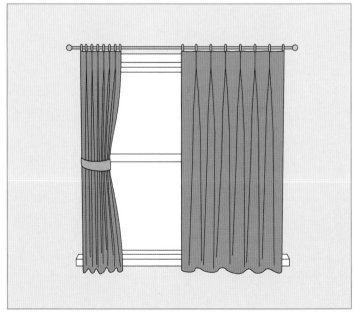

PENCIL PLEAT

Pencil pleats give a simple, classic look. Curtain tape with three hook positions—compatible with all types of track and rod—is used.

THE WIDTH of pencil pleat curtains can be altered slightly by pulling the draw cord on the heading tape.

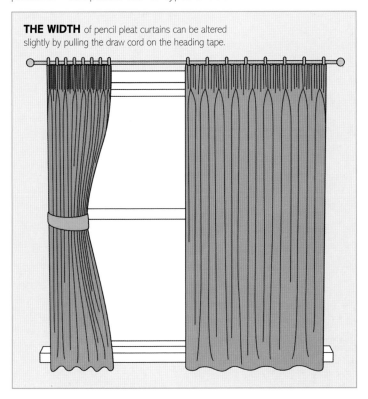

TAB TOP

These stitched loops make curtains look simple yet modern, although they are not quite as easy to open and close as other styles.

TAKE THE LENGTH of the tabs into consideration when measuring for this type of curtain.

TIE TOP

A pretty choice that suits bedrooms, tie-top curtains have ties that are sewn onto the curtain heading and then tied to a rod.

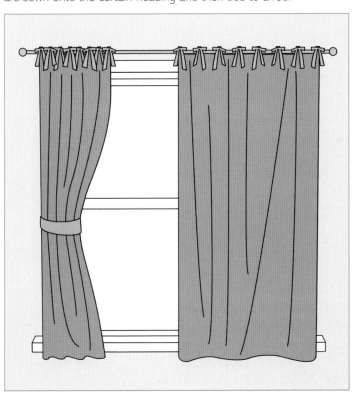

TRIPLE PLEAT

A triple-pleat heading encourages curtains to hang in elegant, formal folds. This makes it a good choice for floor-length curtains.

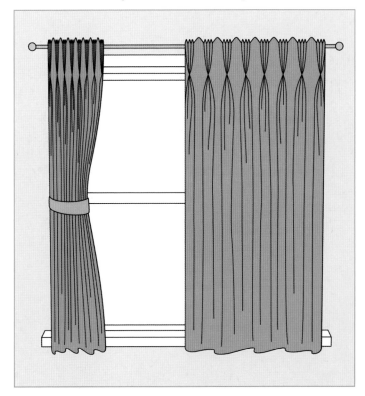

MAKE
LONG CURTAINS

Making your own curtains is a surefire way to ensure that they are the perfect size and material for your room. These tab-top curtains loop directly on to the rod for a modern look that doesn't require curtain hooks. Make them floor length or, for a more luxurious look, longer so that they pool on the floor.

WHAT YOU NEED

- Tape measure
- Fabric—use curtain-weight cotton material (see page 384 for quantity)
- Scissors
- Sewing machine, or needle and thread
- Iron
- Pins
- Curtain rod

1 MEASURE AND CUT

1 TAKE A MEASUREMENT from the bottom of the rod to the floor. (If you want the curtains to finish just above the floor, use this measurement as your starting point; if you want the curtains to pool on the floor, add on an extra 8–12in/20–30cm).

2 CUT THE FABRIC to length, adding an extra 10in (25cm) for hem and top edge allowance.

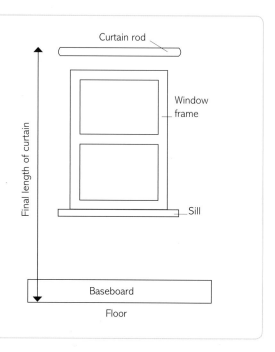

2 JOIN THE FABRIC

JOIN TOGETHER lengths of fabric to make up the necessary width (for these curtains to hang nicely, the width of each should be approximately half to three-quarters the length of the rod). To join, place the lengths together, right side to right side, and sew a seam along one edge. Then open up and lay flat, right side down, and press the seam open with an iron.

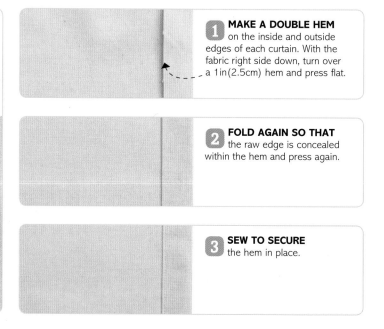

3 HEM THE SIDES

1 MAKE A DOUBLE HEM on the inside and outside edges of each curtain. With the fabric right side down, turn over a 1in (2.5cm) hem and press flat.

2 FOLD AGAIN SO THAT the raw edge is concealed within the hem and press again.

3 SEW TO SECURE the hem in place.

4 HEM THE BOTTOM

1 **TURN UP THE BOTTOM** of the curtains in a similar way but with a 4in (10cm) hem. Fold over and press, then fold and press again, and sew in place.

2 **SEW THE SIDES** as well so that the hem space is completely enclosed.

5 MAKE THE TABS

1 **TO MAKE THE TABS** that will attach the curtains to the rod, cut lengths of fabric that are 8in (20cm) wide and long enough when doubled over to wrap all the way around the rod, with some space for movement, as well as a seam allowance of ½–¾in (1–2cm). If in doubt, make them slightly longer than you need—the excess will be hidden when the curtain is finished.

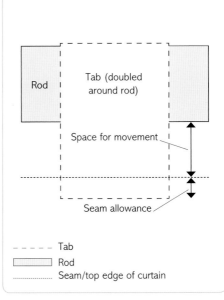

Rod

Tab (doubled around rod)

Space for movement

Seam allowance

- - - - - Tab

▭ Rod

.... Seam/top edge of curtain

2 **FOLD EACH TAB** in half lengthwise, right side to right side, and stitch along the raw edge to make a tube.

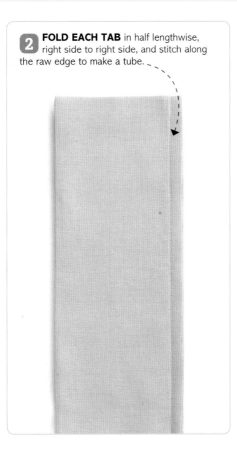

3 **TURN EACH TUBE** the right way around and, with the seam centered, press flat.

6 POSITION THE TABS

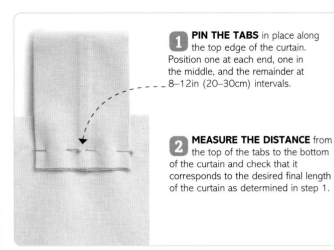

1 PIN THE TABS in place along the top edge of the curtain. Position one at each end, one in the middle, and the remainder at 8–12in (20–30cm) intervals.

2 MEASURE THE DISTANCE from the top of the tabs to the bottom of the curtain and check that it corresponds to the desired final length of the curtain as determined in step 1.

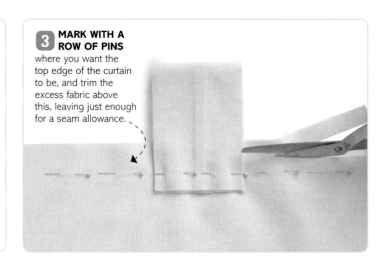

3 MARK WITH A ROW OF PINS where you want the top edge of the curtain to be, and trim the excess fabric above this, leaving just enough for a seam allowance.

7 SEW ON THE TABS

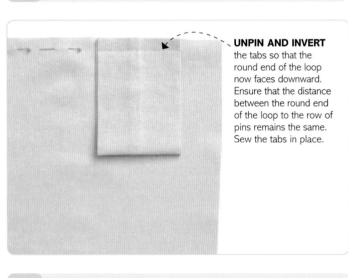

UNPIN AND INVERT the tabs so that the round end of the loop now faces downward. Ensure that the distance between the round end of the loop to the row of pins remains the same. Sew the tabs in place.

8 PREPARE THE BACK PANEL

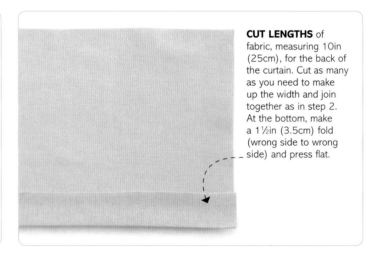

CUT LENGTHS of fabric, measuring 10in (25cm), for the back of the curtain. Cut as many as you need to make up the width and join together as in step 2. At the bottom, make a 1½in (3.5cm) fold (wrong side to wrong side) and press flat.

9 JOIN THE FRONT AND BACK PANELS

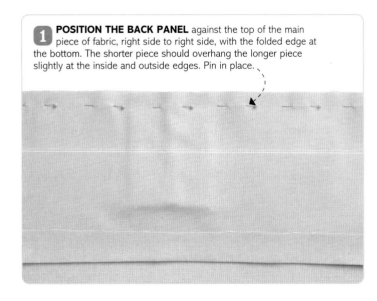

1 POSITION THE BACK PANEL against the top of the main piece of fabric, right side to right side, with the folded edge at the bottom. The shorter piece should overhang the longer piece slightly at the inside and outside edges. Pin in place.

2 SEW ALONG THE ROW of pins to attach the back panel.

10   SEW THE BACK PANEL

1 FLIP THE BACK PANEL over so that the fabric is wrong side to wrong side and the tabs are exposed. Press with the iron.

2 PIN THE BACK PANEL in place and then sew to join.

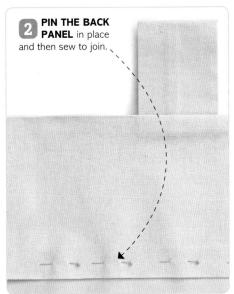

3 AT THE SIDES, neatly fold the overhanging fabric inside and sew the sides as well.

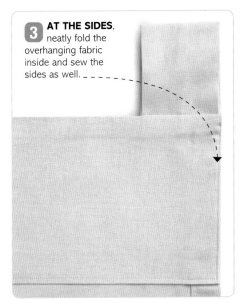

11   HANG

PASS THE CURTAIN ROD through all the loops and secure back in the brackets.

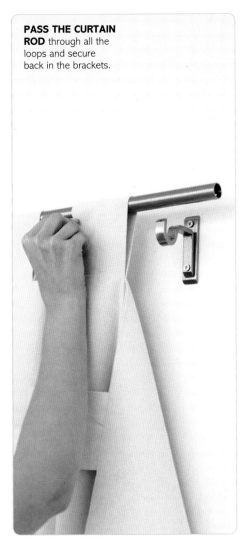

11 CHOOSE A FIREPLACE

Before buying a fireplace for your living room, ask a professional to assess whether you have a working chimney or flue and what condition it is in, the type of fuel you can use, and the required heat output. Armed with this information, you'll be able to choose from the various types of fireplace that are available.

CHOOSE THE TYPE

Start by deciding whether you want a traditional fireplace or stove set into an existing or faux chimney, or whether you prefer to create a more contemporary look with a modern fireplace that's set into or mounted on the wall.

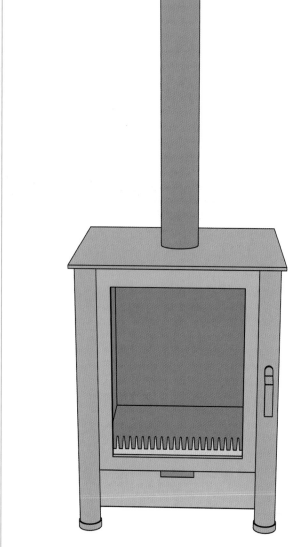

STOVE

More efficient than open-fronted fireplaces, stoves can either be freestanding on a hearth, inserted into the fireplace opening, or—provided the stove has an external flue—positioned centrally in the room to create a focal point. Traditionally found in country homes, stoves are also becoming increasingly popular in contemporary houses.

INSERTED

Inserted fireplaces sit neatly inside a fireplace opening behind the hearth. Most can be installed into a standard-sized fireplace opening, although this may need to be enlarged for a bigger firebox. They are typically placed within a stone or wood mantel, or flush against a tiled, stone, brick, or other noncombustible surface.

WALL-MOUNTED

Wall-mounted fireplaces are contemporary and don't take up any floor space. Depending on the type of fuel used, the fireplace can either be installed fully recessed into an existing or false chimney breast or hung directly on the wall. They are available in portrait, landscape, and square formats.

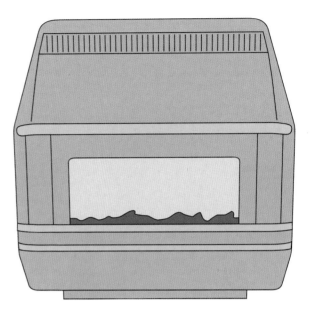

SEMI-RECESSED STOVE

Semi-recessed stoves are installed on the hearth in front of the fireplace opening of a working chimney. These tend to be fairly traditional in design, with a glass front and black surround and quite often with brass detailing. Semi-recessed stoves are only available as gas stoves.

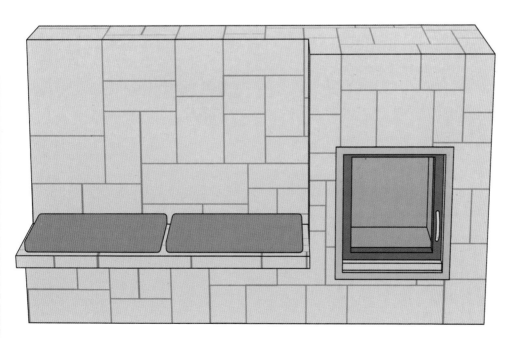

MASONRY HEATER

Made of brick- or stonework, masonry heaters store heat while the fireplace burns, then slowly and evenly release the heat over the next 12 to 24 hours. Some versions combine the main heating function with a smaller stove for cooking, and even built-in heated benches. They require a chimney.

FUEL TYPES

The type of fuel you want to burn is fundamental to the style of fireplace you choose. Here are some points to consider before you buy:

● **Solid fuels** include wood, coal, smokeless fuels, and wood pellets. Many fireplaces and stoves are multifuel, so they can burn any of these alternatives. If you do choose a solid-fuel fireplace, you will need to have somewhere dry to store the fuel.

● **Many gas fireplaces** require a traditional flue and need to be inserted into an existing chimney breast. If you don't have a chimney or flue, a direct-vent gas fireplace can be positioned on, or ducted to, an outside wall.

● **Electric fireplaces** can be positioned anywhere in a room with a power point. More expensive fireplaces are very realistic and may have an optiflame mirror effect, hologram, or even a built-in smoke machine for a more authentic appearance.

5 WAYS WITH
LIVING ROOM DISPLAYS

Displaying your accessories and personal possessions in a creative way will give your living room a neat, stylish look. Pick out objects that look attractive (rather than those that are purely functional) and follow these tips to work out how to display your collections in the best possible way.

GROUPING OF VASES

A good way to display vases is in a grouping of three or five. Use color-coordinated vases of varying heights and arrange them into a loose pyramid shape.

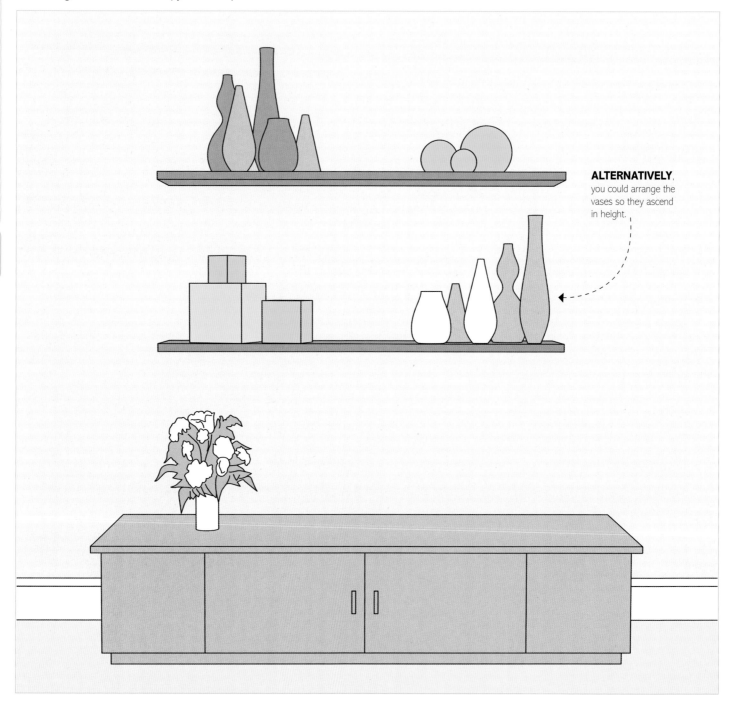

ALTERNATIVELY, you could arrange the vases so they ascend in height.

COLOR-CODED BOOKSHELF

A prominently placed bookshelf will look more ordered if you limit it to books where the colors suit your decorating scheme.

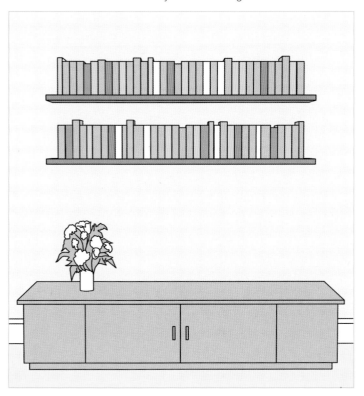

MEMENTOS ON BOX SHELVES

Open box shelves provide a narrow shelf on which to display collections and mementos, and create a neat border around them.

BELL JARS

Use a glass bell jar to show off a small collection. Choose mementos or even delicate dried flowers for your visual displays.

YOU CAN CREATE this effect with an attractive glass cheese dome instead.

SHELVING UNIT ARRANGEMENT

Balance your shelf displays by placing larger accessories in the corners of alternate shelves to create a zigzag pattern.

POSITION SMALLER OBJECTS at the other ends of the shelves.

5 WAYS WITH
DECORATIVE PILLOWS AND THROWS

Decorative pillows and throws on a sofa shouldn't be arranged haphazardly or left to chance. There are many ways—from formal to relaxed—to dress a sofa so that it looks different every time. Choose a look that suits the style of your living room, or change the arrangement according to your mood or the occasion.

INFORMAL

For an eclectic, informal look, cover the seat cushions of your sofa with an animal print throw, tucking it in underneath and around the sides, and add throw pillows in bright colors and prints.

LOOK FOR SCARVES and fabric remnants that you can use to cover your seat cushions if you don't want to use an animal print throw.

NEAT—TWO THROWS

Cover each seat cushion of a two-seater sofa with a small plain throw, then add a single striped pillow to each seat.

CHOOSE POLYESTER PILLOWS, which are firm and keep their shape, for a more formal look, or squishy feather pillows for a more relaxed vibe.

STYLISH—SINGLE THROW

Team a single light-colored wool throw with luxuriously covered plain pillows (all of the same size) for a uniform look.

FOR INTEREST, add one pillow in a patterned fabric.

VINTAGE CHIC

A checkered picnic-style blanket with pillows in a mix of floral and striped designs will give your sofa a vintage look.

MAKE SURE the decorative pillows you choose are in proportion to your sofa.

JUST PILLOWS

Use pillows of different sizes, but in similar colors and prints, to make an interesting visual mix.

FOR A CRISP LOOK, keep your pillow arrangement symmetrical.

12 CHOOSE RUGS

Rugs come in a variety of sizes, materials, and shapes, and can be used to add texture, color, and pattern to otherwise plain rooms. Adding a rug to an area of the house with exposed floorboards will help to minimize drafts and make any rooms with hard flooring look and feel warmer and more inviting.

1 CHOOSE THE SHAPE

The rug you choose largely depends on the shape and look of the area or room in which you place it. For contrast, try a round or natural-shaped rug (made from animal hide) in an angular room. If you are in doubt about the size, bigger is usually better.

ROUND

Incorporating a round rug is a good way to soften hard edges in a room if the furniture has lots of sharp angles. Adding a couple of small, colorful round rugs is also a fun way to brighten a child's bedroom.

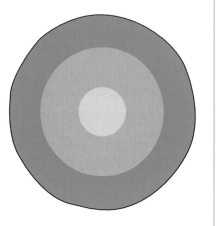

SQUARE

Square rugs work well in small square rooms, where they can act as a great focal point underneath a square coffee or dining table, for example. Try using two or three square rugs to break up the space if you have a long rectangular room.

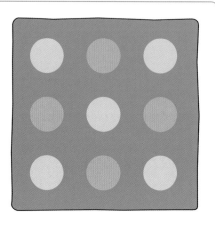

RECTANGULAR

These rugs are the most popular option and can be positioned in the middle of a room in front of a sofa, or practically right up to the edges of a room to give the impression of a fully carpeted space.

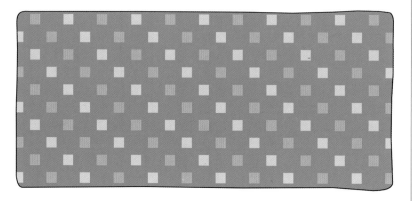

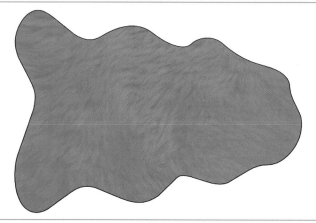

NATURAL/ANIMAL

Rugs made from natural hide or sheepskin are often left in their natural shape, giving them an authentic look. They are ideal for living rooms and bedrooms, and particularly enhance wood or stone floors. Sizes and shapes vary, so be prepared to be flexible.

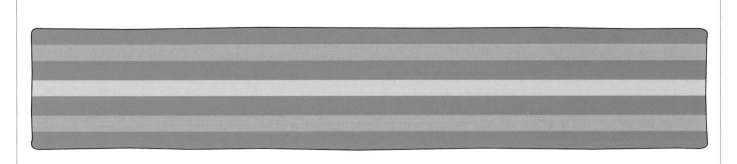

RUNNER

Mostly found in hallways, runners are long, thin, rectangular rugs available in a variety of lengths and widths, and often striped. They can add color and texture while protecting your floor, and also tend to make a space look longer.

2 CHOOSE THE MATERIAL

The fiber and weave you choose for your rug really comes down to personal preference and where you will use it. Long pile is good for creating a cozy ambience, while leather and sheepskin are perfect for modern interiors.

LONG PILE

Medium-priced long pile, or "shag," rugs add texture, comfort, and warmth. They come in a range of materials, from wool to durable synthetics, but have a tendency to shed.

FLAT WOVEN

Flat-weave rugs are made from wool or synthetic fibers such as polypropylene or polyester, hence their wide range of prices. They are suitable for use in all rooms.

NATURAL FIBERS

These medium-priced rugs made from natural fibers such as seagrass, sisal, and jute add texture, but do not have the same warmth and softness as other materials.

SHEEPSKIN

Sold in a choice of shades and sizes (which can be sewn together), these rugs are averagely priced; the pricier rugs are thicker and heavier, with denser wool.

LEATHER & HIDE

Medium to high in price, a rug of natural leather or hide is unique in its markings, color, and size. Shaggy, patchwork leather, and hide rugs are usually cheaper.

PEBBLE

Designed to look like pebbles, these expensive modern textured rugs made of pure wool stitched in various configurations are soft and comfortable underfoot.

CARING FOR YOUR RUG

With a little care and attention, you can keep your rug looking its best for years.

● If your rug is in a room that receives direct sunlight, prevent uneven fading by rotating the rug regularly; turning it every six months or so should be adequate.

● To prevent the fibers from being crushed, do not place sharp casters or narrow legs directly on your rug, or at the very least, move the furniture from time to time so that the pressure is on a different point.

● New rugs with long pile yarns and those made of wool are likely to shed fibers when you first lay them down. This should reduce during the first few weeks of use with the help of light vacuuming. However, some rugs will continue to shed throughout their life cycle.

● Clean up any spills immediately, scraping up solids and blotting up liquids (never rubbing) with a clean damp cloth.

● If you cannot remove a stain yourself, it may be worth consulting a specialized cleaner—they can often work wonders. Professionals may also be able to repair burns and holes.

5 WAYS WITH
RUGS

Rugs can be used to great effect in a living room, whether to add color or pattern, provide a focal point, or create an optical illusion. They can also make a room look more inviting and comfortable, or define a particular area if you have a large, expansive room. Decide which of these looks will suit your room.

AREA RUG

Place a large rectangular or square rug in an open-plan space and group your furniture around it or on it to help define the living or relaxing area of the room.

DON'T LIMIT YOURSELF to just one rug in a large space, but do make sure that your rugs at least complement one another if they don't match exactly.

ROUND RUG

If you have a contemporary living room and modern furniture with sleek, sharp angles, use a large round rug to soften these lines.

ROUND RUGS create a less formal look; they can be used effectively in traditional spaces, too.

THREE SLIMLINE RUGS

If you can't find one rug to occupy your space, lay three slimline rugs next to one another to fill the desired area.

HALL RUNNERS are a good buy for this type of effect. For a more relaxed look, don't line up any patterns exactly.

GROUPING OF DIFFERENT RUGS

For a really laid-back look, use a combination of different-sized patterned rugs to fill the space.

FOR THE BEST EFFECT, make sure the rugs share the same color palette.

STRIPED RUG

Make a small room appear larger with a striped rug. Horizontal stripes will make the room feel wider; vertical stripes will make it look longer.

NEUTRALLY COLORED stripes will give a more subtle effect than bright, bold colors.

5 WAYS TO
REFRESH A LIVING ROOM

A living room sometimes just needs refreshing rather than a complete renovation or redecoration. This doesn't have to cost a fortune and can be achieved within a matter of hours. Make some or all of these changes to lift the look of your living room and make it appealing again.

ADD NEW DECORATIVE PILLOWS

New throw pillows will change the look of your sofa instantly. Change all the pillow covers, or just add two or three new decorative pillows in a pattern or color that complements your sofa fabric.

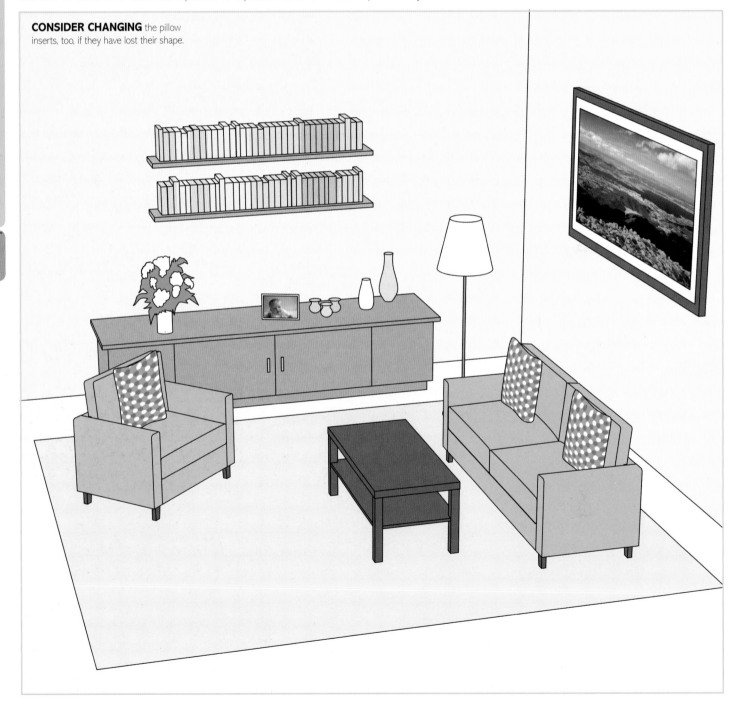

CONSIDER CHANGING the pillow inserts, too, if they have lost their shape.

CHANGE A LAMPSHADE

Lamps are easy to update: change the size, shape, and color of the lampshade to give your lamp a completely different look.

MAKE SURE that the shade is in proportion to the size of the lampstand: if it's too big or small, the overall effect will look unbalanced.

REARRANGE FURNITURE

By simply moving your sofa and coffee table to new positions, you can give your living room a fresh feel and look.

IN SUMMER MONTHS, position the sofa so that it faces the windows, and in winter turn it toward a fireplace.

RE-COVER YOUR SOFA

Pick new sofa covers, whether unfitted or custom fit, or cover individual seat and back cushions with large fabric remnants.

SWAP ACCESSORIES

Change your accessories: Why not swap smaller items such as vases, candles, and picture frames for versions in a new color or shape?

LOOK IN OTHER ROOMS for accessories that you can borrow to use in this room, too.

BEDROOM

1 WHAT TO DO WHEN
RENOVATING YOUR BEDROOM

When redoing your bedroom, or any bedroom in your house, it's essential to schedule the work in a certain order. By doing so, you'll save time, money, and the prospect of having to redo certain jobs that you might have already tackled. Follow these steps to get the schedule right.

1 DEVISE YOUR BUDGET

How much do you have to spend? Once you've decided on your budget, it's vital to use it effectively. So, if the walls need to be repaired, don't spend the majority of your budget on a new bed. Always allow yourself a contingency of at least 10 percent, too, especially if you live in an old property that might pose unforeseen problems.

2 PLAN THE LAYOUT

Draw a scale floorplan of the room and include all doors, windows, and radiators. Figure out where the furniture will be placed and use this as a guide to position electrical receptacles, ceiling and wall lights, light switches, and a TV jack, if needed.

3 REVIEW THE HEATING

Look at how the room is heated and consider whether it would be beneficial to make changes—for instance, could you gain useful wall space by moving the radiator? Would a larger radiator be more suitable for the room?

4 SCHEDULE TRADESPEOPLE

Contact an electrician, carpenter, HVAC contractor, and painter for quotes. If you're not moving walls, now is a good time for a millworker to provide a quote for built-in wardrobes or closets. Ask if other tradespeople's work will affect the job so you can get each person in at the right time.

5 ORDER YOUR MATERIALS

Once your quotes are in, order any flooring, woodwork, doors, radiators, and windows. Furniture, wallpaper, paint, carpets, and lights can be ordered once the main jobs are under way.

6 STRIP THE ROOM

Remove old wallpaper to see if the walls and ceiling need to be patched before painting or repapering. Rip out old woodwork, damaged moldings that can't be repaired, and old or unsatisfactory flooring, and remove old electric and plumbing for heating.

7 HVAC—ROUGH-IN

If you are having new pipes laid for new radiators, have this done first, since it may delay other steps.

8 ELECTRICAL ROUGH-IN

The electrician's rough-in will include running wire beneath the floors and into the walls and ceiling to provide boxes for light switches. If you are installing recessed lighting in the room, the electrician can begin the necessary work for these lighting fixtures now. Make sure that wiring for any phone and TV jacks is installed now, too.

9 INSTALL NEW WINDOWS

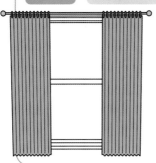

This task can be put in the schedule once the room is gutted and before sheetrock walls are closed. If windows are being renovated, prepare them for painting. While this is under way, get ready to close sheetrock walls.

10 CLOSE SHEETROCK CEILING AND WALLS

Close wall framing with sheetrock, tape the joints and screw heads, apply a skimcoat of plaster, and sand in preperation for paint.. Now is the time to have any plaster moldings repaired, or purchase new moldings.

11 LAY THE FLOORING

After the walls and ceiling are closed, you can lay hard flooring, such as wood, or a subfloor if you are having a carpet laid later.

12 HAVE WARDROBES INSTALLED

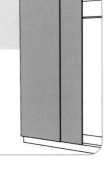

If you are having custom-made or off-the-rack wardrobes built in, have them installed now before new baseboards and moldings are put in.

13 TACKLE THE WOODWORK

Once the plaster is dry, start installing any new wood moldings—baseboards, crown trims, doors, door frames, and picture rails—ensuring first that the carpenter or millworker knows the position of any underlying plumbing and wires.

14 DECORATE

Fill any fine cracks, then paint the ceiling, walls, and woodwork, and, finally, put up wallpaper, if you are using it.

15 ORGANIZE THE FINAL INSTALL

With the decorating complete, the electrician and HVA contractor can return to install the radiators and install the light fixtures and electrical receptacles.

15 ADD FINISHING TOUCHES

Put up curtain rods or blinds, attach the door hardware, and lay a carpet if it is part of your design scheme.

2 CREATE A MOOD BOARD
FOR YOUR BEDROOM

A bedroom is a private sanctuary, a place where you should really feel at peace and be able to relax properly. So choosing the right style for your bedroom isn't just about selecting a decorative scheme or experimenting with colors and patterns, it's also about finding a look that will allow you to unwind completely and feel comfortable. With that priority in mind, you can begin to build ideas using a mood board.

1 **FIND PICTURES OF BEDROOMS YOU LIKE** by looking through books, magazines, and on the internet and either tearing them out, printing, or color-copying them. You should soon find that a theme begins to emerge or a specific style or color scheme appeals to you. Edit the pictures you've selected down to a manageable number to act as a starting point for your scheme. If you are redecorating, it's worth noting what you don't currently like about the room so you don't repeat the same mistakes.

Select a picture or two that you like, or you want to take elements from, to stick to your board as inspiration.

2 **PICK A FAVORITE ITEM**, which could be something you absolutely must include in the room—a beautiful bed, picture, or pillow, for example. Use it as a starting point for colors, patterns, shapes, or a theme.

If you're wallpapering the room, use colors within the wallpaper design as the basis for your accent colors.

3 **PICK A BACKGROUND COLOR** early on, since your walls are the biggest area to decorate. Consider how you'll use the room: should it be light so you can dress and apply makeup, or do you want a cozy, calm setting? Pin wallpaper samples and paint colors onto the mood board, keeping them in the same proportions they'll be used in the room.

Use a third accent color, if required, minimally in the room's scheme.

Choose one color as your main accent shade and aim to use the second color fractionally less.

4 **INTRODUCE ACCENT COLORS**, which can either be a subtle variation of your base color or a dramatic contrast to it (or both). Choose at least two colors, but no more than three. Play around with color combinations using swatches and samples to see if they work together successfully, then pin your favorites to the board.

5 **CHOOSE NEW FURNITURE** that you'd like to include in the room. Use the same approach as you did for choosing your color scheme to pick the right shade of fabric for a headboard or the best type of wood for wardrobe doors or a chest of drawers. To work out if the pieces will sit comfortably in the space, plot the dimensions of the room on graph paper and draw the furniture to scale.

Shape and size are important considerations in a bedroom, especially if you want to buy a new bed.

Think about whether you'd like any beside furniture to be the same style and material as, or in complete contrast to, that of your bed.

6 **ADD PATTERN AND TEXTURE** to provide visual interest and a dimension of comfort. If your wallpaper is patterned, you can still use other patterns in the room, provided that the colors are the same tones as those of the wallpaper. Or introduce texture with a rug, wall-to-wall carpeting, bedspread, or throw pillows so the room doesn't feel plain and unwelcoming. Add samples or pictures of your preferences to the mood board.

A chunky knitted throw or bedspread over the bed is an easy way to include texture in your bedroom.

If you choose a carpet or deep pile rug to add texture and extra comfort, check that it complements or tones with your mood board colors.

Accessories should either match your restricted palette or be in colors that you find calming and restful.

7 **ADD FINISHING TOUCHES** such as throw pillows, bedside lamps, pictures, and rugs. These items don't have to match perfectly, but they should be cohesive in terms of color (this is where you'll use your accent colors), style, or theme if the room is to work well. These subtle touches can make or break a room's success, so use the limited color palette and design scheme of your mood board to help you make your final choices.

3 LAYOUT CONSIDERATIONS IN THE BEDROOM

Your bedroom is inevitably a room that takes the overflow from other parts of the house, so you will need to include as much storage as you can to accommodate everything you use daily. Add to that the fact that it also has to fit in the largest pieces of furniture you'll probably own – a bed and dressers or perhaps wardrobes – and you'll realise you've got a challenge on your hands. Follow these tips to make the most of your space.

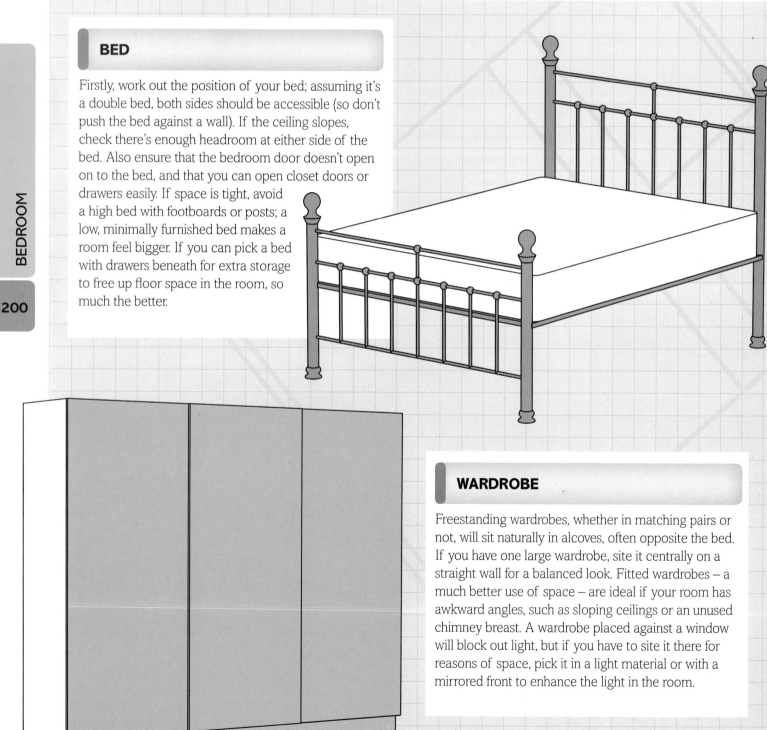

BED

Firstly, work out the position of your bed; assuming it's a double bed, both sides should be accessible (so don't push the bed against a wall). If the ceiling slopes, check there's enough headroom at either side of the bed. Also ensure that the bedroom door doesn't open on to the bed, and that you can open closet doors or drawers easily. If space is tight, avoid a high bed with footboards or posts; a low, minimally furnished bed makes a room feel bigger. If you can pick a bed with drawers beneath for extra storage to free up floor space in the room, so much the better.

WARDROBE

Freestanding wardrobes, whether in matching pairs or not, will sit naturally in alcoves, often opposite the bed. If you have one large wardrobe, site it centrally on a straight wall for a balanced look. Fitted wardrobes – a much better use of space – are ideal if your room has awkward angles, such as sloping ceilings or an unused chimney breast. A wardrobe placed against a window will block out light, but if you have to site it there for reasons of space, pick it in a light material or with a mirrored front to enhance the light in the room.

BEDSIDE TABLES

Bedside tables are all about creating a balanced look and should always come in pairs—they don't have to match exactly, but they should be similar in size. If you think you only have room for one bedside table, try sliding the bed across slightly and fitting in two mini tables or table-height shelves instead so that you don't throw off the room's balance.

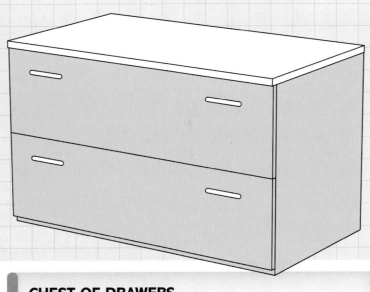

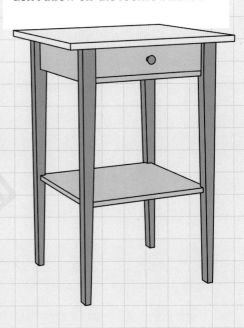

CHEST OF DRAWERS

If your bedroom is large, consider matching chests of drawers to sit on each side of the bed in place of bedside tables. This option will give you plenty of storage for lamps, books, and clothes that don't need to be hung. If there's room for only one chest of drawers, place it centrally on an empty wall and put a mirror above it as a focal point. It can also double as a vanity, but without a chair. If it has to share a wall with a wardrobe, buy one that matches the depth and style of the wardrobe for a streamlined appearance. Or, for a sleek look, place it within a run of built-in wardrobes.

VANITY

If your bedroom is big enough to hold all the essential furniture you require comfortably and you still have plenty of floor space, a vanity is a real luxury item to include. Ideally, it should be placed where the natural daylight is good—in a bay window (with a stand-alone mirror) or at right angles to a flat window (with a wall-hung mirror), for example. Ensure that there's room to sit comfortably in a chair at the vanity and that there is sufficient space for a partner to move around behind it.

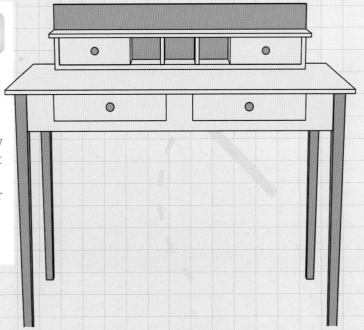

4 CHOOSE FLOORING

Comfort is likely to be high up your wish list when you choose the flooring for your bedroom. However, you should also consider what part it will play in your decorating scheme; the floor is often referred to as the fifth wall in a room. It's worth thinking, too, about how easy it will be to keep clean.

1 CHOOSE THE LOOK

If you want a cozy, relaxing look, carpet is an ideal choice, and a good way of introducing color to a room. Tiles or wood flooring give a sleek look and can be used in either a contemporary or a rustic-looking bedroom.

TILED

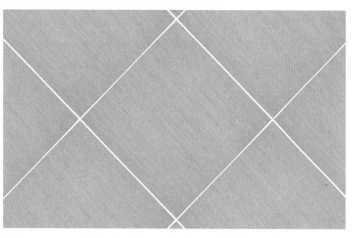

Tiles are a good choice for any bedroom, helping to keep a room cool in summer and, when teamed with underfloor heating (which is strongly recommended), warm in winter. They are also practical. Opt for large-format tiles, and consider using pale colors.

WOOD

Wood can create a contemporary or traditional look, depending on the finish and tone you choose. There are various choices: plank floors (boards that are 6–8in/15–20cm wide); strip floors (narrow boards), and parquet (laid in blocks or a herringbone design).

CARPET

Carpet feels soft and luxurious underfoot, and is available in a range of colors and designs. Solid color carpets will show more marks than flecks or patterns. Natural floor coverings like sisal are not as soft underfoot, but are an aesthetically pleasing alternative.

CHECKLIST

● **Concrete subfloors** must be clean, dry, and flat. Correct any errors using a self-leveling compound, making sure it is completely dry before laying any flooring over it.

● **If you are laying tiles over floorboards**, overlay the boards with hardboard, smooth side up. Timber treated with wood preservatives is not suitable as a subfloor.

● **Carpets are best laid** over an even surface such as plywood or chipboard. Anything with grooves creates marks in the carpet. A good-quality underlay will also ensure that it looks its best, as well as making it more comfortable underfoot.

A bedroom doesn't have as much foot traffic as the rest of the house, so you can choose the flooring almost on looks alone, if you wish. However, since you're likely to be walking around barefoot, consider comfort underfoot in summer and winter.

TILED

PORCELAIN
Porcelain flooring comes in both glazed and unglazed finishes. It is highly durable and easy to keep clean, but it can feel cold and hard underfoot. Prices vary.

CERAMIC
Low-cost ceramic tiles are less expensive than natural stone and porcelain. They won't stain, don't need sealing, and are available in many styles, shapes, and colors.

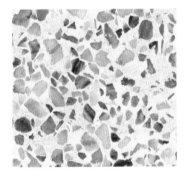

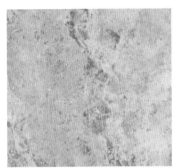

TERRAZZO
Made of marble chips in cement with a color pigment added, terrazzo has a highly polished finish. It is expensive and must be installed by a professional.

TRAVERTINE
Made from natural stone, high-cost travertine has either a sleek, polished finish or a natural tumbled look with soft edges and a spongelike appearance.

LIMESTONE
Limestone tiles are available in a highly polished gloss or rough, matte finish and a range of colors. Although expensive, their good looks make them worth the cost.

WOOD

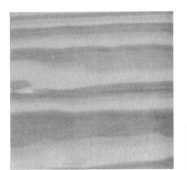

HARDWOOD
Medium to high in price, hardwood floors withstand lots of wear and tear, and can be resanded many times over to restore their natural beauty.

SOFTWOOD
If you want to paint your wood floor, softwood is a cheap or medium-priced option. Only use special packs dried in a kiln so shrinkage is kept to a minimum.

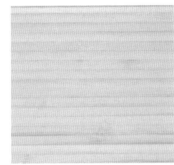

ENGINEERED WOOD
Medium-priced engineered wood has the look and feel of a solid wood floor. It can be laid as a floating floor with an underlay—a good choice for uneven floors.

BAMBOO
Medium- to high-cost bamboo flooring, which looks like wood, can be laid as a floating floor or glued or nailed down, making it suitable for most level subfloors.

LAMINATE
Cheaper than hardwood and engineered woods, laminated planks comprise a decorative wood effect image attached to a base of compressed fiberboard.

CARPET

TWIST PILE

Low- to medium-priced twist piles are extremely affordable, which makes them a popular choice. They have a coarse, rugged appearance and are very hard-wearing.

VELVET PILE

This medium- to high-priced carpet has a dense, low-cut pile and a soft, smooth appearance like suede. Its plush, luxurious finish makes it ideal for a bedroom.

LOOP PILE

A medium-priced loop pile carpet has level, uniform loops, or loops of different heights for a textured appearance. It looks like coir and sisal flooring, but has added comfort.

SAXONY

Medium- to high-priced saxony carpet is woven in loops and then sheared to make an even surface. Its deep, dense pile feels soft and smooth underfoot.

COIR

Low-cost coir, made from coconut husk fibers, has a highly textured finish that can feel rough underfoot, but it is extremely hard-wearing and nonslip.

SISAL

Medium-cost sisal has a fine texture and a subtle sheen. It is available in a range of weaves as well as a choice of colors—either used as blends or solid tones.

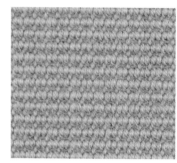

JUTE

Medium-priced jute is comprised of flat woven designs, which give it a stylish appearance. It is softer than other natural floor coverings, but not as hard-wearing.

SEAGRASS

Medium-priced natural seagrass grows in coastal meadows on riverbanks. When woven, it has a chunky appearance and a waxy texture, making it stain-resistant.

ADDING A RUG

If you have opted to use hard flooring, such as wood or tiles, in your bedroom, you should consider placing a rug beside—or on each side of—your bed.

- **Choose a deep pile** for a feeling of luxury in a color that complements the room's scheme.

- **Make sure that the rug** is weighty enough that it won't move or crease when you walk on it, causing a tripping hazard.

- **Before you finalize your decision**, check that the rug will be the right size by measuring and cutting a template out of newspaper and placing it on the floor where the rug will go.

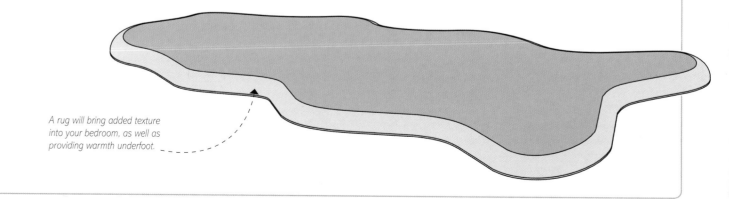

A rug will bring added texture into your bedroom, as well as providing warmth underfoot.

THE PARALLEL STRAIGHT LINES of a wood floor can help create the visual effect of a longer or wider room.

5 CHOOSE WALL COVERINGS

When choosing how to cover your bedroom walls, your main priority should be the look you want to create; you don't need to worry so much about paint or wallpaper being hard-wearing in a bedroom. So, unless your walls are very badly cracked or uneven, you have free reign to use your imagination.

1 CHOOSE THE MATERIAL

In addition to creating the right visual effect in a bedroom, you also need to consider the condition of your walls. If they are newly plastered, do as you choose, but if the walls are old and uneven, wallpaper or paneling may be a more practical choice.

PAINT

Painting your walls is a fairly quick and inexpensive way to decorate a bedroom, but don't underestimate the amount of paint you will need—between two to three coats. Light colors stretch the sense of space; deeper, rich colors create a cozy, cocoonlike feel.

WALLPAPER

If the paper you've fallen in love with is particularly expensive, or you don't feel brave enough to paper all the walls, paper a feature wall (normally the wall behind or facing the bed). Patterned wallpaper has a pattern repeat, so calculate the amount you need before starting.

PANELING

Wainscot paneling, which has a picture framelike effect and is made from solid wood or MDF, gives a traditional feel, simple tongue-and-groove paneling creates a nautical or country look, while flat wood veneer panels seem contemporary.

CHECKLIST

● **When buying wallpaper** it is worth getting an extra 10% as a contingency. Make sure that it is all from the same batch, so that the colors match perfectly, and that you will have enough paper to match up the repeat pattern of a patterned wallpaper.

● **Have you prepared** your walls correctly? Whether you paint or paper the walls, fill and sand any cracks and holes and smooth uneven areas.

● **Sample jars allow you** to check the finish of paint as well as the color; where possible, avoid matte paints that are chalky, since they cannot be easily cleaned if they become marked.

2 CHOOSE THE TYPE

The type of paint, wallpaper, or paneling you choose will have a dramatic effect. Paint is sold in various finishes, each giving a different look; wallpaper is available in a variety of styles and textures; and paneling comes in a wide range of looks.

PAINT

MATTE

Matte emulsion is a nonreflective water-based paint that minimizes imperfections on uneven walls. It suits both modern and traditional bedrooms. Prices vary greatly.

SATIN

A good choice for small or dark bedrooms, medium-priced satin paints have a subtle sheen that reflects light. These paints are durable, too.

METALLIC

For a touch of luxury, use a medium-cost metallic emulsion paint. Or buy metallic shimmer paints that can be painted over a matte color to create a subtle sheen.

SUEDE EFFECT

Suede-effect, medium-priced emulsion, available in a range of rich colors, has miniscule grains that give a brushed look. Apply it with random brush strokes.

WALLPAPER

PLAIN OR PATTERNED

Use plain paper as an alternative to paint, or use patterned paper for a decorative effect. Machine-printed paper is cheap; hand-printed designs cost much more.

FLOCK

Flock wallpaper has a velvet texture and is available in rich colors, so it can be used to create a dramatic look. It is more expensive than other wallpapers.

METALLIC

Medium to high in price, metallic wallpaper comes in a variety of patterns, including contemporary florals and retro geometric designs, and plain and textured finishes.

TEXTURED

Medium-priced textured wallpapers are thicker than other papers and are typically white with a choice of raised patterns. Use it left white or painted on uneven walls.

PANELING

TONGUE & GROOVE

Cheap- or medium-cost tongue-and-groove paneling can give a nautical, country, or retro look. The boards are usually made of pine—or buy ready-made MDF panels.

FLAT WOOD VENEER

Cover a wall in medium- to high-priced veneer panels to create a mid-century look. Iron-on wood veneer on a sheet of MDF that is then attached to the wall is best.

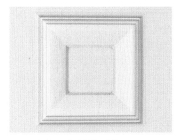

WAINSCOT PANELING

This medium-priced paneling can add interest to plain walls in a traditional or contemporary room. Consider wallpapering inside the paneled frame itself.

HANG
WALLPAPER

Wallpapering is a skill that is worth mastering for the money you can save on installation fees. Each wallpaper requires a particular thickness of paste, so always check the instructions before you mix the solution—a paste that is too thick or too thin will cause the wrong amount of expansion in the paper.

WHAT YOU NEED

- Wallpaper
- Tape measure
- Pencil
- Wallpaper paste
- Paste applicator/brush
- Level
- Wallpaper brush
- Scissors
- Knife
- Sponge
- Small sponge roller

1 PREPARE THE PAPER

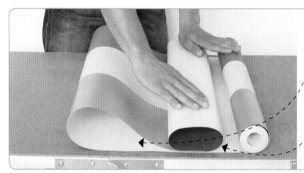

1 UNROLL A SECTION of paper and turn it back on itself. Be aware that it will have a tendency to spring back into a roll.

2 ROLL IT UP in the opposite direction until it will lie flat.

3 MEASURE TO SIZE (allow 4in/10cm more than the height of the room), then line up, mark, fold, and cut along the fold. For a pattern with a repeat you want to run across a wall, take this into account when deciding on the sheet size.

2 PASTE THE PAPER

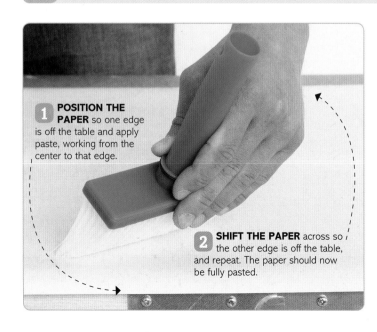

1 POSITION THE PAPER so one edge is off the table and apply paste, working from the center to that edge.

2 SHIFT THE PAPER across so the other edge is off the table, and repeat. The paper should now be fully pasted.

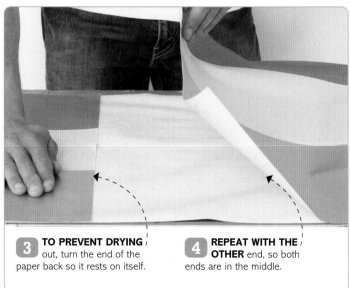

3 TO PREVENT DRYING out, turn the end of the paper back so it rests on itself.

4 REPEAT WITH THE OTHER end, so both ends are in the middle.

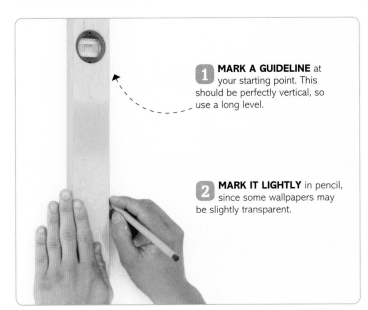

1 **MARK A GUIDELINE** at your starting point. This should be perfectly vertical, so use a long level.

2 **MARK IT LIGHTLY** in pencil, since some wallpapers may be slightly transparent.

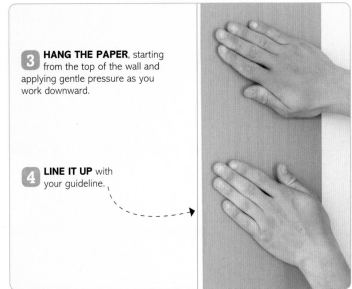

3 **HANG THE PAPER**, starting from the top of the wall and applying gentle pressure as you work downward.

4 **LINE IT UP** with your guideline.

5 **USE A BRUSH** to smooth the paper, working outward to remove any bubbles that are below the surface.

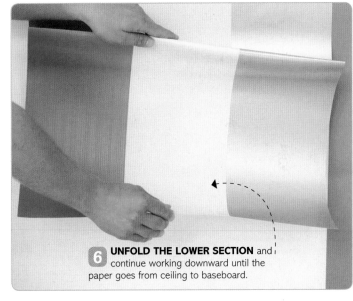

6 **UNFOLD THE LOWER SECTION** and continue working downward until the paper goes from ceiling to baseboard.

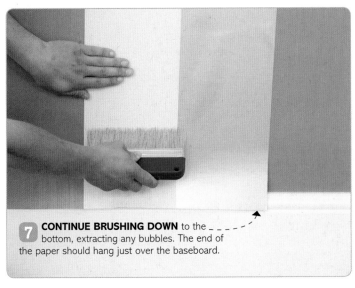

7 **CONTINUE BRUSHING DOWN** to the bottom, extracting any bubbles. The end of the paper should hang just over the baseboard.

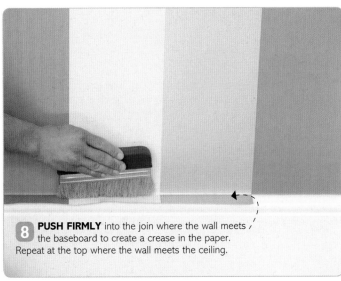

8 **PUSH FIRMLY** into the join where the wall meets the baseboard to create a crease in the paper. Repeat at the top where the wall meets the ceiling.

4 TRIM THE PAPER

1 EMPHASIZE THE CREASE using a hard, pointed, but blunt implement such as a closed pair of scissors.

2 THE CREASE where the wall meets the baseboard should now be sharply defined.

3 TO TRIM THE PAPER, leaving a good, straight edge, take a sharp razor or craft knife and cut along the crease. You can use the baseboard itself as a guide.

4 USE THE BRUSH once more along this edge to ensure that the very bottom of the paper is stuck down firmly—otherwise, it could start to peel away as it dries.

5 WIPE ALONG THE BASEBOARD using a damp sponge to remove any traces of paste left on the woodwork. Repeat these steps at the top of the wall.

1 **HANG THE NEXT SHEET** as close as possible to the first, using the same procedure as before.

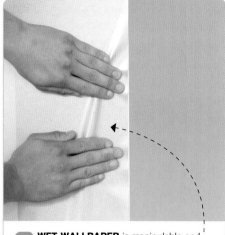

2 **WET WALLPAPER** is manipulable and you will be able to ease it across until it is just touching the first sheet.

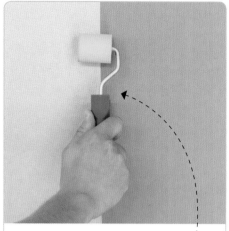

3 **USE A SPONGE ROLLER** along the seam between the two sheets. This will ensure that they are stuck down at the edges and absorb any excess paste.

6 CHOOSE A BED

As is often the case with the largest piece of furniture in a room, your bed will be a major focal point and will undoubtedly set the tone for the style of your bedroom. Do not think solely about its appearance though—never forget that your bed needs to be as comfortable as possible.

1 DECIDE ON SIZE

The first thing to consider before buying your bed is size. Check how much floor space you have in your bedroom, and buy the biggest bed you can fit comfortably into the room. It's advisable to buy a bed that is 4–6in (10–15cm) longer than the tallest person who sleeps in it.

2 CHOOSE THE STYLE

Box springs are essentially a base for the mattress, and will either have a platform top or springs. Bedframes are chosen more for their looks, and come in a wide range of designs and materials.

STORAGE BED

With a deep, fabric-covered base that often incorporates storage, these are a popular type of bed. Remember that you will need a bedskirt to cover the base if yours is not upholstered in a good-looking fabric. If you choose a model with drawers, make sure that the layout of your room will not prevent you from opening them fully.

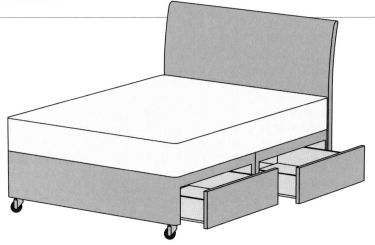

UPHOLSTERED BOX SPRING WITH LEGS

A box spring on legs will look more contemporary than a basic box spring and, provided that the legs are tall enough, give you the opportunity for under-bed storage. You won't need to use a bedskirt with this type of box spring, but you should make sure that the material it is covered in fits with your room's décor.

BOX SPRING

A box spring bed consists of a wood-framed and sprung base (the box spring) upon which the mattress rests, plus a metal framework that elevates everything off the floor. Since box springs and mattresses are engineered to work together as a set, mixing and matching is not advised.

PLATFORM BED

Platform beds come in a huge range of designs, including elegant sleigh beds, romantic four-poster beds, and country-style paneled or slatted beds. Solid wood bedframes are more expensive than wood-effect frames, but will last considerably longer. Choose from cherry, birch, ash, and walnut wood, to name but a few.

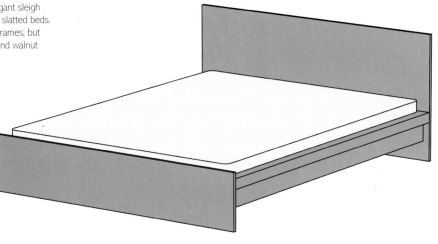

METAL BEDFRAME

Metal bedframes are available in both traditional and contemporary designs and in a variety of colors and finishes, including antique brass, nickel, and powder-coated steel. The design of metal frames is often very ornate.

UPHOLSTERED BEDFRAME

Upholstered bedframes are available in choice of fabric, leather, or leather-effect material. You can often choose the fabric used to upholster your bed, making it completely custom to you. The covers are attached, so can only be wiped clean if they become dirty.

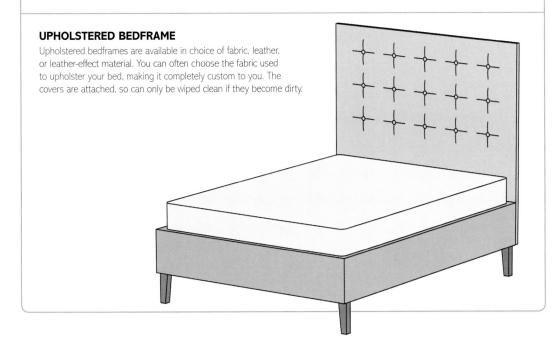

MATTRESS TYPES

Choosing a mattress is just as important, if not more so, as buying the bedframe. It is also often more expensive.

● Open-spring mattresses are made of coiled springs wired together, which move as one and evenly distribute body weight over the surface of the mattress.

● Pocket-spring mattresses are generally of a superior quality and more expensive. The springs are individually wrapped in fabric pockets and packed closely together, working independently to respond to your weight and ensure that two people on the mattress don't roll together.

● Memory-foam mattresses respond to individual weight, pressure, and body heat to form the perfect support. This type of mattress helps to prevent aches and pains.

● Latex mattresses also conform to your body's contours and can help to minimize pressure on joints. They are hypoallergenic, so beneficial for people who suffer from respiratory problems.

6 WAYS WITH
HEADBOARDS

Make a statement in your bedroom with a decorative headboard. Whether it's made of fabric or painted directly onto the wall, a headboard creates impact by making your bed look more substantial and inviting. It can be as high as you like, but keep its width the same as, or just slightly greater than, that of the bed.

BEDROOM

214

FABRIC STRETCHED OVER A FRAME

Make your own headboard using a favorite fabric stretched and stapled onto a wood frame the same width as the bed.

YOU DON'T HAVE TO STICK TO PLAIN FABRICS for a headboard: if your bedding is mostly plain, you can use the headboard to bring pattern into the room.

DECORATIVE PANELS

Fretwork, or cutwork, panels create an unusual backdrop to your bed. Use different-sized panels to form a rectangular shape.

FOR GLAMOROUS APPEAL, spray the panels with metallic paint before securing them in place.

CLASSIC

For a classic look, choose an upholstered headboard with button detailing. This will give your bed a chic, boutique hotel feel.

DON'T ALWAYS OPT for a flat fabric—choose a textured velvet if you want to create a luxurious feel.

WALLPAPER

You can create a decorative headboard effect on the wall itself— hang lengths of patterned wallpaper where the bed will be situated.

FABRIC-COVERED PANELS

Cover foam rectangles in fabric to make two individual headboards. Leave a gap of approximately 4in (10cm) between panels.

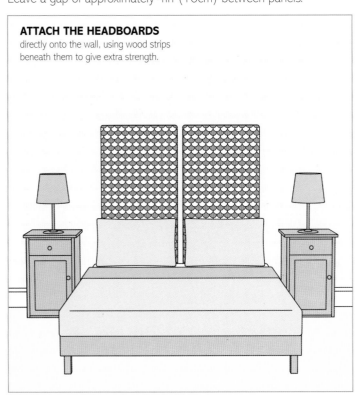

ATTACH THE HEADBOARDS directly onto the wall, using wood strips beneath them to give extra strength.

PAINTED PANELS

If you're not brave enough to decorate your walls with a bright color or pattern, painted MDF panels attached to the wall are a good alternative.

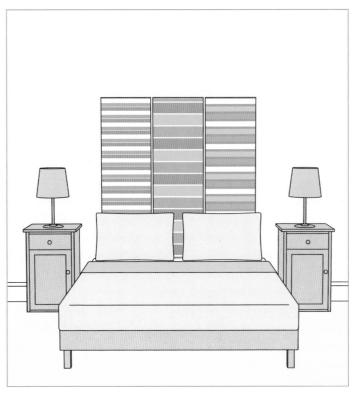

MAKE
A HEADBOARD COVER

Adding personalized touches can help to pull the look of your bedroom together, as well as incorporate an extra element of color, texture, or even glamour that makes it truly yours. To give your bed a more defined structure and accentuate it as a focal point, add a headboard and cover it in your choice of fabric.

WHAT YOU NEED

- Colored fabric
- Scissors
- Pins
- Needle and thread, or sewing machine

1 MEASURE THE FABRIC

1 MEASURE THE SIZE OF THE HEADBOARD before you buy, measure, and cut your fabric; you need to know the width, height, and depth.

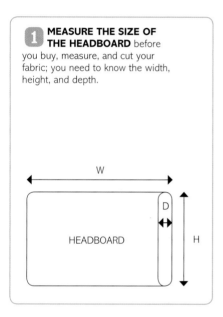

2 CUT THE FABRIC to the width of the headboard plus ¾–1½in (2–4cm) seam allowance. The length should be twice the height of the headboard plus the depth, plus a similar seam allowance. For the ties, cut out 12 pieces of fabric measuring 20in (50cm) by 3in (7cm).

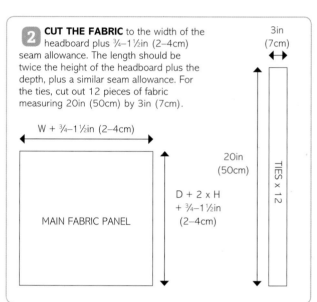

2 PREPARE THE HEM

1 CLIP A SMALL TRIANGLE from each corner of the large piece of fabric to reduce the bulk of material when sewing the seams.

2 FOLD OVER THE EDGES of the fabric, about ½in (1.5cm), and iron them all flat.

3 **FOLD OVER ONE EDGE** once more and pin it in place.

4 **FOLD IN** the corner neatly, making a small triangle.

5 **FOLD OVER** the adjoining edge of fabric again and pin it in place. Repeat with the remaining edges and corners.

3 STITCH THE HEM

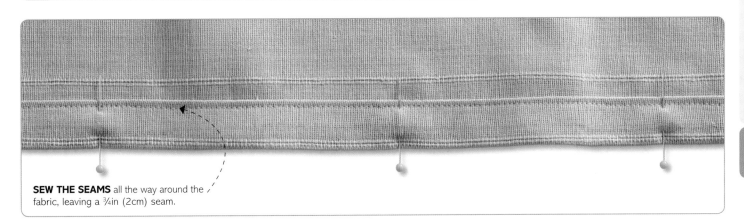

SEW THE SEAMS all the way around the fabric, leaving a ¾in (2cm) seam.

4 MAKE THE TIES

1 **FOLD OVER THE SHORT ENDS** of each tie and iron them flat.

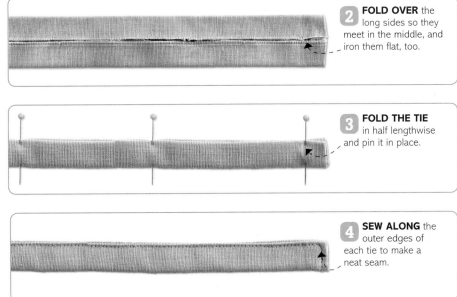

2 **FOLD OVER** the long sides so they meet in the middle, and iron them flat, too.

3 **FOLD THE TIE** in half lengthwise and pin it in place.

4 **SEW ALONG** the outer edges of each tie to make a neat seam.

5 ATTACH THE TIES

1 PIN THE TIES to the inside edges of the fabric. Pin four ties along each side, plus two along the top and two along the bottom.

2 ENSURE THE TIES are positioned correctly so that when the cover is folded in half, each tie aligns with one on the other side.

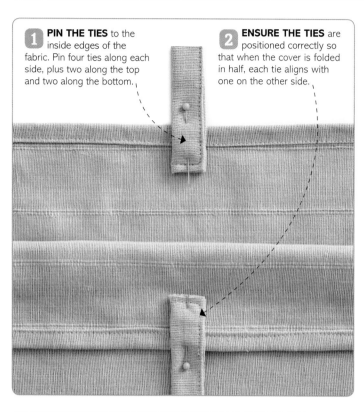

3 SECURE EACH TIE in position with a square seam, which will help to reinforce the join.

6 COVER THE HEADBOARD

PLACE THE FABRIC COVER over the headboard and secure each pair of ties in a bow.

5 WAYS TO
DRESS A BED

There are many ways to dress a bed to create a range of looks, from formal to relaxed. It is worth spending a bit of time getting the look you want just right, since your bed is the main focal point of the bedroom and the area you want to look most inviting when you walk into the room.

MIX AND MATCH PATTERNS

Cover most of a white comforter with a striped bedspread or quilt, arranged so that the stripes are vertical. Add throw pillows that use matching colors and tones, but in a different pattern.

TURN DOWN the top of the bedspread so that a little of the white comforter shows at the top.

COUNTRY

Arrange a folded plaid blanket across the end of the bed. Add a single decorative pillow with a folk art design in front of the pillows.

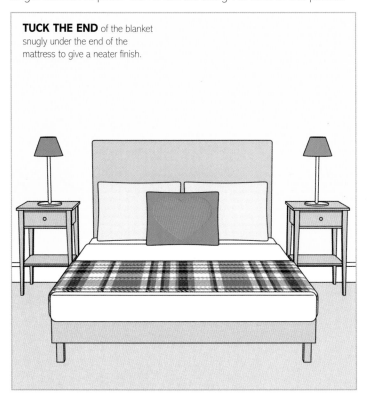

TUCK THE END of the blanket snugly under the end of the mattress to give a neater finish.

FLOOR LENGTH

Not only is a floor-length bedspread a good way to conceal an unattractive boxspring and frame, it also creates a feeling of opulence.

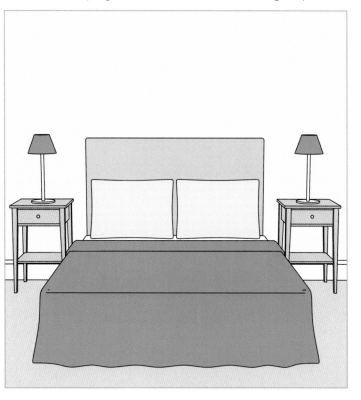

CONTEMPORARY

Place a folded satin or velvet bedspread at the end of the bed. Team it with two matching throw pillows and add a patterned bolster pillow.

ARRANGE YOUR BEDSPREAD at the end of, or about three-quarters of the way down, the bed.

TEXTURED

Lay a wool blanket diagonally across the bed, then add a small faux fur blanket. Finish off the look with textured and furry throw pillows.

USE AN UNEVEN NUMBER of throw pillows for a more laid-back look.

MAKE
ACCENT PILLOWS

Accessories can be easily added to a bedroom to lift the atmosphere from plain and simple to cozy, relaxing, or luxurious. If your bedroom needs freshening up, or you want to make it feel more inviting or sumptuous, make accent pillows in a fabric (or fabrics) of your choice to scatter over the pillows on the bed.

WHAT YOU NEED

- Colored fabric
- Iron
- Pins
- Sewing machine, or needle and thread
- Buttons
- Buttonhole cutter (optional)
- Polyester pillow

1 MEASURE AND CUT THE FABRIC

FOR EACH ACCENT PILLOW, measure and cut a piece of fabric: use the following dimensions (right) to cover a 24 x 16in (60 x 40cm) pillow, or adjust these measurements if your pillows are a different size. The upper and lower sections of fabric identified by the dotted lines (2 x 12in/ 30cm) will be folded over each other to make an "envelope" front to the pillow.

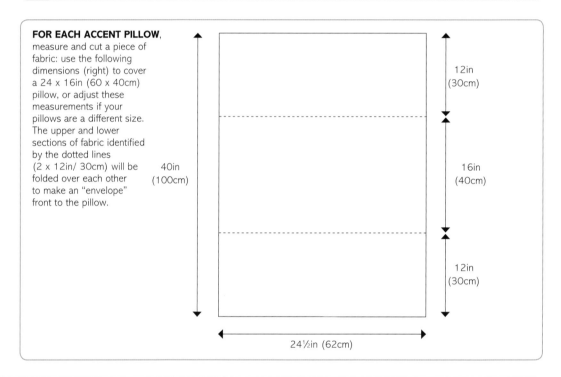

40in (100cm)

12in (30cm)

16in (40cm)

12in (30cm)

24½in (62cm)

2 STITCH THE HEM

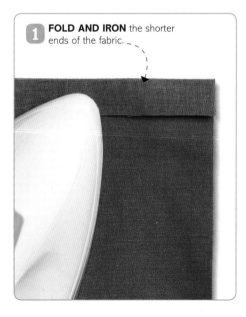

1 FOLD AND IRON the shorter ends of the fabric.

2 FOLD THE SAME ENDS over again, iron them once more, and secure the hem in place with pins.

3 SEW THE SEAM. This will make the front of your pillow, so make this seam as neat as possible.

3 FOLD THE FABRIC

1 **LAY THE FABRIC** out flat, right side up, and measure the distances 12in (30cm) and 28in (70cm) from the top of the fabric. Mark each point in the center of the fabric with a pin.

2 **FOLD THE TOP** of the fabric over at the point of the top pin, then fold the bottom of the fabric on top of it at the point of the bottom pin (the fabric is folded like this initially to identify where to place the buttonholes).

4 MAKE THE BUTTONHOLES

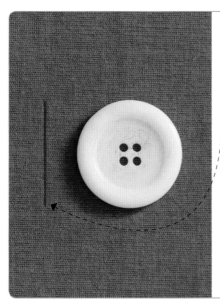

1 **MEASURE FOUR EQUIDISTANT POINTS** along the length of the bottom flap of fabric. Make a short mark with a pen at each point. The mark should be the same length as the buttons you have chosen.

2 **SEW ALONG** either side of the marked line. If you are using a sewing machine, make this a zigzag stitch with a width of 3 and a length of ½ stitch.

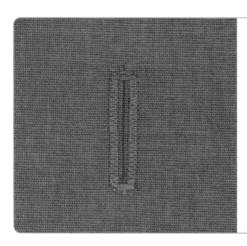

3 **NOW SEW EACH END** of the buttonhole. If you are using a sewing machine, use the maximum stitch width and hold the fabric still while you sew. Make sure you cover the sides with this stitch to secure them.

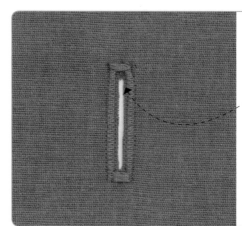

4 **CUT ALONG** the marked line, using a specialized buttonhole cutter if available. Cut carefully, making sure you don't cut the stitching.

5 SEW THE SEAMS

1 **REFOLD THE FABRIC,** this time with the top flap covering the bottom flap (hiding the buttonholes), then pin the fabric together at the sides.

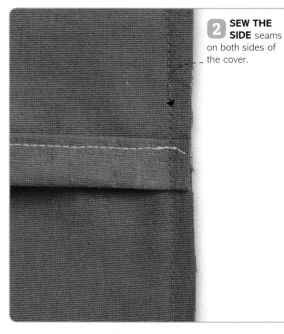

2 **SEW THE SIDE** seams on both sides of the cover.

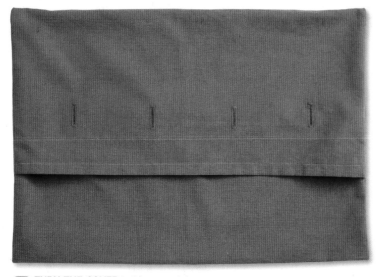

3 **TURN THE COVER** inside out so it is the right way around and lay it out flat.

4 **SEW ON THE BUTTONS** with a needle and thread, then insert the polyester pillow.

7 CHOOSE A WARDROBE

Since it is one of the largest pieces of furniture in your bedroom, you will want your wardrobe to be as attractive as possible. However, the size of the wardrobe and its storage options should be your most important considerations, or you may end up with a beautiful piece of furniture that isn't at all practical.

1 BUILT-IN OR FREESTANDING

When considering whether to choose built-in or freestanding wardrobes, ask yourself which look you prefer, which would suit the style of your home, which would be more space efficient for the shape of your room, and what your budget can handle.

BUILT-IN

Built-in wardrobes are more space efficient, so are an ideal choice if you need lots of clothes storage or if your room is an awkward shape. They can be fully custom, or at least to your specification, so you can get what you need without compromise.

FREESTANDING

Available in a wide range of materials, designs, and styles, freestanding wardrobes offer a versatile choice of looks. They tend to come in standard sizes, so you should search for one that best suits the space you have available.

2 CHOOSE TYPE OF DOOR ACTION

The type of door action you choose may be a style choice, but there are also practical considerations. If you're short on space, sliding doors may be best, as you won't need quite the same amount of space you would require to open hinged doors.

HINGED

Hinged doors on your wardrobe will allow you to see the entire contents of the unit when open. If your wardrobe will occupy a somewhat cramped space, though, check that you will be able to open the doors fully. Before you buy, make sure that the construction of the hinges is tough enough to withstand years of use.

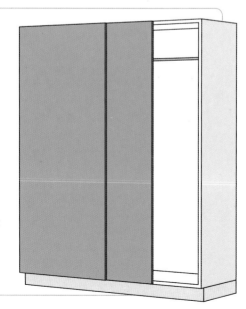

SLIDING

Many larger or built-in wardrobes come with full-height (often floor to ceiling) sliding doors. Two- or three-door combinations are usual. Bear in mind that with these doors you won't be able to see all of your clothes at once—one section will always be hidden by a door. Always ensure that the sliding action is well constructed.

3

CHOOSE THE SIZE

Choose your wardrobe according to how much space you have and how many clothes you want to hang (if you own more clothes that need to be folded rather than hung, a greater amount of drawer space will prove more valuable).

SINGLE DOOR

The most slimline option, a single-door wardrobe will offer limited storage but may be the only choice in a small room. Check the depth of the door to make sure that you have enough space to open it fully.

TWO DOOR

Two-door wardrobes are a classic freestanding choice. This design often comes with a drawer, or set of drawers, at the bottom, although check that they are deep enough to be practical.

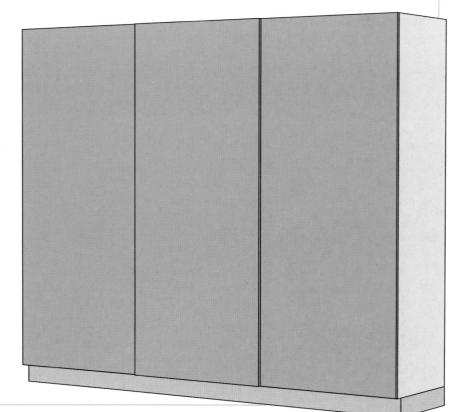

THREE OR MORE DOORS

Larger wardrobes with three or more doors provide plenty of space to include storage options such as shelving, drawers, or shoe racks alongside your hanging space. This allows you to keep all your clothing in one place, without the need for additional chests of drawers or other storage.

4 INTERNAL STORAGE OPTIONS

Your wardrobe's internal storage is every bit as important as its external appearance. Consider all your storage needs, weighing up how much hanging space—long and short—and how much shelf and drawer space you need.

FULL-LENGTH HANGING ONLY

If you want to hang long items, such as dresses, pants, and coats, choose a full-length wardrobe so the clothes can hang without obstruction. With this option, you will need other furniture, such as a chest of drawers, to store any clothes that you do not want to hang.

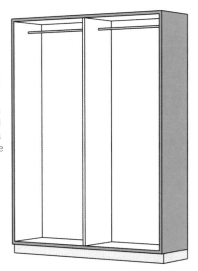

MULTIPLE-HEIGHT HANGING

Multiple-height hanging combines a full-height rail for long clothes with half-height rails for items such as shirts. Bear in mind that the interior of a man's wardrobe will look very different from that of a woman, who is more likely to need more full-height space for her clothes.

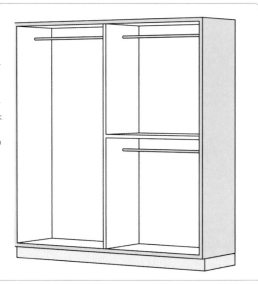

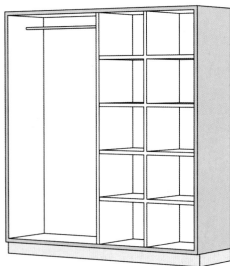

HANGING AND SHELVES

A combination of hanging space and open shelves works when you have clothes that you need to hang and those that you prefer to keep folded. Make sure the shelves are wide enough for the items you plan to store, and ensure that they are adjustable so you can arrange them to suit your needs.

HANGING AND INTERNAL DRAWERS

If you don't have space in your bedroom for a separate chest of drawers, look for a wardrobe that includes an integral one. Choosing one with different-sized drawers will allow you to store everything from scarves to bulky sweaters.

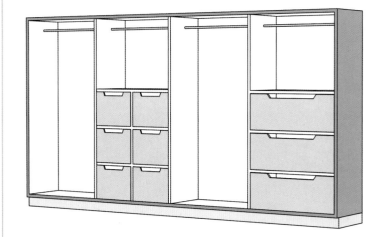

ALL STORAGE TYPES

Some wardrobes, especially built-in options, come with all types of storage: multiple-height hanging, shelves, and drawers. Consider carefully whether you have the right combination for the type of clothes you own and how you would like to store them.

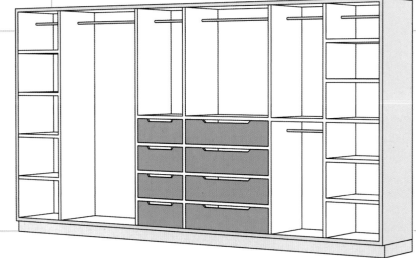

CHOOSE THE HARDWARE

A wardrobe with sliding doors may have just a groove or rail for your fingers rather than knobs, but if it does need hardware, choose pieces that are in proportion to the piece of furniture and will complement its look.

BAR PULL

These angular handles come in various lengths and different finishes, the most common being stainless or polished steel. Bar pulls best suit very contemporary wardrobes and chests of drawers or dressing tables.

D

These pulls are similar to a bar pull, but are curved at the corners for a softer shape. Available in a range of lengths and finishes, they also suit contemporary furniture, but are a better match for pieces with curves within their design.

BOW

Shaped as a single smooth, streamlined curve, bow pulls are simple and elegant. They can be narrow or wide, round or flat, so they can suit a variety of different furniture styles. They are available in a variety of finishes.

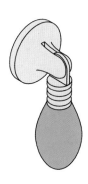

TEARDROP

The design of this classic pull shape gives a neat look to your furniture. It is available in a wide range of metal finishes; the teardrop is usually made from the same metal as the rest of the pull, or from ceramic.

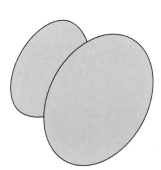

KNOBS

Knobs are available in a huge selection of sizes, materials, and shapes. For traditional-style bedrooms, choose a wood or porcelain finish, or for a more modern room, choose brushed or polished metal.

DECORATIVE KNOBS

If you want to have a bit of fun with the design of your bedroom hardware, look for something that is designed to look like a flower for grown-up bedrooms, or footballs or fairies for children's rooms. These knobs are made from a range of materials, from plastic to metal.

CLOSET ORGANIZERS

If you are designing your closet interior from scratch, you will find it easy to make sure your storage needs are met. However, you may find the storage offered by your closet is less than ideal if you have picked it primarily for its outward appearance or you have redone an existing closet. If so, there are ways to remedy the situation: various organizers are available that enable you to use the space in your closet differently.

● A hanging organizer (right) can be fastened to a hanging pole to provide soft shelving for folded clothes, shoes, and accessories. A typical organizer has six compartments and measures 12in (30cm) wide. Narrower versions specifically designed to store shoes are also available.

● An organizer with three or more rows of storage pockets that hangs against the inside of the closet door can be suspended from the top of the door on hooks. These over-the-door organizers are useful for storing flat shoes, belts, scarves and other small items and accessories.

● Wire cube organizers are another good way to divide up your closet space. Their modular design means that you can create a framework of cubes to suit the space. Sit the framework inside the closet to create extra shelving.

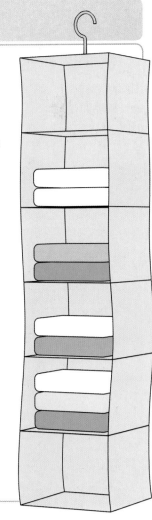

PLAN THE PERFECT
WALK-IN CLOSET

If you have a storage room or an otherwise unused, awkward space in your bedroom, turning it into a walk-in closet will use the space efficiently, help you to organize your clothes properly, and allow the bedroom itself to be a space reserved purely for relaxation and rest. Follow these tips for the best results.

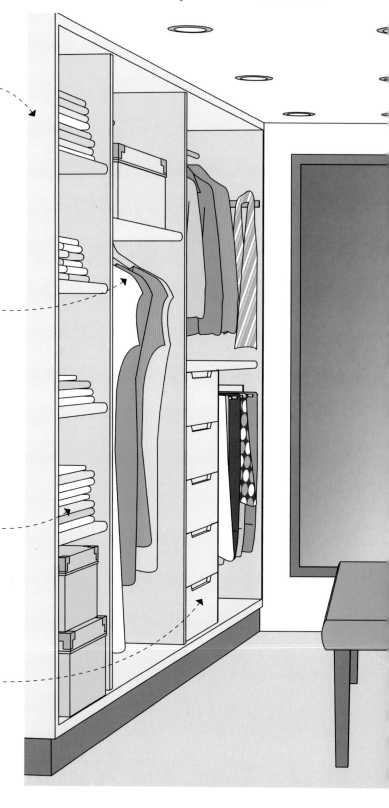

BEDROOM

230

USE BUILT-IN FURNITURE

Professionally custom-fit furniture allows you to maximize your storage space from floor to ceiling and work around any awkward angles and sloping ceilings. If your budget is low, try off-the-shelf modular furniture, but plan it down to the last detail. It's best not to include doors on the cabinets: your clothes will be concealed by the door to the room, or you can use a screen or curtain if your closet is within another room.

INCLUDE HANGING SPACE

Assess your current closet and try to gauge how much hanging space you need, and of what type. Allow room for long garments, shorter clothes such as shirts and skirts, and consider including slide-out pants hangers. The hanging rods don't have to be together; it makes more sense to group clothes according to type and season (all winter clothes together, all skirts together, all shirts together, and so on).

INSTALL OPEN SHELVING

Open shelving is useful for clothes that you wear regularly and that do not require hanging, such as T-shirts, vests, and light sweaters. Also install open shelving overhead for items you rarely need to access.

INSTALL DRAWERS OR BASKETS

Whether you choose drawers in which to store bulky sweaters that don't need to be hung or baskets for lighter items such as underwear, you will find them a useful addition. If you can, create a dressing table by incorporating a drawer for makeup at tabletop height, with legroom beneath and a mirror above.

INSTALL GOOD LIGHTING

Effective lighting is a must. Install lights within cabinets with deep hanging spaces and above or around a dressing table. Make sure the room is well lit, if not by daylight then by recessed downlights or overhead spotlights.

COMPARTMENTALIZE YOUR SPACE

If you share a wardrobe with your partner, it makes good sense to divide it in two and design each half separately. This will help you to make better use of space, keep you from mixing up your clothes, and create a more organized closet overall.

HANG A MIRROR

A full-length mirror is a must in a walk-in closet or dressing room. Mount it on an empty wall or on the back of a door. If you have ample floor space, opt for a freestanding mirror in one corner. Make sure that the light around the mirror is good, and if you will be applying makeup at a dressing table, add a second mirror above your makeup drawer.

MAKE ROOM FOR SHOE STORAGE

Divide your shoe storage into separate sections for sports shoes, everyday and evening shoes, and boots. Install sloping shelves for shoes (or shelves with a rod for the arch of each shoe to rest on) and open shelves for boots with space above. Never underestimate how much shoe storage you need.

MAKE SPACE FOR SEATING

It is always helpful to have somewhere to sit in a walk-in closet, and especially important if you have included a dressing table. A simple stool, that you can approach from all sides, is a practical choice. Alternatively, consider a bench running down the center of the space, or one built into a run of cabinets against the wall.

ADD A LAUNDRY BASKET

If you will be undressing in the walk-in closet, include a laundry basket in your scheme. It should be lidded to keep the space smelling fresh and looking neat. To save space, it could even double up as a bench with a lift-up lid and storage within.

REVAMP
A WARDROBE

If you have wooden furniture that is still good but doesn't suit your new decorating scheme, consider whether you can revamp it rather than replacing it. This sequence shows you how to transform an old pine wardrobe, giving it an aged, antique look.

WHAT YOU NEED

- Medium-grade sandpaper
- Tack cloth or all-purpose cloth
- Shellac
- Wood primer
- Two tones of interior wood paint (one lighter, the other slightly deeper or a subtly contrasting color)
- Paintbrushes (including a natural bristle brush)
- Fine-grade sandpaper (wet-to-dry)
- Clear lacquer

1 PREPARE THE WOOD

1 SAND ALL THE WOOD surfaces of the wardrobe (including the insides of the doors if you want to paint them) to get rid of as much old varnish as possible and create a "tooth" for the paint to adhere to.

2 WIPE DOWN THE WOOD with a tack cloth or a slightly damp all-purpose cloth.

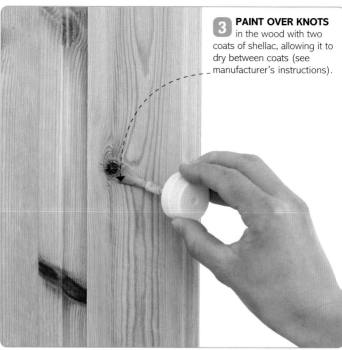

3 PAINT OVER KNOTS in the wood with two coats of shellac, allowing it to dry between coats (see manufacturer's instructions).

1 **APPLY A LAYER** of primer to the wardrobe and allow it to dry (see the manufacturer's instructions).

2 **APPLY AN UNEVEN COAT** of colored paint using a natural bristle brush with loose bristles. Drag the paint roughly over the wood in any direction. Keep the brush as dry as possible by dabbing any excess paint from the brush with a cloth.

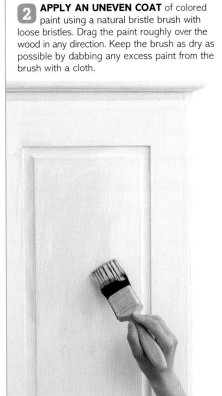

3 **BUILD UP THE TEXTURED LAYERS** of paint until you are happy with the color. The more layers of paint you apply with the bristle brush, the deeper the color and the stronger the texture. Allow to dry.

4 **PAINT A DEEPER** or subtly contrasting color into the recesses and corners of the wardrobe using the same rough, dry-brush technique. Allow to dry.

5 **APPLY ANOTHER LAYER** of primer using the dry-brush technique so that the layers of colored paint beneath still show through. Allow to dry.

3 SAND DOWN THE WARDROBE

1 **LIGHTLY SAND** areas of the wardrobe with fine-grade sandpaper to create the impression of aging.

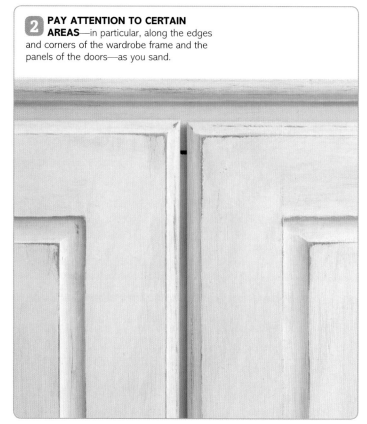

2 **PAY ATTENTION TO CERTAIN AREAS**—in particular, along the edges and corners of the wardrobe frame and the panels of the doors—as you sand.

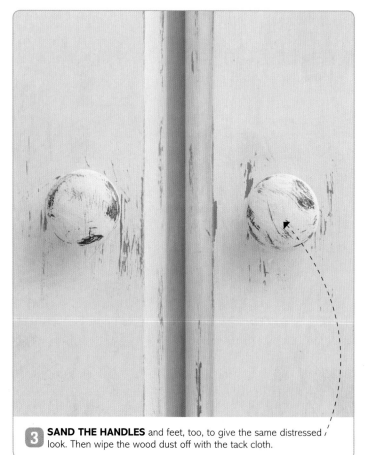

3 **SAND THE HANDLES** and feet, too, to give the same distressed look. Then wipe the wood dust off with the tack cloth.

4 COAT WITH LACQUER

APPLY A COAT or two of lacquer to protect the surfaces of the wardrobe, if you wish.

BEFORE

8 CHOOSE
BEDSIDE UNITS

Usually bought in pairs for double bedrooms, bedside units come in modern and traditional styles and a variety of materials, including wood, acrylic, and mirrored glass. Whether you match them to your other bedroom furniture or go for an eclectic, contrasting style, make sure they suit your storage needs.

CHOOSE THE TYPE

When considering which type of bedside unit you want, think how you will use it and whether it has to provide you with storage. Bedside units are available in many different designs, from simple tables to those with open shelving or drawers.

TABLE
If you only want something on which to stand a lamp and an alarm clock, go for a neat, streamlined table. Many such units have a single drawer or shelf to provide limited storage.

DRAWERS
Bedside units with drawers are a good option for small bedrooms where other storage space is limited. They will also help an otherwise cluttered space feel more tidy.

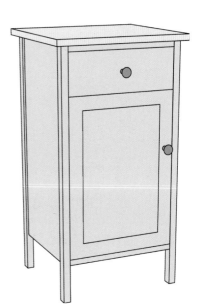

CUPBOARD
A cupboard unit allows you to store larger items that may not fit easily into a drawer. Remember though that cupboard space is more difficult to organize than drawer space.

SHELVING
In a contemporary room, open shelving within a bedside unit is a good choice, assuming you can keep the contents neat. Or use the unit as a mini bookcase.

CHOOSE
A DRESSING TABLE

A dressing table can be a useful addition to a bedroom: as well as providing a place to get ready in the morning, it can also free up valuable storage space in the bathroom, and can even double as a spot where you can sit and do some paperwork.

CHOOSE THE TYPE

If your dressing table is purely to provide a place where you can do your hair and makeup, most types will be suitable; however, if you need it to double as a desk, check that there is adequate table space and make sure you can keep it free of clutter.

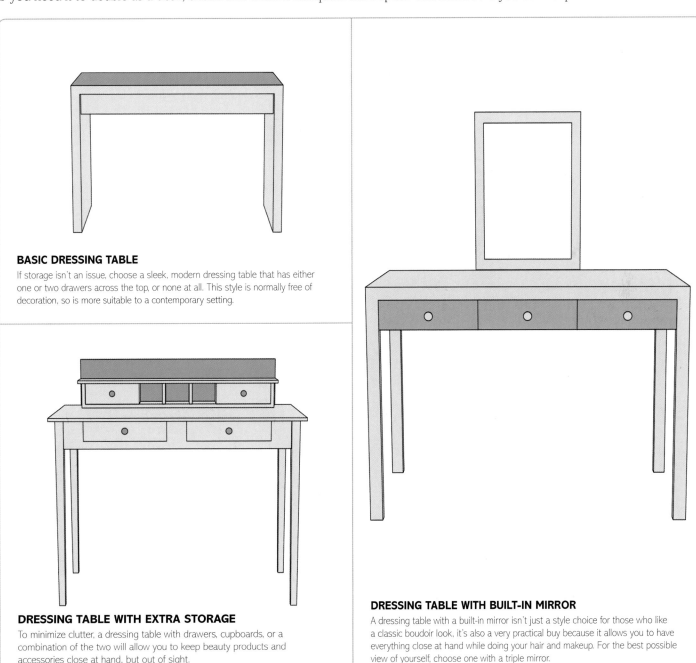

BASIC DRESSING TABLE
If storage isn't an issue, choose a sleek, modern dressing table that has either one or two drawers across the top, or none at all. This style is normally free of decoration, so is more suitable to a contemporary setting.

DRESSING TABLE WITH EXTRA STORAGE
To minimize clutter, a dressing table with drawers, cupboards, or a combination of the two will allow you to keep beauty products and accessories close at hand, but out of sight.

DRESSING TABLE WITH BUILT-IN MIRROR
A dressing table with a built-in mirror isn't just a style choice for those who like a classic boudoir look, it's also a very practical buy because it allows you to have everything close at hand while doing your hair and makeup. For the best possible view of yourself, choose one with a triple mirror.

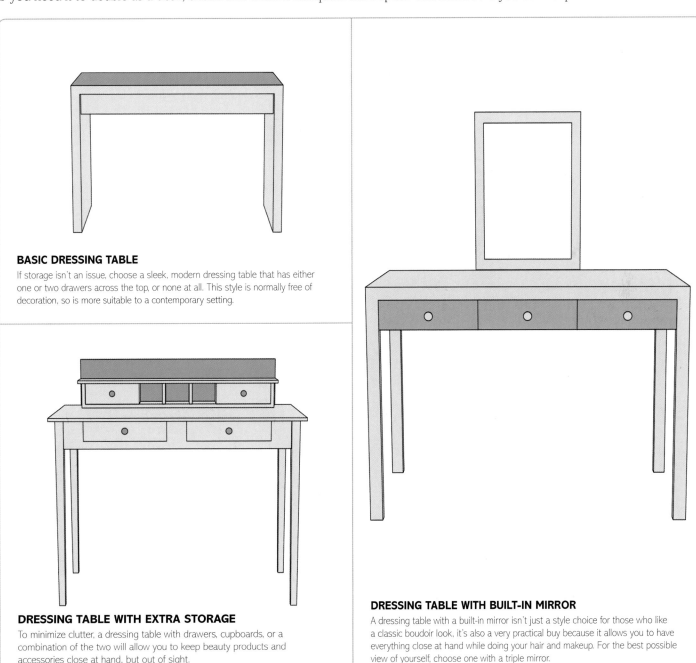

5 WAYS WITH
BEDSIDE LIGHTING

Good bedside lighting is essential for both practical and decorative purposes. From a decorative point of view, low-level lighting is vital for making a bedroom feel welcoming; from a practical angle, a bedside light to read by—or save you from having to get out of bed to turn off an overhead light—is a must-have.

SWING ARM

An swing arm lamp, either a small version that stands on the bedside table or a large version that stands on the floor, gives you lots of scope to adjust the angle and height of the lamp.

RETRO-STYLE swing arm lamps are available in a range of colors, so choose one that suits the look of your bedroom.

TABLE LAMPS

Table lamps are a classic choice for bedside lighting. Look for ones that will complement the style of the other lights in the room.

THE SIZE of the lamps you choose should be in proportion to the size of your bedside tables.

CLIP ON

If you have a tall headboard or a shelf behind your bed, clip-on lighting provides a versatile solution that can be moved easily.

PENDANT

Pendant lighting over bedside tables creates a contemporary look. Make sure that the size of the shade doesn't dwarf the table below.

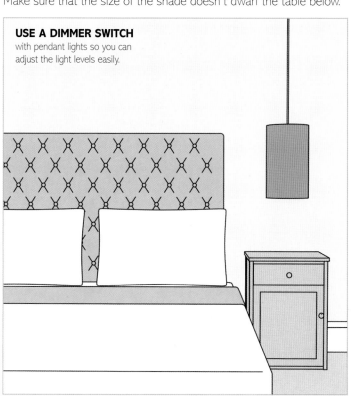

USE A DIMMER SWITCH with pendant lights so you can adjust the light levels easily.

WALL SCONCES

Wall sconces won't take up any space on your bedside table, and in small rooms they won't dominate the space.

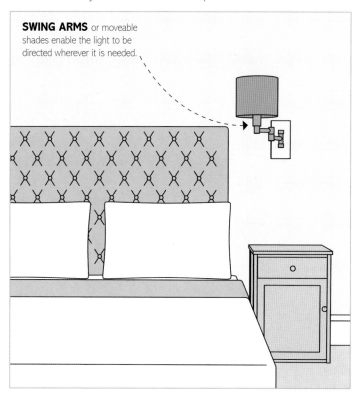

SWING ARMS or moveable shades enable the light to be directed wherever it is needed.

Whether you spend time in your bedroom during the day or not, you will need good lighting first thing in the morning—ideally natural daylight, or at least effective task lighting—and soothing lighting at night. You might also want your lights to improve the room's proportions, and naturally you'll want them to look good.

1 DECIDE ON A STYLE OF LIGHTING

Just as in other rooms, aim for a combination of lighting styles that can achieve a variety of moods in the room at any given time. If you apply makeup, do your hair, or dress in the room, you'll also need good task lighting to see what you're doing.

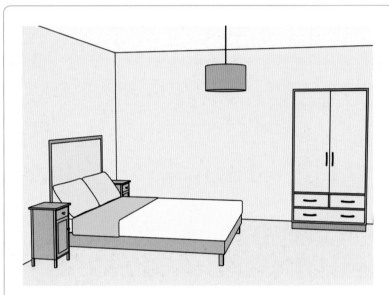

AMBIENT

Ambient lighting is vital in a bedroom. Particularly in the evenings, you will undoubtedly want to dim the lights to help you unwind before bed. Lamps and overhead lights are usually the primary sources of ambient lighting; make sure you include a dimmer switch for adjusting the latter.

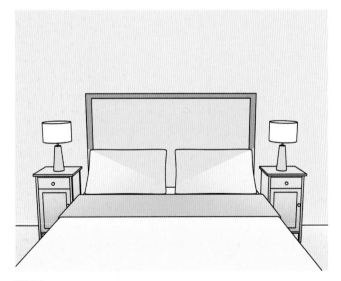

TASK

Task lighting in a bedroom may be a lamp that you use for reading in bed or an over-mirror light that allows you to see yourself clearly close-up. In the mornings, daylight is often the best source of light, so don't ignore this in favor of artificial light if you can arrange your room in such a way as to use natural light effectively.

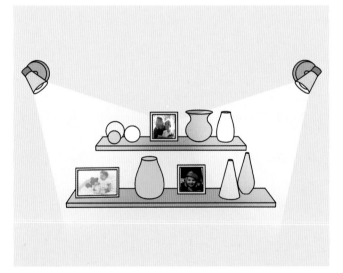

ACCENT

Accent lighting is typically used to show off a piece of art or sculpture, or perhaps illuminate a focal point such as an architectural detail. In a bedroom, you can also use it to illuminate a bookshelf or a favorite collection. You won't need a high level of accent lighting in a bedroom, so use it sparingly.

An average-sized bedroom may only have two or three lights, so make sure they work together design-wise and provide the right levels of light. You don't have to choose coordinating pieces, but they shouldn't compete with each other for attention.

CEILING LIGHTS

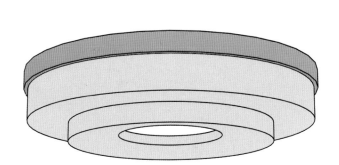

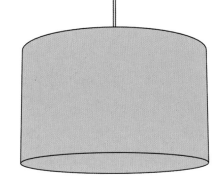

PENDANT LIGHT

Pendant lights tend not to give off the brightest light, but that may suit you if you want your overhead light to be atmospheric rather than bold. Bear in mind that you can also use small pendants on each side of the bed in place of bedside lamps.

SURFACE-MOUNTED CEILING LIGHT

If your bedroom is low-ceilinged and its proportions modest, a surface-mounted ceiling light hung snugly to the ceiling will help to make the ceiling feel as high as possible; lower-slung pendants will invade the vertical space and lower it visually. If the room is large, you can afford to go for a show-off fixture that hangs lower down.

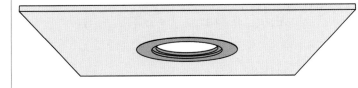

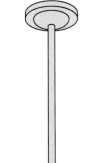

STATEMENT LIGHTING

If you have a large bedroom, choose a statement light as your centerpiece and make sure it can be used with a dimmer switch. Otherwise, you'll find that you only switch it on occasionally. Match it with bedside lamps that match in style but don't compete for attention.

RECESSED DOWNLIGHTS

A contemporary bedroom that's north-facing or has a low ceiling will benefit from recessed downlights, especially on dark mornings when you'd really prefer natural daylight. However, don't use recessed downlights as your only source of bedroom lighting—team them with some lamps and use a dimmer switch so that you can adjust the light levels as you wish.

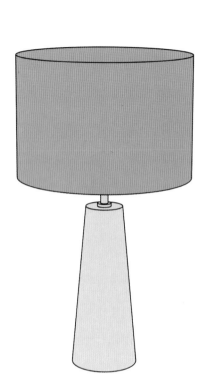

TABLE LAMPS

Just as table lamps in a living room create soft pools of relaxing light, bedside lamps conjure up a similar atmosphere. Bear in mind when installing them that they need to sit at the right height so that when you lie in bed reading, the light illuminates the space but doesn't shine right into your eyes.

FLOOR LAMPS

If you have room in your bedroom for an armchair, a floor lamp standing next to it makes a nice decorative feature, but it may also encourage you to sit and read there or spend time doing craft projects. Make sure the shade isn't too large for the room and that it provides you with decent task lighting if you will be using the light in this way.

CLIP-ON LIGHTING

Clip-on lights, attached to a headboard or a shelf above the bed, are a good lighting solution in bedrooms where there isn't the space for a bedside table and lamp. You could also consider including them, regardless of what other lighting you have, if you need an extra light source for discreet late-night reading.

WALL-MOUNTED LIGHTS

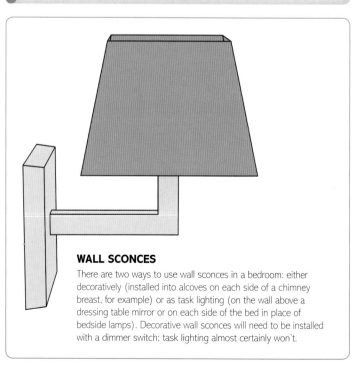

WALL SCONCES

There are two ways to use wall sconces in a bedroom: either decoratively (installed into alcoves on each side of a chimney breast, for example) or as task lighting (on the wall above a dressing table mirror or on each side of the bed in place of bedside lamps). Decorative wall sconces will need to be installed with a dimmer switch; task lighting almost certainly won't.

11 CHOOSE WINDOW TREATMENTS

There are two considerations to think about when choosing bedroom window treatments. First, will the combination of window treatments keep out light, noise, and cold efficiently? Second, does your choice work decoratively to help you create a scheme that's comfortable and relaxing?

1 CHOOSE A TYPE

The style of your room—contemporary and pared back, or traditional and layered—will help you choose whether to opt for more than one type of treatment, such as blinds with curtains, or stick to a single, subtle treatment such as sleek shutters.

BLINDS

Fabric roller and Roman blinds are a good choice if you want to introduce layering, color, and pattern to a bedroom. Their design means you can pull them fully up or down, or anywhere in between. Venetian blinds are typically left down with the slats open or closed.

CURTAINS

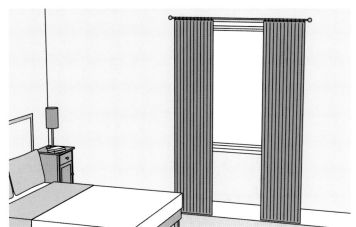

Curtains, whether full- or sill-length, are a good way of adding color, pattern, and texture to your room's scheme and, depending on the fabric and curtain heading you choose, can be used in both traditional and modern homes.

SHUTTERS

Shutters are a popular choice for period homes, but they look stylish in modern homes, too. Solid shutters are available in limited designs. Louvered shutters can be designed with either two or three panels and in styles including full-height and tier-on-tier.

> **CHECKLIST**
>
> ● **To keep out as much** street lighting as possible at night, consider adding blackout roller blinds under curtains, or buying blackout-lined Roman blinds.
>
> ● **If your windows** are not double-paned, heavy, lined curtains will help prevent heat loss. They can also give the room a visual warmth.
>
> ● **Consider the amount of space** around your window and make sure that you will be able to pull back curtains fully or open shutters. By doing so, you can make the room seem larger and let in more light.

2 CHOOSE A STYLE

Each type of window dressing can look traditional or modern, depending on its materials, its pattern or design, and what it's matched with—bed linen, wall coverings, and flooring. Base your choice on these other elements so that they all work together.

BLINDS

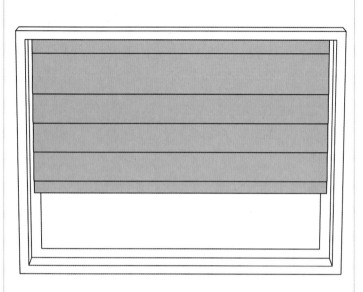

ROMAN

Roman blinds have soft pleats that hang flat against the window when lowered and fold neatly together when raised, which gives them a more layered look than other blinds. Available in a wide choice of fabrics, they are particularly attractive when matched with curtains.

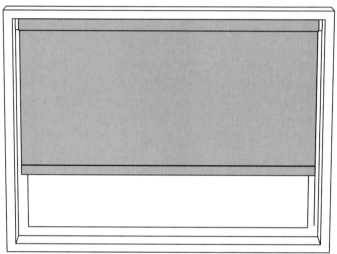

ROLLER

Roller blinds are a relatively inexpensive option and, providing you're fairly handy, are easy to install. Blinds are made from stiffened fabric and available in a wide range of colors and designs, and can be pulled up or down to block out or let sun in. Many ready-made roller blinds can be cut smaller to fit your window exactly.

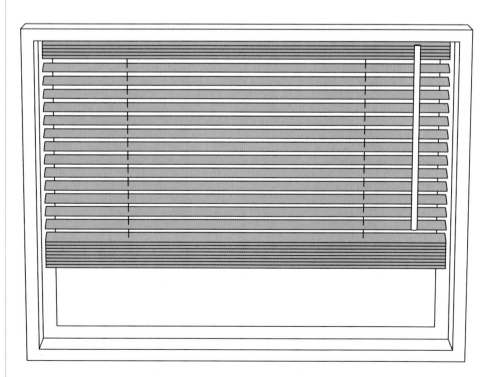

VENETIAN

Venetian blinds have adjustable slats that you can open and close, allowing you to control the amount of light coming through the window. The angled slats also make them good for windows that may be overlooked by neighbors. They are available in a choice of materials, colors, and slat widths.

CURTAINS

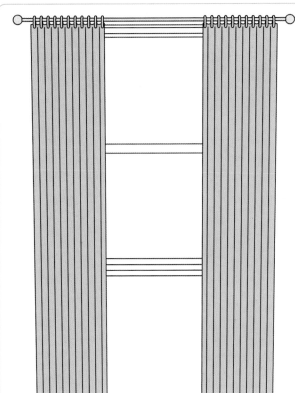

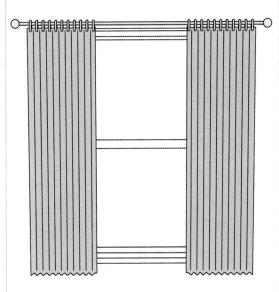

FULL LENGTH

Full-length curtains should typically finish ½in (1cm) from the floor, but if you want a more luxurious finish, have them made longer so that they drape—or pool—onto the floor. Lined curtains hang better than unlined, and the lining also improves both the insulation and the appearance of the top fabric.

SILL LENGTH

For small windows, or country-style bedrooms, sill-length, or just below sill-length, curtains may be a more practical choice, since they sit neatly at your window. These curtains are also worth considering if your radiators sit directly below a window. This curtain length can look old-fashioned, however, so pick your fabric carefully.

SHUTTERS

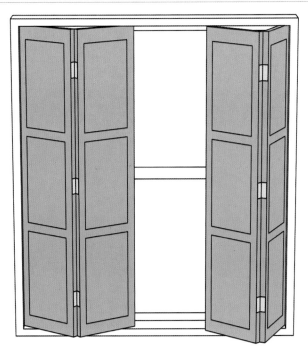

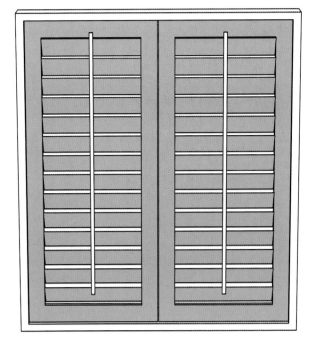

SOLID

Made from solid wood, solid shutters can assist in reducing noise levels, so they are a good choice if you live on a busy street. Designed to be closed shut at night and folded back against the wall during the day, this style of shutter particularly suits tall, thin windows, but is also good for bay windows.

LOUVER

Louvered shutters suit both modern and traditional bedrooms. The best options are tier-on-tier or full-height shutters with a mid-rail, which allows you to control the top and bottom sections independently, so you can close the bottom half for privacy and leave the top slats open to let in light.

MAKE
BLACKOUT CURTAINS

Curtains lined with a blackout lining will keep unwanted light out of a bedroom, helping you get a peaceful night's sleep. The curtains made in this sequence are just below sill-length, with a pencil pleat heading that can be used with any kind of rod or track.

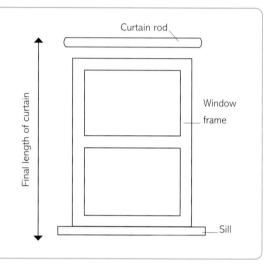

WHAT YOU NEED

- Tape measure
- Fabric—use curtain-weight cotton material (see page 384 for quantity)
- Blackout lining (see page 384 for quantity)
- Scissors
- Sewing machine, or needle and thread
- Iron
- Pins
- Pencil pleat tape
- Curtain hooks
- Curtain rod

1 MEASURE AND CUT

1 **DETERMINE WHAT LENGTH** the finished curtains need to be by measuring from the top of the curtain track or rod to just below the sill.

2 **CUT THE FABRIC** to length, adding an extra 10in (25cm) for hem and top edge allowance.

Curtain rod

Window frame

Final length of curtain

Sill

2 JOIN THE FABRIC

JOIN TOGETHER lengths of fabric to make up the necessary width (for these curtains to hang nicely, the width of each should be roughly equivalent to the entire length of the track or rod). To join, place the lengths together, right side to right side, and sew a seam along one edge. Then open up and lay flat, right side down, and press the seam open with an iron.

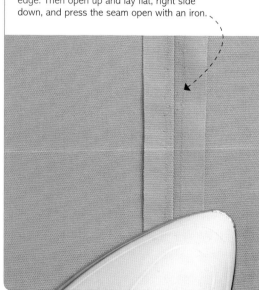

3 HEM THE FABRIC

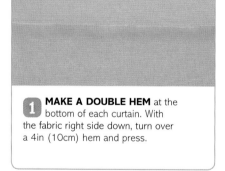

1 **MAKE A DOUBLE HEM** at the bottom of each curtain. With the fabric right side down, turn over a 4in (10cm) hem and press.

2 **FOLD AGAIN** so that the raw edge is concealed within the hem, and press again.

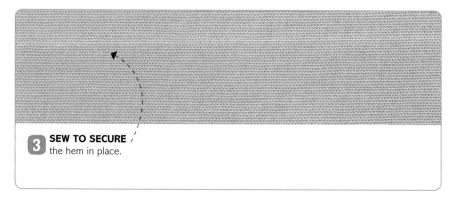

3 **SEW TO SECURE** the hem in place.

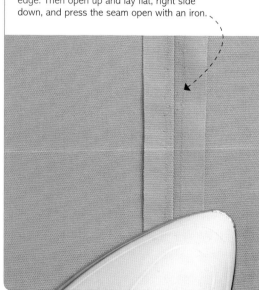

BEDROOM

246

4 JOIN THE LINING

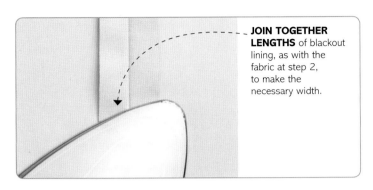

JOIN TOGETHER LENGTHS of blackout lining, as with the fabric at step 2, to make the necessary width.

5 HEM THE LINING

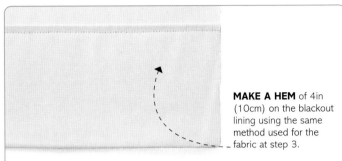

MAKE A HEM of 4in (10cm) on the blackout lining using the same method used for the fabric at step 3.

6 JOIN THE FABRIC AND LINING

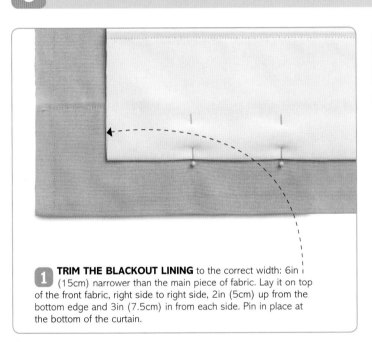

1 **TRIM THE BLACKOUT LINING** to the correct width: 6in (15cm) narrower than the main piece of fabric. Lay it on top of the front fabric, right side to right side, 2in (5cm) up from the bottom edge and 3in (7.5cm) in from each side. Pin in place at the bottom of the curtain.

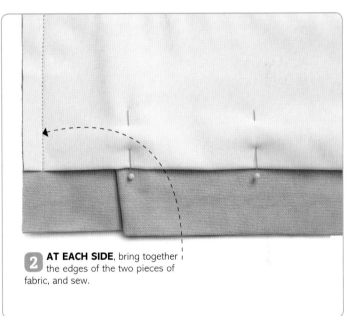

2 **AT EACH SIDE**, bring together the edges of the two pieces of fabric, and sew.

7 SEW THE CORNERS

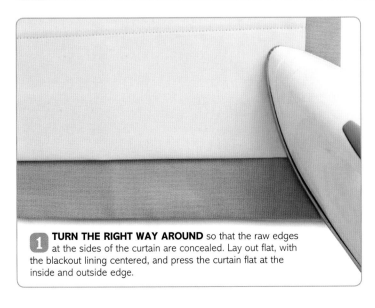

1 **TURN THE RIGHT WAY AROUND** so that the raw edges at the sides of the curtain are concealed. Lay out flat, with the blackout lining centered, and press the curtain flat at the inside and outside edge.

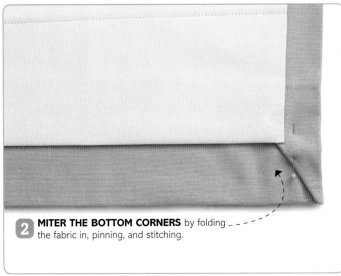

2 **MITER THE BOTTOM CORNERS** by folding the fabric in, pinning, and stitching.

8 SEW THE TOP EDGE

1 MEASURE UP FROM THE HEM and put in a row of pins where you want the top of the curtain to be.

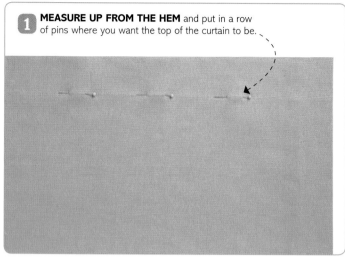

2 FOLD THE FABRIC back along this line.

3 PRESS DOWN along the line.

4 FOLD THE FABRIC in to create a neat, mitered corner.

9 ATTACH THE PENCIL PLEAT TAPE

1 LAY A LENGTH of pencil pleat tape along the top of each curtain. Trim to size, pin in place, and sew to secure.

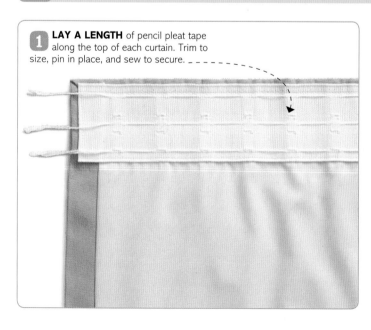

2 LEAVE THE THREADS loose at the outside edge. At the inside edge, tuck them around the back of the tape before you sew it down.

10 DRAW IN THE PLEATS

1 **PULL THE LOOSE THREADS** at the outside edge to create a row of pleats at the top of the curtain.

2 **LOOP THE CURTAIN HOOKS** through the holes in the pleats. Tie the threads together to secure and wrap up the loose ends so they are out of the way.

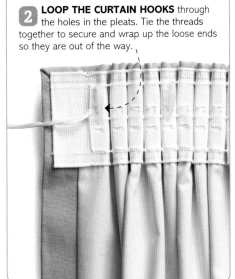

11 HANG

HOOK ON TO the curtain rings if using a rod, or hang directly on to the track.

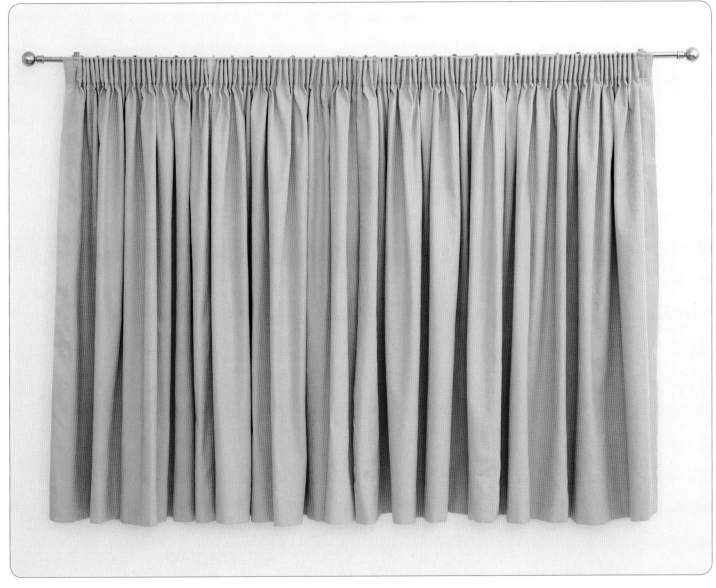

PLAN THE PERFECT
CHILD'S BEDROOM

Planning a child's room takes real thought, since it needs to accommodate activities such as playing and homework as well as sleeping, and it also needs to be able to evolve over time as your child grows. The following pages 250–267 are all about bedrooms for younger members of the family.

MAKE CLOTHES ACCESSIBLE

From the time children are about four—and often before they can even dress themselves—they want to select their own clothes to wear, so it makes sense to store their clothes in an accessible place. Look for versatile closets with hanging space and adjustable shelves to cope with your child's growing needs. Arrange everyday clothes in the lower drawers of a dresser or closet and save the top of the closet for less well-used or out-of-season items. Secure any tall pieces of furniture to the wall so they can't be pulled over accidentally.

WORK IN STORAGE SPACE

When investing in storage, don't be tempted by anything themed or with a particularly fussy finish. Ideally, large pieces of furniture shouldn't have to be replaced—their style should endure and appeal for years. They should also remain as useful as when you first bought them: buy a changing table that can become a teenager's chest of drawers; a bookshelf for story books that can in turn hold CDs and study folders; and a closet with shelves for a small child's outfits that is easy to convert into hanging space for an adult-sized teen's clothes.

PROVIDE A STUDY SPACE

Once children start to get homework, they need a dedicated, quiet space to study. Look for a desk that's adjustable so it can be used by both a 10-year-old and an 18-year-old. Make sure that it has enough built-in storage, too, to hold stationery, exercise books, and files.

CHOOSE FLEXIBLE FURNITURE

Your best option is to choose furniture that grows with your child. The bed will be your biggest buy, so consider one in a neutral color that can be lengthened as the years pass. Or, pick a crib that can be transformed into a small bed. If you can buy a bed with built-in (or under-bed) storage, do so—the amount of storage space a baby requires can't begin to compare with that of a teenager. Whatever you buy, make sure it's stable, of a good enough quality to withstand the wear and tear of being in a child's room, and is easy to clean.

CREATE ZONES

However small your child's bedroom is, structure it so that there are defined areas for sleeping (the bed), playing (a rug and toy box or play table), and reading (a chair) or homework (a desk). Make sure that each area has its own, very functional, piece of furniture and handy storage nearby so that the areas don't become confused. Zoning the room like this will help to make it feel tidier and will make it easier for your child to keep it neat, too.

MAKE SPACE FOR PLAY

If you want to encourage your child to play in his or her bedroom, it's important to devote some floor space to this activity. Small children may want a table to color at or an accessible toy box next to a comfortable rug; older children will appreciate a cozy corner with a beanbag or chair near a bookshelf for reading. If space is tight, you might have to furnish the room cleverly—with a bed on stilts and a play area beneath, for example.

1 CHOOSE
FLOORING

When choosing the flooring for your child's bedroom, comfort is likely to be high on your wish list. However, you may also want to consider what part it plays in the decorating scheme and how easy it is to clean if the bedroom is used for activities other than sleeping.

CHOOSE THE MATERIAL

Children's bedrooms are likely to be subject to more wear and tear than an adult's bedroom, so you will need to choose something that is hard-wearing and easy to clean. Softness underfoot and noise-reducing properties are also worth considering.

TILED

Vinyl tiles are an inexpensive floor covering and come in various colors and designs suitable for kids' rooms, including wood and metal treadplate. Rubber tiles are more expensive, but are hard-wearing and are available in a huge range of colors and textures.

WOOD

A wood floor is a good choice for a child's room, since you can update the rest of the décor around it. Engineered wood can be installed with an acoustic underlay, so is ideal for teenage bedrooms. Softwood, laminate, and wood-effect vinyl are cheap, practical options.

CARPET

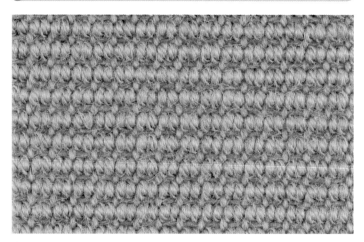

Carpet is soft underfoot and is available in a wide range of colors and designs, such as stripes, that are suitable for kids' rooms. If opting for a solid-color carpet (which will show marks more easily than one with a fleck or pattern), look for an easy-to-clean material.

SEAMLESS

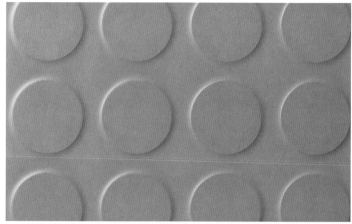

Vinyl, linoleum, and rubber sheet flooring are soft underfoot and any spills are easy to clean. Seamless floors, whether textured, plain, or patterned, are particularly good for small spaces, since the lack of joints give a neat finish.

2 CHOOSE
WALL COVERINGS

You can really have some fun decorating your child's bedroom walls. However, don't get too carried away with using a favourite theme throughout the room—your child is sure to grow out of it before too long and you may face the prospect of having to redecorate again.

CHOOSE THE MATERIAL

When choosing how to decorate your child's bedroom, your main concern should be how it looks. Remember, too, to make sure that it has a surface that is simple to wipe clean and can be touched up or repaired easily.

PAINT

The cheapest and quickest of choices, paint is available in a variety of finishes, but you are best off using satin or eggshell paints, which are more durable than matte emulsions, and any marks can be wiped off without damaging the paint.

WALLPAPER

There are endless designs of patterned wallpaper available, although choose a design your child won't outgrow too quickly. It's also best if you pick a wallpaper that can be easily wiped clean of grubby fingerprints.

PANELING

Tongue-and-groove paneling works well, since it's hard-wearing and can be painted any color you choose. The boards are usually made of pine (although you can buy preformed, routed MDF panels), and installed vertically between the chair rail and baseboard.

CHECKLIST

● **If you choose a paint with a matte finish**, use a sample pot first and check that the finish is not too chalky; if it is, it won't wipe down well if you need to remove marks or scuffs.

● **Do you have enough wallpaper** to decorate the whole room? It's worth buying an extra 10% wallpaper as a contingency, but ensure it's all from the same batch so the colors match perfectly.

● **Prepare your walls properly.** Whether your walls are being painted or papered, any cracks and holes need to be filled and sanded back and any unevenness needs to be smoothed out.

MAKE AND APPLY
A WALL STENCIL

If you have chosen a theme for your child's bedroom, a wall stencil may help to pull the design scheme together. This sequence uses a simple frog shape, a template for which can be found on page 387. Stippling (see step 3) is not essential, but it does help to give the image a little more depth and interest.

WHAT YOU NEED

- Paper (optional)
- Pen or pencil (optional)
- Acetate sheet
- Magic marker
- Craft knife
- Masking tape
- Wall paint
- Small sponge roller
- Stippling brush
- Acrylic varnish
- Paintbrush

1 MAKE THE STENCIL

1 DRAW AN IMAGE onto a piece of paper (skip this step if you are copying your image from an existing source).

2 TRACE THE SHAPE of the image onto a sheet of acetate using a magic marker.

3 CUT OUT THE SHAPE with a craft knife. Discard the cutout and use the sheet of acetate as a stencil.

2 APPLY THE PAINT

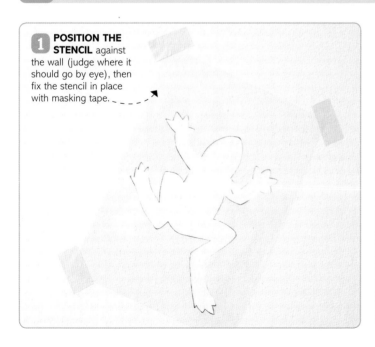

1 POSITION THE STENCIL against the wall (judge where it should go by eye), then fix the stencil in place with masking tape.

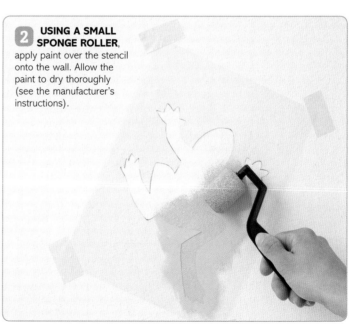

2 USING A SMALL SPONGE ROLLER, apply paint over the stencil onto the wall. Allow the paint to dry thoroughly (see the manufacturer's instructions).

1 **TO CREATE A STIPPLING EFFECT**—a dry-brush technique that gives a fine additional layer of paint—dab a slightly darker hue of paint over one half of the stencil with a dry stippling brush. Use a cloth to dab excess paint from the brush to keep it as dry as possible.

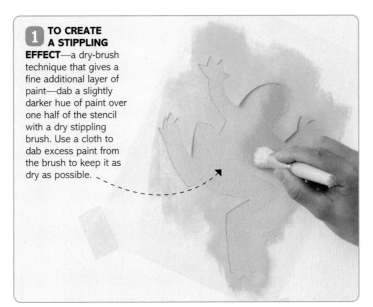

2 **REMOVE THE MASKING TAPE** and gently lift the stencil off the wall. Place it elsewhere on the wall to repeat the process.

4 **VARNISH THE WALL**

IF YOU WANT TO PROTECT the stencils (they may prove tricky to touch up later), apply a thin coat of acrylic varnish over the whole wall with a paintbrush.

3 CHOOSE A CHILD'S BED

Children's beds aren't always chosen as carefully as adult beds. Consider how comfortable a bed will be, now and in the future, and also how the bed can help you make good use of space in what is often a smaller room. Think, too, about its longevity and how soon your child might outgrow it.

1 CHOOSE A BASIC TYPE

Each type of child's bed has its own benefits, whether it be storage, accessibility, or additional floor space beneath. If you want the bed to last, opt for a wood or painted finish that will work with different decorating schemes.

TODDLER BED

Slightly shorter than a regular bed, this is an ideal first bed, especially if the room is small. It usually features two short side rails to prevent your child from falling out, and is often adjustable, so you can lengthen it as your child grows.

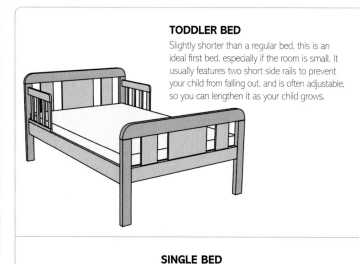

SINGLE BED

Single beds that will see a child through from toddler to teens are available in a wide choice of finishes, styles, and with or without headboards and footboards. If you are happy to buy for the short term, you can also opt for themed bed frames, such as race cars or fairy-tale castles.

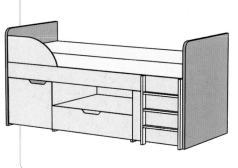

CAPTAIN'S BED

This type of bed has built-in storage beneath it, making it a good choice for rooms that are short on space. There is a huge range of storage combinations available, including shelving, drawers, wardrobes, and desks.

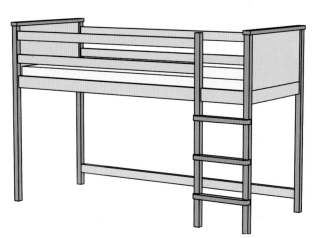

LOFT BED

If a bedroom is short on floor space, a loft bed is a practical option for children of five years and over. The bed is raised much higher than a standard bunk bed (often high enough for an adult to stand beneath), allowing space below that can be used for other furniture or simply as a play space.

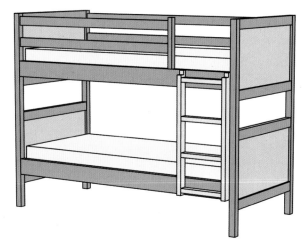

BUNK BEDS

Where children share a room, or a spare bed is needed for guests, bunk beds are an ideal solution. In addition to the classic single-over-single bunk beds, there are other options available, such as a larger bed on the bottom, with storage drawers, or a pull-out trundle that provides even more sleeping space.

2 CONSIDER ADDITIONAL FEATURES

There are many ways in which a child's bed can offer extra functionality. In a small bedroom, this can help compensate for limited storage space, play space, or workspace elsewhere in the room.

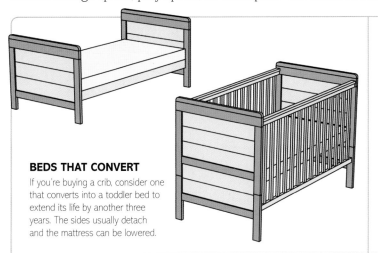

BEDS THAT CONVERT

If you're buying a crib, consider one that converts into a toddler bed to extend its life by another three years. The sides usually detach and the mattress can be lowered.

EXTRA SLEEPING CAPACITY

Whether you have houseguests regularly, your children have sleepovers, or you want to sleep near them when they are sick, an underbed trundle—a slimline beds on wheels—is an invaluable buy. Simply pull it out when you need it.

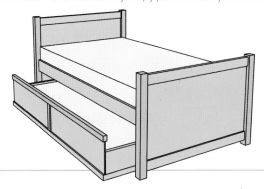

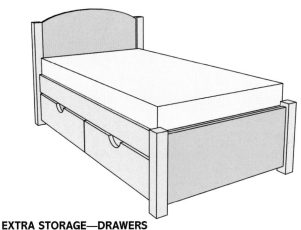

EXTRA STORAGE—DRAWERS

Drawers—whether built-in or separate—that occupy the space under a single bed are always useful. If the drawers are separate units, look for ones that roll out on wheels and have a lid, since dust tends to gather beneath a bed.

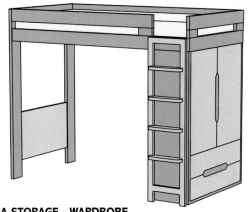

EXTRA STORAGE—WARDROBE

A raised bed with a wardrobe is the ideal buy if you need to store the maximum number of items within the minimum amount of floor space. Shop for a wardrobe with both hanging and concealed drawer/shelving options, since flexibility is key.

PLAY BED

If choosing a bed for a small child, you could opt for one with fun elements such as a slide or a playhouse or "fort" area. If possible, choose one where the extra features can be stripped away when the child gets older.

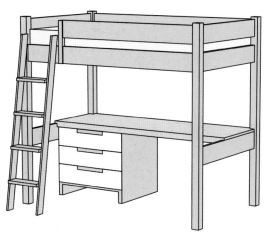

BED WITH WORKSPACE

If your child needs a quiet place to study, a desk incorporated into the space under a raised bed will prove very useful. A model that also offers some storage, such as a chest of drawers, will ensure that you make the best use of the space.

5 WAYS WITH
CHILD'S DISPLAY SPACE

Young children produce lots of paintings, models, and drawings that they—and you—will want to keep on show. However, the challenge is often in knowing how best to display them to create an attractive arrangement on your walls without it overtaking a room.

CORD AND CLOTHES PINS

For a simple display that can quickly be taken down if you need the room to look neater for visitors, fix lengths of cord across a wall and use clothes pins to hang artwork and photographs.

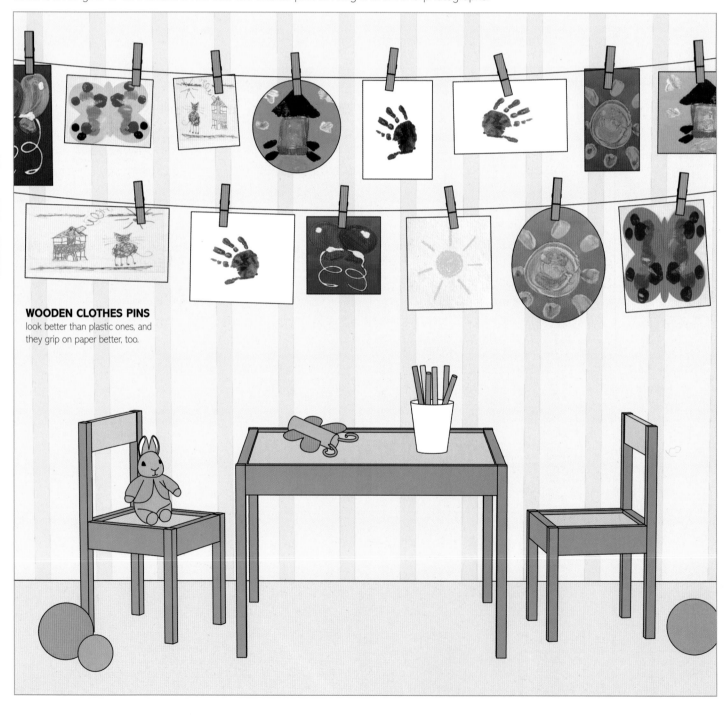

WOODEN CLOTHES PINS look better than plastic ones, and they grip on paper better, too.

BOX FRAMES

Painted box frames displaying models, collections, and awards can be hung on the wall or positioned on a shelf.

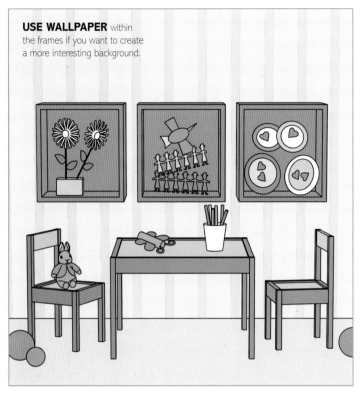

USE WALLPAPER within the frames if you want to create a more interesting background.

CORK BOARDS

Turn cork floor tiles into a bulletin board or series of bulletin boards. Adhere the tiles to the wall in different arrangements and shapes.

LEAVE THE TILES as they are or paint them to match or complement the wall color.

BULLDOG CLIPS

Make a framework with slim wood strips and attach it to the wall with tacks. Attach bulldog clips to the horizontal strips with thumbtacks.

MAGNETIC WALL

Magnetic paint, applied as an undercoat before your chosen paint or wallpaper, can give you a whole wall on which to display artwork.

MAKE
A BEAN BAG

Children love the squishy feel and comfort of a bean bag molding itself around their bodies. It's best to buy polystyrene beads ready-packed, so you can keep the feather-light beads contained while you insert them into the shaped cotton cover.

WHAT YOU NEED

- Pencil
- Large roll of brown paper
- Scissors
- About 10ft (3m) fabric—use curtain-weight cotton material
- Zipper (at least 8in/20cm long)
- Seam ripper
- About 5 cubic ft (140 liters) of polystyrene beads

1 PREPARE THE TEMPLATES

MAKE TWO CIRCULAR brown paper templates, one 30in (76cm) in diameter and the other 15in (38cm) in diameter (you may find it easiest to fold the paper in half, and then in half again, then measure, mark, and cut out a quadrant shape; when opened out, this will form a circle). Make another template in a trapezoid shape, 12in (30cm) wide at one end, 24in (60cm) wide at the other, and 26in (66cm) long.

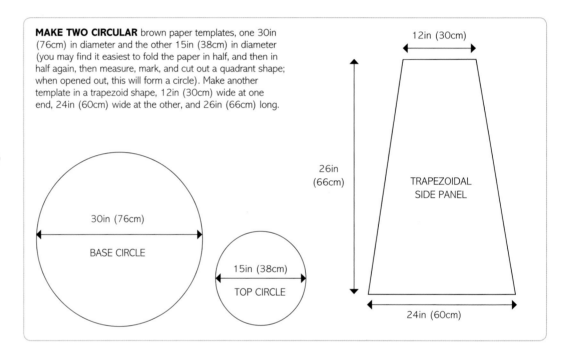

30in (76cm)

BASE CIRCLE

15in (38cm)

TOP CIRCLE

12in (30cm)

26in (66cm)

TRAPEZOIDAL SIDE PANEL

24in (60cm)

2 CUT THE FABRIC

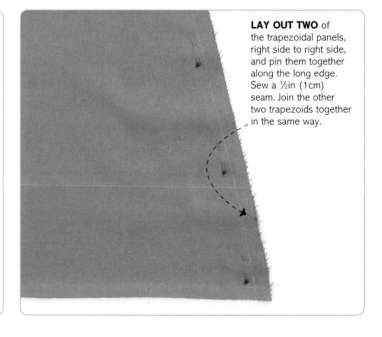

LAY THE FABRIC out on a flat surface and pin the templates onto it. Cut out four trapezoid shapes and one of each of the circles from the fabric.

3 JOIN THE PANELS

LAY OUT TWO of the trapezoidal panels, right side to right side, and pin them together along the long edge. Sew a ½in (1cm) seam. Join the other two trapezoids together in the same way.

4   ATTACH THE ZIPPER

1 TAKE ONE of the joined panels, open it out and iron the seam flat.

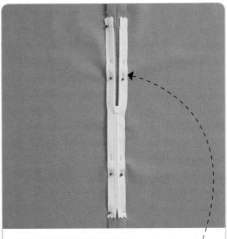

2 PLACE THE ZIPPER over the ironed seam two-thirds of the way down the fabric at the larger end, and pin it in place. Then sew along its sides and across the ends to secure it in place.

3 UNPICK THE FABRIC SEAM from the other side with a seam ripper to reveal the zipper.

5   FINISH AND FILL

PIN THE TWO JOINED PANELS of fabric together (right side to right side, and with the inside of the zipper on the outside). Sew them together with ½in (1cm) seams to make a large tube shape. Pin and sew the smaller circle to the smaller end of the tube on the inside. Repeat with the larger circle at the bottom of the tube. Turn the bean bag inside out through the zipper opening so it is the right way around, fill with polystyrene beads, and close the zipper.

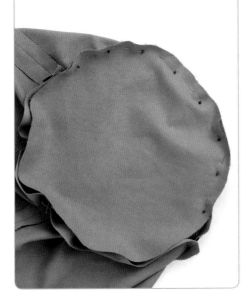

7 WAYS WITH
STORAGE

Children's bedrooms require storage for everything from clothes and equipment to toys and games. Unlike other rooms, the storage will need to be accessed easily—often at a low level, if your children are small—and be almost constantly on show, so it needs to be both functional and good-looking.

HANGING STORAGE BASKET

If you don't have free floor space, use baskets that hang from the wall or ceiling, and that are ideal for light items such as stuffed animals.

MAKE SURE THE BASKETS are attached to the rafters within the ceiling so they won't fall down and damage the ceiling or hurt a child if pulled or swung from.

WALL POCKETS

Colorful wall pockets are fun, practical, and decorative. Position them low enough for a small child to be able to look inside the pockets.

CAPTAIN'S BEDS

Make use of space under a bed with integral drawers in a captain's bed or add under-bed storage boxes, which are ideal for clothes and toys.

SHELVING ON WHEELS

A storage unit on wheels gives you the flexibility to move it when space is needed for playing or other activities.

MAKE SURE there's a locking mechanism on the wheels.

SHELVING UNIT WITH BOXES

A shelving unit with a mixture of boxes or drawers and shelves is a good way to keep clutter out of sight and a room looking tidy.

BASKETS OR BOXES in a low-level shelving unit are ideal for concealing toys and encouraging a child to keep the room neat.

STORAGE BENCH

A storage bench provides handy seating, in addition to somewhere to store away toys and games.

STORAGE BAGS

Large bags can be used permanently or temporarily for clothes, blankets, and toys, and are easy to store away when not in use.

MAKE
AN APPLIQUÉ PILLOW

A colorful appliqué pillow can provide an attractive personal touch in a child's room. This sequence is for a strawberry motif (a template can be found on page 386) on an 18 x 18in (45 x 45cm) pillow, but it can be customized to incorporate a different design or to fit a different sized pad.

WHAT YOU NEED

- Scissors
- Plain base fabric
- Textured red fabric
- Textured green fabric
- Ruler or tape measure
- Pins
- White paper
- Fusible webbing
- Pencil
- Iron
- Darning or tapestry needle
- Tapestry thread (red, green, and white or yellow)
- Sewing machine and thread
- Square pillow pad 18in (45cm) square

1 MEASURE AND CUT THE BASE FABRIC

1 **CUT A RECTANGLE** 46in (115cm) by 18½in (47cm) from the base fabric to form the pillow cover.

2 **MEASURE WITH A RULER** and use pins to mark 14in (35cm) from each end. The area bounded by these lines will be the front section of the pillow, to which the motif will be attached.

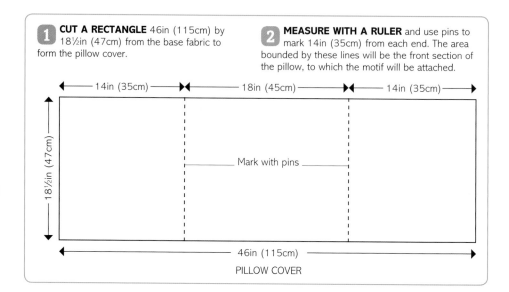

14in (35cm) — 18in (45cm) — 14in (35cm)

18½in (47cm)

Mark with pins

46in (115cm)

PILLOW COVER

2 DRAW THE MOTIF

1 **DRAW A LARGE STRAWBERRY** motif with a stalk on a piece of white paper.

2 **PLACE A PIECE OF FUSIBLE WEBBING** over the motif, secure it in place with a pin, and trace over the motif with a pencil.

3 **CUT AROUND THE WHOLE** motif with a pair of scissors.

4 **THEN CUT OUT THE STALK** so that the strawberry and stalk form two separate cutouts.

3 TRANSFER THE MOTIF ONTO THE FABRIC

1 **IRON THE STRAWBERRY FUSIBLE WEBBING** cutout onto the reverse side of the textured red fabric and the fusible webbing stalk onto the back the textured green fabric.

2 **CUT AROUND** each fabric shape with the scissors.

4 PLACE THE MOTIF ON THE BASE FABRIC

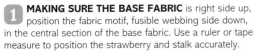

1 **MAKING SURE THE BASE FABRIC** is right side up, position the fabric motif, fusible webbing side down, in the central section of the base fabric. Use a ruler or tape measure to position the strawberry and stalk accurately.

2 **IRON THE STRAWBERRY** cutout onto the base fabric (adjust the heat of the iron according to the manufacturer's instructions), then iron on the stalk.

5 SEW AROUND THE MOTIF

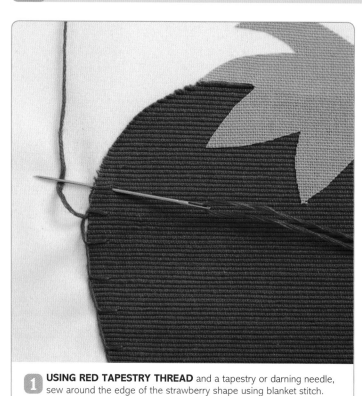

1 **USING RED TAPESTRY THREAD** and a tapestry or darning needle, sew around the edge of the strawberry shape using blanket stitch.

2 **SEW AROUND THE STALK** with green thread using blanket stitch. Then decorate the strawberry with individual running stitches of white or yellow thread to represent the pips.

6 SEW UP THE PILLOW COVER

1 **TURN THE BASE FABRIC** around so the reverse side is facing up. Fold over the short ends (which are 18½in/47cm in length) and hem each end using a sewing machine.

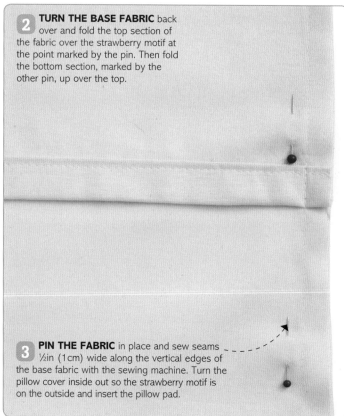

2 **TURN THE BASE FABRIC** back over and fold the top section of the fabric over the strawberry motif at the point marked by the pin. Then fold the bottom section, marked by the other pin, up over the top.

3 **PIN THE FABRIC** in place and sew seams ½in (1cm) wide along the vertical edges of the base fabric with the sewing machine. Turn the pillow cover inside out so the strawberry motif is on the outside and insert the pillow pad.

HALLWAY

1 WHAT TO DO WHEN
REDECORATING YOUR HALLWAY

Redecorating your hallway should be left until you have finished work on any other rooms you are renovating, due to the possible wear and tear from workmen and their deliveries passing through. There is a logical order in which to decorate a hallway, so follow these steps to get the best finish.

1 DETERMINE YOUR BUDGET

Establish how much you are able to spend on the job. Most hallways are limited in terms of space, so what you save on furnishings you can spend on quality flooring, good lighting, and decorative accessories. Allow a contingency of at least 10 percent in case of hidden problems.

2 PLAN THE WORK

Create a list of storage needs and work out the positions of new lights. If you want to convert an under-stairs space into a storage area or a powder room, draw a scale plan of the space.

3 REPLAN THE HEATING

If the hallway is heated by a radiator, consider replacing it with underfloor heating, which will be more efficient, effective, and save vital wall space.

4 BOOK TRADESPEOPLE

Contact an electrician, plumber, carpenter, HVAC contractor, and painter to get quotes. Tell each tradesperson what you have in mind so that you can work out a schedule and get them in at the right time.

5 ORDER MATERIALS

Once you have quotes and booked your tradespeople, order—or get them to order—major materials (heating products, flooring, new doors, or plumbing fixtures). Also order any storage units or parts, such as a new staircase, that you want made by a carpenter.

6 STRIP BACK THE ROOM

Remove old wallpaper to see if the walls and ceiling need to be replastered or patched. Strip down old woodwork. Rip out damaged flooring, old wiring, and pipes for heating. If you're having a new staircase installed, the old one will come out now so preparation work can be done.

7 INSTALL PLUMBING—ROUGH-IN

New plumbing for heating should be put in now, as should any plumbing fixtures you are having installed.

8 ELECTRICAL INSTALL—ROUGH-IN

The electrician will install the wiring for new lights, reposition electrical receptacles and light switches, position the controls for underfloor heating, and install an extractor fan if you want an under-stairs powder room.

9 INSTALL DOORS AND WINDOWS

If you're installing a new front door, it will probably require a new frame and good insulation, too. If any windows are being replaced or refurbished, do this now.

10 INSTALL THE NEW STAIRCASE

A new staircase may dent walls, so it's best to install it now before the plastering is done.

11 ORDER DECORATIVE ITEMS

Order or buy wallpaper, paint, light fixtures, and door hardware now.

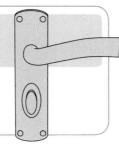

12 PATCH WALLS AND CEILING

Patch or replaster the walls and ceiling if this needs to be done.

13 LAY THE FLOOR

If you are having underfloor heating installed, this should be done now, with the new flooring laid over the top and sealed, if necessary.

14 CALL THE CARPENTER

The carpenter can now replace baseboards, chair or picture rails, crown trim, decorative moldings, and door frames, measure for the boxing-in of pipework and electric cabling, and install, or make on-site, your storage units.

15 DECORATE

Paint the ceiling, then the walls and woodwork, and wallpaper last.

16 ORGANIZE THE FINAL INSTALL

The plumber and electrician can return to install light fixtures, light switches, and plumbing fixtures, if required, and finish any details. Boxing-in can be completed and painted.

17 FINISH THE JOB

Add door furniture and decorative touches such as mirrors, runners, carpets, pictures, and furniture.

2 CREATE A MOOD BOARD
FOR YOUR HALLWAY

A hall provides a transitional point between the outside world and domestic life. Despite its function of essentially being a confined, practical area that links to other rooms and accommodates outdoor wear, it also needs to be a space that is inviting and organized. Use a mood board to create the best possible look to make your busy hallway feel calmer, bigger, brighter, and more welcoming.

1 FIND PICTURES OF HALLWAYS YOU LIKE by looking at books and magazines and on websites. Photocopy, print off, or cut out images of rooms or elements that appeal to you, and include any ideas—even if they're not in a hallway—that you would like to incorporate. Edit these pictures down to a favorite few and attach them to your mood board. This will help you to narrow down what color scheme and other elements to choose.

Study your favorite picture and decide which elements— lighting, furniture, storage, or wall and floor finishes—will work in your own hallway.

2 FIND A KEY ITEM that will be a focal point in the hallway. It might be fabric for a door curtain, wallpaper to hang on one wall, a large, ornate mirror, an antique console table, or something you already own. Pin a picture of the item to the mood board and use it as a starting point for your design scheme.

The focal piece you choose may inspire you to follow a theme, pick out a certain color palette, or opt for a particular period look.

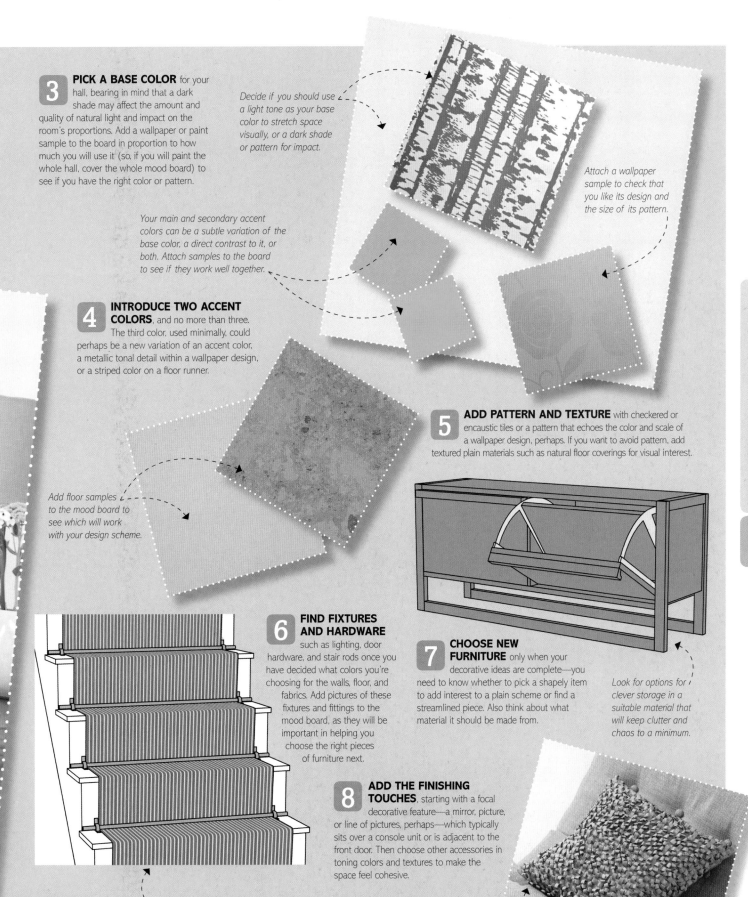

3 **PICK A BASE COLOR** for your hall, bearing in mind that a dark shade may affect the amount and quality of natural light and impact on the room's proportions. Add a wallpaper or paint sample to the board in proportion to how much you will use it (so, if you will paint the whole hall, cover the whole mood board) to see if you have the right color or pattern.

Decide if you should use a light tone as your base color to stretch space visually, or a dark shade or pattern for impact.

Attach a wallpaper sample to check that you like its design and the size of its pattern.

Your main and secondary accent colors can be a subtle variation of the base color, a direct contrast to it, or both. Attach samples to the board to see if they work well together.

4 **INTRODUCE TWO ACCENT COLORS**, and no more than three. The third color, used minimally, could perhaps be a new variation of an accent color, a metallic tonal detail within a wallpaper design, or a striped color on a floor runner.

5 **ADD PATTERN AND TEXTURE** with checkered or encaustic tiles or a pattern that echoes the color and scale of a wallpaper design, perhaps. If you want to avoid pattern, add textured plain materials such as natural floor coverings for visual interest.

Add floor samples to the mood board to see which will work with your design scheme.

6 **FIND FIXTURES AND HARDWARE** such as lighting, door hardware, and stair rods once you have decided what colors you're choosing for the walls, floor, and fabrics. Add pictures of these fixtures and fittings to the mood board, as they will be important in helping you choose the right pieces of furniture next.

7 **CHOOSE NEW FURNITURE** only when your decorative ideas are complete—you need to know whether to pick a shapely item to add interest to a plain scheme or find a streamlined piece. Also think about what material it should be made from.

Look for options for clever storage in a suitable material that will keep clutter and chaos to a minimum.

8 **ADD THE FINISHING TOUCHES**, starting with a focal decorative feature—a mirror, picture, or line of pictures, perhaps—which typically sits over a console unit or is adjacent to the front door. Then choose other accessories in toning colors and textures to make the space feel cohesive.

Look for pictures of fixtures and fittings, such as floor runners and stair rods, in a style and finish that suit your design scheme.

Pick out ideas for small accessories like throw pillows, which will turn a functional chair into an inviting seat, and add them to the board.

3 LAYOUT CONSIDERATIONS FOR THE HALLWAY

A hallway is usually a long, thin area, with little room for maneuvering, that has to accommodate a variety of bulky items, while also making a good first impression. However, there are still ways in which you can improve the space immeasurably, both decoratively and functionally, and avoid ways of getting the layout wrong. Follow these layout tips to get it right the first time.

CONSOLE TABLE

If your hallway is long and thin, you may only have one place for a console table—usually up against a left- or right-hand wall by the front door. If the hallway is too narrow for a table, hang a shelf at tabletop height on sturdy brackets in the same position, or perhaps over a radiator. If your hallway is wide, consider where the table might be best positioned from a decorative point of view. If you place it against a wall by the front door, position it centrally for balance; if it will stand opposite the front door, position it so it's the first thing you see as you step inside.

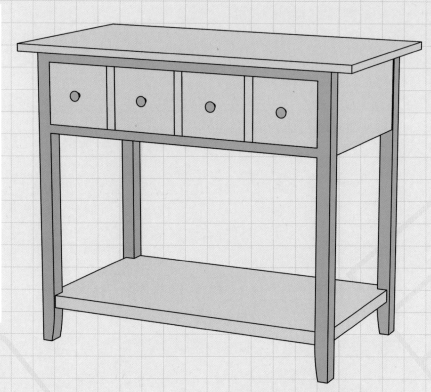

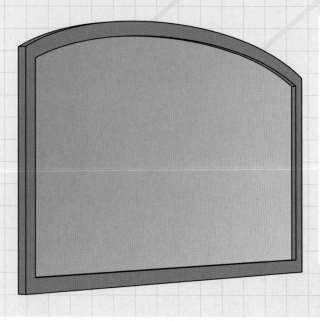

MIRROR

If you have room for a console table, hang a mirror centrally above it for a practical and decoratively attractive look. A wide mirror that matches the length of the console table will give a balanced look and help the hall to seem longer. If the room is too small for a table, place a long—even floor to ceiling—mirror adjacent to the front door (assuming the door has a glazed panel) to reflect natural light and make the hall seem wider. Or improve a small hall by hanging a large mirror opposite the front door.

COAT RACK

A wall-hung coat rack is the best choice for a small hallway, since it takes up no floor space. Hang it on a wall with space on each side so bulky coats won't be in the way. Think about how to conceal the rack and its contents—in a recessed space with a sliding panel or door in front, perhaps, or in a closet—or buy a modern design in contemporary materials so that it looks as attractive as possible. A coat rack looks good in a hallway, but takes up floor space, so is best placed in a corner of a large hall.

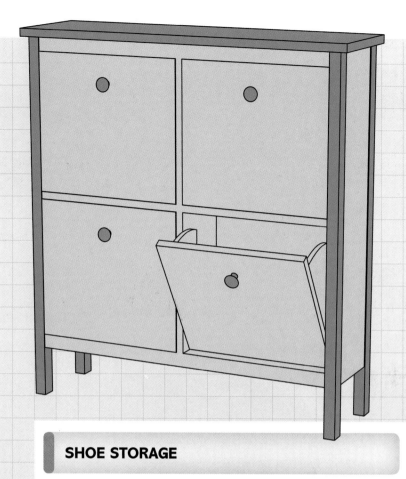

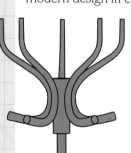

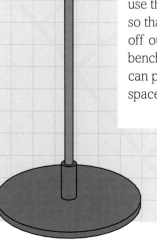

SHOE STORAGE

If you have a wall-hung coat rack, the natural place for shoe storage is beneath it (ideally, not on show). Or store shoes in lidded baskets beneath the console table or in any deep drawers or shelves that the unit has. Narrow shoe storage units with hinged drawers that tip out (above) are also available, and you can use the top of the unit as a console tablelike surface.

SEATING

If you have room near the front door, use the space for a bench or seat so that you can sit down to take off outdoor shoes. Or look for a bench with a lift-up lid so that it can provide more useful storage space for shoes and boots.

4 CHOOSE FLOORING

A hallway is the first impression you and your visitors have of your home, so the floor needs to look attractive. There's a huge range of good-looking yet hardy flooring available, but remember that this floor in particular is subject to lots of foot traffic, so it needs to be extremely durable and easy to care for.

1 CHOOSE THE LOOK

While practicality is paramount, you will also want something that is stylish and consistent with the rest of your home. Carpet is inviting, tiles look sleek or rustic, and wood floors can be both highly practical and attractive.

TILED

Tiled floors are the most practical choice for hallways, since they are easy to keep clean and generally easy to care for. Choose tiles in colors that hide dirt well. Lay the tiles diagonally to stretch the space visually if your hallway is small.

WOOD

Wood floors add warmth and character and, depending on which way you lay the planks, can make a short space feel longer or a narrow space look wider. Use parquet for pattern and interest if you have a plain scheme. Choose from a wide range of tones.

CARPET

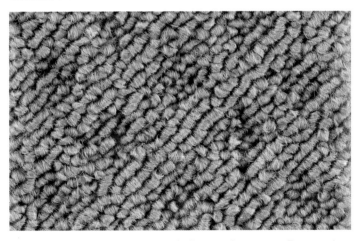

Bring color and texture to your hallway with a carpet. Patterned designs are particularly good at hiding dirty marks and add interest to a plain room. The palest shades will show dirt quickly, but don't be put off light tones, which will help a small space feel larger.

SEAMLESS

In open-plan ground-floor hallways, poured concrete and poured resin floorings give a contemporary look. Think about the color and finish when you consider this option—lighter gloss finishes will stretch the space visually, but may also show marks and smudges.

2 CHOOSE THE MATERIAL

The material you choose for the floor needs to be resilient, easy to clean, and in a shade or finish that hides dirt. Tiles or wood are a practical option unless you are in the habit of taking off your shoes at the door, in which case a carpet will last well.

TILED

PORCELAIN

The smooth, nonporous surface of porcelain is easy to keep clean. It is available glazed (which may become slippery when wet) and unglazed in a range of prices.

CERAMIC

Ceramic tiles are inexpensive and therefore a good choice if you have a large area to tile. They won't stain and don't need to be sealed, so are easy to look after.

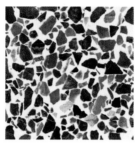

TERRAZZO

These expensive, highly polished tiles of marble chips, cement, and color pigment are hard-wearing. They can be slippery if wet, so avoid them if you have children.

CONCRETE

Concrete tiles come in a range of colors and finishes, including polished, matte, or with exposed aggregates. These tiles are expensive yet hard-wearing.

TERRA-COTTA

This medium-priced porous tile is a good choice if you want a warm, inviting look for your hallway. Choose presealed tiles or have your installer seal them.

TRAVERTINE

These expensive natural stone tiles come in various sizes and shades. They are also available with a sleek polished finish or a natural tumbled look.

LIMESTONE

High-cost limestone tiles are a good choice for brightening up dark hallways. Choose between highly polished gloss tiles or rougher matte finishes.

SLATE

The naturally uneven surface of dark slate tiles makes them less slippery than smooth tiles, and they won't show dirt. They are medium to high in price.

LAMINATE

These low- to medium-cost tiles offer a cheaper alternative to natural materials like slate and travertine, and you can install them yourself to cut costs.

WOOD

HARDWOOD

Medium to high in price, this option is hard-wearing and can be sanded to remove scratches and scuffs. To add more interest, consider using parquet flooring.

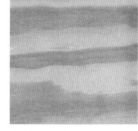

SOFTWOOD

If you like hardwood but don't have the budget for it, a low- to medium-priced softwood like pine is a good option. It may dent and mark, but it can be repaired.

ENGINEERED WOOD

This medium-priced floor looks like a solid wood floor, but can be installed as a floating floor with an underlay, making it good for uneven floors and apartments.

BAMBOO

Bamboo flooring is hard-wearing, good-looking, and is medium to high in price. Choose a bamboo floor with an oil finish, which can be patch-repaired.

LAMINATE

If you're on a low- or medium-priced budget, laminate is a great choice. For the best effect, look for planks with realistic textured finishes and detailing or parquet.

CARPET

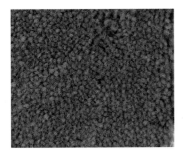

TWIST PILE

This low- to medium-priced hard-wearing carpet has a coarse, rugged appearance. Patterns and heathers are better at hiding stains, so are good for hallways.

VELVET PILE

Medium to high in price, velvet pile carpet is hard-wearing and feels comfortable underfoot. It has a dense low-cut pile and a stylish, elegant look.

BERBER

Berber carpet is made from yarn that forms loops on the surface of the carpet. Avoid it if you have pets, since their claws catch on the loops. It is medium priced.

SEAMLESS

CONCRETE

A modern option, polished concrete will give your hallway a contemporary, industrial look. Although expensive, it is extremely durable, and comes in a range of colors.

RESIN

Poured resin flooring comes in matte and gloss finishes and a range of colors. This expensive option suits open-plan spaces where the hall is part of the living area.

INSTALLING FLOOR LIGHTS

Recessed floor lighting can illuminate and add interest to your hallway, but it needs to be wired up before your flooring is installed.

● **The lights themselves will sit flush** with the floor, so they need to be recessed into the subfloor. Get professional advice if your lights have to be recessed into a concrete subfloor or you want to combine them with a carpet.

● **This type of lighting** creates a contemporary feel, so is best matched with a hard flooring such as tiles or wood.

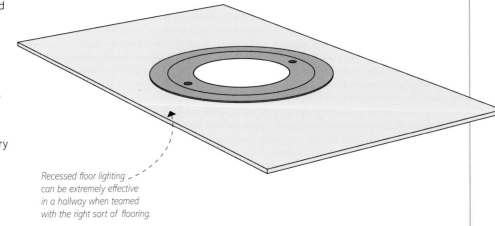

Recessed floor lighting can be extremely effective in a hallway when teamed with the right sort of flooring.

5 CHOOSE WALL COVERINGS

Since hallways are often narrow rooms that people move through to get in and out of the house, the walls need to stand up to more wear and tear than the walls in other rooms. These walls also need to look attractive, since it is the hall that makes the first impression when guests enter your home.

1 CHOOSE THE MATERIAL

When considering which type of material to use, keep in mind the size of your hallway and your lifestyle. If the hallway is narrow, choose something tough that is easy to repair. If space is not a concern, decoration can take priority over functionality.

PAINT

Paint is a good choice for family hallways, since it can be touched up easily if gets very dirty or nicked. If your home is full of children or pets, look for paint finishes that can be wiped down with a cloth, and choose colors that won't show dirt and scuffs easily.

WALLPAPER

Matte wallpapers will hide minor imperfections on walls, and are a great way to introduce pattern into a space that may be otherwise plain. Find a finish that can be wiped clean, and bear in mind that designs with a sheen will help to reflect light around the hallway.

PANELING

In addition to adding visual interest to your walls, paneling is a good way of protecting them. Tongue-and-groove and traditional-style paneling can be used either beneath the chair rail on the lower half of the wall, or from floor to ceiling.

CHECKLIST

● **If you've chosen to paint** your walls or paneling, it's worth keeping enough extra paint on hand so that you can touch up the walls when they get marked or scuffed.

● **Make sure that your wallpaper** adheres well to the wall, since it can easily be torn at the edges in a heavy traffic area. If it becomes loose, reapply wallpaper adhesive immediately.

● **While reflective wallpapers** and paints with a sheen are good for small hallways because of their light-reflecting properties, your wall will need to be perfectly flat and even, since the surface will highlight any lumps or cracks.

2 CHOOSE THE TYPE

The two main factors to remember when choosing which type of paint, wallpaper, or paneling you want in a hallway are durability and style. Ideally, you want to pick something that is both tough and space-enhancing.

PAINT

MATTE

Water-based matte emulsion paints come in an endless choice of colors, and the nonreflective finish minimizes imperfections on uneven walls. Prices vary greatly.

SATIN

A great medium-priced choice for family hallways, satin paints are easy to clean, so marks come off quickly. Satin paints also help to reflect light around a space.

METALLIC

Medium-priced metallic emulsion brings a touch of luxury to a hall. It reflects enough light to make a room seem bigger. Use this paint on a focal wall for the best effect.

EGGSHELL

Acrylic eggshell paint is tough enough to resist staining and wear and tear. It is suitable for use on walls and woodwork. It is a medium-priced paint.

WALLPAPER

PLAIN OR PATTERNED

If your walls have fine surface cracks, use plain wallpaper that is easy to wipe clean. Prices will vary hugely, depending on the design you buy.

FLOCK

For a grand entrance, medium- to high-cost flock wallpaper, with its raised velvet texture, is ideal. Stains can be carefully sponged or dusted with a soft brush.

METALLIC

Add glamour by using a paper with a metallic sheen. Choose a pale background and a subtle design to maximize space in a small hallway. It is medium to high in price.

TEXTURED

Thicker than other papers, this medium-priced wallpaper is hard-wearing and can disguise uneven walls. Buy a raised design to paint or an embossed colored paper.

PANELING

TONGUE & GROOVE

Low- to medium-priced tongue and groove can withstand knocks and scrapes. It is usually made of pine, although MDF designs are available. It can be painted.

FLATWOOD VENEER

Medium to high in price, this is available in various finishes. Sheets come in various sizes, and it's possible to bond multiple pieces side by side for large projects.

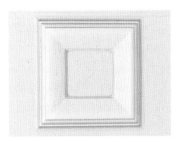

WAINSCOT PANELING

Medium-priced wainscot paneling adds texture and interest to your walls. Paint the inside of the panels a different color from the wood itself for added interest.

6 CHOOSE LIGHTING

A hallway is a tricky space to light because it tends to be a long, thin space, often with little natural daylight. The trick with lighting a hallway is to use light to make the space feel brighter and bigger. There are a number of ways to do this and many different lighting styles and types to help you achieve your goal.

1 DECIDE ON A STYLE OF LIGHTING

If you are reworking your lighting plan from scratch, try to use a combination of accent and ambient lighting, however small your space, to allow you to create a range of lighting levels and atmospheres in what could otherwise be a characterless space.

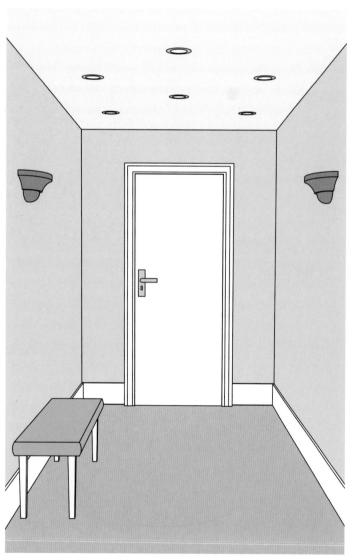

AMBIENT

The ambient lighting in your hallway should mimic natural daylight as closely as possible, so, unless yours is a very small space, it is best not to rely on a single pendant bulb that may be too weak to light the space effectively. Instead, consider recessed downlights or an arrangement of spotlights along the length of the ceiling, and find space for a table lamp to soften the mood when needed.

ACCENT

Accent lighting is all about creating an effect or an atmosphere. In a hallway, baseboard lights, or step lights on the stairs, can provide low-level accent lighting, while highlighting pictures on the walls is another good option. Clever use of accent lighting can make a hallway more interesting and even exaggerate its proportions.

2 CHOOSE YOUR LIGHT FIXTURES

Consider your space first: a low ceiling won't suit a large pendant, but a grand hallway can accommodate a chandelier. Then think about the style of the lighting. A period home doesn't need traditional lighting if contemporary options will work wonders.

CEILING LIGHTS

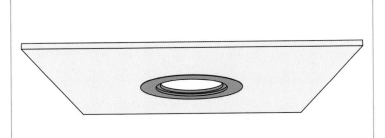

RECESSED DOWNLIGHTS

Recessed downlights are the perfect buy for a small, low-ceilinged hallway that needs to feel bigger and brighter, or a very long, thin hall, since the light they create tends to closely mimic daylight and is strong enough to throw light in every direction.

PENDANT LIGHT

If your hallway is small, a pendant light might suffice. Make sure that the shade hangs close to the ceiling so the tallest person in the house won't hit it if stretching up to put on a garment. Choose a shade, too, that's designed to throw light upward and downward—doing so will help to exaggerate space. If your hallway has a low ceiling, avoid pendants altogether.

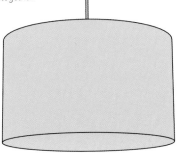

STATEMENT LIGHTING

A statement light is ideally suited to a large, high-ceilinged hallway and may need to be matched with other lighting styles, such as recessed downlights, to light the whole length of the hallway practically. Don't feel that you have to stick to one piece if the hallway is large—a line of three or five smaller lights can be equally effective.

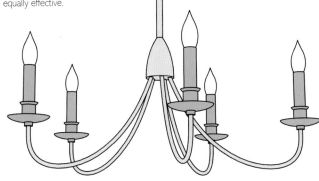

SURFACE-MOUNTED CEILING LIGHT

A surface-mounted ceiling light should be picked for decorative effect. This means choosing a large chandelier or contemporary piece with a multitude of bright bulbs for a big, high-ceilinged hallway, or a line of attractive lamps for a long, narrow space that needs character.

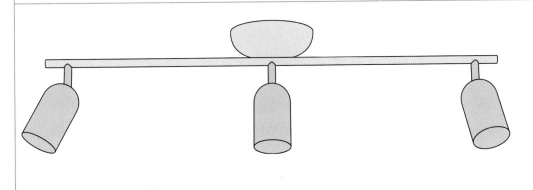

SPOTLIGHTS

A single lighting unit with directional spotlights will allow you to light the space practically and throw light onto elements of the room that you want to illuminate. This is an ideal choice if you are renovating a contemporary-style home.

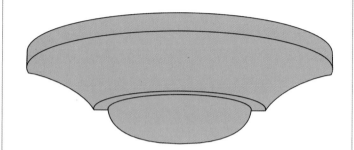

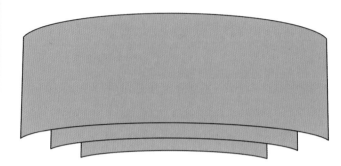

UPLIGHT SCONCES

If your hallway has a low ceiling, you should use every trick in the book to improve its proportions. The most effective way to do so is to use uplights placed about two-thirds up the wall. These lamps will throw the light upward to create a visual trick of raising the ceiling.

DECORATIVE SCONCES

Wall-mounted sconces are all about making the space look more interesting and playing with its proportions. A line of slim decorative pieces running the length of the hallway just above head height makes the hallway feel welcoming and, importantly, much longer.

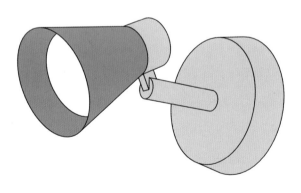

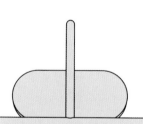

SINGLE SPOTLIGHTS

Single spotlights should be used to highlight an architectural detail, a picture, or a particularly attractive accessory such as a sculpture. The fittings themselves don't need to be immediately visible, but the effect they create should be.

PICTURE LIGHTS

Picture lights won't light your hallway at all, but they will subtly highlight a favorite picture. They should ideally be used on medium to large pictures and, if you have a number of pictures, you should either light all of them, just the largest, or the picture hung in the focal point of the room—above the console table, for example.

FLOOR LIGHTS

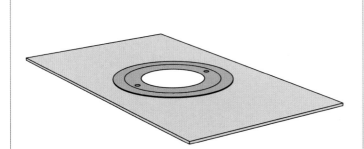

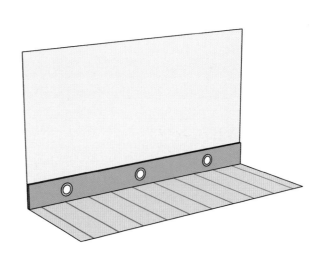

RECESSED FLOOR UPLIGHTS

Recessed floor uplights should be installed along the length of a hallway, ideally on both sides. They are designed to sit close to the wall and subtly light it upward; get a dimmer switch installed so that you can vary the height the light travels, and bear in mind that it will highlight imperfections in the texture of the wall.

BASEBOARD LIGHTING

Typically set into the baseboards that run up the length of one side of a flight of stairs, usually on every other step, baseboard lights can also be set into a flat floor every three feet (1m) or so. Make sure that these lights are set low enough to skim the floor with light.

LAMPS

TABLE LAMPS

If you have a console table in your hallway, putting a lamp on it or, better still, a pair of matching lamps at each end, will make the room look more interesting decoratively and—once the task lighting is switched off—much more welcoming. If you only have room for a small corner shelf in your hallway, make space on it for a table lamp.

FLOOR LAMPS

A tall, floor-standing lamp, placed in a corner, is a good way to bring ambient lighting into a hallway that doesn't have room for a table. Make sure the shade isn't too bulky and won't be in the way as you walk past it, and that it's set at the right height—too low or too high and you'll be looking into the bulb as you walk past it.

TORCHIERE FLOOR LAMPS

Torchiere floor lamps are generally placed behind or adjacent to furniture to throw light upward onto a wall. They create a similar effect to sconces in improving the hall's is less uniform and more about creating a dramatic effect.

5 WAYS WITH
MIRRORS

Putting a mirror in a hallway isn't just about having somewhere to check your appearance before you leave the house—or even about having a decorative piece to admire. Its main function is to improve the light and proportions of what might otherwise be a narrow, light-starved space.

LARGE MIRROR

A mirror hung over a console table just inside a glazed front door will reflect any light that comes through the door or a transom window, if you have one.

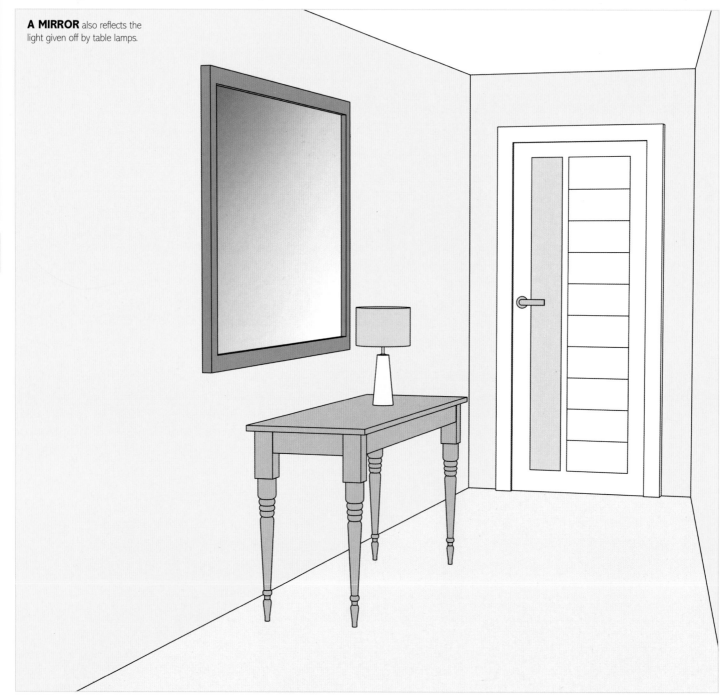

A MIRROR also reflects the light given off by table lamps.

FLOOR-TO-CEILING MIRROR

Small hallways will appear to expand when you hang a tall mirror. The taller the mirror is, the higher the ceiling will seem, too.

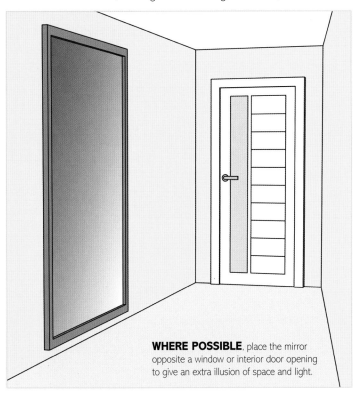

WHERE POSSIBLE, place the mirror opposite a window or interior door opening to give an extra illusion of space and light.

GROUPING OF VINTAGE MIRRORS

An assortment of vintage-style mirrors in varying shapes and sizes, and with different frames, will create a decorative and eclectic look.

TRY THIS look on a stairway wall, too.

END MIRROR

Hanging a floor-to-ceiling mirror at the far end of a short hallway will make the space seem longer.

MAKE THE MIRROR as wide as possible so it fills the wall space; this will help to widen the hall, too.

REGULAR GROUPING

Instead of hanging just one mirror over a console table, hang a grouping of smaller mirrors in a regular grid layout.

THIS WORKS with square, rectangular, and circular mirrors.

7 CHOOSE HALLWAY STORAGE

As the first room you—and any visitors—will see when entering your home, your hallway should be kept as neat as possible. Choosing the best storage solutions will help you achieve this goal. Since hallways are generally narrow, busy areas, opt for streamlined pieces that can withstand everyday knocks and scuffs.

CHOOSE ITEMS

What you choose depends on your household's storage needs, so assess what you actually want to keep in the hallway: if you don't have space to store shoes in a bedroom closet, for example, would a shoe rack in the hall be a satisfactory solution?

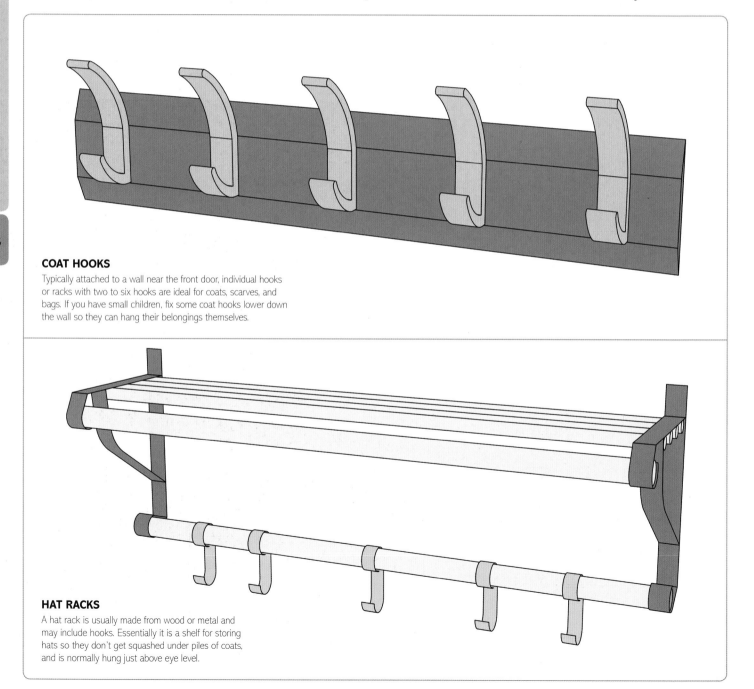

COAT HOOKS

Typically attached to a wall near the front door, individual hooks or racks with two to six hooks are ideal for coats, scarves, and bags. If you have small children, fix some coat hooks lower down the wall so they can hang their belongings themselves.

HAT RACKS

A hat rack is usually made from wood or metal and may include hooks. Essentially it is a shelf for storing hats so they don't get squashed under piles of coats, and is normally hung just above eye level.

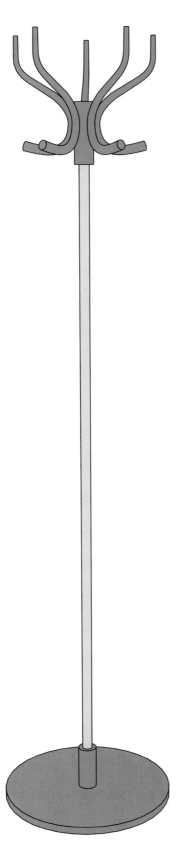

COAT STAND

Floor-standing coat stands are available in traditional and contemporary designs, with some also featuring storage space for umbrellas and hats. Try not to overload them with occasional-wear items, since they can take up quite a lot of space when full.

UMBRELLA STAND

If you regularly take an umbrella with you when you go out, a neat umbrella stand positioned near the door will help ensure you always have one in a convenient place, without taking up too much space.

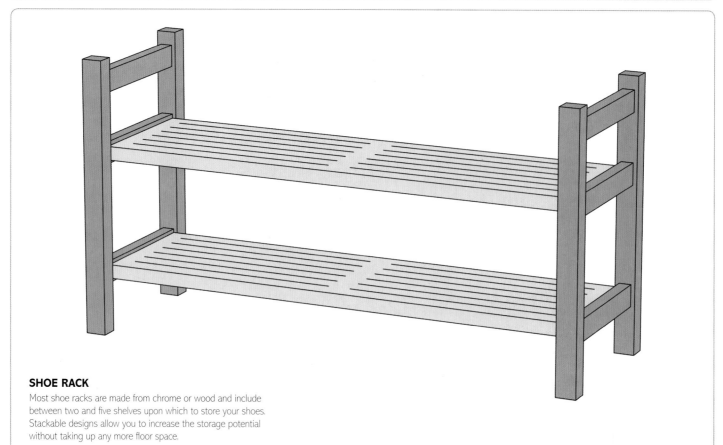

SHOE RACK

Most shoe racks are made from chrome or wood and include between two and five shelves upon which to store your shoes. Stackable designs allow you to increase the storage potential without taking up any more floor space.

SHOE CABINET

These slimline units allow you to hide your shoes away inside pull-down compartments. These cabinets take up minimal space and sit neatly against a wall. Due to their narrowness, though, they may need to be attached to the wall so they don't fall forward.

CONSOLE TABLE

Console tables are an ideal choice for hallways, since they provide you with a surface on which to place your telephone, letters, and keys. If you pick one with drawers, you can also store bigger items like telephone directories.

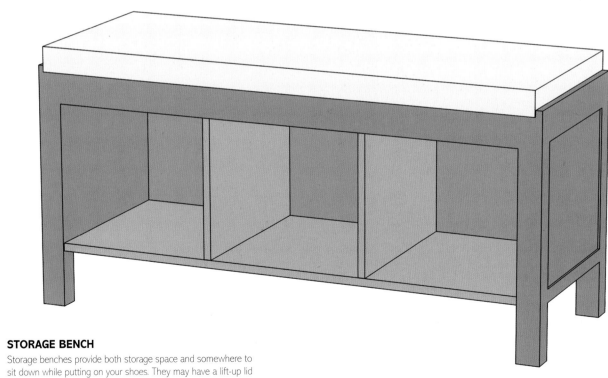

STORAGE BENCH

Storage benches provide both storage space and somewhere to sit down while putting on your shoes. They may have a lift-up lid or drawers that are large enough to store hats and gloves, shoes, bags, and sports gear.

7 WAYS TO
ADD CHARACTER TO A HALLWAY

While it is sensible to leave the hallway until after you have redecorated any other rooms, doing so means you risk running out of steam and creating a featureless space that doesn't work as hard as it should. Here are some tips on how to give your hallway a more stylish finish.

ADD A RUNNER

Add interest to a plain floor by adding a patterned or colorful runner. It will also add comfort underfoot in halls that have hard flooring.

A STRIPED RUNNER will give the appearance of a longer or wider space.

ADD STATEMENT LIGHTING

Make a statement with a striking ceiling light or, if you have low ceilings, an attractive table light.

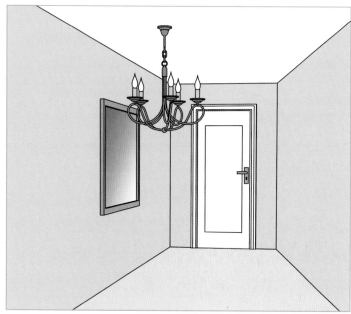

PICTURE GALLERY

Create a picture gallery using framed photos or art. This works successfully even in the narrowest of hallways.

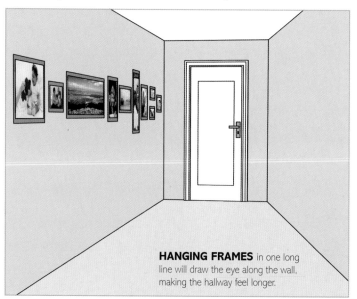

HANGING FRAMES in one long line will draw the eye along the wall, making the hallway feel longer.

OPEN SHELVING

Wider hallways are the perfect place to add open shelving to store an overspill of books and display decorative objects.

IN SMALLER HALLWAYS consider hanging shallow shelves above and around door frames.

COLORFUL FURNITURE

If you have space, use a sideboard or table painted in a bright color, or a long footstool upholstered in a decorative fabric, to lift the room.

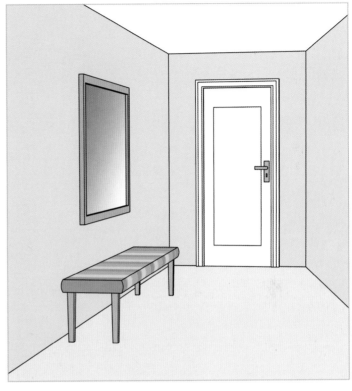

PAINT A WALL

One of the easiest ways to add character to a plain hallway is to create a feature wall using paint.

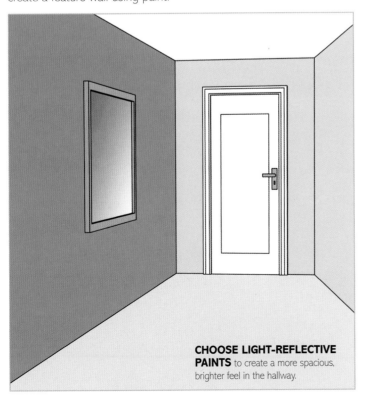

CHOOSE LIGHT-REFLECTIVE PAINTS to create a more spacious, brighter feel in the hallway.

STATEMENT WALLPAPER

Add personality to your hallway using a dramatic wallpaper with a large floral or geometric design.

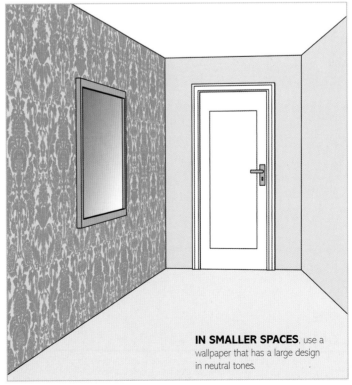

IN SMALLER SPACES, use a wallpaper that has a large design in neutral tones.

6 WAYS WITH
STAIRS

Although a staircase is an essential requirement if you live in a house or townhouse, you can turn it into an attractive feature or showpiece by adding character and individuality. Here are six durable, but good-looking, treatments for your stairs.

RUNNER

Lay a carpet runner, or use paint; apply a base color to the whole staircase, then paint the central section in a contrasting shade.

PAINT BOTH the tread and riser of each step to create a continuous block of color down the whole staircase.

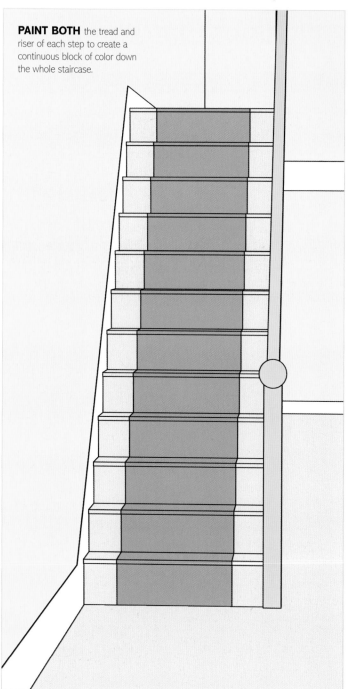

VARNISHED TOP, PAINTED RISER

For a classic look, varnish or stain the tread and paint the riser to match the rest of your woodwork.

TO GIVE THE VARNISHED SECTION a washed-out look, choose a varnish tinted with white or pale gray.

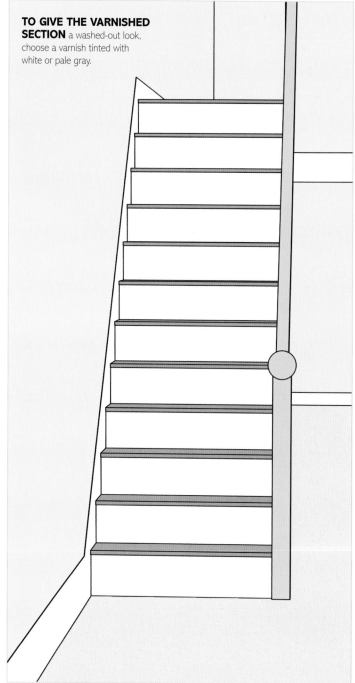

CORK TREADS

Update tired treads by attaching corkboard floor tiles to each stair tread to provide a softer feel underfoot.

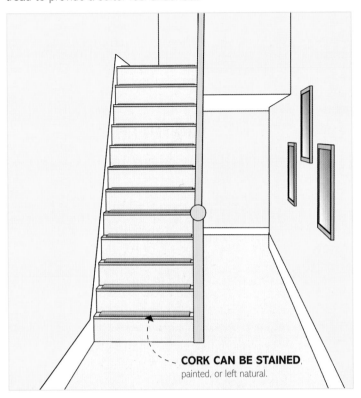

CORK CAN BE STAINED, painted, or left natural.

FULLY CARPETED

If your staircase is not made of an attractive wood that you would want to show off, fully carpeted stairs are a good option.

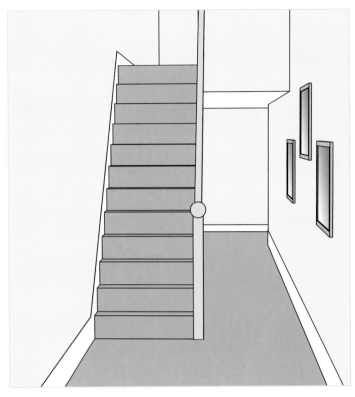

NUMBERED RISERS

Number each of your stair risers using either a painted stencil, transfer, or a number cut from paper.

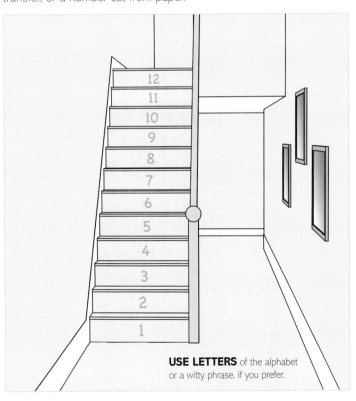

USE LETTERS of the alphabet or a witty phrase, if you prefer.

WALLPAPERED RISERS

Introduce pattern to your stairs by wallpapering the risers. Stick the paper down using wallpaper adhesive, glue, or double-sided tape.

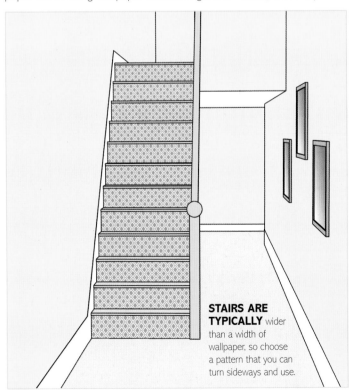

STAIRS ARE TYPICALLY wider than a width of wallpaper, so choose a pattern that you can turn sideways and use.

6 WAYS WITH
UNDER-STAIR SPACE

The area under the stairs is wasted in many homes, but with careful planning and design it can become an invaluable space. Measure the dimensions to see what you can realistically do with it, and consider whether custom-made furniture will help you to use the space more efficiently.

MEDIA UNIT

If your stairs are part of your living room, use the under-stair space to hide your TV and other media equipment.

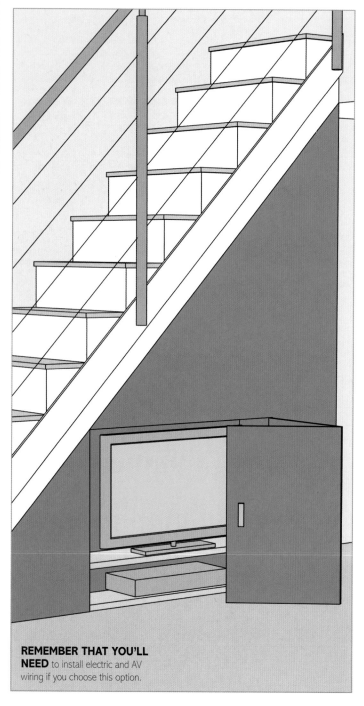

REMEMBER THAT YOU'LL NEED to install electric and AV wiring if you choose this option.

UNDER-STAIR SEATING

Built-in seating can create a cozy nook for quiet reading, or provide extra seating in your living room.

CONSIDER INCLUDING A WALL SCONCE or clip-on light to illuminate the space.

DRAWERS

Custom-built drawers use the space well and can be used to store shoes, scarves, gloves or equipment for outdoor games.

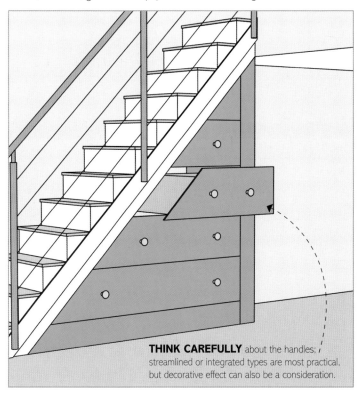

THINK CAREFULLY about the handles; streamlined or integrated types are most practical, but decorative effect can also be a consideration.

PULL-OUT CABINETS

Tall cabinets on runners are a good use of under-stair space. Shelving within will help keep them organized.

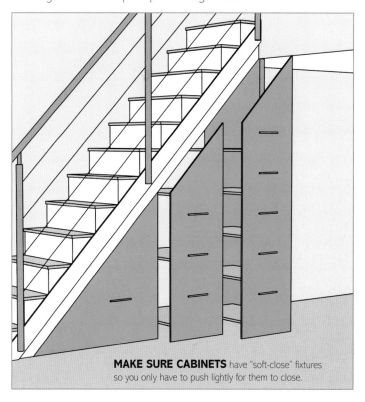

MAKE SURE CABINETS have "soft-close" fixtures so you only have to push lightly for them to close.

HANGING SPACE

Hang your coat rack under the stairs so that bulky outdoor clothes and bags won't encroach on the thoroughfare of the hallway.

YOU COULD ALSO add a shoe rack in the space underneath.

HOME OFFICE

If there's enough headroom, you can create a small home office area. Be sure to find furniture that will make good use of the space.

KEEP THE COLOR SCHEME the same as the rest of the room so the workspace doesn't attract attention.

7 WAYS WITH
COLOR TRICKS

By using some simple decorating tricks you can make a hallway feel more inviting and improve its proportions, too. Think carefully which of these looks will suit the dimensions and style of your space, and which will link well to other rooms that lead off the hallway.

DIAMOND PATTERNED FLOOR

To make a narrow hallway feel wider, lay floor tiles diagonally or paint a diamond pattern onto your floorboards.

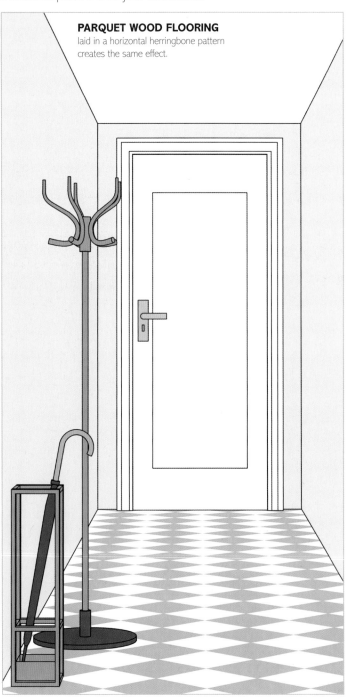

PARQUET WOOD FLOORING
laid in a horizontal herringbone pattern creates the same effect.

STRIPED RUNNER

Make a short hallway seem longer by adding a striped runner—either a carpet or painted directly onto the floor—along its length.

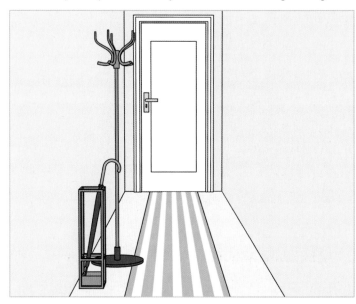

CHAIR RAIL

Make your hallway feel taller by adding a chair rail. Paint the walls a dark color beneath the rail and a lighter color above.

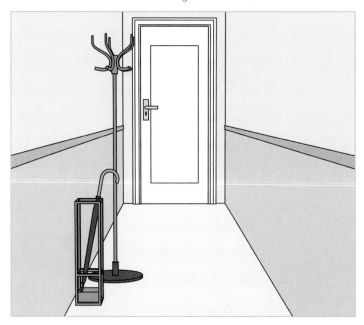

VERTICAL STRIPES

Make a low ceiling feel higher by painting vertical stripes in different tones of the same color on the walls to draw the eye upward.

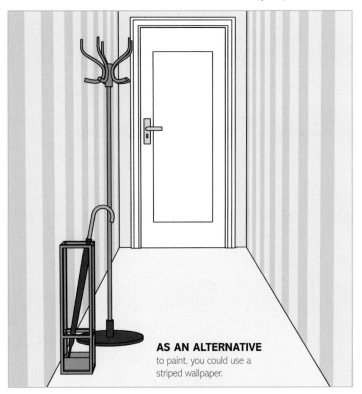

AS AN ALTERNATIVE to paint, you could use a striped wallpaper.

HORIZONTAL STRIPES

Make a short, narrow space seem longer and wider by painting horizontal stripes in similar tones on the walls.

STICK TO PALER shades to create a calm scheme.

DEEP COLOR ON AN END WALL

To make a long, narrow hallway feel shorter, and therefore wider, paint the wall at the far end a deep color.

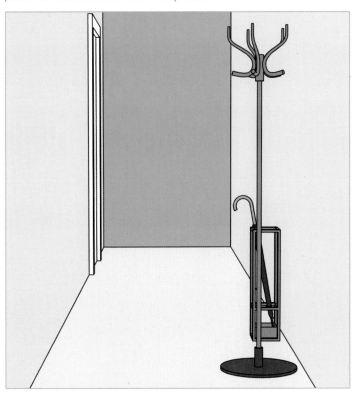

DEEP COLOR ON LONG WALLS

To make a short, uninviting hallway seem more welcoming, paint the longer wall, or walls, a deeper shade than the shorter wall, or walls.

HOME OFFICE

A home office will not be included in every home, but if you do want one it will require careful planning to make sure it works not just decoratively but also functionally. Follow this schedule to get the appropriate tradespeople in and the work done at the right time.

1 DEVISE A BUDGET

If you're starting work from scratch, include costs for decorative finishes in your budget list. Include extra money for any wiring, equipment, and a good office chair, and allow yourself a contingency of at least 10 percent.

2 PLAN THE LAYOUT
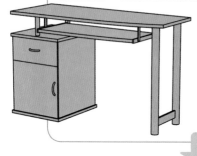

Draw a scale plan and include all doors and windows. Plot the position of the desk and, based on this, work out where to place the lighting and the phone/internet and electrical outlets.

3 RETHINK THE HEATING

Consider whether you need to make changes to the heating system. You can easily become cold when sitting still at a desk and if the room was not an office to begin with, it may need better or more easily adjustable heating. Similarly, can you open the windows easily to cool the room?

4 BOOK TRADESPEOPLE

Contact an electrician, HVAC contractor, plasterer, and painter to give you quotes. Ask a custom furniture company for a quote for built-in storage, too. Ask them what their job entails so you get everyone in at the right time.

5 ORDER THE MATERIALS

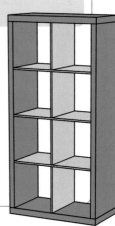

Once the quotes are in, order flooring, woodwork, doors, radiators, and windows, if being replaced. Furniture, wallpaper, paint, carpet, and light fixtures can be ordered once the main jobs are underway, unless you have space to store them. If you are ordering new furniture, find out about lead times for delivery, since it may need to be ordered now.

6 GUT THE ROOM

Remove old wallpaper to see if the walls and ceiling need replastering or patching, rip out damaged woodwork and unrepairable moldings, and pull up old flooring. Old wiring and obsolete plumbing should also be removed.

7 HVAC ROUGH-IN

Have new radiators or ductwork installed, since it is a disruptive job and may stop other steps from progressing.

8 ELECTRICAL—ROUGH-IN

The electrician will run wiring beneath the floor and into the walls and ceiling for the lighting system. The wiring and points for the phone/internet and additional equipment such as a printer should also be done now.

9 INSTALL NEW WINDOWS

Tackle this task now before the walls are patched. If the windows are being renovated rather than replaced, prepare them for painting now.

10 PATCH THE WALLS AND CEILING

Patch any holes in sheetrock walls and ceiling. Tape, sand, and skimcoat for a smooth finish.

11 LAY THE FLOORING

After the walls are patched, lay hard flooring, such as a wood floor, or a subfloor for a carpet.

12 INSTALL BUILT-IN FURNITURE

If you have chosen custom-fit office furniture, have the millworker install it before putting in baseboards and moldings.

13 INSTALL THE TRIM

Once the built-in furniture is in place, the new woodwork—baseboards, crown trim, doors, door frames, and picture rails—can be installed by the carpenter or millworker.

14 DECORATE

Fill fine cracks or dents in the walls. Prime and paint the ceiling, walls, and woodwork, and put up wallpaper last.

15 ORGANIZE THE FINAL INSTALL

The electrician can return to install lights and electrical outlets, and the HVAC contractor can put in the radiator.

16 LAY THE CARPET

If you have chosen a carpet (or carpet tiles), now is the best time for it to be laid.

17 ADD FINISHING TOUCHES

Any new furniture such as a desk, filing cabinets, and an office chair can be delivered now. Put up curtain rods or blinds, install door hardware, connect computer equipment, and hang items like a bulletin board on the wall.

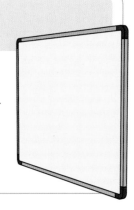

2 CREATE A MOOD BOARD FOR YOUR HOME OFFICE

Whether your home office is large or small, it needs to feels calm and organized. Getting the color palette, patterns, and furnishings right the first time will enable you to create an office that's not only well put together and uses space effectively, but is also an inviting and comfortable work area. Using a mood board will help you to create the most successful design for this often overlooked room.

1 FIND PICTURES OF HOME OFFICE ROOMS you like the look of by searching the internet and looking through magazines and books. Tear them out, print them off, or copy them and lay them all out on the floor. You might notice a theme begins to emerge, whether it's a liking for a type of wood or a furniture shape. This will be the starting point for your room design scheme.

Edit your selection of home office pictures down to one or two favorites and pin them to your mood board.

2 PICK A KEY ITEM or a theme to help you find a direction for your scheme. Use it as inspiration for everything from colors and shapes to patterns and textures when searching for the other components of the room.

Your favorite item could be a retro filing cabinet, an interesting lamp, or antique desk.

3 **PICK A BACKGROUND COLOR** for the room. Whether you choose a light, soothing shade or a deep, welcoming tone depends on how much natural light the room receives, but both these options will be easy to live with. If you're covering most of the walls with shelving, storage units, and bulletin boards, your background color (whether paint or a wallpaper) will be less of a feature.

Paint a larger proportion of the mood board (or pin on a wallpaper swatch) in your background color.

The intensity or subtlety of your main accent color will also influence the atmosphere of your working space.

Second accent colors can help to add more depth and interest to your design.

A third accent color might be a subtle variation of, or a complete contrast to, your main color.

4 **CHOOSE TWO OR THREE ACCENT COLORS**, which can be a subtle variation of your wall color or a dramatic contrast to it. One will be your main accent shade; use the second fractionally less and the third minimally. Paint color samples onto the board in the same proportions as they'll be used within the room to check that you have the right balance.

5 **ADD PATTERN & TEXTURE** with a rug, bulletin board, or fabric blind, for example; only small splashes are needed in an efficient environment like this. Keep the furnishings simple if you choose patterned wallpaper or, if the walls are plain, add wood shutters or a desk with a grainy wood surface.

Stick some floor swatches to the mood board to help you decide which flooring will suit your scheme.

6 **CHOOSE NEW FURNITURE** Using the same tricks you used to narrow down your room's color scheme, begin to look for furniture for your office. If the look of the room seems fairly plain so far, aim to add interest with a curvaceously shaped upholstered office chair, for example.

Displays of well-ordered colorful box files on shelves will add visual interest.

Stick any pictures of functional yet attractive furniture onto the board to build up your ideas.

7 **ADD FINISHING TOUCHES** Adding accessories and final touches, such as lighting, a chair cover, or picture frames, to a home office can turn it from purely functional to personal and individual, and help to pull your design scheme together. This is the time to pick pieces in your third accent color, whether they tone or contrast with your main color scheme. These subtle touches will ensure the success of your scheme, so refer your choices back to the color palette and style of your mood board first to ensure that they will be right.

3 LAYOUT CONSIDERATIONS FOR THE HOME OFFICE

A home office will invariably be a small room—or perhaps even a corner of a large room—so it's important to consider the layout of your office thoroughly before you start to purchase furniture, storage units, and accessories. You should also make a careful note of the room's measurements at this stage so that the furniture you buy will fit the proportions of the space you have available.

DESK

The desk you choose should be in proportion to the size of the room and placed correctly so that you are comfortable when working. If you use a computer, don't sit at the desk with your back to a window or the screen will be almost invisible. Similarly, don't sit facing a window unless it's north-facing or you're prepared to keep the blinds closed. Ideally, position the desk adjacent to, or pulled back from, the window and angle your computer screen away from the light. Also, allow enough space for an office chair to be pulled back. The desk needs to be conveniently placed for the wiring, too. Electric outlets can be installed in the floor instead of the wall if the desk will sit centrally, but make sure you work this into your rewiring plan.

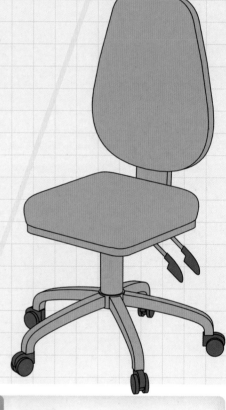

CHAIR

Choose an office chair that doesn't dominate the room or make it impossible or uncomfortable to sit at the desk. Allow at least a 4ft (1.25m) gap from the edge of the desk so the chair doesn't bump against a wall or other furniture when you push back to stand up. If your room doubles as a living space, you might want to incorporate the chair into the existing seating area—if so, make sure you don't have to lift the chair up and over other furniture whenever you want to use it.

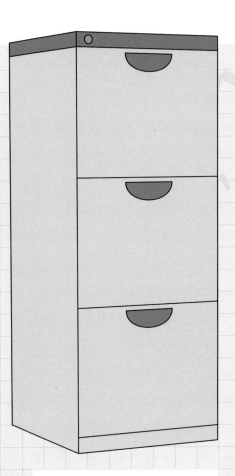

WALL-MOUNTED STORAGE

To be useful, wall-mounted cabinets and shelves should be just a little deeper than a file or three-ring binder. Search for wide, streamlined cabinets with sliding doors if you don't have enough space for the doors to open out, and hang the cabinets and shelves at eye level so you can easily see inside or reach items. Make sure they don't block natural light, either. If you have an alcove, use it for shelving; if you have no other space, install a high shelf to store files and items that you rarely need.

FILING CABINET

The most convenient place to position a filing cabinet is within (or beneath) your desk, so you don't need to get out of your seat to open a drawer. If a set of desk drawers isn't large enough for your files, consider the amount of floor space you have: tall, thin filing cabinets are ideal for rooms with little space for anything else. If you have more room, lower, wider units set behind, or adjacent to, the desk are a good solution and will provide you with another work surface on which to store extras such as in-box trays.

BULLETIN BOARD

A bulletin board is a must-have for a home office: it can be used to display paperwork and notes such as reminders, timetables and calendars, bills, lists, and other relevant information. Position the bulletin board where you can easily see and reach it—to one side of your desk, for example. If you find it hard to keep it looking neat, use an area of wall that is not immediately visible upon entering the room.

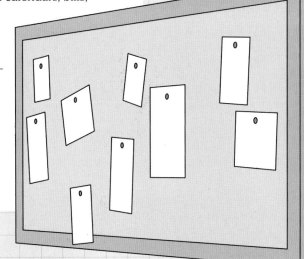

4 CHOOSE A DESK

With so many people now working from home, the choice of desks available is huge. Check that the desk you want to buy is the right size for your room and appropriate for the tasks you will be undertaking. Also make sure that you are able to open and close the door to the room easily once the desk is in position.

CHOOSE THE TYPE

The type of desk you choose depends on your workload. Do you work from home and need desk space for a laptop and files, or is it simply a place to do home administration? Does it need built-in storage or will you have extra storage in the room?

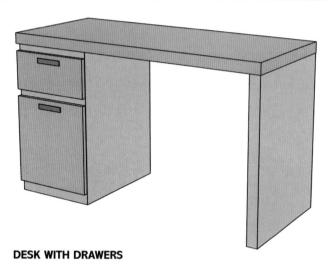

DESK WITH DRAWERS

This classic design suits most people's requirements for a home office desk, since it has ample surface space and storage for paper, files, and other small items. This style of desk is available in a huge range of sizes, designs, and materials so there's bound to be something to suit your home office décor.

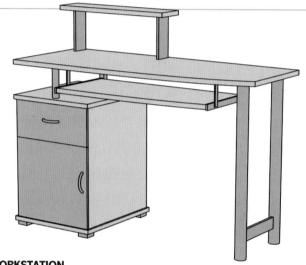

WORKSTATION

Workstations are made specifically with the intention that a computer and its accessories will be housed on or inside it. Some also have doors that you can close at the end of the day to keep all your equipment hidden away—ideal if your office is in an area of your living room or bedroom.

TRESTLE

A trestle has a larger-than-average desk surface, which sits on two trestle legs. Despite being larger, its skeletal structure means that it doesn't dominate a room. It is typically used by writers, architects, and people who need plenty of tabletop space, but can work equally well as a conventional desk.

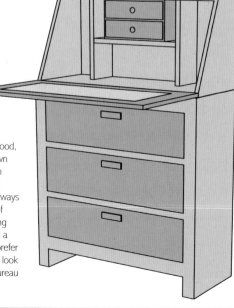

BUREAU

Generally made from wood, a bureau has a pull-down front section that, when opened, creates a desk surface. They are not always the most comfortable of desks to work at for long periods, but if you want a desk for light use and prefer something that doesn't look like office furniture, a bureau is a good choice.

5 CHOOSE AN OFFICE CHAIR

If you work from home and spend long hours sitting at a desk, buying the right office chair is of utmost importance. The seat and backrest should be padded firmly enough to support you, and if you spend lots of time using a keyboard, armrests are an important feature.

1 CHOOSE THE TYPE

The chair you choose depends on your budget, how often you use it, and how comfortable you want it to be. A simple office chair is fine for occasional use, but if you work full-time from home, an ergonomic "executive" chair is worth the extra expense.

BASIC OFFICE CHAIR
A basic office chair is all you need if you are only going to be sitting in it now and again. If other family members will also use it, look for one with an adjustable seat height and back.

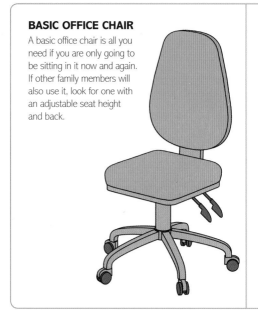

"EXECUTIVE" OFFICE CHAIR
Executive chairs are built for maximum comfort, and high-end products are ergonomically designed with a high curved back for back and neck support. These chairs mean business, and are often priced accordingly.

CLUB-STYLE OFFICE CHAIR
These chairs have added comfort and style in addition to all the benefits of a basic office chair. They are often available in decorative fabrics, which is a

2 CHOOSE THE MATERIAL

The style of chair you have selected may well determine the material you choose. Unless you're picking something that suits your room's decoration, you may prefer a practical or comfortable fabric that is available in the chair design you want.

FABRIC
Low in cost, natural fabrics like wool or cotton are also breathable and warm to the touch. Office chair fabrics typically have a textured, tweed, or patterned appearance.

LEATHER
Durable and hard-wearing, leather is a practical, medium-priced option. Prolonged exposure to heat (either central heating or the Sun's rays) may cause it to crack.

MESH
Mesh is comfortable, since it shapes itself to your body and allows air to circulate to keep you cool. It ranges from cheap to expensive, but color choices are limited.

6 CHOOSE LIGHTING

Your home office needs to be carefully lit to get the right balance of practical task lighting and ambient atmosphere. You also need to consider whether you need different levels, or types, of lighting (mainly task-based) throughout the day and evening, if you or other family members use the room frequently.

1 DECIDE ON A STYLE OF LIGHTING

While you may be able to add accent lighting to a larger home office, the reality is that this room is first and foremost a functional space and is also likely to be fairly small. Therefore, make ambient and, especially, task lighting your main focus.

AMBIENT

Determine what level of ambient lighting you need. It's worth making sure that the ambient lighting in this room is bright enough to illuminate the whole room efficiently without task lighting, if necessary. Also use a dimmer switch so that you can dim the overhead lights when desired.

TASK

It might be that you only need a single desk lamp to light the space by your computer or work area, but if your home office has more than one work surface, or perhaps a single large stretch of desk, you may want to think about adding some more task lighting.

2 CHOOSE YOUR LIGHT FIXTURES

If your office is a small, low-ceilinged room, or the natural daylight in the room is poor, a spread of efficient spotlights sunk into the ceiling or close to it are a practical buy; reserve a pendant light, or lights, for a larger home office.

SURFACE-MOUNTED CEILING LIGHT

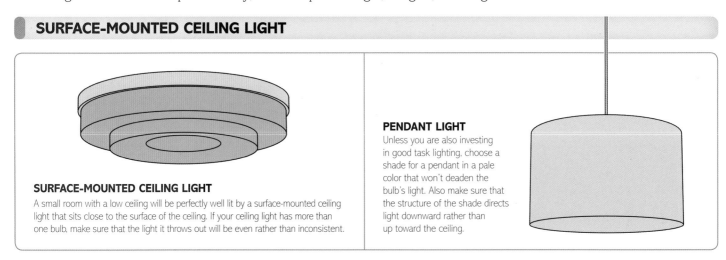

SURFACE-MOUNTED CEILING LIGHT

A small room with a low ceiling will be perfectly well lit by a surface-mounted ceiling light that sits close to the surface of the ceiling. If your ceiling light has more than one bulb, make sure that the light it throws out will be even rather than inconsistent.

PENDANT LIGHT

Unless you are also investing in good task lighting, choose a shade for a pendant in a pale color that won't deaden the bulb's light. Also make sure that the structure of the shade directs light downward rather than up toward the ceiling.

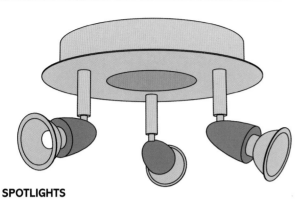

SPOTLIGHTS

Spotlights are a good choice for a small, dark room, especially if they can be directed to suit your needs. Bear in mind, however, that ceiling spotlights will throw shadows around the room, so if you sit at a desk with your back to a central spotlight, it's likely that the space in front of you will be in shadow.

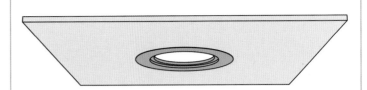

RECESSED DOWNLIGHTS

Recessed downlights are a stylish option for a small, contemporary room, especially if it has a low ceiling that won't suit pendants or lights jutting out from the ceiling. These lights tend to be very bright, so don't install too many in a tight space—aim to install one light every three feet (1m) or so.

WALL-MOUNTED LIGHTS

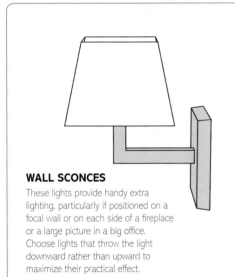

WALL SCONCES

These lights provide handy extra lighting, particularly if positioned on a focal wall or on each side of a fireplace or a large picture in a big office. Choose lights that throw the light downward rather than upward to maximize their practical effect.

SINGLE SPOTLIGHTS

A wall spotlight can be used as task lighting, providing a strong pool of light over a desk surface, but it can also be directed onto a bookshelf, for example, to both show off your books and make them easier to see.

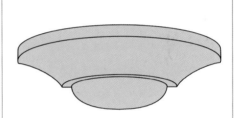

WALL UPLIGHTS

Wall uplights as soft ambient lighting can create a welcoming atmosphere—often overlooked in a home office. They throw light upward to highlight the ceiling and give walls the illusion of added height.

LAMPS

DESK LAMPS

Desk lamps are a must-have in a home office, and the best are those that can be directed up and down and from side to side. Ideally, the lamp should sit just behind and to the right or the left of your computer or main writing space.

CLIP-ON LIGHTS

If you have no room for a desk lamp, or need extra lighting in other areas of the room, clip-on lights are a good solution. They can be easily attached to the edges of shelves and numerous other surfaces. Make sure that you buy clip-on lights with directional heads.

7 CHOOSE WINDOW TREATMENTS

The window treatment you choose for your home office really depends on how and when you use the room. If you work from home and use the office during the day, choose something that can be adjusted as the light changes. If you only use the room in the evenings, you can choose something purely decorative.

1 CHOOSE A TYPE

Decide what will be practical for your home office and whether what you'd like will provide enough shade or insulation, and be easy to clean. It's also worth checking if the window will be easy to open and close if your desk is positioned at the window.

BLINDS

Blinds are unobtrusive and sit neatly against your window frame, taking up minimal space—which, if your desk is by the window or the room is small, is an important consideration. If a blind on its own is too stark a look for you, match it with curtains or dress curtains.

CURTAINS

If your desk sits against your window, dress curtains matched with blinds or shutters may give you the look you want without having to be drawn. Curtains are an option in a larger room if you want a cozy look that also gives some insulation.

SHUTTERS

Shutters are a stylish choice for a home office, and are available in a wide range of wood finishes and color choices. Louvered shutters can be designed with two or three panels and in a choice of styles including full-height, café, and tier-on-tier.

CHECKLIST

● **Consider the light** that comes through the window at different times of day, and if you need a window treatment that will help you to control this. If you really want curtains, consider teaming them with a venetian blind, for example.

● **If your windows aren't double-paned,** you could use heavy lined curtains to prevent heat loss through the windowpanes at night and give the room a visual warmth during the day.

● **If your room is overlooked,** consider using a translucent fabric such as muslin, voile, or lace net that offers privacy while still letting in light. Half-depth shutters fulfill the same function.

2 CHOOSE A STYLE

Home office windows seldom receive the decorative attention they should, since they're usually seen, like the rest of the room, as a purely functional feature. However, furnishing them attractively will have a major impact on how good the room looks.

BLINDS

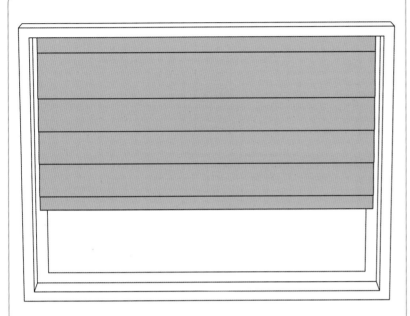

ROMAN

The most decorative of the blinds recommended for a home office, Roman blinds are formed of soft pleats that hang flat against the window when lowered, and fold neatly together when raised. Available in a wide choice of fabrics, they are particularly attractive when matched with curtains.

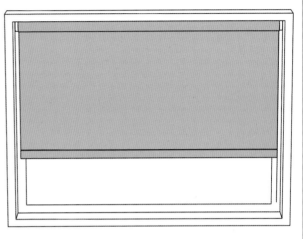

ROLLER

Roller blinds are an inexpensive option, and, provided that you are fairly handy, are easy to install. Blinds are made from stiffened fabric in a wide range of colors and designs, and can be pulled up or down to block out or let in sunlight. Many ready-made roller blinds can be cut smaller to fit the size of your window.

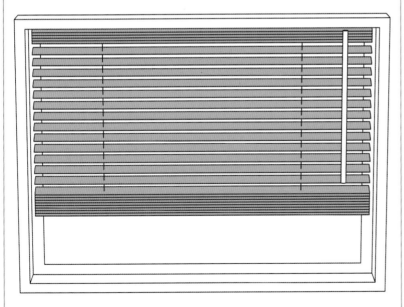

VENETIAN

With their adjustable slats, Venetian blinds are a practical choice for a home office, since you can easily control the amount of light coming through the window simply by moving the slats up or down. They are available in a choice of materials, colors, and slat widths.

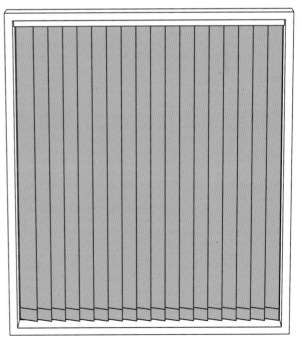

VERTICAL

Vertical blinds are available in a wide range of colors and fabrics, and are made up of vertical strips of fabric that can be tilted or drawn. These blinds are more suited to floor-to-ceiling windows, and fit best in a contemporary rather than a traditional space.

CURTAINS

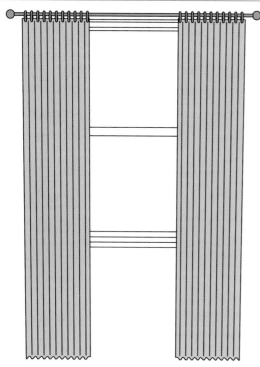

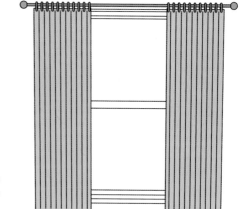

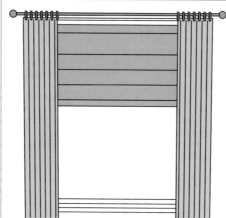

SILL LENGTH

Sill-length curtains are perhaps more practical in rooms where space is at a premium, since they sit neatly against the window and don't infringe on the wall space below. This curtain length can look old-fashioned, so pick your fabric carefully.

FULL LENGTH

Full-length curtains in your office are only an option if your desk or other office furniture isn't near the window (otherwise you may find they become caught up in a drawer or under the wheel of your chair). Use a curtain rod that is wider than your window so the curtains can be pulled all the way back to let in as much light as possible.

DRESS CURTAINS

If you have chosen to use roller or Roman blinds for practical purposes, but still want to add curtains for a decorative touch, combine them with dress curtains, which are narrower than normal curtains and are not designed to be drawn.

SHUTTERS

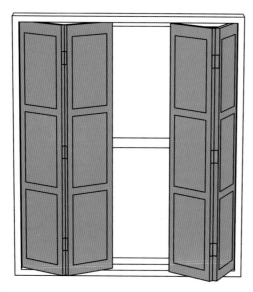

SOLID

Solid shutters are a popular choice for period, particularly Victorian, homes. Made from solid wood, they can assist in reducing noise levels, so they are a good choice if you live on a busy street. However, bear in mind that they do not let in any light when closed, so should only be used at night.

LOUVERED

Louvered shutters look stylish and are an excellent choice for home offices, since you can adjust the slats to control the amount of light flooding into the room. The best options for home offices are tier-on-tier shutters or full-height shutters with a mid-rail so you can control the top and bottom sections independently.

8 CHOOSE
OFFICE STORAGE

Keep your office from becoming cluttered by investing in the right kind of storage. This may mean buying one single multipurpose unit or a combination of pieces that can meet your needs. You don't have to stick to office furniture—items meant for a living room or bedroom can work, too, so use your imagination.

1 CHOOSE THE PIECES

The pieces you choose will depend on what you need to store and the space available. Take time to work out what you will need to file, what you would like to keep hidden away, and what needs to be within easy reach.

WALL-MOUNTED STORAGE

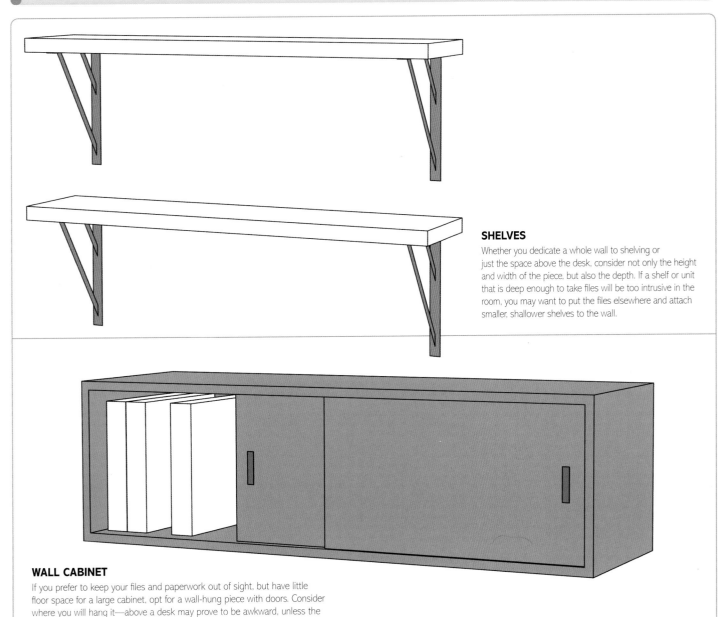

SHELVES

Whether you dedicate a whole wall to shelving or just the space above the desk, consider not only the height and width of the piece, but also the depth. If a shelf or unit that is deep enough to take files will be too intrusive in the room, you may want to put the files elsewhere and attach smaller, shallower shelves to the wall.

WALL CABINET

If you prefer to keep your files and paperwork out of sight, but have little floor space for a large cabinet, opt for a wall-hung piece with doors. Consider where you will hang it—above a desk may prove to be awkward, unless the doors slide open rather than open outward.

FILING CABINET

A traditional filing cabinet is useful if you need lots of hanging file space. This type of cabinet usually consists of three or four deep, lockable drawers, making it a good option if you have private files that need to be locked away.

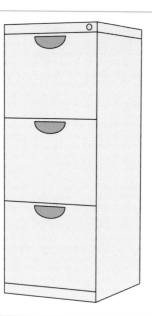

DRAWER UNIT

Drawer units designed for office use are available in various heights and widths—some will sit neatly under your desk—and are often on casters so you can move them around easily. They can either have uniformly sized drawers or drawers in a range of sizes.

BOOKCASE

If your home office is mostly used for family administration and homework, you may simply need storage for books or files that you don't have space for elsewhere. For flexibility, look for one that allows you to tailor the shelf heights to suit your specific—and changing—needs.

TALL CABINET

Tall cabinets provide lots of storage for anything from a computer to files that you'd rather not have on display. In a small room, a part-glazed unit will help to increase the feeling of space, but only invest in one of these if you're confident you can keep what's on show neat.

LOW CABINET

Low cabinets are a good choice for small, narrow rooms, since they won't dwarf the space. Choose one that's deep enough to store files inside and has enough surface space to place a printer on top.

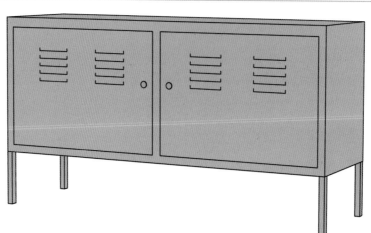

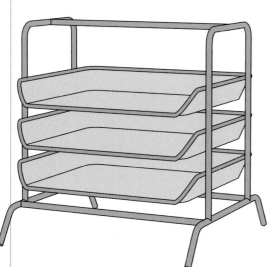

LETTER TRAY

Letter trays are handy for paperwork that you're not ready to file away. They are available in single, double, and triple layers, or you can use stackable trays to create a many-tiered configuration.

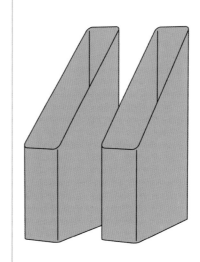

MAGAZINE FILE

These upright files are useful for storing brochures, folders, and paperwork, as well as magazines. Their size means they will fit into a storage cabinet or sit neatly on shelves or a desk. Cardboard files are the cheapest option, but not as durable as plastic or wooden ones.

HANGING FILE BOX

Lidded suspension file boxes provide extra storage for hanging files that allow you to keep your papers neat and organized. They can be easily accessed and are also portable. They are available in a wide range of materials and sizes.

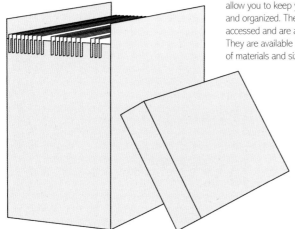

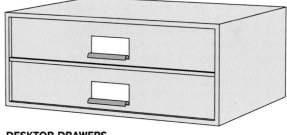

DESKTOP DRAWERS

Keep your paperwork organized and out of sight with storage drawers that sit neatly on your desk, a shelf, or in a cabinet. Use one on its own or stack several together to provide extra storage space.

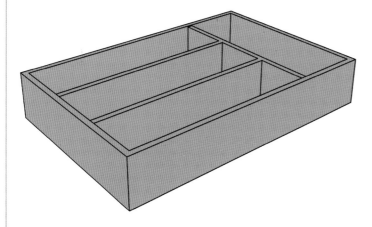

DRAWER ORGANIZER

Keep your drawers neat and tidy with a drawer organizer. Similar to a cutlery tray, it is made up of different-sized compartments that are ideal for storing pens and other small stationery items.

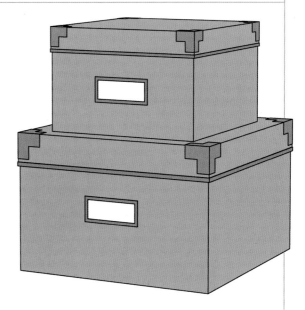

STORAGE BOXES

Basic storage boxes are useful for storing anything from receipts to small office supplies. Choose a color or pattern that will suit the room and keep the contents organized by labeling the boxes.

5 WAYS WITH
OFFICE WALL DISPLAYS

Your office doesn't have to be just a functional, businesslike space, it can be decorative and inviting, too. If you're feeling creative, you can adapt functional items to produce a decorative effect. Choose a display that is appealing and useful, although not so exciting or extreme that it will distract you from your work.

BULLETIN BOARD

Stick self-adhesive cork tiles onto a wall and pin up anything from a calendar and useful phone numbers to posters and family photos or a montage of a favorite theme. Whatever you pin up, keep it all organized to give an orderly feel.

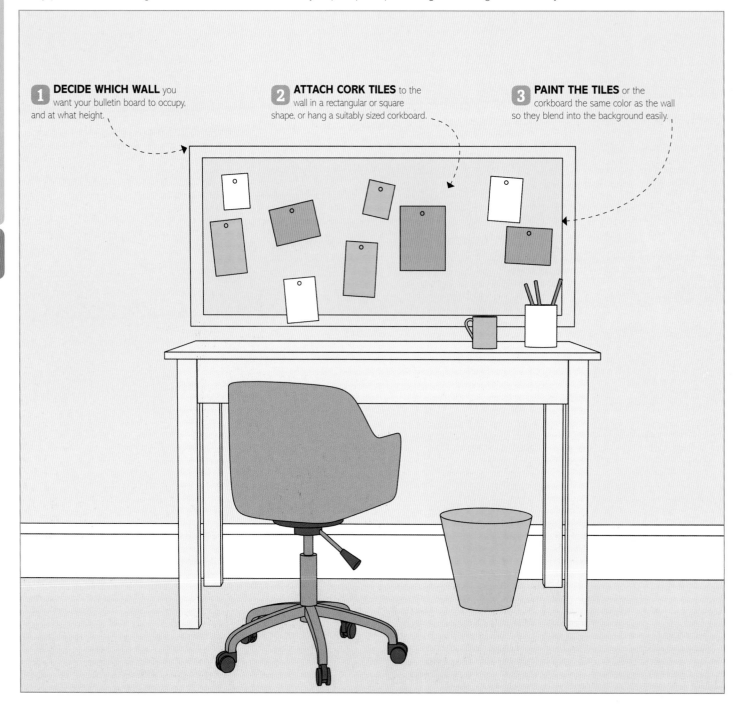

1 **DECIDE WHICH WALL** you want your bulletin board to occupy, and at what height.

2 **ATTACH CORK TILES** to the wall in a rectangular or square shape, or hang a suitably sized corkboard.

3 **PAINT THE TILES** or the corkboard the same color as the wall so they blend into the background easily.

MAP

Hang a large map on the wall, or frame some smaller maps, as a decoration. It can also function as a device for planning trips away.

CLOCKS

Whether it's to check the time elsewhere in the world or for decoration, a group of clocks on the wall telling different times is a stylish display.

CLIPBOARDS

Clipboards on a wall will provide somewhere on which to attach items such as letters, invitations, and tickets. Hang as many as you need.

CHOOSE CLIPBOARDS that are color coordinated, or cover them in a pretty wallpaper before you hang them.

BLACKBOARD

Paint a large square on one wall with chalkboard paint and paint a grid in chalk to create a weekly or monthly calendar.

9 CHOOSE FLOORING

While a home office is primarily a functional room, the more of your personality and style you inject into it, the happier you'll be spending time there. To that end, the right flooring deserves careful thought. Don't overlook practical considerations though; think about wear and tear in the area around the desk, for example.

1 CHOOSE THE LOOK

Not all floor types are suitable for office chairs, so there are fewer options here than in most other rooms. Wood gives a sleek contemporary look, while carpet offers a cozy and traditional feel.

WOOD

Wood floors can add character and warmth to your room's design scheme. Wood planks make a room appear visually longer and wider, so they are a good choice for small rooms. Light-colored woods will help enhance the sense of space further still.

CARPET

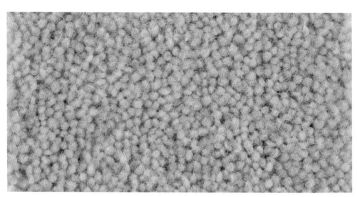

Carpet, by its very nature, will always make a room feel warm and cozy. Using carpet is also a good way of adding texture and color to a home office; you could even opt for a patterned carpet if the walls of your office are plain.

2 CHOOSE THE MATERIAL

A home office floor needs to be hard-wearing around the desk itself, so choose a material that is durable, easy to clean, and that you can repair if it gets damaged. The following are all worthy of consideration.

WOOD

HARDWOOD

Hardwoods like oak, maple, and ash are stylish yet tough and hard-wearing. Their cost is medium to high and they should be laid by a professional to get the best finish.

SOFTWOOD

Low- to medium-priced flooring brings a sense of warmth to a home office. Use floor planks dried in a kiln so that shrinkage is kept to a minimum.

ENGINEERED WOOD

Layers of hard and softwood boards and a hardwood veneered surface make up medium-priced engineered wood, giving it the look and feel of a solid wood floor.

LAMINATE

Made by laminating a decorative wood-effect image on to a base made from compressed fiberboard, laminate planks are low to medium in price.

CARPET

TWIST PILES
Low- to medium-priced hard-wearing twist piles have a coarse, rugged appearance. Made of wool or man-made fibers, they come in plains, heathers, or patterns.

VELVET PILE
This carpet has a dense low-cut pile and a soft, smooth appearance, somewhat like suede. Despite its luxurious look, medium- to high-cost velvet pile is hard-wearing.

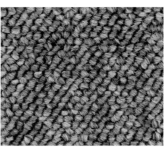

CARPET TILES
Low-cost carpet tiles allow you to replace squares as they become worn-out—for instance, under your desk and chair—without having to change the whole floor.

COIR
Low-cost coir is made from coconut husk fibers that are softened in seawater and then woven. It has a highly textured finish that is extremely hard-wearing.

SISAL
Made from the Agave Sisalana plant, sisal is medium-priced with a fine texture. It is available in a range of weaves and a choice of colors.

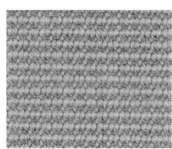

JUTE
Softer than other natural floor coverings, jute is available in flat woven designs, including a tight boucle and herringbone in its natural color. It is medium priced.

SEAGRASS
Medium-priced seagrass grows in coastal meadows on banks of rivers. It has a chunky appearance once woven, and a waxy texture that is stain-resistant.

OFFICE CHAIRS AND YOUR FLOOR

An office chair on casters that is in constant use will put more pressure on your flooring than any other chair in the house. If you regularly move your chair backward and forward on casters, check which type of floor covering will suit your space best:

● **Look for a carpet** with a wool/nylon mix, since this is more durable than other carpets.

● **Hardwood and engineered wood floorings** may scratch a little, but they are likely to stand up well to wear and tear, and both can be sanded back to restore their appearance; softwood flooring, however, will be more easily damaged.

● **Laminate flooring** is likely to become quite scratched or scuffed by casters, and metal and hard plastic casters can also cause chipping, so this option may not be suitable if you are after long-term durability.

● **Whatever flooring you choose**, it's wise to protect the area beneath your chair with a protective mat or low-pile rug.

If you buy a good office chair that has casters, it's also worth investing in a durable flooring material.

COVER
STORAGE BOXES

Practical accessories in bright colors will lift the atmosphere of your home office to make it a more attractive place in which to work. For a coordinated, streamlined look, choose a colored felt that fits in with the rest of your color scheme.

WHAT YOU NEED

- Flat-packed storage box
- Felt fabric
- Scissors
- Double-sided adhesive tape
- Bradawl or screwdriver

1 CUT THE FELT FABRIC

1 **LAY THE FELT FABRIC** on a flat surface, then place one of the flat box panels on top and cut out the fabric around it. The fabric should be slightly larger than the panel to allow for overlapping for a neat finish (it can be trimmed later).

2 **LAY THE SECOND BOX** panel flat on the remaining felt and cut out the fabric, leaving the same allowance for overlapping.

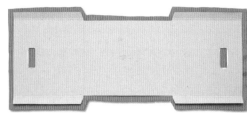

2 COVER THE BOX

1 **STICK DOUBLE-SIDED TAPE** along the outside edges of the box panel. Lay the fabric cutout flat (use a little tape at the edges, if necessary, to hold it in place). Pull the fabric gently as you anchor it down to get rid of any wrinkles or creases). Peel the backing off the tape and carefully position the box panel centrally on the fabric.

2 **REPEAT WITH THE OTHER BOX** panel and piece of fabric.

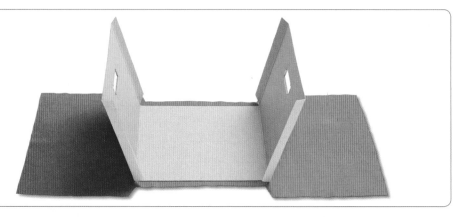

3 **TRIM THE EDGES** of the fabric neatly with scissors.

4 **REPUNCH THE HOLES** on the sides of the box panels with a bradawl or small screwdriver.

5 **RECONSTRUCT THE BOX** using the nuts and bolts provided with the flat pack kit.

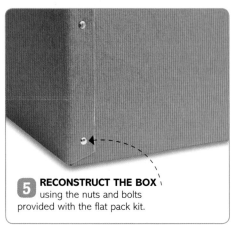

3 COVER THE LID

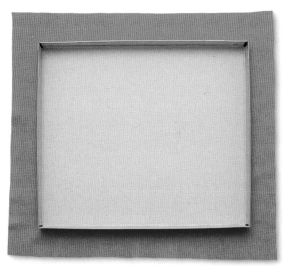

1 USING THE LID AS A TEMPLATE, cut a square of fabric that is larger than the lid (to allow for overlapping), then draw around the lid with a pen.

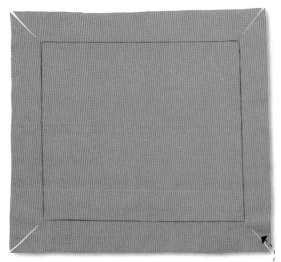

2 ANCHOR THE FABRIC down with tape (as before), if necessary. Then, using the scissors, make a diagonal cut from each corner of the fabric to the edge of the pen square.

3 STICK THE DOUBLE-SIDED TAPE around the outside and inside edges of the lid, peel the backing off, and place the lid on the fabric, aligning it with the pencil square. Fold in the corners, then fold the fabric over the edges of the lid and press it down.

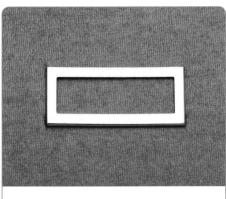

4 REAPPLY THE LABEL holder onto the side of the box.

MAKE
AN UPHOLSTERED MESSAGE BOARD

Inject a shot of color and texture into a home office with a handsome message board. It's up to you how padded you want the message board to be (depending on which thickness of polyester padding you choose). It's also worth buying plenty of ribbon (around 15ft/5m, to be safe), since you will use a lot of it.

WHAT YOU NEED

- Cork bulletin board
- Polyester padding
- Cotton fabric
- Staple gun and staples
- Ribbon
- Scissors
- Thumbtacks or upholstery tacks

1 CUT THE FABRIC AND PADDING

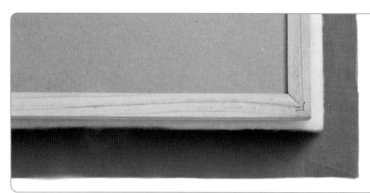

CUT A RECTANGLE of polyester padding that is slightly bigger than the bulletin board. Cut a rectangle of fabric that is 2in (5cm) larger on all sides than the bulletin board. Lay the fabric, face side down, on a flat surface, place the padding on top, then place the bulletin board face down on top of the padding.

2 STAPLE THE FABRIC

FOLD OVER the edge of one side of the fabric and gently stretch it over the back of the frame, fold over the edge, and secure it in place with a staple using a staple gun. Repeat the process on the opposite side, then follow this suggested sequence (see right) to staple the rest of the fabric to the bulletin board, leaving the corners for last.

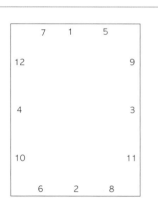

3 SECURE THE CORNERS

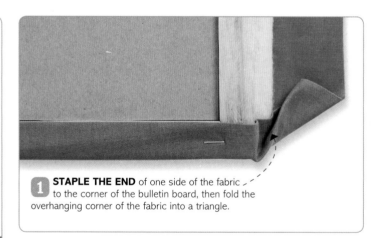

1 **STAPLE THE END** of one side of the fabric to the corner of the bulletin board, then fold the overhanging corner of the fabric into a triangle.

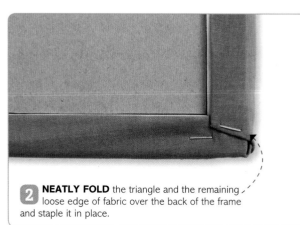

2 **NEATLY FOLD** the triangle and the remaining loose edge of fabric over the back of the frame and staple it in place.

1 **STAPLE ONE END** of the ribbon to the back corner of the board and stretch it across the front in a diagonal line. Cut and staple the end of the ribbon to the opposite back corner. Attach more lengths of ribbon in the same direction, judging the distance between each length by eye rather than measuring it.

2 **CREATE A DIAMOND PATTERN** by attaching diagonal lengths of ribbon in the opposite direction.

3 **PUT A THUMBTACK**, or upholstery tack, in the front of the board at each ribbon intersection.

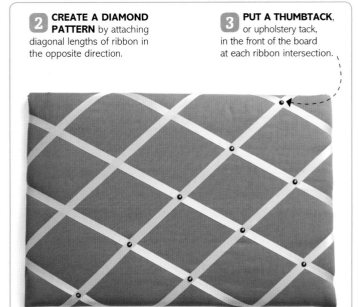

PLAN THE PERFECT
DUAL-PURPOSE OFFICE/LIVING ROOM

If your work area is set up in an area of your living room, it is important that you find suitable furniture and enough storage to cope with all your practical requirements, while still making the room look good. Follow these guidelines to make the most of your multiuse space.

USE FABULOUS FILES

If you only have space for wall-hung shelves on which to store your paperwork, pick uniform filing boxes and folders covered in a printed design or in a color that tones with your room. Alternatively, cover them yourself in wallpaper and fabric remnants. This will help you both to stay organized and keep the space looking good.

CHOOSE A DESK

Opt for a slimline console table, small dressing table, or corner unit, which are all compact and ideal for dual-purpose rooms. If you want your work area to blend into the room, choose a desk in a material that complements your other furniture. Sit at the desk in the store before you buy and be sure there's enough room for a laptop, lamp, phone, and in-box at the very least.

HIDE IT AWAY AT THE END OF THE DAY

A folding screen can be used to conceal your work space if you want to keep it hidden from visitors or shut it off from the rest of the room in the evening. Choose a good-looking screen that will suit the rest of your scheme or even enhance it (you can buy either ready-made screens or versions that you assemble and decorate yourself).

FIND STORAGE FOR TECHNOLOGY

Equipment such as a printer or scanner isn't attractive to look at, so hiding these large pieces of equipment away is a must if your room doubles as a living or sleeping space. Instead of choosing office furniture, which isn't always good-looking, search for a credenza, antique armoire, or cabinet deep enough to house everything inside.

DUAL-PURPOSE OFFICE/BEDROOM

If your home office is housed in the corner of your bedroom, many of the same principles apply. Choose furniture that suits the design of the bedroom and conceals unattractive equipment, and check that your desk has enough surface space to accommodate office necessities. If your bedroom is large, consider using modular shelving units instead of a screen to conceal the office area, and store files, books, picture frames, and decorative items on both sides of the shelving. Make sure you have enough natural light (and suitable window treatments) and task lighting, such as a swing-arm lamp, to illuminate your work area, too.

SAVE SPACE WITH DUAL-PURPOSE FURNITURE

Every piece of furniture must work twice as hard in a multipurpose room, so when you look for furniture that's not designed for a home office—a coffee table or a footstool, for example—shop for clever designs with storage incorporated, or pieces that are designed to be dual-purpose. For example, some coffee tables have deep drawers in which you can store phone books or lids that pop up to create computer tables. The key to buying this furniture is research—be prepared to put some effort in to finding the right items.

FIND MOBILE FURNITURE

Mobile furniture on casters is a good choice for multipurpose rooms so that it can easily be rolled aside if you need to create extra space to unfold a sofa bed, for example. The furniture must be solidly built and the casters sturdy enough to stand up to wear and tear.

PLAN FOR GUESTS

If you're using your living room as somewhere to work, the probability is that you don't have a spare guest room. If this is so, it's a good idea to buy a sofa bed rather than a conventional sofa for guests to sleep on when they visit.

LAUNDRY ROOM

1 WHAT TO DO WHEN
RENOVATING YOUR LAUNDRY ROOM

If you're lucky enough to have the space for a laundry room, you'll want it to be as useful a space as possible, so plan the room carefully to get both the layout and work schedule right the first time. Follow the timeline below to ensure that you include everything you need, when you need it.

1 PLAN YOUR LAYOUT

Draw a plan of the room to scale on graph paper and include all the items you require. It's worth keeping all plumbing to one side of the room to cut down on costs. Include a water supply for the sink and washing machine plus drainage, electrical receptacles, task-focused lighting, an extractor fan, and space for a duct and exterior vent for the dryer, if needed.

2 CONSIDER STORAGE AND DRYING OPTIONS

For storage, look for a combination of deep closet and drawer space; kitchen cabinets are ideal. Plan in some countertop space to accommodate a laundry basket and folded laundry. Also consider whether you want wall- or ceiling-hung drying racks installed or floor-standing racks that can be folded flat when not in use. Think about where you'd like these to go.

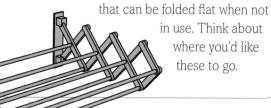

3 GET QUOTES FOR THE WORK

Line up quotes from at least three different plumbers, electricians, HVAC contractors, and carpenters, and possibly tilers and painters. Or ask one general contractor to take on the work and line up all workmen.

4 ORDER YOUR MATERIALS

Ask your contractor when flooring, fixtures, plumbing, electrical, and other supplies should be delivered. The washing machine and accessories can be ordered once work is underway.

5 GUT THE ROOM

Clear the room of everything that is no longer needed, such as old woodwork, plumbing fixtures, and flooring.

6 INSTALL ELECTRICAL AND PLUMBING—ROUGH-IN

The electrical install for everything from underfloor heating to receptacles, and the plumbing for laundry appliances can start now. The electrician and plumber will need to return later to finish installing these (final install).

7 CLOSE THE WALLS

Once the plumbing and wiring are in place, the walls and ceiling can be patched and skim coated for decoration (some parts of the room may need some minor filling later). Be sure to use moisture-resistant tile-backer board at tiled, wet areas.

8 LAY THE FLOOR

If you are having electric underfloor heating, ensure that the subfloor is level before installing it, then protect it with a hard floor suitable for a laundry room; tiles and concrete are practical choices. Seal the new floor, if necessary, and keep it well protected until other work is finished.

9 INSTALL WOODWORK

Once the walls are dry, new baseboards, door frames, and any other decorative moldings can be put back into the room. If you are having built-in storage installed, this could be done at the same time.

10 PREP AND PAINT

Fill, prime, and paint over any fine cracks or damage to the walls as a result of woodwork installation. Start with the walls and ceiling, then the woodwork. Choose paint that is water-resistant, since condensation will be an issue.

11 FINAL INSTALL—ELECTRICAL AND PLUMBING

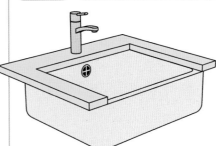

The plumber and electrician can return to install the sink and connect the electrical receptacles and lighting.

12 TILE THE WALLS

Tiles withstand knocks and scrapes well, are easy to wipe clean, and are a good surface for rooms with moist conditions, so the more tiled surfaces, the better. Painted wood paneling around dry areas is another option.

13 INSTALL HANGING STORAGE

Install wall- and ceiling-hung drying racks, hooks, and shelves. Vary the height of the hooks to accommodate clothes of differing lengths (fold-up, floor-standing drying racks can be stored on wall hooks, too, when not in use).

14 ADD FINISHING TOUCHES

Include some fun details, such as pictures, old-fashioned laundry signs, clothes-pin bags, or decorative boxes to hold laundry products.

2 LAYOUT CONSIDERATIONS
FOR THE LAUNDRY ROOM

A laundry room will rarely be a very large space—more commonly it will be just about big enough. Planning the layout down to the last detail is therefore a must to ensure that you can fit in all the equipment you need, that everything is easily accessible, and that the room functions well. Follow these tips to find out how to plan your laundry room effectively.

WASHING MACHINE

Your washing machine, or washer-dryer, and a sink will be the two most important elements in the room, so position them first. They don't need to be next to each other, but it will cut your plumbing budget if the water supply and drainage for the two are nearby, preferably along the same wall. Check that there is enough room to kneel in front of a front-loading washing machine and that opening the door to the room will not impede access to the drum.

CLOTHES DRYER

If you have enough floor space, a clothes dryer should sit next to the washing machine so you can transfer a load of laundry easily. If there isn't enough room, put the clothes dryer on top of the washing machine (don't try it the other way around, since the washing machine will be too heavy). Most dryers will need to be vented, so consider how best to work this into your layout so that the dryer is placed on an outside wall.

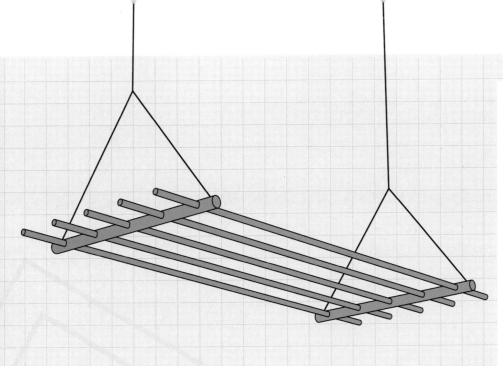

DRYING RACK

Wall- or ceiling-hung drying racks are useful, since they take up no floor space. Position them near a source of ventilation such as a window and above a sink or drain board so clothes can drip-dry. Also hang them high enough so that you can hang long items without them touching the floor or another surface. Otherwise, buy drying racks that will fold flat against the wall when not in use.

SINK

If you can place the sink near your washing machine, you will find it more practical: anything left to soak can be neatly transferred to rinse and spin in the machine without water dripping over the floor. Try to leave space on either side, or to one side, of the sink for a drain board, and space below to hold laundry detergent.

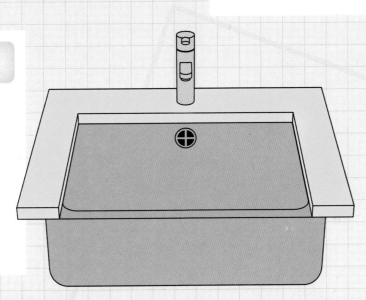

SHELVES OR CABINETS

Any spare wall space within a laundry room can be filled with shelves or, for a neater look, wall-hung cabinets. If the room is doubling as a downstairs powder room, install shelves or a cabinet above the toilet and use the space above the sink to incorporate a medicine cabinet with a mirrored front.

3 CHOOSE APPLIANCES

Your washing machine and clothes dryer are probably the most important purchases you will make when equipping your laundry room. Think about where the appliances will be located, in addition to your household's requirements, since this too may have a bearing on which models you opt for.

1 CHOOSE A COMBINATION OF APPLIANCES

When planning what appliances you need, consider the cost, the available space, and your lifestyle. With separate machines, you will get through laundry more quickly, but if space is at a premium, a single machine may be more practical.

WASHING MACHINE

The budget option: a one- or two-person household may be able to get by with just a washing machine. To do this comfortably, though, you will need space—indoors or outdoors—for line drying.

WASHER-DRYER COMBO UNIT

A combined washing machine and dryer is a good option if you only have space for one appliance. Keep in mind, that these machines do not always dry clothes as well as a normal clothes dryer would.

SEPARATE WASHING MACHINE AND CLOTHES DRYER

If you have enough space for separate appliances, this is usually the best option, particularly for households of several people. The great benefit of this is that you can run both machines at the same time, thereby getting through more laundry at once. Arrange them side by side or stack vertically (see panel opposite), depending on what works best in your space.

2 CHOOSE THE MODELS

With all laundry appliances, you should check that you are happy with the capacity, the cycles available, and the energy efficiency rating (check the unit's ENERGY STAR rating). Beyond that, consider the following.

WASHING MACHINES

FRONT LOADING

Usually the preferred option, front-loading washing machines can be built into a run of units under a countertop—often the best use of space in a kitchen or laundry room. These machines also typically use less water than top loaders, so are more energy efficient. If you are stacking your appliances, a front loader is more space efficient.

TOP LOADING

Top-loading washing machines tend to be harder on clothes than front loaders, although you may find them more accessible if you have difficulty bending down to reach the drum. Top loaders tend to be cheaper than front-loading machines, so are a better buy if you are on a budget.

CLOTHES DRYERS

GAS OR ELECTRIC

Gas-powered clothes dryers are more energy efficient than electric models, and hence cheaper to run. However, they must be installed by a professional. Electric machines are easier to install, although bear in mind that a vented machine must be vented with a duct to an outside wall (more expensive condensing models can sit anywhere in a well-ventilated room).

STACKING APPLIANCES

Stacking your washing machine and clothes dryer can offer a better use of space than positioning them both on the floor. Here's how to do it:

● Buy a suitable stacking kit or stacking frame. Try a "universal" kit or, for the best fit, see if the manufacturer of your appliances offers a more custom stacking kit option.

● Always put the dryer on top of the washing machine, and make sure that the washing machine is on a sturdy, level base.

● Choose a washing machine that has a low vibration level when it's spinning to ensure that the dryer isn't damaged.

● Stacked appliances can easily be hidden within a tall closet or cabinet built around them. Make sure that the door, or doors, open in the same direction as those of the washer and dryer, and add a louver to the top and bottom of the doors to allow ventilation around the units.

LAUNDRY ROOM

335

4 CHOOSE
FLOORING

Whether your laundry room is adjacent to your kitchen or garage, or is accessed from outside, you'll want flooring that is hard-wearing and easy to keep clean. If the room is small, it's best to choose something in a medium to light tone so that the room is light and bright enough to complete chores.

CHOOSE THE MATERIAL

The material you choose in your laundry room needs to be hard-wearing as well as nonslip when wet. If you use the room for doing ironing as well as laundry, you may want a surface that is not cold underfoot.

TILED

A good choice for laundry room floors, tiles are very durable and easy to clean. Porcelain and ceramic tiles are both ideal for use in this room, as are some natural stones, including slate and terra-cotta. Also consider laminate and vinyl tiles.

WOOD

Provided they're well sealed, solid wood, softwood, and engineered wood floors can be used in a laundry room. However, if you are on a tight budget, consider a wood-effect laminate or vinyl: both of these, if of good quality, will be durable enough.

SEAMLESS

Vinyl, linoleum, and rubber sheet flooring or poured concrete and resin are all tough and easy to clean. Seamless floors come in a wide range of designs and textures and are good for small spaces, since the lack of seams give a neat finish.

CHECKLIST

● **This is a room where** you should consider having under-floor heating installed—it's an efficient way to heat a space where there will probably be damp laundry hanging out to dry on a regular basis.

● **Make sure that your floor** is perfectly flat, especially in areas where washing machines and dryers will sit; positioning them on uneven surfaces will damage them.

● **If your laundry room** is upstairs, make sure that the subfloor is fastened down firmly to cut down on vibration. You could also consider sound-proofing the joist cavity.

5 CHOOSE
WALL COVERINGS

Although a laundry room isn't a room visitors will wander into, you should still inject some personality into it. One way to do this is with wall coverings. If the laundry room is next to the kitchen, it makes sense to carry the same theme and materials through into it. Otherwise, choose something simple but stylish.

CHOOSE THE MATERIAL

Ask yourself what tasks you will be doing in the laundry room and how water-resistant the walls need to be. This will help you to designate wet areas, just as you would in a bathroom or kitchen, and choose materials that suit the area.

TILES

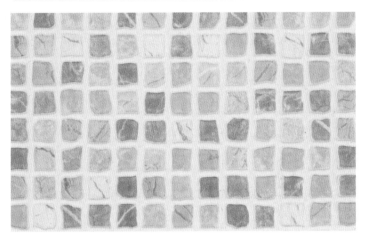

Tiles are a practical choice for a laundry room. Plain, unfussy, easy-to-clean tiles are the best choice for a small room. Don't feel you have to put the tiles everywhere—they can be used as backsplashs around wet areas only.

PAINT

Painting at least some of the walls is a practical choice, especially if you plan to cover the majority of the wall space with shelving and hanging racks. If are installing a clothes dryer, use a kitchen and bathroom paint or acrylic eggshell, which are resistant to moisture.

WALLPAPER

Vinyl wallpapers are specially made for rooms with a high moisture content, although don't use them in areas that get wet, such as behind a sink. Designs include florals, geometrics, and tile effects, but stick to simple patterns in muted tones in a small room.

PANELING

Tongue-and-groove paneling works well, since it's hard-wearing and can be painted any color you choose. The boards are usually made of pine, although you can buy ready-made MDF panels, which you attach directly onto the wall. Install paneling at half- or full-wall height.

LAY
VINYL TILES

Laying floor tiles is not a standard procedure; it's very much a visual exercise to ensure that cut tiles around the edge of the floor look appropriate to the size of the room, and that whole tiles are laid straight and at right angles. It's best to plan out a grid system first so the cut tiles around the edges are equal in size.

WHAT YOU NEED

- Vinyl tiles, self-adhesive
- Vinyl floor tile primer
- Large paintbrush
- Tape measure
- Piece of chalk
- Long metal ruler
- Pencil
- Wood strips
- Hammer and nails
- Rolling pin
- Hardboard
- Craft knife
- Profile gauge

1 PREPARE THE FLOOR

CLEAR THE FLOOR of any debris and dust with a vacuum cleaner; pull out, or hammer in, any protruding nailheads; and fill and smooth any gaps or cracks. To help maximize the adhesion of the tiles, seal the surface of the floor with a vinyl floor tile primer using a large paintbrush, and allow to dry. (It's also worth checking the tile manufacturer's instructions about applying a vinyl tile floor primer.)

2 PLAN HOW TO LAY THE TILES

1 MEASURE THE LENGTH of each wall and mark the central point of the wall with a pencil. Draw a straight line on the floor from one mark to the other on the opposite wall. Repeat with the two other walls. The two chalk lines that cross in the middle mark the center point and divide the floor into four quarters.

2 POSITION TILES in an L shape along the chalk lines of one quarter. The space between the end of the tiles and the wall is where the cut tiles will be placed. If this area is too thin, remove a tile from each line, adjust the tiles slightly, and use the outside edge of the central tile as your new center point. Repeat in the other quarters to make a cross of tiles on the floor.

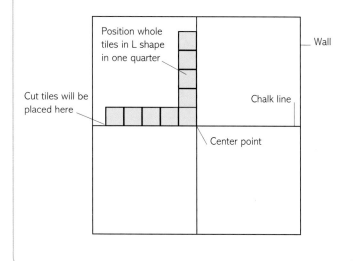

Position whole tiles in L shape in one quarter

Wall

Cut tiles will be placed here

Chalk line

Center point

3 CREATE A BOUNDARY

Pencil line to mark the edges of the whole tiles

DRAW A STRAIGHT PENCIL LINE along the edge of the floor in front of each wall where the cross of tiles finish. This line identifies where the edges of the whole tiles will be laid, and helps keep the tiles in a straight line as you fix them to the floor. Place wood strips along these pencil lines to create a boundary within which to lay the tiles. Knock a couple of nails through each wood strip into the subfloor to keep them firmly in place.

4 LAY THE TILES

1 REMOVE THE ADHESIVE backing from a tile, butt the tile up against one inside corner of the boundary of wood strips, and stick it down. It's best to lay the tiles systematically in each quarter from the corner of the room toward the center point.

2 STICK MORE TILES down in an L shape or in a row, ensuring that each tile is butted right up against the wood strips.

3 WHEN YOU HAVE LAID a few tiles, use a rolling pin to press each tile down firmly. Once you have laid the tiles in a quarter of the room, follow the same process in the remaining quarter sections, then remove the boundary of wood strips.

5 | TILE THE EDGE OF THE ROOM

1 **PLACE A TILE ON TOP** of one of the whole tiles that is adhered to the edge of the floor.

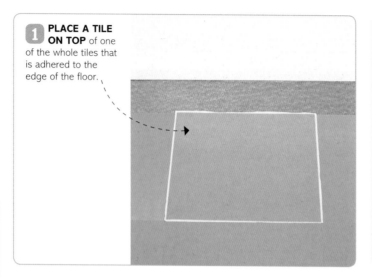

2 **LAY A SECOND TILE** on top so that it butts up against the edge of the wall. This should create a gap between the two tiles that is the same depth as the untiled edge of the floor. Mark this distance on the lower tile by drawing a pencil line across it using the edge of the upper tile as a guide.

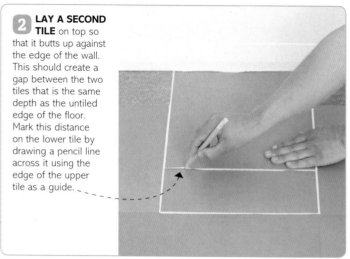

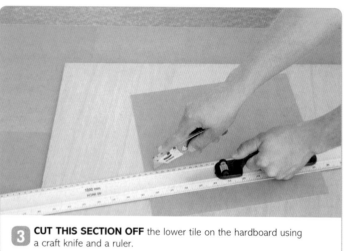

3 **CUT THIS SECTION OFF** the lower tile on the hardboard using a craft knife and a ruler.

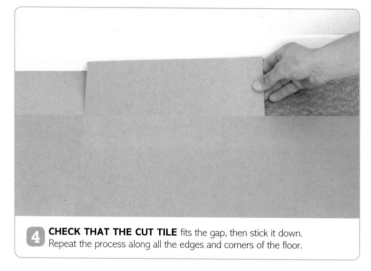

4 **CHECK THAT THE CUT TILE** fits the gap, then stick it down. Repeat the process along all the edges and corners of the floor.

6 | CUT AROUND AWKWARD CORNERS

1 **USE A PROFILE GUIDE** to help you cut the tiles for irregularly shaped spaces. Place the profile gauge into the space where the tile will be laid. Push the sliding elements of the profile gauge up against the edge of the door frame (or wall) so it echoes the shape of the frame.

2 **PLACE THE PROFILE** gauge on a tile, lining up the corners for an accurate fit. Trace around the shape of the profile gauge with a pencil.

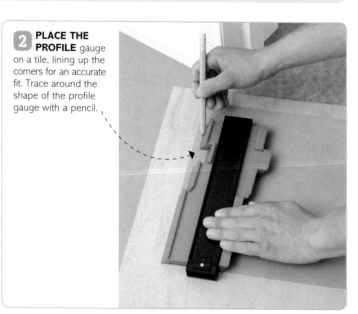

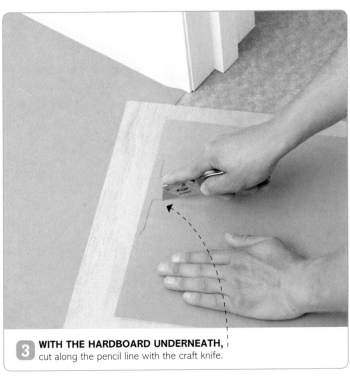

3 **WITH THE HARDBOARD UNDERNEATH,** cut along the pencil line with the craft knife.

4 **CHECK THAT THE TILE FITS**, then stick it down onto the floor and press it down evenly with the rolling pin.

PLAN THE PERFECT
LAUNDRY ROOM

Your laundry room is, overall, a very practical space, and it's unlikely that many visitors will see it. However, that doesn't mean it can't look inviting while also being functional. Follow this guide to making your laundry room look as good as possible, while still accommodating all the equipment you need.

INSTALL SHELVING

It's helpful to have everything on hand in a laundry room, so don't underestimate the amount of shelving you should put up. Ideally, keep the shelves uniform—either running at the same height all the way around the room at just above head height or in a stack on a free wall—and within arm's reach of the washing machine. Choose a theme for your laundry room (such as shabby chic, French laundry, or rustic country) and find shelves that will fit your look.

DISGUISE WITH BOXES AND BASKETS

You will find you have a whole array of things to put on your shelves, from detergent to spare lightbulbs, and pet supplies to candles. Don't feel they all have to be in their original packaging—the room will soon look like a supermarket storage room if they are. Instead, buy a range of lidded boxes and baskets to hide things away. They'll still be accessible, but disguised by, for example, a country print fabric or a 1950s enamel tin.

INSTALL A STYLISH SINK

Don't be tempted by the cheapest laundry-room sink you can find. Instead, look for a sink that will finish the room perfectly and can sit near the washing machine. Ideally, it needs to be roomy and flat-bottomed so you can hand-wash clothes, and there should be, if not a drain board, then a space for drip-drying clothes nearby. Look in flea markets and on the internet for old recycled ceramic sinks for a laid-back look, or hunt for old industrial stainless-steel units.

STOW AWAY YOUR IRONING BOARD AND IRON

Add a couple of hooks to a wall or the back of a door at head height so you can hang your ironing board so it is off the floor and out of the way. The iron can sit on a shelf alongside your laundry detergent. If you're opting for a contemporary look for the room, you can buy combined ironing board/iron holders that can be wall- or door-hung (assuming you have a solid door and it can take the weight).

HANG A DRYING RACK

If your laundry room is contemporary, there is a huge range of wall-hung or floor-standing metallic or plastic-finished hanging racks that will work perfectly and will not look out of place. However, if you hunt around—at flea markets, for example—you may find something more appropriate for a traditionally styled room, such as a Victorian ceiling-hung drying rack or a vintage-style linen rack in an attractive solid wood.

FIND INTERESTING FLOORING

Whatever you choose for your floor, it must be as water-resistant as possible or it will be stained within no time. Since this is usually a small room, it makes sense to choose a light color, and you can also stretch the space visually by setting any tiles diagonally. If you want to be adventurous and make the room look more fun, choose tiles, vinyl, or rubber in a bold pattern or bright color.

CHOOSE A LAUNDRY BASKET

Even if you have a laundry basket elsewhere in your house— in your bedroom, family bathroom, or master bath—it's handy to have an extra basket in the laundry room where you can transfer laundry. If floorspace is tight, look for a basket with a lid that can sit on top of your washing machine, a quarter-circle- or triangular-shaped lidded basket that can sit in a corner, or bags that can hang on a wall or the back of a door.

6 WAYS WITH
CLOTHES DRYING RACKS

There are many different kinds of drying rack, with floor-standing, wall-mounted, and ceiling-hung models all providing good solutions for certain room layouts. Consider the styles below to see which is the best option for your laundry room.

HANGER WITH CLOTHESPINS

Ideal for drying smaller items, hangers with clothespins are hung from the ceiling: hang your laundry using the clips or clothespins.

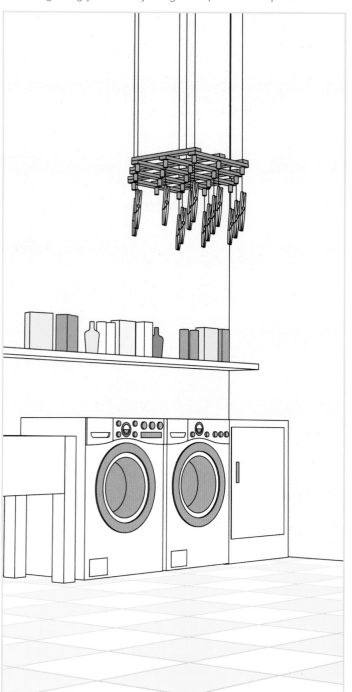

PULLEY RACK

Save floor space by choosing this option. It is fixed to the ceiling and can be pulled neatly up and out of the way.

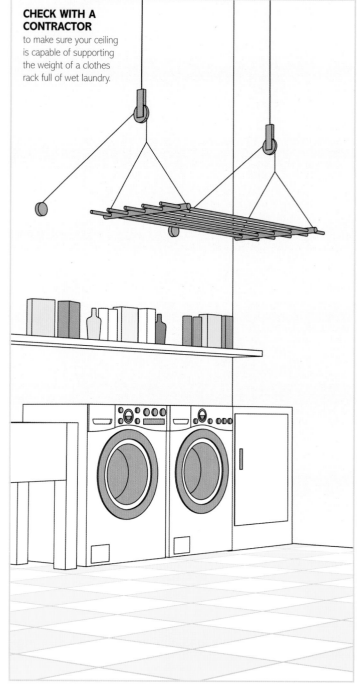

CHECK WITH A CONTRACTOR to make sure your ceiling is capable of supporting the weight of a clothes rack full of wet laundry.

RETRACTABLE LINE

This line is attached to a wall with brackets on the opposite wall to hold it when pulled out. It's ideal if you need lots of hanging space.

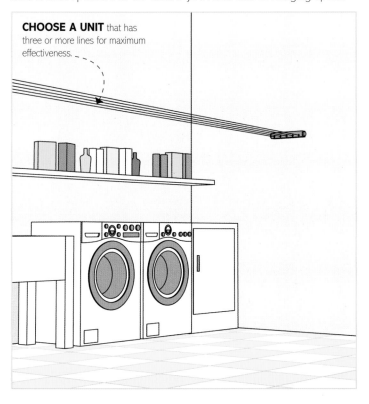

CHOOSE A UNIT that has three or more lines for maximum effectiveness.

FOLD-DOWN WALL-MOUNTED RACK

A wall-mounted drying rack is attached to the wall at its base and simply folded out from the top when needed.

CHOOSE A UNIT (or have one made) with knobs or hooks at the base for extra hanging space.

PULL-OUT WALL-MOUNTED RACK

This collapsable clothes rack can be folded back to be almost flush against the wall when not in use, so it is ideal for a small room.

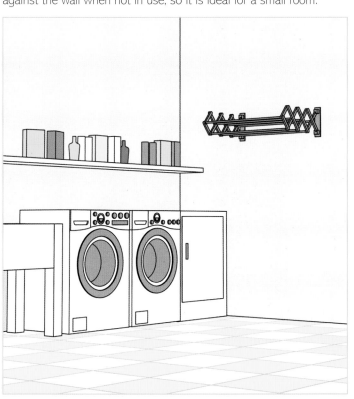

FLOOR-STANDING RACK

A floor-standing clothes rack provides generous space for drying clothes while occupying relatively little floor space.

PLAN A SPACE within your laundry room where you can stash the rack away when it is folded flat.

OUTSIDE SPACE

1 WHAT TO DO WHEN REDECORATING YOUR OUTSIDE SPACE

If you're considering redesigning your outdoor space—whether a patio, deck area, or small courtyard garden—it pays to plan well in advance. That way, you can get everything delivered at the right time, have workmen ready to spring into action, and get the whole job done efficiently.

1 MAKE A PLAN

Draw a rough plan to scale and include your needs— a sun deck, shed or storage unit, dining or barbecue area, or a garden structure or planting for privacy, for example.

2 CONSIDER YOUR BUDGET

Work out what you are able to spend, and what this will allow you to do, bearing in mind that the more structures and hard landscaping involved, the greater the cost. If you have to spread the cost over time, invest in landscaping first.

3 PLAN THE ELECTRICAL AND WATER FEATURES

Check if you can afford decorative features such as lighting (controlled from within the house) and water features, which require electrical work, excavation, and plumbing. (Save money by buying solar-powered lighting and water features, although they are not as effective as electrically powered versions.)

4 CONSULT A GARDEN DESIGNER

Just as if you were designing any room in the house, get the opinion of professionals. Some may offer a design service for free and others will charge, but the cost can be taken off their services, should you decide to retain them. A professional can be more cost-effective—although not cheaper—because he or she can project-manage, order materials at good rates, and offer clever design ideas.

5 GET QUOTES AND BOOK WORKMEN

Ask at least three people or companies (including general contractors, electricians, and plumbers) for quotes. Ideally, engage one landscaping company to do the clearing and hard landscaping for you (most will see the jobs all the way through), but if you have a very tight budget, getting people in separately may be cheaper. Do your homework now to save yourself money later.

6 ORDER MATERIALS

Ask your tradespeople to help you figure out what materials you need for hard landscaping and garden structures. If they offer to order them for you, find out what discounts they get, and how much of this saving they are willing to pass on to you. If you're ordering in bulk, you may be able to negotiate a good deal with suppliers, but it is unlikely to be as good as a trade rate. Order any water features and lighting now, too.

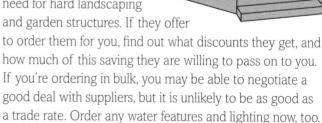

7 CLEAR THE PLOT

Clear the space of anything that won't be needed, including old plants, weeds, storage units, paving, decking, and so on. Unless your outdoor space has direct access to the street, garbage (and new materials) will be transported through your home. If you have ordered a dumpster that will sit on the street, be sure to secure the necessary permits first.

8 BEGIN HARD LANDSCAPING

The hard landscaping can now begin: leveling or shaping the plot, digging the foundations for walls, steps, structures, and the patio or deck, and excavating soil for any water features.

9 ELECTRIC AND PLUMBING— ROUGH-IN

As the hard landscaping begins, other tradespeople will need to lay pipes and hoses for the water features and electrical wiring for the garden lighting, powering the water features, and electric points. If you are having an outside hose bib installed, get this done now.

10 ORDER PLANTS, TOPSOIL, AND FURNITURE

As the space takes shape, think about ordering the topsoil, plants, mulch, and garden furniture. The best time to plant is fall and spring, so delay planting if the work takes place in midsummer or midwinter.

11 FINISH HARD LANDSCAPING AND ORGANIZE THE FINAL INSTALL

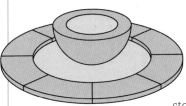

At this stage walls should be built and possibly stuccoed, steps and structures—whether pergolas or outdoor storage—constructed, and ponds or water features assembled. The plumber and electrician must return now to finish their work.

12 EXTERIOR PAINTING

Once any concrete or stucco is dry, and before you bring in bags of soil, paint or stain the outside walls, fences, trellis, pergolas, garden structures, or storage. Give them all at least two coats of stain or paint for effective protection.

13 FILL A WATER FEATURE

If you have a water feature, it can be filled now. Before populating it with fish or aquatic plants, follow the supplier's instructions to prepare the water properly.

14 PLANT

Fill flower beds with soil and plants, either with mature specimens (if you have the budget for an instant, finished look) or seedlings that, with care, will soon shoot up to fill the beds. If you don't have flower beds, dot pots of plants that grow to different heights around the outdoor area to create the impression of a verdant space.

2 CREATE A MOOD BOARD
FOR YOUR OUTDOOR SPACE

Just as with rooms inside the house, creating a mood board for your yard, courtyard, or balcony will help you to decide whether all the elements you are considering will sit successfully together. Before you begin, it's also worth thinking about what type of atmosphere you want to create, especially if the space is to be used both as a relaxing and a dining area.

1 **FIND PICTURES OF OUTDOOR AREAS** you like, or can use as inspiration, in magazines, on websites, and in books. If the space will have a dual purpose—as a dining and lounging area, perhaps—decide which element is more important to you. Then gather pictures of that type of outdoor area and figure out how you can incorporate the other element within the space. Edit the pictures down to a manageable few and see if a color scheme or decorative theme starts to emerge.

Stick a favorite image, or images, to the mood board as a starting point for your own outdoor design scheme.

2 **CONSIDER THE SUNLIGHT** and where it falls on your space, since this will have a bearing on which color palette you choose as a background, what type of plants you will buy and where you will position them, and where your outdoor furniture will sit.

Decide if you want a bright, neutral, or cool scheme, according to how much sun or shade your space receives.

3 **PICK A BACKGROUND** for the room. Just like walls indoors, perimeter walls or fences provide a backdrop and dictate the look of other elements. Your choice won't just be paint shades for walls or stains for fences—you also need to consider the effect of the colors and textures of natural materials, whether brick, stone, or wood. Pin pictures of materials to the board or paint part of it in your chosen color in proportion to how it will be used outdoors. This will also help you to choose other colors.

Your background should blend with both your furniture and planting plan.

Stick swatches of accent colors onto the background to see if they work together.

4 **INTRODUCE ACCENT COLORS**, which can be a subtle variation of your background color or a contrast to it, or both. If you want a well-designed, space, keep the color palette to fewer than three colors other than green (although you can add a whole range of colors with flowers, if you wish). Use the first accent color in greater proportion to the second, and the third minimally.

A contrasting accent color will make your scheme look dynamic and stimulating.

Add images of furniture and other outdoor items to see if they will coordinate with your scheme.

Pick out one or more of your accent colors with particular plants and flowers.

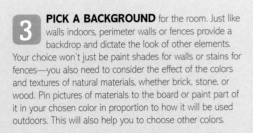

5 **CHOOSE NEW FURNITURE** using the same methods as you did for your paint and plant colors. Work out if your choices offer what you need practically, but also if they will enhance the space decoratively. Sketch the layout of the space to be certain that everything will fit.

6 **ADD PATTERN** in the form of a design on your garden chair covers or cushions. This should be sufficient for an outdoor space, since flowers and plants can provide added pattern and color. Stick pictures or fabric samples to your mood board to ensure that you're working along the right lines.

Pictures of various accessories in similar colors and tones on your mood board will help you get the mix right.

Look for a fabric design and flower pots that match your color palette.

7 **ADD FINISHING TOUCHES** such as outdoor candles, dishes, lighting, and flower pots. You can choose individual pieces rather than a matching set of dishes, for example, to give your outdoor room a more individual look, but they should all blend in terms of color, material, or texture if the room is to work successfully.

3 LAYOUT CONSIDERATIONS FOR OUTSIDE SPACE

If you have an undeveloped outdoor space, you really have a blank canvas on which to impose a layout. However, there are several things to consider that will affect your plans, such as how to gain privacy if you are overlooked, where the sunlight falls and when, and even how well you can hide some components of this area. Follow these layout tips to create the most successful space possible.

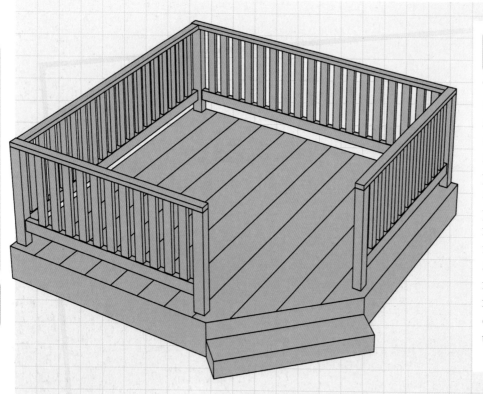

PATIO OR DECKED AREA

Think about how much of your patio or deck you want in the sun, in dappled shade, or in full shade. If you want to combine space for sunbathing, dining, and a kids' play area, you might want to position part of it in full sun for lounging and part in dappled shade for dining and playing. If you'll only be using this space for dining, it makes sense to position it right outside the back door. Ideally, this area should be screened from your neighbors' view: you may have existing features, such as a wall or trees, that you can take advantage of, or create a screen using trellis, pergolas, or planting.

DINING AREA

Where you position your dining furniture depends on where your patio or decking area is, where you have dappled shade (if your yard is south-facing, you may have to create shade with a pergola, planting, or a large umbrella), and how close to the house you want to dine. When calculating what size of table to buy, allow an extra 3ft (1m) all around it for the seats to be comfortably pulled in and out.

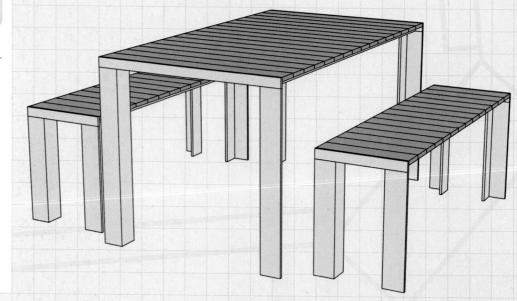

COOKING AREA

The most convenient place for an outdoor cooking area is near the house. If you are planning a fully functioning outdoor kitchen, it will also be easier to install electric and/or gas if the house is nearby. Choose a shady spot for your cooking area, or create one using a pergola or ingenious planting—but be careful not to create a fire hazard.

WATER SUPPLY

Install a hose bib in the back wall of the house next to a perimeter wall (not centrally, where it will take up space), with a stashable hose attached to the wall next to it. If you have children, consider adding a hot-water supply so you can fill a wading pool. If you want an outdoor shower, locate it in a sunny spot where the shower area will dry out quickly.

STORAGE

Tuck a shed or storage unit out of sight at the end or the side of the yard, or hide it with creative planting such as climbers or tall, bushy plants. If your space is very small, a bench with a lift-up lid and storage beneath is a good option. Any small units can sit against a wall of the house so they aren't visible from indoors.

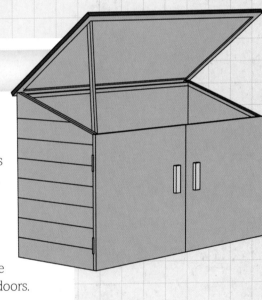

PLANTING

Plants can be used as screening for privacy, to hide ugly views or features, for shade, or simply as decoration. Plant tall trees around your boundaries if you need to screen your outdoor space, or train climbers over a pergola or a trellis to hide a seating area. Hide an ugly view with tall, bushy planting or climbers trained over a trellis.

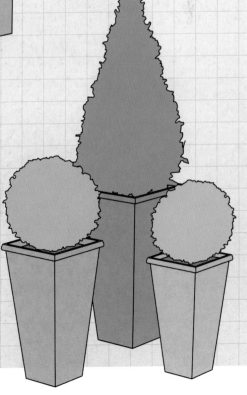

4 CHOOSE OUTDOOR FLOORING

Shop for outdoor flooring in the same way that you would when deciding what to lay on your floors indoors. Think about the style and finished look of the outside space, its size, how you'll be using it, whether you want a low-maintenance surface, and, of course, what your budget can accommodate.

1 CHOOSE THE TYPE

Paving, decking, and gravel are the three main types of hard outdoor flooring. Selecting the right one is as important as selecting the right plants, so consider how it will go with your overall scheme.

PAVING

Paving sizes range from small stones to large slabs laid in various patterns for different effects (opt for a sawn edge for a contemporary look). Prepare the ground with gravel or a cement foundation and lay out the blocks as you want them before securing them in place.

DECKING

This is a versatile surface that can be used to create a patio leading out from the house, a separate raised area, or for leveling off a sloping yard. Lay the decking on a frame so it is clear of the ground and air can circulate underneath, and make sure there is good drainage.

AGGREGATE

Gravel, or aggregate, is the cheapest hard surface, so it's a practical option for large areas. Check that the ground is compacted, cover it with a weed-suppressing membrane, and scatter the gravel over it to a depth of at least 1in (2.5cm). Weed the area regularly.

CHECKLIST

- **Make sure that the flooring** you choose—whether tiles or decking—is nonslip when wet.

- **Rainwater needs to runs off** a patio or deck, so ensure that there is adequate slope and drainage.

- **Decide whether you want** your outdoor flooring to match that of the connecting room indoors. Doing so will unite the two spaces and make both seem larger.

- **Is the flooring you've chosen** suitable for your family? If you have children you may be better off with a softer floor, such as wood, for example.

2 CHOOSE THE MATERIAL

Each type of outdoor flooring is available in various materials, sizes, and colors. Look at all the available choices—taking samples home, if possible, to see what they look like in the place first—before making up your mind.

PAVING

SLATE

Ideal for contemporary patios, this red-black stone can run from indoors outside via a wall of glass doors. Its low-to-medium cost makes it good value for money.

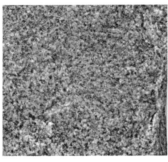

GRANITE

Hard and extremely durable, granite comes in a variety of grays, reds, and greens. Run it from inside onto the patio for a seamless transition. Its cost is medium to high.

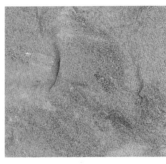

LIMESTONE

Available in various shades, limestone is smooth, low-maintenance, and hard-wearing, and suits minimalist modern patios. Prices range from cheap to expensive.

SANDSTONE

Sandstone has a subtle texture, varies in color, and is very hard-wearing, which makes its low-to-medium cost good value for money. It may need sealing once laid.

FLAGSTONE

Comprised of flat stones with a nonslip surface that provide rustic charm, flagstones develop an attractive weathered look. The medium-cost tiles are irregular in shape.

CONCRETE

Hard-wearing concrete can be colored, textured, or patterned. Choose slabs or blocks, depending on how you want your patio to look.

TRAVERTINE

The advantage of medium-to-high cost travertine is that it doesn't heat up, which makes it ideal for sunny patios, as it always stays cool underfoot. It is slip-resistant.

BRICK

Brick paving is made of clay or concrete that is then dyed, which is cheaper but less durable than clay. This medium-cost surface is available in different shapes.

DECKING

HARDWOOD

Durable hardwood decking is medium to high in price. Oil it occasionally to prevent it from drying out. It can become slippery when wet, so opt for a textured finish.

SOFTWOOD

Easier to work with than hardwood, though not as long-lasting, softwood requires regular painting or staining. Its prices range from low to medium.

MAN-MADE

Weather-resistant UPVC lacks the aesthetic appeal of timber, but is nearly maintenance-free. Medium-cost composite decking is low-maintenance and looks like solid wood.

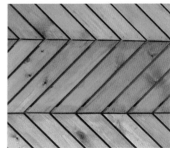

DECK TILES

Wooden tiles, which are low to medium in cost, can be laid over an existing patio to create a deck without the need for a frame. They are slip-resistant and easy to lay.

AGGREGATE

SLATE CHIPS
These low-cost flattish stones in varying sizes are easier to walk on, and wheel a barrow over, than gravel. They also deepen in color and intensity when wet.

LIMESTONE CHIPS
Pale gray or buff limestone chips are bagged according to the size of stone, so check which size suits your space. Their low cost makes them good value for money.

FLINT CHIPS
This low-cost, hard-wearing, angular gravel is available in tones of gray, white, or gold. Its warm, mellow appearance makes it a popular choice for outdoor surfaces.

BEACH ROCKS
These large, smooth, medium-cost pebbles give a relaxed, seaside feel. They are hard to walk on, so use sparingly in borders, or in place of randomly selected paving stones.

PEA GRAVEL
Composed of crushed stones through a sieve, low-cost pea gravel is available as a rounded or slightly jagged shape. The bags may be mixed or uniform in color.

RUBBER CHIPS
Made from recycled tires, low-cost rubber is economical because it goes much further than other aggregates. It's also a child-friendly alternative to sharp stones.

LAWNS

There are dedicated gardening books and resources that provide much more advice on lawns than this book is able to do, but lawns are, of course, a major consideration when it comes to planning your outdoor flooring.

● **Is your outdoor space** suitable for a lawn? Grass does best in a well-drained site that has some sunlight—too much shade will make the lawn patchy. Find out which grass type will best suit your garden's exposure to sunlight (establish, too, which type will be best for your planned usage).

● **Thinking about how** you will use your lawn will help you decide the most suitable shape for it. If it is to be a practical play area, a simple square, oval, or circular lawn will be best. If you want to enhance your yard's design, consider a more dynamic shape, with curves carved out to create interesting edges for borders.

● **You can create** a lawn by laying down turf or sowing seed. Either way is simple enough to do, with seed being the cheaper option and turf being quicker. Whichever approach you choose, be prepared to give it lots of water in the early days.

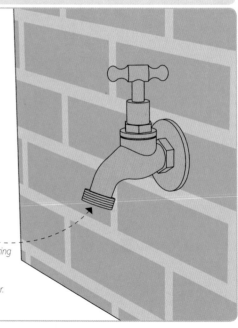

An outside hose bib is useful for watering a lawn, especially a newly laid one that needs plenty of water.

WOODEN OUTDOOR FLOORING gives a warmer feel than stone or concrete, but requires careful weather-proofing.

6 WAYS WITH
PATIO AND DECK SHAPES

Add extra interest to your outdoor space by including a patio or deck in a dynamic shape, or enhance a regular rectangle or square patio with clever seating and planting arrangements. Choose a design that fits the dimensions of your space and complements the style of your planting scheme.

DIAMOND

If you have space, create an interesting patio design using two squares interlinked to form a diamond design, with planting displayed around it. This works well in a courtyard garden.

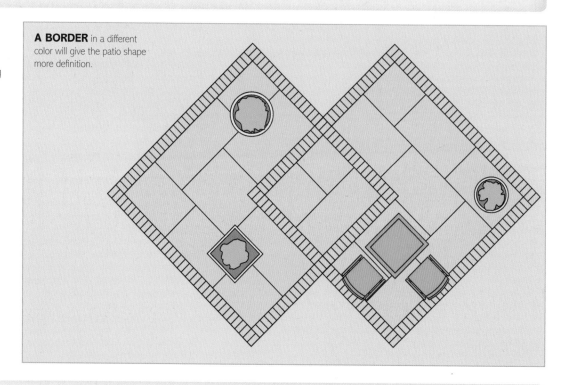

A BORDER in a different color will give the patio shape more definition.

STRAIGHT EDGE

A straight-edged patio or decked area will usually run the full width of your house and can be any depth, depending on the space you have available in your backyard.

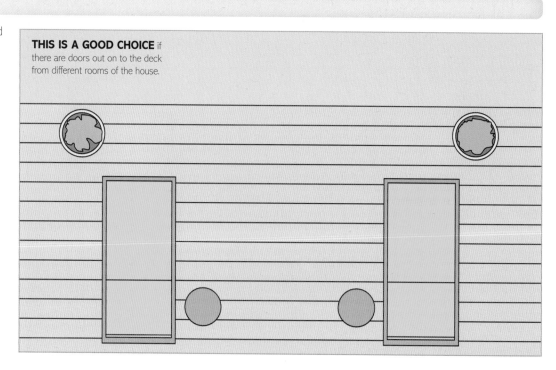

THIS IS A GOOD CHOICE if there are doors out on to the deck from different rooms of the house.

45° CORNERS

Add interest to a square or rectangular area of decking with 45° corners at the ends. Planting in the corners will give privacy.

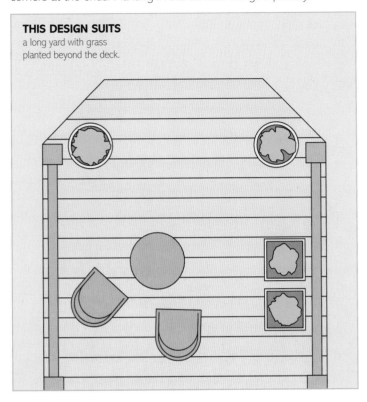

THIS DESIGN SUITS
a long yard with grass planted beyond the deck.

CURVED

Curved edges can give a less formal look to your yard and the soft edges will blend in with the planting beyond.

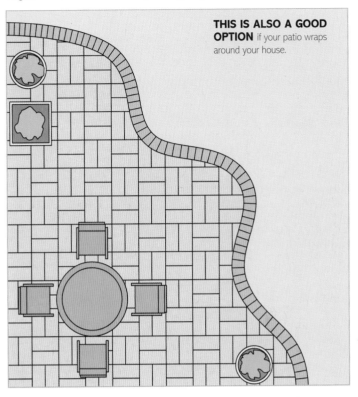

THIS IS ALSO A GOOD OPTION if your patio wraps around your house.

ROUND

A round patio creates a focal point in the center of a yard and softens any hard edges. Highlight the shape by planting around it.

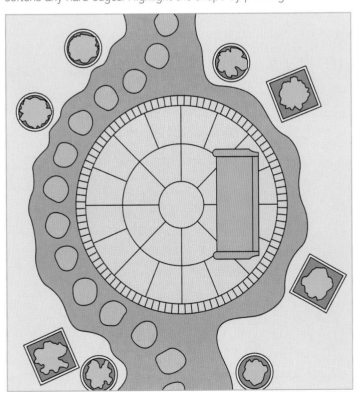

SQUARE

In small yards, square patios and decked areas work well. Break up their formal look with planting among the paving or with large pots.

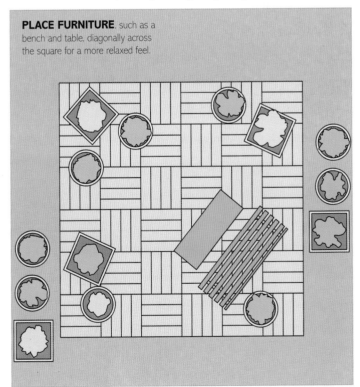

PLACE FURNITURE, such as a bench and table, diagonally across the square for a more relaxed feel.

6 WAYS WITH
SLAB PATTERNS

Laying a patio isn't as basic as it might seem—there are a great many different designs you can create by using certain slab shapes in particular arrangements. Achieve a modern, traditional, ordered, or relaxed look to suit your outside space. Here are a few ideas to consider.

HERRINGBONE

Laying bricks or concrete blocks in a herringbone pattern will create a stylish, neat look that works for wide expanses and pathways alike.

IF YOU LIVE in an old property, use reclaimed bricks for a more authentic look.

DUTCH

This design is created by laying two different sizes of square slab in a repeating pattern.

USE ALL THE SAME color or two different colors— one for the large squares, another for the small squares.

FIELDSTONE PAVING

Irregular sizes and shapes of stone or concrete paving can be used to create a random, organic pattern.

A FIELDSTONE PATIO, with its loose feeling, requires sensitive selection and chipping of stones to get it just right.

ASHLAR

Obtain slabs of four or five different sizes and shapes, ensuring they will tessellate, and arrange them into a random pattern.

THIS DESIGN will require careful planning to ensure that the slabs all fit.

SLABS AND COBBLES

Create your own design using a mixture of slabs and cobbles. Use the cobbles to form borders to the slabs.

LIKE OTHER DETAILED PATTERNS, this design will make your patio look "busy," so keep the pots and planting simple.

COBBLES OR SETTS

The rustic look of cobbles or setts will give a relaxed, country feel, but you can make them feel more formal by using geometric patterns.

IF YOU ARE PLANNING an intricate pattern, draw it out to scale on graph paper first.

MAKE
A SAIL SHADE

Create a lightweight triangular shade to give you a retreat from the sun on warm summer days. The shade can be secured to trees, fence posts, or whatever else you have in your outdoor space, as long as the fixtures are sturdy enough to take the extra stress. Avoid using in high winds.

WHAT YOU NEED

- Fabric
- Needle and thread, or sewing machine
- Scissors
- D rings
- Cord

1 MEASURE THE FABRIC

MEASURE THE AREA where you want the shade to go and sketch out a scale drawing, including the points where you want to attach the corners. Use this drawing to determine the size of your shade. It is very likely that you will need to attach two pieces of fabric to make the necessary width, so make a plan for where the seam should go and where the fabric will need to be cut.

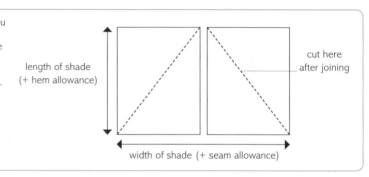

length of shade (+ hem allowance)

cut here after joining

width of shade (+ seam allowance)

2 JOIN THE FABRIC

1 PLACE THE TWO PIECES of fabric together, right side to right side, and sew a ¾in (2cm) seam to create the central join.

2 TRIM BACK THE SEAM fabric to half its width on one side.

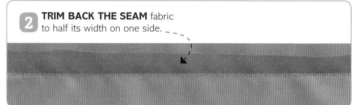

3 OPEN OUT FLAT and fold the wider side of the seam fabric around the narrower side.

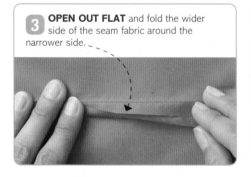

4 FOLD DOWN FLAT against the fabric so that the raw edge is tucked away.

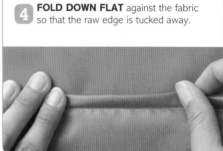

5 SEW AGAIN to secure, creating a flat seam. Now you can make the diagonal cuts to create your triangle.

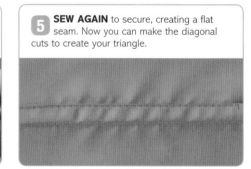

3 HEM THE SIDES

1 ON EACH OF THE THREE SIDES, create a double hem by folding once, then folding again to conceal the raw edge, and sewing.

2 AT THE CORNERS where the folded hems meet, a tail will be created. This can be left loose for now.

1 **PASS THE TAIL** through a D ring at each of the corners. Fold the fabric over the straight edge of the ring and stitch to hold in place.

2 **TRIM THE TAIL**, fold the raw edge underneath, and sew again.

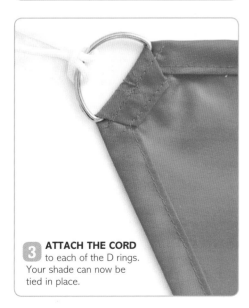

3 **ATTACH THE CORD** to each of the D rings. Your shade can now be tied in place.

5 CHOOSE
OUTDOOR LIGHTING

As in the house, good use of lighting in your outdoor room will help enhance the space, highlight attractive features, and provide the necessary illumination for whatever activities are to take place there. Opt for a combination of different lighting types—maybe three or four types if it is a large space.

CHOOSE YOUR LIGHT FIXTURES

Consider how you use your outside space—and how you would like to use it—and try to identify lighting that will meet your practical needs, as well as suiting the proportions of the area.

WALL-MOUNTED LIGHTS

WALL LIGHTS
Wall lights are best used singly above or in pairs on each side of a door. They are most useful if they also have a security function. As with all outdoor electric lighting, make sure the switch is positioned inside, by the door.

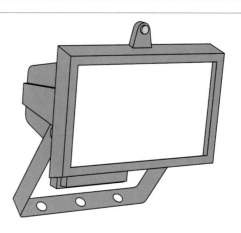

FLOODLIGHTS
If you have a large outdoor space and regularly use it at night, for entertaining, sports activities, or as a play area, a floodlight will provide the most generous illumination. Remember though, if you live in close quarters with your neighbors, to be careful how a light like this is aimed.

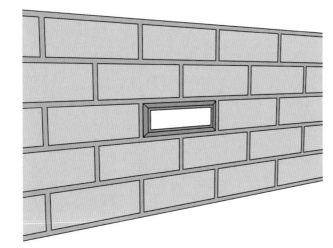

BRICK LIGHTS
If you want to create subtle lighting around a patio area, set brick lights into the wall of the house or boundary. They can be positioned comfortably at ankle, shoulder, or just above head height, although each variation will create a different effect: the lower the lights, the softer the overall lighting will be.

CEILING LIGHTS

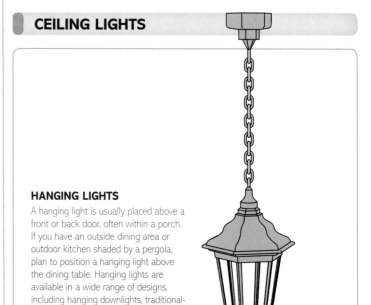

HANGING LIGHTS
A hanging light is usually placed above a front or back door, often within a porch. If you have an outside dining area or outdoor kitchen shaded by a pergola, plan to position a hanging light above the dining table. Hanging lights are available in a wide range of designs, including hanging downlights, traditional-style lanterns, and opulent chandeliers.

FLOOR LIGHTS

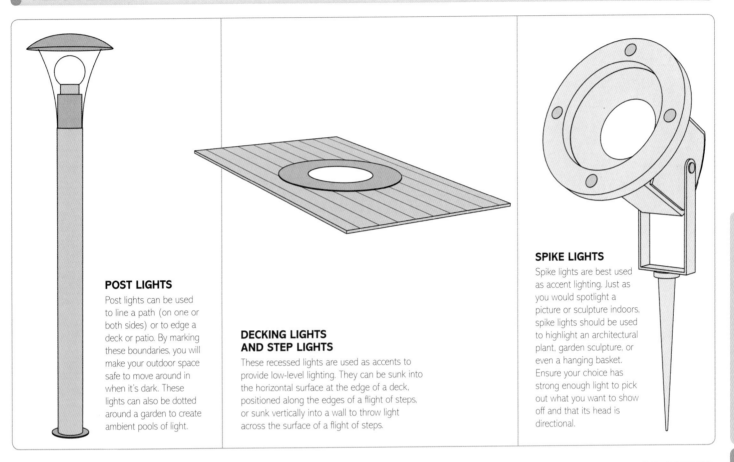

POST LIGHTS

Post lights can be used to line a path (on one or both sides) or to edge a deck or patio. By marking these boundaries, you will make your outdoor space safe to move around in when it's dark. These lights can also be dotted around a garden to create ambient pools of light.

DECKING LIGHTS AND STEP LIGHTS

These recessed lights are used as accents to provide low-level lighting. They can be sunk into the horizontal surface at the edge of a deck, positioned along the edges of a flight of steps, or sunk vertically into a wall to throw light across the surface of a flight of steps.

SPIKE LIGHTS

Spike lights are best used as accent lighting. Just as you would spotlight a picture or sculpture indoors, spike lights should be used to highlight an architectural plant, garden sculpture, or even a hanging basket. Ensure your choice has strong enough light to pick out what you want to show off and that its head is directional.

DECORATIVE LIGHTING

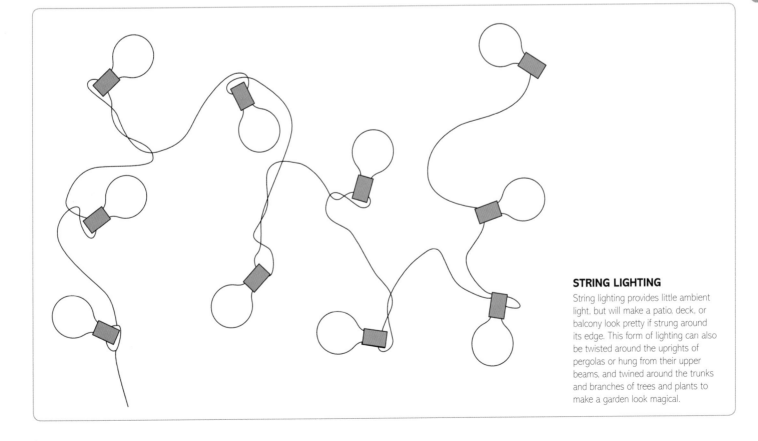

STRING LIGHTING

String lighting provides little ambient light, but will make a patio, deck, or balcony look pretty if strung around its edge. This form of lighting can also be twisted around the uprights of pergolas or hung from their upper beams, and twined around the trunks and branches of trees and plants to make a garden look magical.

7 WAYS WITH
PLANTERS

Potting plants in planters isn't just about creating a bright, pretty display of your favorite flowers. It can also be about defining the style of your yard or garden, delineating a certain area, or screening an ugly view. Carefully choose planters in styles that complement both the plants and the design of your outdoor space.

BORDER

Use planters to create a low border around the edge of your lawn, patio, or path. They can also create a safety barrier at the edge of a raised deck.

RECTANGULAR PLANTERS
work well, but you can use any planter shape you like.

WINDOW LEDGE

Instead of window boxes, use several pots of flowers or herbs to brighten up a window ledge, provide privacy, or screen an ugly view.

USE PAINTED POTS
that will add color if the flowers aren't in bloom.

DIFFERENT HEIGHTS

For a relaxed look, create an interesting grouping of different-sized pots. Mix the shapes and colors of the pots, too.

GROUP THE POTS
and plants in odd numbers for best effect.

ON EACH SIDE OF A DOORWAY

Position identical pots on each side of a front or back door to frame it. This look works very well with large pots and architectural plants.

FOR THE BEST EFFECT, the planting in both pots should match.

ON STEPS

If you have backyard steps, place one pot at the edge of each step. Mix the pot shapes for variety, or use the same style for uniformity.

IF YOU HAVE WIDE STEPS, consider placing groups of several pots on each step.

WALL MOUNTED

Add visual interest to a plain wall or fence by vertically mounting a series of pots that diminish in size the higher up they are.

DISGUISE A FENCE or wall by planting a combination of trailing plants.

ÉTAGÈRE

Add interest and height to a corner of your yard using an étagère, which allows you to display many pots at different heights.

SEMICIRCULAR and circular étagères allow you to plant against flat walls and around trees.

6 CHOOSE OUTDOOR FURNITURE

The outdoor furniture you choose will depend on a number of factors, such as the type of material you like, how contemporary or traditional your space is, and its size. Small spaces require compact pieces, while a bigger yard may lend itself to large pieces. Check, too, how easy furniture will be to store, move, and clean.

1 CHOOSE A DINING SET

Start by thinking about the dining area. What size and shape of table will be best for your space? Tables are often sold in a set with matching seating, but you could also buy separate pieces that complement each other more subtly.

TABLE AND CHAIRS

Separate tables and chairs are available in a wide range of sizes, from neat café-style tables that seat two people up to large rectangular, circular, and oval tables that can seat many people. You can buy these pieces in sets or individually, which means you can choose chairs that suit your space and comfort requirements.

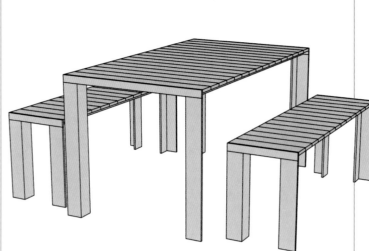

TABLE WITH BENCHES

A table with benches is a good choice if you often need to seat lots of people, (although bear in mind that benches are not suitable for children under three), to eat at the same time. Benches are not always comfortable to sit on for long periods, so if possible, complement them with at least a couple of chairs.

PICNIC TABLE

Picnic tables have fixed benches, so you don't have to buy separate seating. However, climbing over the benches to sit on them can be awkward. They are a good choice for families and small yards. You can buy rectangular and round versions.

CHOOSE ADDITIONAL FURNITURE

When choosing additional furniture, think about what you want to do in your outside space. Do you want a chair on which to sit and read or drink a cup of coffee, or are you looking for something you can stretch out on and sunbathe?

CHAIR

If you intend to leave garden chairs outside all year round, choose a material that is durable and weather-resistant. If you want to store them away, it makes sense to buy folding or stackable chairs. Consider buying separate seat cushions to make the chairs more comfortable.

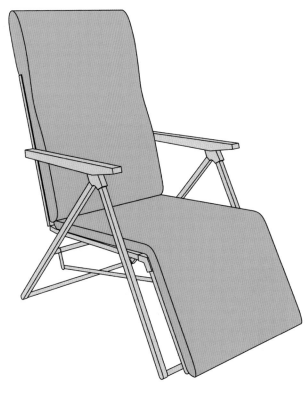

RECLINER

Recliner chairs adjust from an upright to near-horizontal position, and are ideal if you have little space to store both dining and lounging chairs, since you can use them for both dining and reclining. They are available in a range of materials and with or without filled cushions.

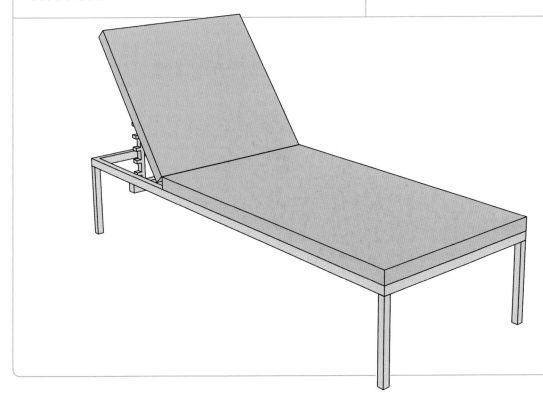

CHAISE LOUNGE

If you like to sunbathe, a chaise lounge—made from wood, plastic, or metal—is the most comfortable option. It features an adjustable back, which can be raised for reading or laid flat for stretching out. Some, usually fixed models, can be left outside all year round, while others can be folded away for easier storage.

BENCH

Available in a wide range of sizes and styles, and in a choice of wood or metal, benches can either be used as extra seating for dining or placed in a quiet corner for you to enjoy your outdoor space. Find a permanent spot for a bench, since it won't provide the same flexibility as individual outdoor chairs.

SOFA

Outdoor sofas are usually made from a woven plastic or a treated rattan. Not all garden sofa materials can be left outside in all weather, so check before you buy if you don't have somewhere to store it in winter. They are often sold with seat cushions for added comfort.

SWING

Garden swings typically have a fixed frame with a hanging swing seat (normally to seat two or three) and a canopy that offers protection from the sun. This furniture takes up a fair amount of space, so is more suited to large outdoor spaces.

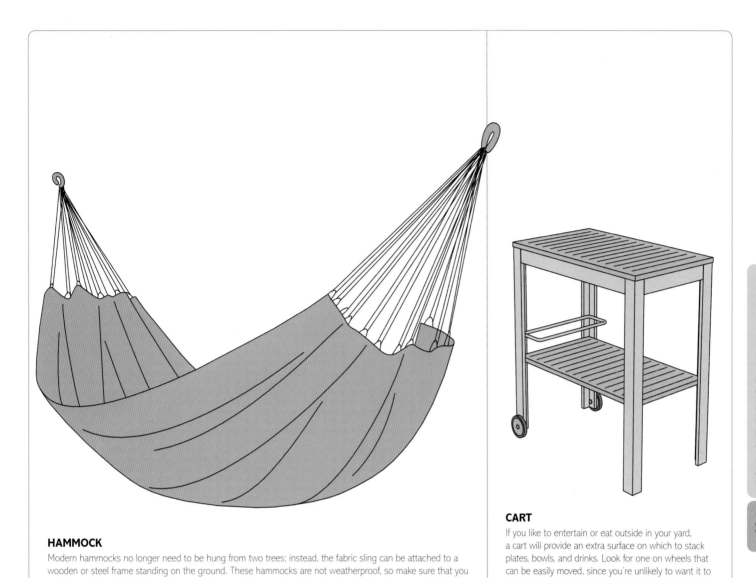

HAMMOCK

Modern hammocks no longer need to be hung from two trees; instead, the fabric sling can be attached to a wooden or steel frame standing on the ground. These hammocks are not weatherproof, so make sure that you have storage space for them in wetter months.

CART

If you like to entertain or eat outside in your yard, a cart will provide an extra surface on which to stack plates, bowls, and drinks. Look for one on wheels that can be easily moved, since you're unlikely to want it to sit outside all the time.

3 CHOOSE THE MATERIAL

When choosing outdoor furniture, consider whether the material it is made from will suit your outdoor scheme, how durable it is, and whether it will need annual maintenance.

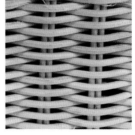

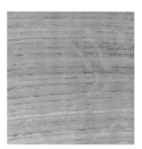

WROUGHT IRON

Medium to high in cost, furniture made of heavy wrought iron is often traditional-looking and ornate. It can be uncomfortable, so consider seat cushions.

PLASTIC

Available in a range of prices, plastic furniture comes in many different colors and designs, and is easy to clean. It is extremely lightweight.

CAST ALUMINUM

Cast aluminum is lightweight, so can be moved around easily. It is typically low to medium in cost and can be left outside all year round.

RATTAN/WICKER

Medium to high in cost, natural wicker and rattan furniture gives a relaxed look. Choose a synthetic version if you will be leaving it uncovered in wet conditions.

WOOD

Wood furniture, available in a range of prices, is durable and hard-wearing, but often heavy. Most woods need to be treated or stained every 6–12 months.

MAKE
CUSHIONS FOR GARDEN CHAIRS

Add an extra touch of comfort to your outdoor seating area with these chair cushions, which can be made to fit any shape and size of garden chair. Covering both the seat and chair back, they have ties to secure the seat pad in position and elastic that loops over the chair back to keep the back pad upright.

WHAT YOU NEED

- 2 flat foam pads (about 1in/2.5cm thick)
- Scissors
- Colored fabric—use curtain-weight cotton material or waterproof, outdoor fabric
- Pins
- Thick elastic
- Sewing machine, or needle and thread

1 MEASURE AND CUT

1 MEASURE THE DIMENSIONS of your chair, recording the height of the chair back, the depth of the seat, and the width of the seat and back. Cut the foam pads to size.

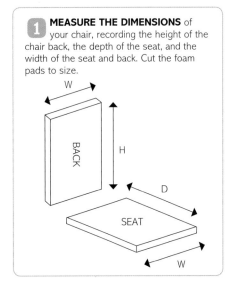

2 FOR EACH CHAIR COVER, cut out two large fabric panels, plus two smaller pieces for the ties, as follows.

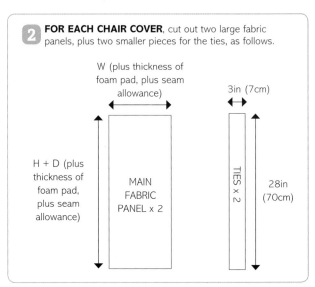

W (plus thickness of foam pad, plus seam allowance)

H + D (plus thickness of foam pad, plus seam allowance)

MAIN FABRIC PANEL x 2

3in (7cm)

TIES x 2

28in (70cm)

2 MAKE THE CUSHION COVER

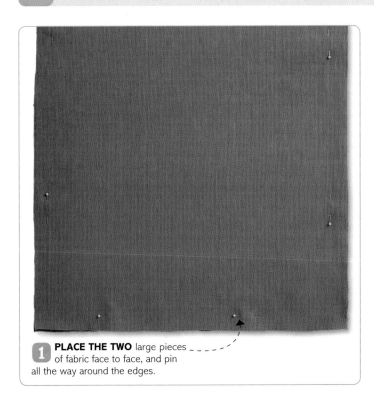

1 PLACE THE TWO large pieces of fabric face to face, and pin all the way around the edges.

2 PIN THE ELASTIC across the width of the cushion cover, about a quarter of the way down from the top of the fabric.

3 SEW AROUND three sides of the fabric, leaving one short end open.

4 TURN THE FABRIC inside out through the open end so it is the right way around. Check that the elastic is firmly attached.

3 INSERT THE SEAT PAD

1 INSERT THE SEAT PAD through the open end of the cushion cover.

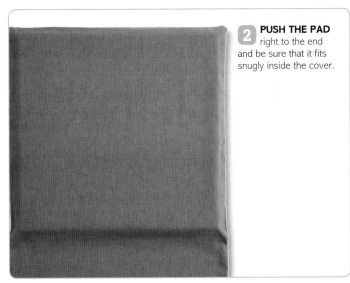

2 PUSH THE PAD right to the end and be sure that it fits snugly inside the cover.

4 MAKE THE TIES

1 FOLD OVER THE SHORT ENDS of each tie, then the long ends, and then fold the tie in half lengthwise.

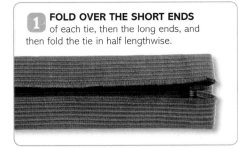

2 PIN THE FOLDS to secure them in place.

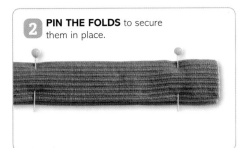

3 SEW neatly around the edges.

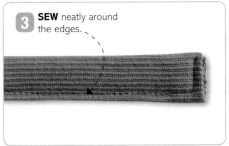

5 SECURE THE TIES

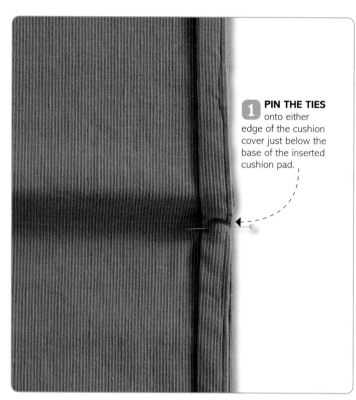

1 PIN THE TIES onto either edge of the cushion cover just below the base of the inserted cushion pad.

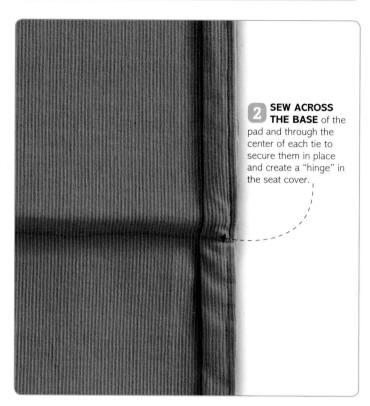

2 SEW ACROSS THE BASE of the pad and through the center of each tie to secure them in place and create a "hinge" in the seat cover.

6 INSERT THE BACK PAD

1 SLIDE THE BACK PAD into the remaining section of the cushion cover through the open end.

2 FOLD AND PIN the open end of the cover so the seam will rest against the chair back.

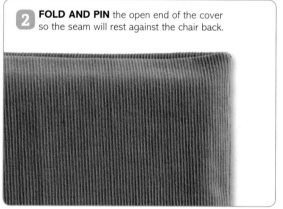

3 SEW UP the open end with a neat seam.

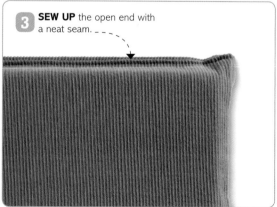

8 WAYS WITH
TINY OUTDOOR SPACES

Having a small yard doesn't necessarily mean that you will be severely limited in what you can do with it; there are plenty of ways to be creative with a restricted space. The key is to build a versatile area with hidden storage, built-in seating, and clever features.

BUILT-IN SEATING

If you can't find furniture that fits the proportions of your yard or makes best use of its space, consider having custom-built furniture made.

BUILT-IN BENCHES can be made from stucco brickwork as well as wood. Provide seat cushions for an extra element of comfort.

WALL ART

Add interest to a plain wall with a decorative wall hanging or some shelves that can be used to display small pots or garden sculptures.

PAINT THE WALL your decoration is on in a contrasting color to create a focal point.

ADD A LIVING WALL

Plant a living wall using specially designed modules or panels that contain soil for plants like herbs, grasses, and ferns to grow.

SOME LIVING WALLS may require irrigation systems and professional installation.

HANG FOLDING CHAIRS

Where space is tight, look for tables and chairs that can be folded flat and hung out of the way on the wall.

ENSURE THE FURNITURE is weather resistant, or have covers made to protect it.

ADD A MIRROR

Using mirrors in a garden will help reflect light, making the space feel larger. Look for a weatherproof acrylic mirror.

FOR SAFETY REASONS, do not place a mirror in direct sunlight.

CREATE A MEZZANINE

A small mezzanine will provide an extra level that you can use for planting or even a seating area. The space underneath will also offer some shade.

CHECK WHETHER you need permission from your building department before doing work.

ADD DECORATIVE LIGHTING

Create a party mood using decorative lighting. Highlight seating and dining areas using hanging lights, string lights, or lanterns.

DUAL-PURPOSE FURNITURE

ALTERNATIVELY, look for furniture that can be used indoors and out.

Make the most of your space by choosing furniture that serves more than one function—such as a bench that has a lift-up lid with space beneath for storing seat cushions.

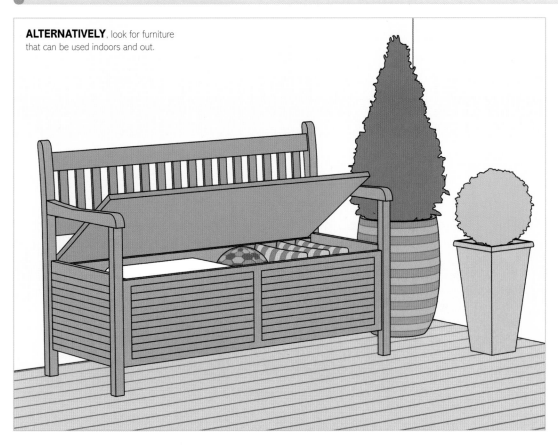

PLAN THE PERFECT
OUTDOOR KITCHEN

If you love entertaining and eating outdoors, you may prefer to have an outdoor kitchen installed so you can cook and serve more than just basic barbecued food. You need to employ many of the same rules as you would for designing an indoor kitchen, and what you include depends on how much space you have.

POSITION THE COOKING AREA

Unless you are an aspiring cook or live in a suitable climate, you will probably only want the most basic of cooking equipment. This is likely to include a grill, perhaps a gas burner, and possibly a stove or cooktop. The cooking you do in an outdoor kitchen will be far more sociable than indoors, so bear this in mind—can you position the cooking area safely so that it faces out on to the rest of your yard or patio, where guests will be sitting waiting for their food?

ALLOW FOR ADEQUATE COUNTER SPACE

You need to allow adequate counter space at either side of your cooking area—at least 24in (60cm), and more, if possible. Don't plan for your cooking area to be at one end of a run of countertops—incorporating enough space for food preparation and serving at each side is a must.

CHOOSE A LIDDED WASTE BIN

Having a waste bin in your outdoor kitchen is essential, because it will allow you to clear plates quickly, which means that you won't be overrun with insects. Either incorporate your waste bin into a self-closing pullout within a run of cabinets or choose one that is freestanding, but sealed with a lid.

ALLOCATE STORAGE SPACE

Lots of efficient storage isn't as important outdoors as it is indoors, but since you're unlikely to have much counter space outdoors, it is good to have somewhere to store cooking utensils, serving dishes, and plates, even if these will all be cleared away once you've finished eating. Open shelving is easy to access, while cabinets with well-sealed doors are also practical.

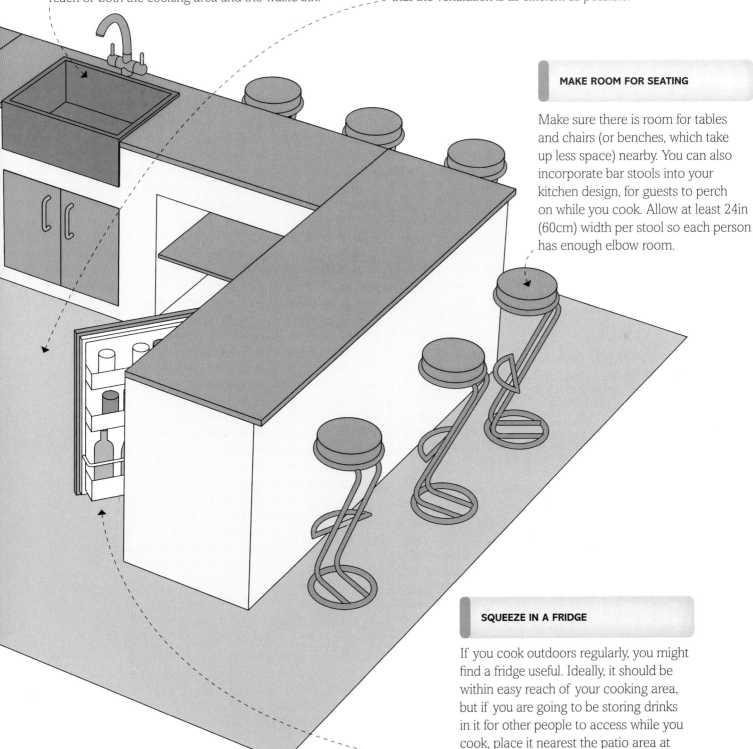

FIND ROOM FOR A SINK

If you have the room to add a sink to your outdoor kitchen, you will find it invaluable. Without one, you will have to make room for a large bottle of water for cooking and a storage area for dirty cooking utensils and pans to be stashed away. Ensure that the sink is within easy reach of both the cooking area and the waste bin.

GIVE YOURSELF SPACE

Build in enough room—at least 4ft (1.25m)—as a thoroughfare for your cooking area, and make sure that people who aren't cooking don't have to use it as a route to and from the house. You may also want to protect yourself (from sun or rain) with a nonflammable roof; make sure it is constructed so that the ventilation is as efficient as possible.

MAKE ROOM FOR SEATING

Make sure there is room for tables and chairs (or benches, which take up less space) nearby. You can also incorporate bar stools into your kitchen design, for guests to perch on while you cook. Allow at least 24in (60cm) width per stool so each person has enough elbow room.

SQUEEZE IN A FRIDGE

If you cook outdoors regularly, you might find a fridge useful. Ideally, it should be within easy reach of your cooking area, but if you are going to be storing drinks in it for other people to access while you cook, place it nearest the patio area at the end of a run of cabinets.

USEFUL RESOURCES

This is a selection of US organizations and companies that cater to the home designer and decorator. Some are big multinationals, others are magazines and websites or smaller companies, but all are good sources of information and products.

General Info

DIY Network
www.diynetwork.com
A helpful how-to site offering guidance on a range of home improvement projects.

NKBA
www.nkba.org/
The website of the National Kitchen and Bath Association offers resources you'll find useful when renovating your kitchen or bathroom. The website has many beautiful images for ideas.

Planning a Room

Elle Décor
www.elledecor.com
Style magazine, with ideas, information, and products to help you design and decorate.

Apartment Therapy
www.apartmenttherapy.com
A blog design magazine with unique solutions for designing small spaces on a budget. Be sure to check the "marketplace" section.

houzz
www.houzz.com
A home design photo database. Includes thousands of images from top designers.

Freshome
www.freshome.com
Blog devoted to latest developments in interior design, with hundreds of pictures and articles.

Better Homes and Gardens
www.bhg.com
A resource-filled website full of design ideas and do-it-yourself projects.

Kitchens.com
www.kitchens.com
A helpful website with lots of links to information to help show you the wide array of options available when choosing appliances.

General Retailers

IKEA
www.ikea.com
Global home products retailer.

Macy's
www.macys.com
Department store.

Sears
www.sears.com
Department store offering appliances.

Container Store
www.containerstore.com
A retail chain offering items for storing, hanging, and organizing just about everything.

Bed, Bath, and Beyond
www.bedbathandbeyond.com
A general retailer selling an array of household goods for all rooms—items range from small appliances to linens, and kitchen goods, organizers, and furniture.

Target
www.target.com
A discount retail chain with a good selection of nicely designed home goods.

Paints and Wall Coverings

Graham & Brown
www.grahambrown.com
Supplier of a wide range of designer wallpapers and paints.

Wallpapers-to-go
www.wallpaperstogo.com
An online retailer with a large selection of wallpapers.

Benjamin Moore
www.benjaminmoore.com
Major paint producer in the United States.

Sherwin-Williams
www.sherwin-williams.com
Supplier of entire range of wall coverings—from paints and primers to faux finishing and stains. Wide variety of wallpapers available.

Behr Paint
www.behr.com
Paint and stains for indoor and outdoor use.

Tiles

The Tile Shop
www.tileshop.com
A regional showroom vendor with a large selection of stone, glass, and ceramic tiles.

Dal Tile
www.daltile.com
A large manufacturer of ceramic and natural material tiles.

Bisazza Mosaico
www.bisazza.com
Glass mosaic tiles offered in a vast array of colors, patterns, and finishes.

Ann Sacks
www.annsacks.com
Tile and stone in beautiful patterns, shapes, colors, and glazes.

Flooring

Lumber Liquidators
www.lumberliquidators.com
National flooring material retailer.

FLOR
www.flor.com
A company offering innovative modular carpet tiles, which are easy to install and replace and can be configured in unique patterns and different shapes.

Armstrong Flooring
www.armstrong.com
Leading manufacturer of resilient flooring materials. Offerings include vinyl tile, linoleum, sheet products, and laminates.

Shaw Floors
www.shawfloors.com
Shaw has offerings in all major flooring material categories: carpet, resilient laminates, hardwoods, and tile and stone.

Plyboo
www.plyboo.com
Bamboo plywood and solid flooring. A good eco-friendly choice.

Kitchens & Bathrooms

Kohler
www.kohler.com
A leading manufacturer of bathroom and kitchen plumbing, accessories, and tile goods.

Waterworks
www.waterworkscom
Vendor of plumbing fixtures, fittings, tile, and coordinating accessories for kitchens and baths.

Franke
www.franke.com
Kitchen and utility sinks, faucets, water filters, and organization systems.

American Standard
www.amerianstandard.com
A collection of brands of plumbing fixtures and bathroom products.

Ceaserstone
www.ceasarstone.com
Leading quartz composite countertop company.

Thomasville Cabinetry
www.thomasvillcabinetry.com
Cabinetry for any room in your home—kitchen, bathroom, home office, living room, laundry room, you name it.

Corian
www.corian.com
Dupont's international solid surface countertop and sink business.

Formica
www.formica.com
Solid surfaces and laminate countertops.

Shades and Curtains

The Shade Store
www.theshadestore.com
A modern selection of window treatments offered by a national retailer with services available in-store, by catalog, and online.

Blinds.com
www.blinds.com
An online retailer of blinds, shades, shutters, and draperies.

Country Curtains
www.countrycurtains.com
Cozy window treatments offered from retail stores in the Northeast, and by catalog and online throughout the country.

Hunter Douglas
www.hunterdouglas.com
The leading manufacturer of custom-made window treatments in North America. Products offered range from sheers, shades and honeycomb shades to blinds and shutters.

Furniture and Interiors

Crate and Barrel
www.crateandbarrel.com
Furniture, interiors, and accessories retailer with a range of styles.

Ethan Allen
www.ethanallen.com
A large, comprehensive selection of stylish interior products.

Design Within Reach
www.dwr.com
Contemporary and modern classic furniture and accessories.

Pottery Barn
www.potterybarn.com
National retailer of classic furniture and accessories; products available in-store, online, and by catalog.

Room and Board
www.roomoandboard.com
A retailer of furnishings, carpet, and modular millwork.

West Elm
www.westelm.com
Mid-century and organic-inspired furniture and accessories.

General Building

Home Depot
www.homedepot.com
Home improvement chain selling a wide array of building materials and finishes. Home Depot offfers a range of installation services, including kitchen installations, landscaping, and plumbing services.

Lowes
www.lowes.com
General building supplies. A large building supply vendor that offers many types of installation services.

Ace Hardware
www.acehardware.com
General hardware and building supply company.

CALCULATING FABRIC QUANTITIES
FOR MAKING CURTAINS

To make curtains like the ones demonstrated on pages 178–181 and 246–249, you will need to know from the outset how much fabric you need. To establish this, follow the steps below. Making these calculations can be tricky if you are inexperienced and it's recommend that you do your calculations twice or more until you are confident that the measurements are correct.

MEASURE THE LENGTH OF THE TRACK OR ROD

You will need to know this later when you establish what width the curtains should be. If you are installing a new rod, aim to use one that extends 6–12in (15–30cm) beyond the window or recess, excluding any decorative ends.

ESTABLISH THE USABLE WIDTH OF FABRIC

With plain fabric, the usable width is simply the width minus any seam allowances. It is likely to be less for patterned fabric, where it will be dictated by the repeat of the pattern.

ESTABLISH THE FINAL LENGTH OF YOUR CURTAINS

You typically figure out the final length of your curtains by measuring from the top of the track or rod to the point where you want the curtain to finish, whether this is just below the sill or just above the floor (if you want curtains that are long enough to pool on the floor, measure to the floor and then add on an extra 8–12in/20–30cm). You will need to bear in mind different headings, however. For instance, with tab tops, the curtain starts lower down, so take your measurements from the bottom of the rod rather than the top.

CALCULATE THE CUT LENGTH OF THE CURTAINS

The cut length of the curtains is the length you will need to cut the fabric to in order to achieve the requisite length of final curtain. To make the curtains in this book, using plain fabric, calculate the cut length by adding 10in (25cm) to the intended final length, for hem allowance and top edge allowance. Again, if using patterned fabric, you will need to take the repeat of the pattern into account

ESTABLISH THE MINIMUM WIDTH OF THE CURTAINS

Curtains should always have a certain "fullness"—essentially, this is about there being enough fabric to hang in attractive loose folds. The fullness is dictated by the headers, and as a result, different styles of curtain need to be made to different widths, even if the window is the same size. For tab-top curtains (pages 178–181) to hang nicely, the width of each should be half to three-quarters the length of the rod. For the pencil pleat curtains (pages 246–249) to hang nicely, the width of each should be roughly equivalent to the entire length of the track or rod.

CALCULATE HOW MANY WIDTHS OF FABRIC YOU WILL NEED

To do this, divide your figure for the intended final width of the curtain by the usable width of fabric. This will almost certainly not result in a whole number—round up, not down, to establish how many widths of fabric will be required to make a curtain of the necessary width.

CALCULATE THE TOTAL QUANTITY OF FABRIC REQUIRED

You now know both the length the fabric needs to be cut to (the cut length of the curtains) and how many widths of fabric are required for each curtain. Multiplying these two figures together will give you the quantity of fabric needed for the main front panel of each curtain.

DON'T FORGET THE EXTRAS

You are nearly ready to order your fabric, but first you need to take any extra pieces into account. Tab-top curtains, for example, have a back panel at the top, which also needs to be accounted for, plus the tabs themselves. You can calculate the extra fabric needed for the back panel by repeating the above steps, assuming a length of 10in (25cm). To calculate how much additional fabric is needed for the tabs, first determine the size of one tab—8in (20cm) wide; length dependent on the thickness of the rod. You then need to work out the number of tabs: they will be positioned at 8–12in (20–30cm) intervals so divide the final width of the curtain by 20, 25, or 30. The resulting figure, rounded up to the nearest whole number, represents the number of tabs. Work out how many tabs you will get from a width of fabric, and calculate the fabric you need accordingly.

REMEMBER THAT for tab-top curtains like these, you will need to order additional fabric with which to make the tabs.

PROJECT
TEMPLATES

If you have been inspired to try the projects in the "Child's Bedroom" section of this book—the appliqué pillow on pages 264–267, or the wall stencil on pages 254–255—and would like to use the same designs, use the templates on these pages. To increase or decrease the size, either photocopy the page using the "enlarge" function or scan and resize. Alternatively, try the projects with designs of your own.

TRACE AROUND THIS IMAGE, or an enlarged version of it, onto a piece of fusable bonding web and you are ready to start your appliqué pillow.

PLACE A SHEET OF ACETATE over this page, or a photocopied enlargement of it, and trace around the shape using a felt-tip pen. You can then cut the shape out to create your template.

INDEX

ACKNOWLEDGMENTS

Author's acknowledgments

Clare Steel would like to thank Gary for his support and patience, and Lucy Searle for her constant guidance and advice.

Publishers' acknowledgments

Dorling Kindersley would like to thank Zoe Browne and Alison Smith for creating the craft-based projects, Jane Coulter for creating the index, Barry Cox and Kit Jolliffe for set building, Sara Emslie for interiors styling, and Samuel Grant for the DIY projects.

Thanks also to the following suppliers, who assisted by donating samples to be photographed:

Bamboo Flooring Company—bamboo flooring
www.bambooflooringcompany.com

Bushboard—laminate countertops
www.bushboard.com

Churchfield sofa bed company—sofa fabrics
www.sofabed.co.uk

Concreations—concrete countertops
www.concreations.co.uk

Decorative Aggregates—rubber and stone chips
www.decorativeaggregates.com

Flooringsupplies.co.uk—wood flooring, engineered wood flooring, laminate flooring, carpets
www.flooringsupplies.co.uk

Fritztile—terrazzo tiles
www.fritztile.com

Furniture Choice—sofa fabrics
www.furniturechoice.co.uk

Glassact—glass countertops
www.glassactuk.com

Granitesolutionsdirect—granite and quartz composite countertops
www.granitesolutionsdirect.co.uk

London Stone—Yorkstone paving
www.londonstone.com

Meadee Flooring—rubber, vinyl, and linoleum flooring
www.meadeeflooring.co.uk

Puur—Seamless concrete and resin floors
www.puur.uk.com

Q Stoneworks—granite and lavastone countertops
www.qstoneworks.co.uk

Sofa.com—sofa fabrics
www.sofa.com

Sofas&stuff—sofa fabrics
www.sofasandstuff.com

The Sofa Company—sofa fabrics
www.sofa-company.co.uk

Tong Ling Bamboo Flooring—bamboo flooring
www.tlflooring.co.uk

Walls and Floors—tiles
www.wallsandfloors.co.uk

Wallpaper direct—wallpaper
www.wallpaperdirect.co.uk

Wilsons Flooring—Saxony carpets
www.wilsonsflooringdirect.co.uk

Wilton Carpets—velvet pile carpets
www.wiltoncarpets.com

Picture Credits

Dorling Kindersley would like to thank the following for their kind permission to reproduce their photographs:

(Key: a-above; b-below/bottom; c-centre; f-far; l-left; r-right; t-top)

Alamy Images: Ivan Barta 51; *The Garden Collection*: Nicola Stocken Tomkins 357; *Getty Images*: Neo Vision 14tr; *IPC+ Syndication*: Hallie Burton / Livingetc 16bl, Ideal Home 135; *Photoshot*: Red Cover / Ed Reeve 16cb, 16crb, Red Cover / Ken Hayden 279, Red Cover / Mary-Jane Maybury 16br; *www.jordicanosa.com*: 205

All other images © Dorling Kindersley
For further information see: www.dkimages.com

About the Author

Clare Steel has worked across a broad selection of national interiors magazines in the UK, from *Ideal Home* to *House Beautiful*, and regularly contributes to property and design websites, such as channel4.com/4Homes. She has spent the majority of her career conceiving, designing and creating rooms and cameos for photo shoots. She has also transformed countless magazine readers' homes with room and house makeovers, and regularly contributes written features to magazines and websites on everything from choosing color schemes to picking out flooring.